The
GRAPE
GROWER

The
GRAPE
GROWER

A Guide to Organic Viticulture

by Lon Rombough

CHELSEA GREEN PUBLISHING
White River Junction, Vermont

Cover designed by Ann Aspell.
Interior designed by Andrea Gray.
Printed in the United States of America.
First printing, October 2002.
12 11 10   10 11 12

Library of Congress Cataloging-in-Publication Data
Rombaugh, Lon, 1949-
      The grape grower / by Lon Rombough.
            p.   cm.
      Includes bibliographical references (p.).
      paperback ISBN 1-890132-82-9
      hardcover ISBN 1-931498-30-X
      1. Grapes—United States. 2. Viticulture—United States.
      3. Grapes. 4. Viticulture. I. Title.
SB389.R76 2002
634.8'0973—dc21 2002023371

Chelsea Green Publishing Company
P.O. Box 428
White River Junction, VT 05001
(800) 639-4099
www.chelseagreen.com

Chelsea Green Publishing is committed to preserving
ancient forests and natural resources. We elected to print
this title on 30-percent postconsumer recycled paper,
processed chlorine-free. As a result, for this printing, we
have saved:

16 Trees (40' tall and 6-8" diameter)
5 Million BTUs of Total Energy
1,518 Pounds of Greenhouse Gases
7,313 Gallons of Wastewater
444 Pounds of Solid Waste

Chelsea Green Publishing made this paper choice because
we and our printer, Thomson-Shore, Inc., are members
of the Green Press Initiative, a nonprofit program dedicated to supporting authors, publishers, and suppliers
in their efforts to reduce their use of fiber obtained
from endangered forests. For more information, visit:
www.greenpressinitiative.org.

Environmental impact estimates were made using the Environmental Defense Paper Calculator.
For more information visit: www.papercalculator.org.

This book is dedicated to
Dr. H. P. Olmo
Elmer Swenson
Byron Johnson
Robert Zehnder
D.C. Paschke
for what I learned from them,
both in information and dedication
to grapes, and especially to my wife
Susan for her love and support
through the effort of producing this book

Contents

Foreword:
Seed Matters

RELIEF FROM THE SUN was what my grandmother had in mind when, early last century, she requested a grapevine be planted outside the kitchen door of her new farmhouse. At midday, in midsummer, in the Midwest, even the cows seek out shade. And shade she got, as the vine topped the arbor of chestnut posts and split rails. Beneath its leafy canopy, peas were shelled, beans snapped, and babies nursed. My mother washed her hair in a bucket there and walked out into the light on her wedding day. I remember, as a young boy lying on the vine-cooled terrace beneath the arbor, the contrast between the cool of the sandstone paving and the hot whine of cicadas in overdrive in the elm branches above the barn.

The Guernsey dairy herd is gone now, so too the American elms, and grandmother herself. But the grapevine lives on. The arbor is on its third generation of posts, but the vine is still an adolescent. Compare it, for example, to the Great Vine at Hampton Court Palace in England, which was planted in 1768 and still bears an annual crop of fruit. Barring someone uprooting Grandmother's vine in a burst of ill temper at having had to sweep the fallen grapes off the terrace one time too many, it will someday be as venerable. Key to its survival is the fact that grapevines are so extraordinarily self-reliant. It helps, of course, that grapes are native to North America, but this vine to my knowledge has never been given much more than earth, water, and sun. Its pruning has been no more sophisticated than cutting back the shoots that attempt to mount the roof, or threaten to seal off the arbor's entrances. Unsprayed, it still yields fruit sufficient to keep the jelly jars filled.

In my own vineyard, the vines receive considerably more attention. The training, pruning, and feeding are all directed at producing the largest and most perfect bunches of grapes that genetics and the land will allow. This is not Ohio but southern

New Hampshire, and a cool mountainside is hardly prime grape-growing terrain. Nevertheless, it has proven hospitable to a score of the earliest-maturing and hardiest selections (two characteristics that are not necessarily linked). Despite the famous unpredictability of New England's weather, these vines reliably produce more grapes than any one family could ever eat.

Our friends think we should be making our own wine. But with only one or two vines of each kind of grape, any wine we might fashion would resemble too closely those blended wines that are available for five dollars a jug at the nearest convenience store. At the end of the season, when killing frosts have turned the leaves brown and crisp, and brought an end to any further accumulation of sugar, we do strip the vines of fruit that's left, turning it into either juice or raisins. Most of our fruit, though, gets eaten fresh.

We entertain by reaching under the leaves for yet another full bunch on a sunny September afternoon, grooming it quickly to remove the imperfections, the fruit that the wasps have discovered first. And then, without disturbing the delicate waxy bloom that coats the individual berries, we offer up the entire bunch to someone's lips. Some guests prefer to feed themselves, but even they exhibit refreshingly little reluctance in sampling whatever is available. Each of these grapes is different, and not just because of their hue. This deep blue one is slip-skin, reflecting its American heritage; this adherent-skin red, on the other hand, has European wine-grape genes. Some of the grapes are unmistakable in their foxiness; some have just the tiniest hint of clove. That last one was solid-fleshed; this one almost pure juice.

But while the grapes being offered usually vary widely, the responses they elicit do not. By now we know what to expect, especially from first-time visitors. "Seeds! Seeds!" the person sputters. "They've got seeds!"

"Of course they have seeds," I patiently counter, "Grapes are supposed to have seeds." Outside of grocery stores, seeds in fruit are the norm. At what point in recent history did we forget that the purpose of a fruit is to deliver its seeds? Fruiting plants, grapevines included, surround their seeds with a layer of edible flesh that only becomes sweet and attractive when the seeds inside are mature and ready to be dispersed. Frugivores, or fruit eaters, including all of us who like the taste of grapes, are supposed to spread these seeds in return for the sweet mouthful. Shirk our responsibility, and natural selection will replace the sweet pulp with dry, paper airfoils (like maple seeds) or whatever other method of seed dispersal that time and evolution happen to serve up.

It's not that seedless grapes are new. They aren't. The word "currant" is a contraction of the name "raisins of Corinth," referring to the small, seedless grapes grown in ancient Greece. But the present preponderance of Flame Seedless, Perlette, and Thompson Seedless in the produce sections of supermarkets is due less to any superiority of flavor than to the pacification of a generation of picky eaters, child and adult alike.

Lest anyone underestimate the importance of seeds, consider what has come from the four or fewer small brown pips contained in a grape. At last count, the world's individual grape varieties numbered over ten thousand. Less than one percent of those have resulted from a mutation to an existing vine. The rest got their start as seedlings.

Just one such seedling eventually yielded Grandmother's vine. In 1843, an amateur viticulturist named Ephraim W. Bull sowed some seeds from a wild grape at his home in Massachusetts. A gold beater by profession, he subsequently named one of the seedlings after his hometown, and exhibited the fruit of the new Concord grape at the Massachusetts Horticultural Society show of 1852. In 1865, it was awarded the Horace Greeley Prize as the best grape for general cultivation. The best known of the eastern table grapes, it continues to be instantly recognizable today.

Grandmother's Concord grapevine found its way west to Ohio as a rooted cutting, a form of vegetative propagation intended to preserve the genetic integrity of the original plant. I, too, have a Concord vine, but only one in four years do I harvest any ripe fruit. The variety needs 140 frost-free days to mature. Mine shakes off temperatures of twenty below zero during the winter but most years the fruits freeze before they have had a chance to sweeten. The grapes that I grow that look, and taste, like Concord are all newer varieties, the fruits of careful selection among seedlings—grapes like Worden, which ripens a critical two weeks earlier, and Alwood and Price, which mature earlier still. For such improvement, we again have grape seeds to thank.

The next time anyone encounters an entire layer of grape seeds coating a log of port wine cheddar at an hors d'oeuvres table, or hears a waiter mention grapeseed oil in the description of the evening's specials, it might be worth noting that these are the very same seeds that people are so quick to spit out when they encounter them inside the grape itself. Spitting grape seeds out is, admittedly, a perfectly acceptable way to disseminate them. It just must be done without any rancor or other objection. Swallowed or spit out, grape seeds are at the heart of all grapes and at the heart of this book. For whether your taste runs to French champagne or grape popsicles, shady arbors or stuffed grape leaves, seeds still remain the price of admission.

Roger B. Swain

Introduction

Over the years, people have asked me questions about grapes and grape culture, and all too often I had to write long, drawn-out explanations because there wasn't any one book I felt comfortable recommending: I had to give them a whole list, with each book covering a different aspect. But even that list didn't cover everything. Some books offer lots of theory and cover commercial practices, but lack the up-close coverage that only comes with hands-on experience. Others focus on only one area of viticulture, such as growing grapes for wine. And while a few general garden books cover a few varieties of table grapes, no previous book since the days of U.P. Hedrick, near the start of the twentieth century, has covered table grapes with much more than a passing mention.

I bring to this book over thirty-five years experience growing grapes. I started as a young teenaged amateur, then took university classes in viticulture, worked for a nursery, and spent years growing and

testing over two hundred varieties and observing many more, as well as breeding grapes. I've corresponded and met with grape growers and breeders in North America and elsewhere. This book is a distillation of my experiences, presented in ways I hope will be useful, easy to follow, and even entertaining for home growers and commercial growers alike.

This is not the ultimate grape book, just an attempt to assemble as much good experience and interesting information as possible in a form useful to the greatest number of people. As they gain experience, every grower will find ways of doing things at least somewhat differently from the book, which is as it should be. Grape growing is a science and also a living art, growing and changing all the time. But this book *will* give you a solid starting point to work from.

This book is also an attempt to show that grapes are much more adaptable than most people think. By using the right varieties and species, one can successfully grow grapes from the tropics to the Far North. And one thing particularly different about the book is the section on grape breeding, which is presented in a way that, I hope, will show the amateur that it can be a surprisingly enjoyable and rewarding pastime.

Techniques in this book may not always be the same ones found in the "classic" texts, but they have worked for me and for people with whom I've corresponded.

And if there was information I couldn't test personally, I got it from people I knew to be experienced, hands-on viticulturists, and, judged its validity, using my own training and background, against reports from a number of other sources.

Most of all, I hope the book "demystifies" grapes enough that more people will take the time to plant and enjoy this wonderful fruit.

1 STRUCTURE of the VINE

THE STRUCTURE AND FUNCTION of the grapevine may seem like a dry subject, but learning the names of the parts of the vine and the sequence of events in its life cycle will enhance your understanding of how to grow grapes successfully. Also, the rest of this book will make more sense if you know the meaning of the terms that I will be using.

MAJOR STRUCTURE of the VINE

Roots are the underground structures that support the vine and, more importantly, interact with the soil's web of life to provide the vine with water and nutrients. A vine that grew from seed has roots that arose from the seedling root. But most vines are grown from cuttings and their roots developed as *adventitious roots*—roots that grew where there were no pre-existing roots.

The *trunk* is the main upright structure of the vine from which shoots and canes arise. In turn, these can be trained to become extensions of the trunk called *cordons*. Vines may have more than one trunk. The juncture of the trunk with the roots is called the *crown*. If the vine is grafted, there will likely be a visible *graft union* close above the crown, showing as a bulge, a difference in diameter below and above the graft union, or a difference in bark.

Bark is the tough external covering of a woody stem or root. Bark is largely composed of dead tissue, which is slowly being shed by the vine. In bunch grapes, the bark on one-year-old shoots is generally tight and smooth, but on two-year and older wood it becomes looser and more shredded. In vines more than three years old, there is usually enough old, loose bark that some can be pulled off without harm to the vine.

Immediately under the bark is the *phloem*, a region of tissues composed of

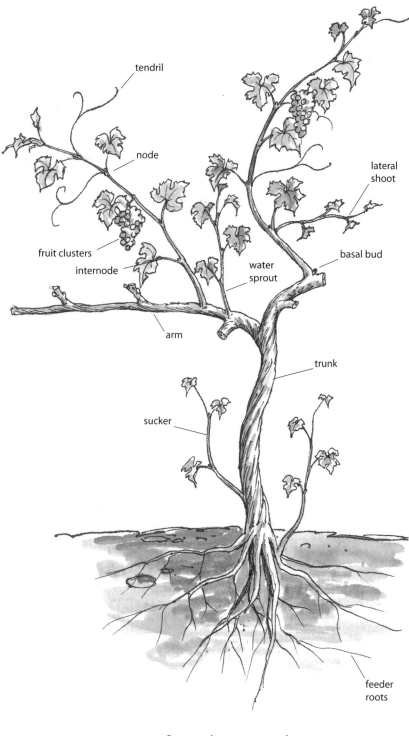

tendril

node

lateral
shoot

fruit clusters

internode

basal bud

water
sprout

arm

trunk

sucker

feeder
roots

Structural components of a grape vine.

sieve tubes and *parenchyma*—living, thin-walled cells that fit loosely together—that translocate food materials produced by the leaves. Vines channel most of the food to the roots for storage, though some food is stored in wood and some is translocated to the fruit.

Under the phloem is the *cambium*, a thin layer of undifferentiated, or *meristematic*, tissue. All tissues in the vine originate from the cambium. That is, the cambium is composed of cells that can become whatever type of tissue is needed. If the cambium is injured in some way, the vine heals it by forming callus. *Callus* is parenchyma tissue that grows over a wound or graft and protects it from drying or injury. Callus also forms at the base and nodes of cuttings being prepared for rooting. Roots cannot arise directly from cambium, so the cambium produces callus, which is undifferentiated tissue that can then give rise to roots.

Directly under the cambium is the *xylem*, the woody portion of conducting tissue whose function is to move water and minerals up from the roots. In grapes, xylem makes up most of the wood and gives structural support.

At the top of the trunk(s) is the head, that portion of the trunk where cordons canes, or spurs originate. *Cordons* are extensions of the trunk composed of permanent wood two years old or older where spurs are located. *Canes* are shoots that are mature, brown, and woody. They are usually called canes only after leaf fall. *Spurs* consist of canes pruned to four or fewer nodes. Spurs serve either for bearing fruit or as renewal spurs, which produce a cane or canes to be used for fruiting in the following season.

Buds are undeveloped shoots, usually located in the axil of a leaf at a *node,* which is the thickened portion of a shoot or cane where the leaf and bud are attached. When the leaf falls off, it leaves a leaf scar right underneath a bud. The leaf scar is a useful "landmark" to be sure a cutting is oriented correctly for planting.

Buds usually are covered by *scales,* protective scale-like leaves that are covered with hairs and impregnated with suberin. In grapes, the buds on the nodes are compound—containing more than one bud. Cut across a bud horizontally and inside the scales you will see a large primary bud, plus a small crescent-shaped secondary bud and a still smaller tertiary bud nestled between the secondary and primary buds. The primary bud contains a highly compressed shoot, complete with flower clusters that will produce fruit in the upcoming season. Both the secondary and the tertiary buds also have clusters, but fewer, smaller ones than the primary. If all three of these buds are damaged or removed, there will be no growth from that node, because grapes cannot make *adventitious buds,* buds that arise out of nondifferentiated tissue. It may appear as though adventitious buds are the source of shoots that seemingly arise out of the wood of the trunk or cordon arms, but these shoots have sprung from *latent buds,* buds that remain dormant indefinitely unless the vine suffers a major injury that makes it necessary to produce new shoots.

A *basal bud* is a small bud at the base of a cane or spur. A whorl of basal buds form when a shoot arises from older wood. For most varieties, when counting the buds on

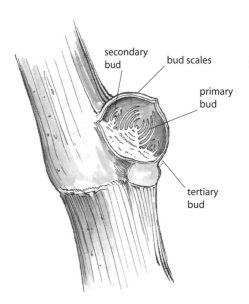

Vertical cross-section of a bud.

a spur or cane, basal buds are not included. Basal buds usually remain dormant unless the buds along the cane fail to grow. For a few varieties that are extremely fruitful, however, the basal buds may often "break" (begin to grow) and produce a crop.

When a bud breaks, it will produce either a fruitful shoot with flower clusters on it or a vegetative shoot without clusters. As the shoot extends, all new growth originates at the *shoot apex* (the tip of the shoot). The effect of *apical dominance* inhibits the lateral buds from growing, through hormones produced by the shoot apex. As the shoot elongates, the apical dominance effect decreases farther down the shoot, and lateral buds along this portion of the shoot may sprout. Generally, the lateral shoots produced from these buds are vegetative, but in some cases, these shoots produce a few small secondary clusters that ripen later than the main crop.

Other types of shoots include *suckers*, which are shoots arising from a bud below ground. On an own-rooted vine, which is a vine that has not been grafted, a sucker can be used to create multiple trunks or layered to replace a missing vine in an adjacent empty space. Properly prepared grafted vines don't produce suckers—the presence of suckers indicates that the rootstock wasn't correctly disbudded before grafting. Vines also may produce *watersprouts*, fast-growing shoots arising from latent buds on branches or trunks. Watersprouts are usually, but not always, unfruitful.

Part of what helps a shoot expand rapidly is the presence of *pith*, the tissue in the central part of shoots or stems, usually made up of soft parenchyma cells. At first, the pith may make up 50 percent or more of the interior of the shoot, but this percentage decreases as the surrounding tissues mature and compress the pith. In healthy, mature shoots, the pith is reduced to being small and round. In soft, poorly hardened growth, the pith may be oval in cross section and take up a large percentage of the shoot.

At first, the shoot starts to expand slowly, so the first three or four *internodes*—spaces between the nodes—are close together. As weather warms, the shoots start to expand faster and internode distance increases until growth begins to slow again in mid- to late summer. This variation in internode length can be "read" in winter as a record of growing conditions during the previous season.

At each node there is a leaf, consisting of a leaf *petiole*, or stem, and a *blade*, the expanded portion of the leaf. The leaf is the primary location of photosynthesis and food production. The term "leaf" is also used in viticulture to refer to the age of a vine: a vine in its "third leaf" is three years old.

The epidermis of leaves and young stems includes pores called *stomata*. Specialized *guard cells* in the epidermis control opening and closing of the stomata, allowing gas exchange to take place. Carbon dioxide needed for photosynthesis enters the leaves through the open stomata.

At the base of the leaf petiole is the *eye*, a compound bud that will become the dormant bud on the cane or spur in winter. Part of the eye is a *leaf bud*, a bud that develops into a stem with leaves, but no flower clusters. A leaf bud will break and become a new apical shoot if something damages the existing one. Most of the time, the leaf bud never breaks and eventually is buried in the wood.

On the opposite side of the node from the leaf, clusters or tendrils arise. A *tendril* is a slender structure that can coil around objects to help support the shoot and allow the vine to climb. Tendrils may be simple (single), bifurcated (forked), or trifurcated (with three tendrils coming off one stem), depending on the species and cultivar. If a tendril fails to contact an object it can hang onto, it usually will dry up and drop off. If a tendril attaches itself to something, such as a support wire, it will thicken and eventually become hard and woody. Tendrils can "recognize" if they are in contact with another shoot and will generally not attach to that shoot unless it is woody. Flower clusters are considered modified tendrils, and tendrils may produce a few flowers.

FLOWERS *and* FRUIT

All wild grapes are basically dioecious: female (pistillate) and male (staminate) flowers are borne on separate plants. Female plants bear pistillate flowers, which have a central structure called a pistil. The pistil consists of an ovary, a style (a column of tissue atop the ovary), and a stigma (an area of the style that can receive pollen). Male plants produce staminate flowers, which have upright, functional stamens but no pistil. Stamens consist of an anther, a structure that produces pollen, a filament, a stem that bears the anther at its tip. In grapes, female flowers often include stamens, but the stamens curve under the base of the flower, and any pollen they produce is sterile. Likewise, some staminate flowers may have a rudimentary ovary and a tiny stigma, but lack a style.

Most cultivated grapes have *perfect* flowers, in which the pistil is fully developed (with a complete stigma, style, and ovary) and the stamens are upright and produce fertile pollen. When a grape flower opens, the petals do not unfurl from the top down, as in most flowers. Instead, the petals detach at the base and remain fused together as a cap, called the *calyptra*. Most perfect-flowered grapes are largely self-pollinating. The anthers have usually begun to shed pollen onto a flower's stigma almost as soon as the calyptra loosens.

Each flower is attached by its own *pedicel* or cap stem. In turn, each pedicel is attached to a larger stem, on up to the *rachis*, the main stem of the cluster. In turn, the cluster is attached to the shoot or cane by the *peduncle* or the cluster stem.

The peduncle has a surprising amount of importance in the fruit cluster and how it can be handled. If the peduncle is too short, the cluster may be so close to the shoot that it becomes difficult to harvest without damaging the fruit. If the peduncle is woody and hard, harvest can require special care to ensure that clusters are not torn in handling. Likewise a peduncle that stays too green and tender may be more prone to breakage and loss of the cluster or to attack by insects or disease.

Depending on how many flowers set fruit on a cluster, the density of the cluster will vary. Cluster density definitions are:

Straggly—plenty of space between berries; berries are unevenly sized and spaced.

Very loose—many visible stems, but berries are more evenly spaced and mostly of the same size.

Loose—berries mostly of the same size; less than half the stems show; cluster will "relax" and spread out to show more stems when laid on a table.

Well-filled—berries evenly distributed; no berry stems show when the cluster is held up, but the cluster can still relax and show stems when laid on a table.

Compact—berries touching each other, cluster is a solid mass that does not relax when laid down; when twisted, berries are knocked off, but juicing is minimal.

Very compact—berries pushed together so hard that many are deformed and flattened, and some may split or burst from pressure. Trying to twist the cluster causes juice to run and dislodges berries.

female
(pistillate flower)

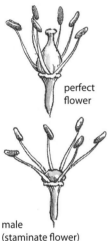

perfect
flower

male
(staminate flower)

Sex of grape flowers.

straggly

very loose

loose

Density of the cluster depends on how many of the flowers set (how many ovaries are fertilized) and become berries. Surprisingly, 10 to 12 percent of the fruit set usually will result in a well-filled cluster. In many varieties, a 20 percent set leads to compact or very compact clusters.

In clusters that have *shoulders*, the basal lateral branches are larger than other laterals. Depending on the size and location of shoulders, the cluster may be one-sided, cone-shaped, cylindrical, or other shapes. Additionally, clusters may have one or more *wings*. A wing is a well-developed basal cluster lateral that projects from the main stem and is separated from the main body of the grape cluster, rather like a small cluster that is attached to the main cluster stem but separate from the rest of the cluster. In extreme cases, the wing may be large enough that the cluster appears to be two separate clusters with a common peduncle. One Asian *Vitis vinifera* variety, Ranspay or Rangspay (meaning "horse's tail"), is a series of several wings each as large as the main cluster, forming a massive spherical cluster as big as a basketball and weighing several pounds.

The majority of the cells in the berries, other than the seeds, are parenchyma cells. Most of these cells have already been produced by the time the flower blooms; the cells simply enlarge after set occurs. In many varieties, if the weather is warm at bloom time, the parenchyma cells will divide more during bloom and the berries will have the potential of being larger than ones set in cool weather.

Development of the fruit proceeds from the green of immature berries to *veraison*, an intermediate stage when the ripening of the berries begins. Veraison is characterized by a softening of the fruit and a color change. White grapes become translucent; red or blue grapes turn red (then blue). Some red grapes turn white first, then red. Maturity continues until the fruit is either picked or reaches its maximum sugar content, which varies according to genetics and conditions. Most labrusca-type grapes rarely reach more than 17 to 19 degrees Brix, while some vinifera grapes can reach as much as 10 degrees Brix higher than that.* As the fruit ripens, the *lenticels*—porelike, slightly raised spots on pedicels and berries—may also become more prominent. Some varieties have more prominent lenticels than others. For example, Interlaken has noticeable lenticels, but its sister variety Himrod does not.

The ANNUAL CYCLE *of the* VINE

Following are the stages a grape vine goes through in a year. They are not individual events, the way the list makes them seem. Instead, they change and move from one to the other on a mostly continuous basis.

Starting in midwinter there is total *dormancy*. The vine is at rest and there is no visible activity.

Activation starts when the vine wakes up. This usually begins when temperatures

* Sugar in fruit is measured in the *Brix* or *Balling* scale. The names are interchangeable as the scale was developed by two different researchers at the same time, so both get credit for it. Measured in degrees, it measures the soluble solids in the fruit and is close enough to percent that for practical purposes, it can be though of as that. Thus, 17 degrees Brix (or Balling) is essentially 17 percent sugar.

well-filled

compact

very compact

reach 51°F (11°C) and the main outward sign of it is that buds begin to swell. As the process proceeds, buds continue to become engorged and shed their scaled sheaths, until they begin to show green. This is the stage known as *bud break*. At this point, young, green shoots begin to grow from the buds.

The shoots proceed through *debourrement*, the period between bud break and the appearance of the first *inflorescence* (flower cluster). During this time, the shoots usually grow about 10 inches (25 cm), moving into *pre-bloom* when all of the shoot's inflorescences have expanded from the compressed state they were in up to this time. During the unfurlment of the flower clusters, the shoots continue to grow, to about 14 inches (36 cm).

When daytime air temperatures reach 68°F (20°C) the flowers *bloom*. The process is also known as *anthesis*. The individual blossoms lose their calyptras (caps) and begin to self-fertilize. During this period the inflorescences take on a characteristic "Chia Pet" appearance due to the fine filaments of the stamens all over the flowers. The grape bloom is also very fragrant. Bloom usually takes about 14 to 21 days (depending on weather).

When the ovaries of the blossoms on each inflorescence have successfully self-fertilized, they become small, hard, green berries. The inflorescences thus are transformed into grape clusters. This is *berry (fruit) set* or nouaison.

Not all ovaries set, and the unfertilized berries fall from the new clusters about 7 to 10 days after bloom. This stage is known as *shatter*. If shatter is excessive, such as from nutrient deficiency, the entire cluster may wither and fail.

After berry set, the shoots continue to grow and unfold leaves, which are known as *first cover*.

When the berries lose their grass-green color and begin to soften and change color, they have started to ripen. This is known as *veraison*. White grapes become translucent, while most colored grapes begin to develop red pigment before turning other colors.

During veraison, the rate of growth slows until the shoots stop growing and begin to show woodiness developing. This is known as *aoutement* (Fr.—"Augusting"). As it proceeds, the shoots and leaves may even start to turn color.

The next stage is when the fruit is ripe, ready for use. It's *harvest* time.

Finally, the vine begins to get ready for winter by *hardening off*. The leaves drop, the shoots become woody to the tips, and the vine gets ready for winter. This is when the vine undergoes *deactivation* and re-enters dormancy.

2 GETTING STARTED: SITE, SOIL, and PLANTING

I N THE RIGHT CLIMATE and growing conditions, grapes can be very long-lived. Even if the top of a vine is killed, such as by cold, new shoots usually arise to replace it, making the vine all but immortal. At the same time, a newly planted vine can take five to seven years to reach full production. Respect these qualities of grapevines, and plan your vineyard carefully. Choose the wrong site and you may waste years having to start over. Plant the right varieties in the right place, and the vines may live to provide your great-grandchildren with fruit.

Site and soil can make the difference between healthy, productive vines and disease-ridden, unproductive ones. Setting up the right trellis at the start will also make training and caring for the vines much easier in the years after. Let's consider site first.

The RIGHT SITE

The ideal vineyard site generally is in full sun with the best possible air circulation through it. The ideal site is not always attainable, nor is it always exactly the same in every situation. For example, in southern locations, where light intensity is higher and temperatures may reach levels that can adversely affect the vines, full sun may not be desirable. It might be necessary to provide afternoon shade, or to position and train the vines so that the vine's own foliage canopy reduces the effects of heat and bright sunlight on the fruit.

The right site has a distinct effect on the health of vines. A grower in Massachusetts planted Concord vines on two sites, an upland slope with good air drainage, and a low pocket where air settled and stagnated.

The vines were only a few hundred feet apart, but the upland vines were healthy and needed no spray in all but the worst years, while the ones in the low area were diseased in all but the most favorable years.

What was the difference? The good air circulation around the upland vines kept them dry, robbing fungus of moisture it needed to grow as well as blowing away spores before they could settle on the vines. The lowland vines sat in a "dead air" zone that allowed dew and moisture to persist on the foliage and fungi to settle on the plants with little disturbance. Treating the diseased vines with fungicides was a possible solution, of course, but since the grower's goal was to avoid spraying, the low-lying site was unsuitable.

Similarly, there is a line between allowing for open air circulation and siting a vineyard where excessive winds may break and damage shoots. A windy site may not be unusable, depending on the time of year the wind is most active and how it blows. Vines are most susceptible to wind damage in spring and early summer, when shoots are tender and more easily broken. By midseason, though, the shoots are tougher and more strongly attached to the older wood. Once the shoots have started to harden, the leaves may become tattered by strong winds before the shoots will break.

Steady winds generally harm vines less than irregular, gusty winds because the vines adapt themselves to steady blowing by producing stiffer, stouter shoots. For example, some of the best Concord vineyards in the United States are located along the shores of Lake Erie, where there is a nearly constant breeze during much of the growing season.

If a windy site is your only option, or if other factors make it a desirable site, one

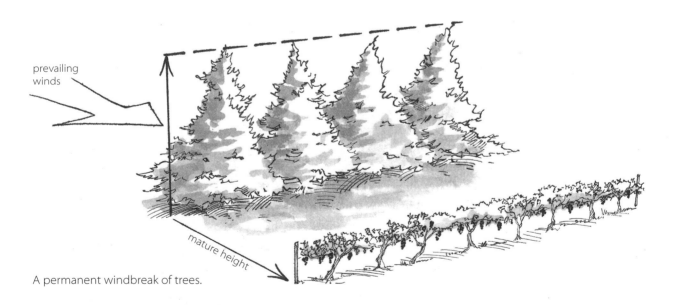

prevailing winds

mature height

A permanent windbreak of trees.

solution is to plant windbreak trees such as fast-growing hybrid cottonwoods. (Some selections grow 8 to 15 feet per year with good care.) With such trees, a permanent windbreak could be planted at the same time as the vineyard and the trees would be big enough to protect the vines by the time the young vines are ready to train. If wind is a problem only part of the season, consider a temporary wind barrier. Windbreak fabric is an option that allows the grower to erect a wind barrier quickly, and it can be taken down when it isn't needed. Depending on the size of the area to be protected, poles as tall as 20 feet or more may be set around the side of the vineyard from which the strongest winds originate. If the wind comes from the east, for example, the windbreak will need to be along

the east side, usually with extensions along the north and south sides. Nor is a simple, solid wall always the most effective windbreak. The goal is not to stop the wind entirely, but to slow it down. Wind speed is reduced proportionately to the proximity to the windbreak, so that vines on the far side from the windbreak may feel almost the full strength of the wind. In some cases, setting up shorter sections of fabric fence that overlap each other creates a baffle effect that slows the wind more than a continuous section would.

In temperate climates, site vineyards on slopes that face south or east. West- or north-facing slopes receive sun too late in the day. Dew and cold air will remain around the vines longer, which can encourage disease and sometimes interfere with pollination. In extremely hot subtropical or tropical climates, the situation may be reversed, with the shelter of a north slope needed to protect vines from desiccating winds and scorching sunlight.

If possible, observe a site for at least a full year before planting. Watch where water collects in wet weather and where the ground dries out first in dry weather. Watch for patches where grasses and other plants turn dry and brown faster than others (this may indicate shallow soil). Observing how water drains can also help you discern how air drains in the same area. Low spots where water collects also tends to be where cooler, denser air collects and stagnates.

To analyze and correct potential site problems, think of cold air as acting like a river. For example, a ring of shrubs and trees on the low side of a hill can act as a cold-air dam, holding back air flow so that stagnant air collects around vines on part

wind

panels 10' high

A temporary windbreak of fabric with baffle effect.

or all of the slope. Cutting a few openings in the "dam" can let cold air drain away, thereby reducing or eliminating frost pockets. On flat land, filling in small low areas may eliminate localized frost pockets. Before filling such areas, however, be sure that the area doesn't have soil problems such as hardpan or dense layers that might keep the surface soil wet or waterlogged even after filling. If that's the case, leveling may just create a spot of soggy soil that is unsuitable to plant.

Observing sun and shade patterns over time also is critical in evaluating a site. If

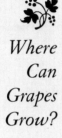

Where Can Grapes Grow?

JUST ABOUT THE TIME I think I've heard of all the possible situations in which grapes can grow, someone manages to surprise me. Grapes are amazingly adaptable as to soil and climate, yet I'm amazed at some of the unusual places that certain creative people have decided to grow grapes. Such as:

- High on the slope of a volcano in Hawaii. The "soil" was pure volcanic cinders, but grapes like poor soils. Why not another spot on the island? Because the slope was the only place where there was any cold in "winter"—meaning that it could actually have frost once or twice in the winter. Grapes generally need cold to help them go dormant and give to them a "rest" before the new growing season. So it would that like this would be a possible site. At that altitude, there was a surprisingly small difference between daytime and nighttime temperatures during the growing season, and uniform temperature often helps the fruit develop more flavor. Did it work? Well, not for the man who contacted me: he couldn't afford the price of real estate there, but there *is* a winery in that area that has been growing a few grapes successfully.

- A few hundred yards inland from the beach along the Oregon coast. The "soil," which was essentially pure beach sand, wasn't a problem since the grower could add compost to boost the nutrient value. He wasn't trying for wine production, just fruit for home use, so it was possible to shelter the vines against the south side of a building, with small "wings" to help block wind from the vine. By choosing the earliest grape possible, he was able to get some fruit, and certainly had bragging rights.

- In shallow soil, where it was only 6 feet to the water table. Since the water table was stable and didn't rise to flood the vines, this would work easily in many cases. Many commercial vineyards are planted in shallower soils than this, with the difference being that the underlayer was rock or heavy clay. The only possible drawback might be if the constant moisture allowed the vines to grow too late into the fall, making them susceptible to freeze damage.

- Two square feet of soil in back of an apartment house. In a spot where the pavement didn't quite come up to the building, a single Niagara vine had been planted and grew clear up the wall, three stories and more. It was estimated that the vine produced as much as a half ton of fruit, which the residents could pick simply by reaching out a window.

In a sloping vineyard site, cold air is trapped by trees and shrubs (above), but drains out when trees and shrubs are removed (below).

trees or other objects surround the vineyard, they may cast shade during a critical time of year. One vineyard I knew suffered from shade cast by a hill to the east. During the spring, the sun didn't top the hill until late morning. The vines in the morning shade took longer to dry from dew and rain. The excess moisture interfered with pollination in many years, and the vines in the shady area often had loose or straggly clusters. The effect was pronounced with a noticeable difference in fruit set on vines less than five feet apart. During the summer, the affected area was in full sun for most of the day, but by that time the damage already had occurred. The grower could have avoided this problem by observing the site for an entire year before planting.

Finally, if you live near a forested area, or if deer frequent your area (and they probably do) look for signs such as trails, deer scat, or trees with bark rubbed off. Analyze a site with deer in mind. For example, a vineyard sited on a hillside with woods above and water below is very likely in the path of a regular deer route, as the deer travel from cover to drink the water. If you suspect deer have a regular route through the site, you will need to plan for deer control right from the start. (See chapter 7 for more on animal pests).

ASSESSING *the* SOIL

The ideal soil for best vine growth and production, especially of table grapes, is a deep, light, silty or slightly sandy loam. Classic wine vineyard soils are often the reverse; thin, rather poor soils that make the vines "struggle" so that they develop more character and more intense flavors. However, grapes can adapt to a wide range of soil types, from sandy soil to heavy clay, depending on the variety of grape, the climate, and how the soil is managed. Nor is rocky soil a hindrance. In fact, rocky soil can be an advantage where the climate is marginal; the outcrops or surface rocks soak up heat during the day and release it at night, moderating temperatures for vines planted nearby.

If you are a home grower, and *especially* if your home is a new one in an area where there is new construction, check your soil condition before finalizing your planting site. Home builders are notorious for leaving "land mines." Builders often scrape off topsoil during construction and spread some sort of "replacement" over the remaining subsoil. If the land was graded and leveled extensively, you may have alternating patches of deep topsoil and shallow (or no) topsoil over poor subsoil. You may discover buried pockets of everything from rock or gravel to globs of leftover cement. In short, dig some test holes 2 or 3 feet deep around the property to learn what kind of soil you *really* have. A good rental shop should have power posthole diggers or soil augers that will make the job simple enough, barring serious rock infestations.

When you evaluate your soil, keep in mind that not all grape varieties like the same type of soil. For example, Ontario (a white grape variety), likes a fertile, slightly sandy loam for best growth. Ontario is a parent of many varieties (such as Alden,

Himrod, Interlaken, Lakemont, New York Muscat, and Schuyler) that also prefer similar soil. In soil that these varieties *don't* like, they exhibit less vigor, smaller berries, and less attractive clusters. In contrast, the wine grape Merlot is an example of a variety that only produces well in poor, sandy soil. Able to "hog" nitrogen from any fertile soil, Merlot will grow rampantly on all but the poorest soils, but will yield little or no crop in anything but very light, sandy soils.

Individual varieties and species of grapes adapt to specific soil types in different ways. Muscadine grapes, for example, grow in the very sandy soils of South Carolina and Florida with seemingly little problem. There are a number of bunch grapes that do best in a very narrow range of soil types. (For specifics on these bunch grapes, see chapters 10 and 11.)

Several factors are involved in helping grapes adapt to less-than-ideal soils. Soil depth can make a big difference. In the Pacific Northwest, soils can be deep. Once the vine's roots have reached at least 3 to 5 feet down, there is no need to irrigate the vines—the subsoil holds sufficient water to supply the vine. By comparison, the Northeast has areas of glacial soils that are quite shallow, with rock little more than 2 or 3 feet below the surface. In such shallow soils, there is no place for a natural reservoir of soil moisture, and irrigation is a must if there isn't regular rainfall during the growing season.

In my experience, the most important factors in helping grapes adapt are developing and maintaining soil structure. This involves building soil structure and fertility while doing as little mechanical damage to the soil as possible. The best way to

Deep Soil Develops Sturdy Vines

IF THE SOIL ALLOWS IT, grape roots will stretch to amazing depths in search of water and nutrients. In parts of Lodi, California, there are old vineyards of Tokay grapes that have grown to look like trees, their trunks are so large. In those districts there are some incredibly deep sandy loam soils estimated to be more than 100 feet deep in places.

Now, Tokay is pure *Vitis vinifera*, and the old vines are susceptible to phylloxera since they are not grafted on resistant rootstocks. Phylloxera *has* infested the Lodi area and the pest can be found in those old vineyards. However, many of the vines have not suffered any ill effects, because their roots have penetrated so far down in the deep soil that they are beyond the reach of the phylloxera. The vines are well nourished by those uninfested roots.

accomplish this is to reduce or eliminate soil cultivation and to mulch (or possibly use herbicides to control weeds under the vines) and plant a permanent ground cover between the rows. Only small, light equipment is used to mow or spray. I'll discuss building soil structure and fertility in detail in chapter 4.

I have grown vines in several types of soils and studied the vines of other growers in a wide range of soils, including heavy clay, silty loam, sandy loam, and very sandy soil. In each case, once the vines were well established and the soil structure had time to reestablish itself, vines did better than they would have been predicted to do based on soil type alone. In one case, Interlaken on heavy clay soil yielded 30 to 35 pounds of fruit per vine, per year, which is 5 to 10 pounds more than the variety ordinarily yields in other soils. However, those vines took longer to reach bearing age than vines planted on lighter soil would and did not achieve their heaviest production until the soil had fully "healed" itself.

By "healed," I mean that compaction layers had disappeared and there were uninterrupted channels through the soil from earthworms and other soil fauna, plus root channels. Further, organic matter content had stabilized and was being renewed by the mowings of the ground cover (mostly wild grasses and some weedy plants) and by the addition of mulch.

Soil testing

Unless you have reason to believe there is something drastically wrong with your soil, soil testing has limited value. For example, plants in soils low in phosphorus are aided enough by good soil life, such as mycor-rhizal fungi, that they may do better than plants in soils with adequate levels of phosphorus, but little soil life. If you want to test, use the results as a baseline to compare after the vineyard has had several years of care to build soil life and organic matter in the soil. You will probably find that the performance of the vines outstrips what the soil test says they should be able to do.

pH Requirements

Some American *V. labrusca* types tolerate soils acid enough for blueberries (pH 5.5 or below), though with high acidity the vines grow slowly and may not bear. On the other hand, *V. vinifera* and some American species, and varieties derived from them, can tolerate alkaline conditions up to pH 8.0, if not higher. Generally, grape vines do best with a pH of between 6.5 and 7.2.

PREPARING YOUR SITE

In an ideal world, your chosen site for a vineyard would already be planted with a soil-building ground cover crop, and you would be able to plant your vineyard with minimal disturbance of the soil. However, in most cases, you'll have to deal with unwanted existing vegetation on your site, which will involve a considerable amount of digging or other work. If the site has never been cultivated, or has lain fallow for years, the first step in preparing it for planting is to get rid of existing perennial plants.

If the perennials are woody shrubs and small trees, and they are few in number, you may be able to dig them out. If they are species that do not resprout from stumps or roots, and they are small enough, you can cut or mow them with a flail mower. I like using a flail mower whenever possible as it grinds up most materials finely enough that they can be left in place to add organic matter to the soil.

A different strategy is required for perennials that resprout from stumps or roots. Unless you can spend more than two years getting the land ready, the usual options are repeated mowing, rototilling, and applying herbicides.

If you repeatedly mow as soon as any sprouts show, the roots eventually will be exhausted and the plants will die. Cultivating the land with a rototiller brings up roots to allow them to dry out and die, and kills any that have started to sprout.

Systemic herbicides can help in eradicating aggressive woody plants. In the Pacific Northwest, for example, the introduced Himalayan blackberry, *Rubus procerus*, is an extraordinarily difficult plant to kill. Able to regenerate from even very small pieces of root, the canes can reach 20 feet or more in length and propagate themselves by tip layering, allowing even a single plant to cover very large amounts of land in just a few years.

Keep in mind that even broad-spectrum herbicides don't often kill perennial plants entirely in one application. Mowing, repeated cultivation, digging by hand, all these tasks take more than one year to ensure complete eradication of weeds.

If you are willing to spend up to three years preparing the site, you can fence goats in the area to eat the unwanted vegetation. For this to work, it is usually necessary to mow the area first so there are only new, tender shoots—the goats may ignore older plants.

For vineyards of one acre or less, solarization may be an option. This process uses the sun's heat to kill plants and seeds. During a sunny part of the summer, mow the grass or weeds as short as possible. Water the area well. Cover the area with clear plastic and seal it down by burying the edges. This is not an easy job. By hand, it can take two people to spread a roll of 6-foot-wide, six mil plastic and hold it in place while two more people bury the edges. Commercial machines are available that will unroll the plastic and plow a ridge of soil over the side edges of it so that the plastic can be laid by one or two people. The cost of renting such a machine may be worth the time and labor it saves.

Once the plastic is laid, the sun then warms the soil and the plastic retains the heat to the extent that the plants, seeds, and microorganisms are killed to a depth of 3 to 4 inches, or more. The process takes four to six weeks or more to ensure a thorough kill, but when it is done, plants can be set directly through the dead sod, which will act as a mulch. Further, if the vines are set directly through the plastic, it can act to keep the soil warm and help the vines begin growing sooner. Cut an "X" in the plastic and plant through that. The hole will act as a vent so the vine won't overheat. If the plastic is ordinary, non-ultraviolet-stabilized plastic sheeting, it will usually break down by the following season and can be gathered up and disposed of.

Solarizing to prepare a site for planting may be a two-year process, depending on the climate in your area. In cooler climates, by the time the soil is sterilized, it may be too late to plant, unless fall planting is possible in your area (or unless the vines have been held in pots, ready to set out as soon as the soil is ready). In the South, it should be possible to solarize the planting area in time to set out vines in late spring. In either case, irrigation will probably be necessary. Drip irrigation should be your first choice, because it allows the kind of deep watering that encourages deep rooting of vines.

Laying Out Rows

Row direction is important. If possible, rows should run parallel to the direction of prevailing winds. This allows breezes to dry vines as quickly as possible after a rain, reducing humidity and removing moisture from leaf surfaces that might help fungal spores to germinate. Thus, if the prevailing wind is from the west, rows should run east to west to let the wind blow through the aisles. I have both north-south and east-west rows. In unusually cool, wet years, the north-south rows (which run perpendicular to the prevailing wind) exhibit more

powdery mildew damage than east-west rows. Keep in mind that if you have hot summers, east-west rows may require a training system that creates a canopy of foliage over the fruit, especially on the south side of the vine, in order to prevent sunscald.

On land with any degree of slope, try to site access roads and paths in low areas; they will act as channels to funnel cold air out of the vineyard. Vine rows planted on the contour of a hill with no break or channel through them will tend to act like dams, holding the cold air back so that lower rows will be more prone to frost damage than they might be with good channels for the cold air.

Spacing

Standard spacing for bunch grapes is 8 feet apart in the row, with rows 8 to 12 feet apart. Wider aisles are preferable for air circulation and activities such as in-row

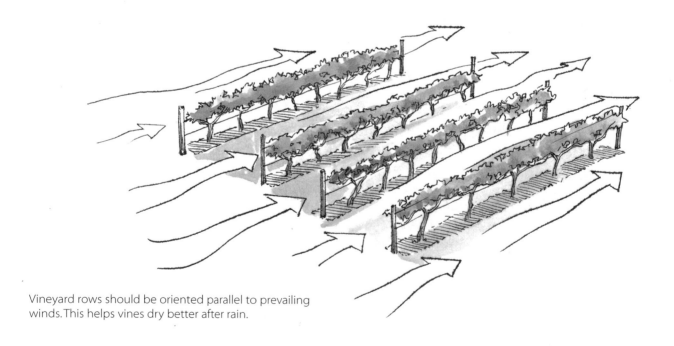

Vineyard rows should be oriented parallel to prevailing winds. This helps vines dry better after rain.

TABLE 2-1

Number of Vines per Acre
with Various Spacing Arrangements

Number of feet between rows	Number of feet between vines*						
	3	4	5	6	7	8	9
3	4,840	3,630	2,904	2,420	2,074	1,815	1,613
4	3,630	2,723	2,178	1,815	1,556	1,361	1,210
5	2,904	2,178	1,742	1,452	1,245	1,089	968
6	2,420	1,815	1,452	1,210	1,037	908	807
7	2,074	1,556	1,245	1,037	889	778	691
8	1,815	1,361	1089	**908**	**778**	**681**	605
9	1,613	1,210	968	**807**	**691**	**605**	538
10	1,452	1,089	871	726	622	545	484
11	1,320	990	792	660	566	495	440
12	1,210	908	726	605	519	454	403

*Boldface numbers are the most common spacings.

mowing, especially if the vines are vigorous and tend to grow out into the aisles during the summer. If you space rows more than the basic 8 feet apart, you are less likely to catch spreading shoots and break them when you mow in the aisles. (This assumes a growing system in which shoots hang down or are otherwise allowed to grow out from the trellis.) Some wine-grape growers train shoots in a vertical "curtain" to catch all available sunlight; they may space rows as close as 3 feet apart. However, this approach is a highly labor-intensive system that requires special-sized equipment as well as intensive summer pruning and training. It is *not* recommended for home growers.

It is possible to grow vines up the trellis the same year they are planted, using drip irrigation and regular fertilizer, but the average home grower is better off letting the vine grow undisturbed the first year to get it well established. The second year, it can be cut back to two buds in late winter, letting the vigor of the established vine be channeled into those new shoots, and trained up that season.

Use table 2-1 to determine the number of vines per acre needed for a particular spacing arrangement. For example, if you space vines 3 feet apart in rows 3 feet apart, you will need 4,840 vines to plant 1 acre. The total vines per acre for the most common row/plant spacing combinations are highlighted in bold.

PLANTING

Most growers find it easiest to plant new vines *before* installing the trellis system, as it can be harder to work around the wires and posts once they are in place. Also, once the vines are planted, the support stakes can be driven closer to the vines than would be possible if the vines were being planted after the stakes were in place.

Plant vines so that they are in-line in the row. If you looked down the row, the trunks would be hidden behind the posts. If the row runs east and west, the vines should be set so that they will all be on either the east or west side of the stakes. This makes cultivation easier, and the stake helps protect the vine trunk from injury by the tractor as it passes when cultivating or mowing.

Most grapes are sold as bareroot stock and need immediate attention on arrival. Inspect your vines. They should have a good root system with at least two large (3/16- to 1/4-inch-diameter) roots and a number of smaller ones. Untrimmed is best, but even roots cut back to 6 inches are acceptable if there are plenty of them and they have no discolored or damaged areas. Cut one to see if it is firm and light-colored inside. Soft, spongy roots that are dark brownish or watery-looking inside may have been frozen. Such a vine may not grow. The condition of the top of the young vine is less critical. A vine may have as little as 2 inches of top growth showing at planting, and still grow well if it has a healthy root system.

New vines need no pruning other than to trim off broken or dead roots and shoots. If the broken roots and shoots are live, just cut off the damaged part. If the vine can't be planted immediately, heel it in soil or moist, aged sawdust (fresh sawdust could burn the roots). Soak the vine in plain water for several hours before planting to replace water lost in storage and shipping. If fall planting is possible where you live, it allows grape roots to grow until the ground freezes, establishing the vine better for faster growth in spring. However, vines are often not available until late winter, for spring planting.

The planting hole should be large enough to accommodate all of the roots. Plant the vine with the roots spread evenly over a small mound of soil. How deep to plant? Cold-climate growers have found that planting a vine deep, as much as 18 inches, helps ensure that some roots and buds will survive even through harsh winters that kill the top of the vine. In my own experience, this is a good strategy for other climates as well because it encourages the vine to send its roots deep. Deeper-rooted vines survive drought better and can absorb minerals from farther down in the soil.

Do not plant grafted vines deeply. The graft union must be above the soil line; otherwise the variety grafted on the rootstock will put down its own roots and invalidate the effects of the rootstock.

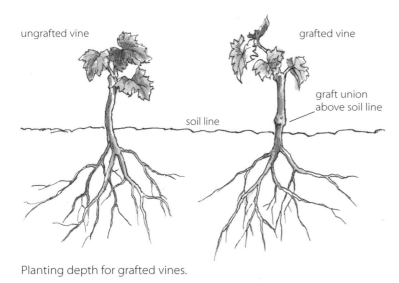

ungrafted vine

grafted vine

graft union above soil line

soil line

Planting depth for grafted vines.

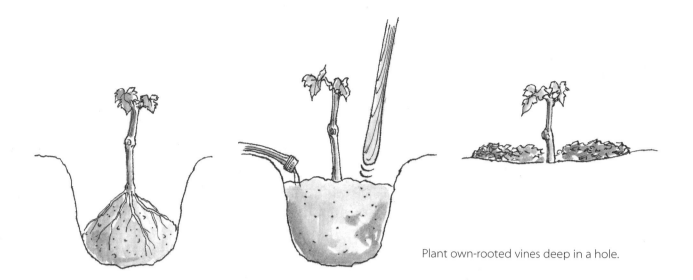

Plant own-rooted vines deep in a hole.

Do *not* add compost or similar soil amendments to the planting hole. This tends to make the vine keep its roots there, as though it were planted in a pot, and the roots are slower to move into the surrounding, untreated soil. Instead, use only small amounts of soluble fertilizer in the hole, putting soil amendments on top of the soil as mulch. Better yet, add a bit of mycorrhizal fungi inoculant (see resources for fungi suppliers), sprinkling it on the roots as you fill in the hole. One or two teaspoons per vine is sufficient. Mycorrhizal fungi encourage root growth, aid nutrient uptake, and help protect the roots from disease.

Fill the hole, tamping the soil with your boot or a stick, and water it in to settle it firmly around the roots. Now is the time to use organic matter, such as compost, as a mulch around the plant, both to keep out weeds and maintain soil moisture. Nothing is harder on new plants than fluctuating moisture levels. Mulch is an excellent way to help ensure even moisture levels between waterings. Further, organic matter on the surface encourages earthworms, which will carry the organic material down into the soil, aerating the soil and rebuilding its structure.

Watering Young Vines

Fertilizing young vines is not as important as keeping them watered. Most vines need a minimum of one to two inches of water per week when they are getting established. Water deeply to encourage roots to grow down. Deep roots will help ensure the vine's ability to withstand drought later on and will help it reach minerals deep in the soil.

If you do need to water your grapes, choose drip irrigation or a soil soaker. Avoid overhead watering, which wets the leaves and increases humidity, two factors that encourage growth of fungus. Stop watering by midsummer, or a minimum of a month before frost, so that vines harden off and fruit ripening isn't delayed.

If you are going to grow vines without irrigation, you will need a way to ensure that young vines don't dry out until they are well established and their roots can reach subsoil moisture. There are several ways to do this.

First, in areas where winters are mild enough (Zone 7 and warmer), it is possible to plant in the fall. This usually involves using planting stock that has been held in pots, as dormant nursery stock is not always available in time. Vines are set out when fall rains have started, usually when the vines are starting to go dormant, though they may still have their leaves. At that time, the soil is still warm enough for the roots to continue to grow and help the vine get established, so that the vines are usually ready to train up in the spring. I have used a variation that saves time by growing vines in 1-gallon pots and training the shoots up a light bamboo pole in the pot. When the vine is set out, the shoot is usually tall enough to reach the first training wire and can be left as the new trunk. If the winter is cold, it may nip this shoot back, in which case I just start the vine up from two buds in the spring. This technique usually saves time.

The second method is one I haven't tried myself yet, but it looks promising. There is a product available called DriWater that comes in a milk-carton-type container. The material is water combined with a biodegradable gel thickener. The carton is opened and the open end is pushed into the soil next to the young vine. As the gel degrades, it releases the water, keeping the vine moist enough to continue to grow for up to six weeks.

The third way is simply to carry water to the vines. I have been able to carry a 55-gallon drum full of water in the bucket of my tractor. The drum has a spout attached.

I could water about forty vines per hour this way, including time to refill the barrel.

Fertilizing

Withhold fertilizer unless symptoms of nutrient deficiency begin to show. (Symptoms are described in chapter 4.) Proper fertilizing helps the wood of grape vines to mature, making them better able to withstand harsh climates. There is also plenty of evidence that lush, over-fertilized vines are more attractive to deer and insects.

When you fertilize, keep applications light. Heavy feeding is mainly useful for young vines to get them up to size. Mature vines fed too much nitrogen become overly vigorous, and dense growth can be hard to keep disease free. Also, excess nitrogen causes flower clusters to "shatter" (flowers fall off), reducing fruit set. In fact, mature vines should not need any supplemental nitrogen when grown in a healthy soil with plenty of organic matter.

A good general rule for fertilizing grapes is to use a mulch of well-rotted compost, which will supply small, but regular essential amounts of nutrients. Regularly adding organic matter in this way will make up for poor soils to a surprising degree. I've grown grapes on very heavy clay soils that shouldn't have been suitable, yet the vines thrived and bore well with regular applications of compost mulch.

Do *not* use chemical fertilizer on vines treated with mycorrhizal fungi; the fertilizer will inhibit or kill the fungi. Use only mild, organic fertilizers such as fish emulsion or pellets. I have never needed to fertilize well-established vines. If an established vine is healthy and shows no sign of deficiency symptoms, there is no need to apply any kind of fertilizer, though adding organic matter such as compost is always beneficial for maintaining soil structure and soil life.

TRAINING *and* TRELLIS SYSTEMS

Like the right site, the right training system makes a *big* difference. In my own vineyard, I use a simple two-wire system, with (mostly) cordon-trained vines. The cordons are trained on one wire, at about 5 feet high, with a second wire 15 inches above that. As shoots grow up, they attach to the upper wire and are supported. If needed, I may tie shoots to the upper wire to be sure they don't break. I'll describe in detail how to set up a system like this. If you want to learn more about other types of trellising systems, turn to chapter 3.

Posts

Two types of support posts are needed for a vineyard: heavy posts that are the main supports of the wire, and lighter support stakes for each vine. The wire-support posts are generally made of wood, while the vine supports may be wood or metal. Wooden posts, unless made of rot-resistant wood such as black locust, should be treated to prevent rot. Black locust posts can last as long or longer than treated posts and have the advantage of being free of chemicals that might leach into the soil. Black locust grows fast enough that it may be worthwhile to plant a row of the trees along one side of the vineyard (preferably the north side where they won't shade the vines) to be a future source of replacement posts. Since black locust trees are vigorous re-sprouters, posts can be coppiced, or cut from the same trees repeatedly. One further advantage is that black locust is a legume, a type of plant that fixes nitrogen, thereby improving the soil in the vicinity.

The wire-support posts should be a minimum of 3 inches in diameter for rows up to 300 feet long. Larger diameter posts, up to about 6 inches in diameter, are needed for longer rows due to the increased weight of the wire and the greater pull on

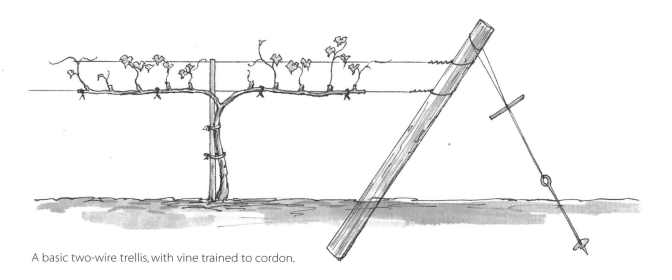

A basic two-wire trellis, with vine trained to cordon.

the posts. The number of wire support posts within the row varies with the type of system used. In my vineyard, I use only two support wires, so the wire support posts are set 100 feet apart. If a vineyard is exposed to a lot of wind, especially when the soil is wet, the heavy support posts may set be as close as 20 feet apart to keep the row from "leaning."

Heavy wire-support posts should be set at least 2 feet deep in average soil. You will need posts at least 8 feet long in order to leave 6 feet above ground for trellis use. In soft soils, such as sand, consider using taller posts and setting them deeper, or setting them with cement to anchor them well. In very rocky soil, posts can sometimes be set less deeply—say 1½ feet deep for an 8-foot post—as rocky ground will hold posts more strongly than loam or other softer soils, though it takes more work to dig the post hole.

Wire

The size wire generally used to support grapevines runs from 9 to 12 gauge, 9-gauge being the heaviest. If you go to a wire dealer, it is usually sold by weight rather than by length; 100-pound rolls are the basic unit. The dealer may sell you smaller amounts, but you will pay a cutting charge for it. In some cases, the charge may be enough that it's cheaper to buy the whole roll.

When I first started with grapes, the main wire available was galvanized steel wire. It served the purpose, but after a few years of being stretched, it would sag and you had to restretch it. Also, rust would start to show. If you are a backyard grower, galvanized wire may work for you. A short run of it won't stretch a lot, and it's not that hard to retighten one or two small rows. Otherwise, I recommend trying tem-

Creative Trellising

MANY CREATIVE VARIATIONS, both in materials and form, of a basic trellis system are possible. For example, one grower used rebar (steel concrete-reinforcing bars or rods, usually ⅜ to ½ inch in diameter) in place of wire. He welded short nipples of rebar on the long pieces, and put matching pieces of short pipe on the support post. This allowed him to set the long bars on top of the posts with the nipples in the pipe sections. The bar was as rigid as wire would be without needing to be stretched, and the grower could lift the whole top "wire" off the trellis at pruning time. It also eliminated the need for anchors or braces at the ends of the rows.

Other growers have used things like telephone wires (the heavy cables hanging from the poles, not the light wire used inside the house), and plastic baling twine (cheap, but it stretches and needs replacing every few years). In cold climates, plastic twine might be an option that would make it easier to remove vines from the trellis to lay them down for winter protection. Twine could be cut loose from the vines more easily than vines could be separated from wire.

The main thing is, don't be confined by a stereotype. If you can find materials or methods that work better for your situation, don't be afraid to experiment.

WHEN I PLANTED MY FIRST VINEYARD, I figured I'd save money by making my own anchors. We were building a house at the time and there were lots of 3-foot pieces of half-inch rebar left from the cement work on the basement. I bent loops on each end of each piece by hooking them through a trailer hitch on the back of our old truck. Then I set one end in the holes in concrete blocks (seconds, from a local factory) or into plastic pots a gallon or larger.

When the cement for the house was poured, odd dabs of cement were left after each load, when the cement trucks were being cleaned, and I used those to fill the pots and blocks. Since the pots were plastic, they could be slipped off the hardened concrete and reused. I made enough anchors for over twenty rows that way. *Then* I realized how much digging would be needed to set all those anchors. Not to mention that they couldn't be used until the dirt settled for several weeks, or tightening the wires would pull them out of the soil, letting the wires go loose quickly. It didn't take me long to decide that commercial wire anchors were a lot easier to use than the homemade kind.

pered, high-tensile, stainless steel wire. It resists rust better than galvanized, and stretches so little you may find yourself replacing posts before you have to tighten wire. However, it does take more work to install high-tensile wire, enough that it's usually a job for two (or more) people. Trying to put up high-tensile wire by yourself is like trying to stretch a giant Slinky.

Wire Anchors

Wire must be stretched tightly to support grape vines. Simply tying wire to the end posts isn't sufficient. There must be some type of anchor, usually buried in the ground, at the end of each row, to which the wire is attached or the end posts must be solidly braced, to allow the wire to be stretched tightly. The easiest type to use is the commercial anchor. This is a heavy iron rod 2 to 3 feet long, with a loop at one end and a split disk at the other. The disk, which ranges from 3 to nearly 6 inches in diameter, acts like a drill. Put a piece of

pipe or iron bar through the loop, turn the pipe or bar, and the disk bites into the ground. Once in the ground, the disk gives the anchor the ability to resist being pulled out. The anchor is usually painted bright orange so that it's easy to see. Anchors come in several sizes: the longer the row, the more wire pulling on the anchor, and the bigger the anchor needs to be to resist the pull.

With a piece of pipe or steel bar through the loop at the top as a handle, a wire anchor makes a good posthole digger. I used an old anchor that way for many years; screw it down a few inches and pull it out, repeating the process until the hole is deep enough. It makes a hole very close to the diameter of a post, so very little backfilling is needed.

When setting the end posts of a row, if you plan to use wire anchors, set the posts at an angle of about 15 degrees off vertical, pointing away from the row. This braces the posts against the pull of the tightened wire. End posts are only set vertical if they

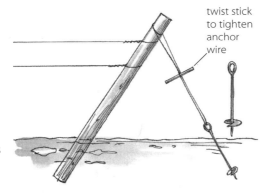

twist stick to tighten anchor wire

End posts set with wire anchors should be about 15 degrees off vertical, pointing away from the row.

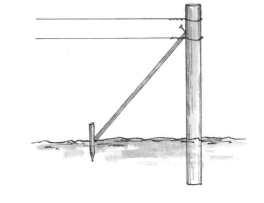

End posts may be set vertically if braced with an angle post inside the row.

are to be braced with an angle post inside the row (see illustration).

Which system is better to use—inside braces or anchors? A brace has the advantage of leaving the end of the row free of anything that might be hit by equipment, and it allows the row to be fit into a closer space if you don't have to allow an extra 3 feet at each end for wire anchors. However, the cost of braces is greater than that of wire anchors in most cases, and braces take more labor to install than wire anchors. Also, the end of the brace that butts against the ground tends to rot or rust more rapidly than the rest, so that braces usually have to be replaced or shored up more often than other parts of the system. How often will depend on climate: hot, humid climates will rot or rust posts more rapidly than cold or dry climates.

In heavy or poorly drained soils, it is a good idea to fill in around posts with gravel, instead of using the soil that came out of the hole. The extra drainage will slow rot and extend the life of the posts, as well as anchoring them more solidly (gravel doesn't compact the way soil does). Put 6 inches of gravel in the bottom of each hole before inserting a post. This will keep the posts out of direct contact with the soil. Use crushed gravel, which packs more solidly than rounded (pea) gravel.

One other trick that extends the life of the posts is to put a "cap" of zinc flashing (sheet metal) on the top of the large diameter posts other than the grape stakes (stakes at the vines). The flashing helps prevent rot by keeping the cut end of the post dry. The zinc also has a fungicidal action to further inhibit decay. Any zinc that washes into the soil is too dilute to cause harm to the soil, and in some cases, will actually provide a needed nutrient to nearby vines.

Attaching the Wires

I didn't develop a really good method of attaching the wires until cordless rechargeable drills came along. These portable drills allowed me to drill ⅝-inch holes through the main posts at any height I wanted so that I could thread the wires through the posts, all the way down the row. Before that, I had tried staples, screws, and nails. Staples pulled out after two or three years; screws took extra work to install and scraped the wires; and nails held the wire too tightly or split the posts. Also, with wire tightly attached at every post, it was nec-

To attach wire, drill two holes in the end post parallel to the direction of the wire. Drill a third hole at the top at 90° to the first two holes for the wire to attach to the anchor wire.

Threading and tightening trellis wire.

essary to tighten each section of wire between each post. However, with the wire threaded through the holes, tightening and later retightening the wire in one place served to tighten the entire length. At the same time, the wire was supported enough to hold the vines easily.

I find it easiest to install the lowest wire first, then stop and drive the posts/stakes for each grape vine. The wire makes a good guide to keep the row straight and is low enough that the post driver doesn't hit it when I drive the posts.*

To attach the wire, I first drill two holes in the end posts at the appropriate height. The holes should be parallel to the direction in which the wires are to run. Then I drill another hole above those two at a 90-degree angle to them, and parallel to the ground. You should be able to look through the two lower holes and see the next post in the row, while the view through the top hole will be of the neighboring row. The top hole is for the anchor.

Run wire through the hole in the top and down through the loop in the anchor. Do this twice, so you have two strands through the hole. Pull up the slack and leave at least a foot or more overlapping in each direction. Twist the ends around and over each other and wrap them thoroughly (see illustrations). Nothing else needs to be done at this point. Repeat this at the other end of the row.

Stretching Wire

Take an end from the coil of wire and thread it through the lowest hole in the end post.

* A post driver is a heavy metal tube with one end sealed. It slips over the end of the post and the user slides it up and down to drive the post in.

Continue feeding out wire and threading it through posts all the way down the row. At the far end, thread the wire through the hole in the other end post, wrap it around the post at least twice, and wrap at least 1 foot of it around itself just back of the point where it enters the hole.

Back at the starting end, you have several options on how to stretch the wire tight. The simplest for a small-scale vineyard is to pull up most of the slack by hand, estimating how much wire should extend through the hole to wrap around the post twice and leave at least 1 foot to wind back over the trellis wire, as at the other end. With the majority of the slack pulled out by hand, hook the wire in the claw of a claw hammer right where it comes through the hole. Alternatively, a fence tool (see illustration) can be used the same way. With the head of the hammer or the tool braced against the post, rock the tool to one side to pull the wire tighter. Have a second hammer/tool to catch the wire right at the hole, and repeat. By "rocking" it this way, you can stretch the wire quite tightly. Bend the wire around the post as you stretch, and it will resist pulling back enough so that you can wrap the wire all the way around the post to hold it, and finally wrap the wire around itself to fix it in place.

This was the way I installed most of my early vineyard. It is about the cheapest method, but not always the easiest. For example, it is now possible to use wire grippers to take much of the work out of tightening wires. Looking like miniature traffic cones, wire grippers are fitted in holes in the end posts and the wire is threaded through them. As the wire is pulled through, the device grips the wire so that it will move only in one direction. It is a simple matter to pull the wire tight with a claw hammer or a fence tool.

At this point, you should install the vine stakes—iron fence posts or wooden stakes to support individual vines (see below). Then you can install the second wire in the same way as you installed the first wire.

After you install the second wire, you'll find that the first will have developed a slight slack. You can take care of that by twisting the wire attached to the wire anchor. Put a heavy stick (1 to 2 inches thick) between the wires of one of the anchors in the row and twist to wind up the anchor wire (like winding the rubber band in a toy airplane). As the wires are twisted, they pull

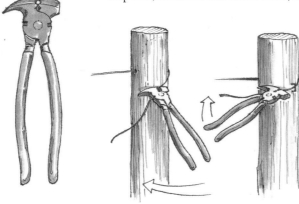

Tightening with grippers. To get the wire really tight, tighten at least twice. First pull the wire tight with one tool, then grip the wire with a second tool, close to the post, and repeat the tightening. If possible, repeat again. Then anchor the wire with a staple, and wrap around post and around itself, as shown on page 25.

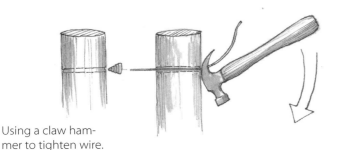

Using a claw hammer to tighten wire.

the post back and tighten the wires in the row. If you have stretched the wires tight to start with, you won't need to wind the anchor wires all the way, so that you will have some slack left to tighten the row more in later years.

Since the time I installed my first vineyard, several types of commercial wire tighteners have been invented. One is a ratchet device that attaches to the post, with the wire attached to it. As the wire becomes slack, the ratchet is turned to re-tighten it. These are a fairly large expense and may not be necessary unless the row is more than 500 feet long.

In some systems, the wires are regularly moved or taken down as shoots are positioned during the growing season. In this case, wires may be attached to sections of chain. Hooks are installed in the end posts and the chains are hooked over them. Thus, the wire can be tightened or taken down, as needed.

Turnbuckles can also be used to tighten wire, but turnbuckles can be fairly expensive and you are limited in how far they can be tightened. Further, the wire has to be fairly tight to start with.

Generally, home and small-scale vine-yardists will usually find the low-tech method I've described above easy and in-expensive enough for their needs. However, higher-tech versions, such as ratchets, might be a helpful option for persons with limited strength.

Supporting Vines

Small posts are needed to support both the vines and the wire in the basic trellising system I've described. In my vineyard, I prefer using steel fence posts to support

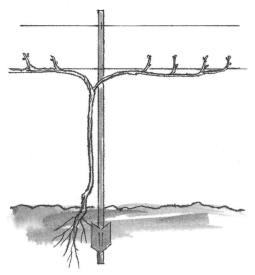

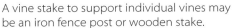

A vine stake to support individual vines may be an iron fence post or wooden stake.

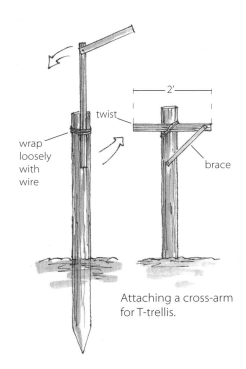

twist

wrap
loosely
with
wire

2'

brace

Attaching a cross-arm for T-trellis.

individual vines. They are widely available, long-lasting, and attractive. Plus, they have attachment points for wire and are easy to install with a post driver.

Pressure-treated, round, wooden grape stakes are an alternative to metal posts. Grape stakes are usually cheaper than metal stakes, but they break more easily, and are harder to drive. If possible, before you buy, inspect the stakes for knots and diagonal grain. Flaws such as these are a sign that the stakes may break easily. If you can, get a replacement guarantee from the seller. When I used these stakes, I found that staples and other fasteners either pulled out or split the wood. The method that worked best for

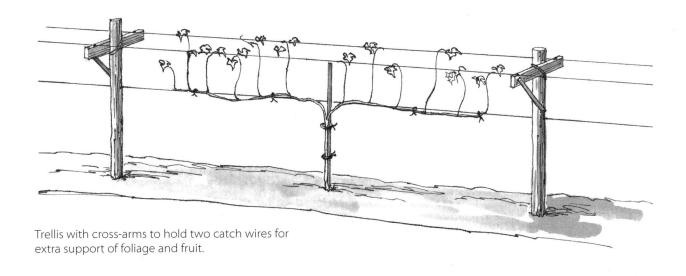

Trellis with cross-arms to hold two catch wires for extra support of foliage and fruit.

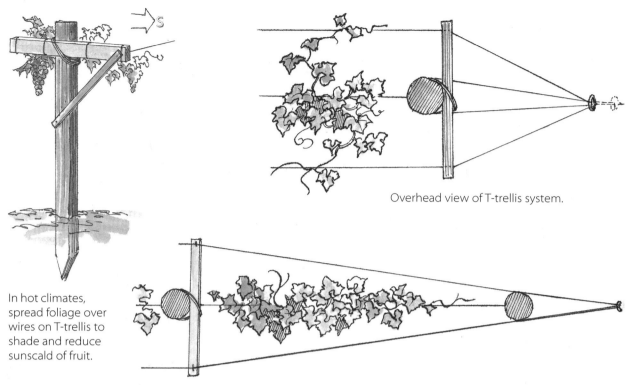

Overhead view of T-trellis system.

In hot climates, spread foliage over wires on T-trellis to shade and reduce sunscald of fruit.

Where turning space at end of row is tight, the last cross-arm can be left off the end post.

me was to drill a hole through a stake and then put a loop of wire through the hole and around the trellis wire. The wire loop supported the trellis wire like a sling, yet allowed the trellis wire to slide freely when it was tightened.

A second type of stake is the stamped metal stake. These light stakes can be used with standard fence clips to hold the trellis wire. However, the stakes lack the stabilizing fin of a standard metal fence post and tend to tilt in the soil, allowing the row to "lean" from the pressure of the prevailing wind. On the plus side, they are cheap, and they are easy to pull out of the ground when they need to be replaced. You probably will have to replace them more often than heavier metal or wooden posts, since they

bend or rust through at ground level. These stakes would be a poor choice in acid or alkaline soil (below 6.0 or above about 7.2 pH), because the thin metal is likely to corrode and weaken more quickly in such soils.

It isn't always necessary to pay full cost for steel fence posts. Watch for used ones for sale. Unless the posts are badly rusted, they will still serve for many years. Slight kinks or bends can often be straightened.

If there is a dealer in steel nearby, you may be able to get "seconds" cheaply. These usually lack paint or the fin at the bottom. I've bought 10- and 12-foot imperfect posts for less than the price of standard 7-foot fence posts. Posts that long can be driven in deep enough to hold well even if they lack a fin at the bottom.

3 *PRUNING and TRAINING*

NOTHING SCARES PEOPLE AWAY from growing grapes more than the fear of pruning them. Fruit trees, at least, will form a recognizable tree shape even if you don't prune them. But left untended, a grape vine becomes a tangle of growth that seems unconquerable, especially if you are an inexperienced pruner.

Proper pruning and training leads to reliable crops of consistently high-quality fruit on a vine that is easy to manage, year after year. The basic principles of pruning grapes are easy to learn and apply and offer enough flexibility to allow for error and inexperience.

In this chapter, I will talk about the reasons for pruning and the basic types of pruning and training systems; the nuts and bolts of how to prune and train, beginning with young vines; and special pruning situations, such as dealing with overgrown vines, and summer pruning. Finally, I'll cover how to train a vine on an arbor and in less conven-

tional places, such as against a wall. I'll also discuss how to grow grapes in a greenhouse.

REASONS *for* PRUNING

The most basic reason for pruning grapes is to regulate the amount of the crop. This, in turn, affects crop quality and ensures uniform annual production.

A vine produces its crop from buds laid down in the previous year's new growth. This means that, during the winter, all new canes already carry flower buds with the potential to bloom and become clusters of grapes. (If you carefully open and dissect a bud, you will find a tiny little compressed shoot and flower bud clusters.) If too many buds set fruit, there will be more fruit than the vine can handle properly. Several things, none of them desirable, can happen when you leave a vine unpruned or prune it too little.

At bloom time, if there are too many flower clusters, available food (carbohydrates) is spread among too many flowers. This means fewer flowers in each cluster get the energy needed to allow them to set and start developing into berries, or they develop as undersized berries. With fewer berries per cluster, the clusters are straggly or loose instead of well-filled or compact. However, because there are many more clusters than usual, the overall weight of fruit is higher than normal. The fruit competes with new shoots and undeveloped leaves for the food stored in the vine. This source is insufficient, so the plant suffers until enough leaves develop to make all the carbohydrates needed by both the new growth and the fruit. By that time, it is too late to improve the fruit set. Plus, there isn't enough growing season remaining for the new shoots to develop size and vigor. The end result is that the berries don't get the sugar needed for ripening until much later than normal, if at all.

If a variety normally ripens late, overcropping can delay ripening past the time of first frost. By the time sugar builds up in fruit on an overloaded vine, the acid in the fruit will have dropped too low for good flavor—the fruit will taste flat and insipid.

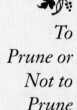

To Prune or Not to Prune

IF ALL YOU WANTED TO DO was keep crop production regular each year, you could pick off flower clusters early in the season, before bloom, without pruning. This would adjust the crop so the vine wouldn't be overloaded, keeping the fruit quality high.

Of course, after a few years of thinning fruits in this way, the vine would be an enormous tangled mess: In addition to adjusting the crop, pruning keeps the vine under control.

Why is this the case? The same buds that produce fruit also produce shoots that bear leaves. On a pruned vine, the smaller number of buds means a much smaller number of new shoots to start growth in the spring. Until the leaves on the new shoots are mature enough to produce food, the vine is living off stored reserves. Even then it takes a while before there are enough mature leaves to offset the drain on the stored food. For instance, a vine pruned to have only 24 fruit buds will have to grow for several weeks before the first new leaves are ready to produce food. Meanwhile, an unpruned vine will have at least ten times as many shoots, 240 leaves producing food as opposed to the pruned vine's 24. Now, if the crop on the unpruned vine had been thinned so that it had the same number of flower clusters as the pruned vine, each flower cluster would have at least ten times as many leaves feeding it early in the season, right at bloom time. This gives the unpruned vine a big jump on the pruned one early in the season. However, the unpruned vine's shoots won't elongate much. The energies of the unpruned vine are divided among many more shoots, so each one may grow only a foot or so, while the pruned vine thrusts its energy into fewer shoots, pushing them to much greater ultimate size. Eventually the shoots on the pruned vine grow long enough to have as many productive leaves total as the unpruned vine. So, while the unpruned vine may have the edge early in the season, the pruned vine will catch up.

Finally, the fruit color on an overcropped vine usually doesn't develop well, making it both unattractive and lacking the pigment needed for wine, juice, or jelly.

Meanwhile, because the new shoots get less food, they develop fewer buds with smaller flower clusters, setting up the vine for a sparse crop the following year.

In short, an unpruned vine may bear more fruit, but fruit quality is likely to be so poor that it's hardly worth using, and in the following year, the vine will bear a small crop.

Even more important, when fruit takes longer than usual to ripen, it diverts energy from helping the new growth harden off and prepare for winter. This can result in more winter dieback of the vine and its canes, weakening or even killing it. Even in mild winters, poorly ripened wood may become diseased and die back to older wood.

The year after a vine is overcropped, it produces very few clusters, though their quality may be surprisingly good. That's because so few fruit buds were laid down the year before, due to the overcropping of the vine. Now, with so few clusters, the ratio of leaves to fruit is higher. Those few clusters have bigger, sweeter berries, and the crop ripens earlier. Trouble is, with a smaller crop, the vine also has energy left over to produce more new growth, including more fruitful buds, which means another large crop looms ahead for the following year. And because there is also more food to allow the wood to harden off better, the odds of all the new growth surviving are increased. In other words, the stage is set to repeat the boom-bust cycle again.

Unpruned vines *can* reach equilibrium and stop the up-and-down cycle. However, the fruit rarely will be as good as on a pruned vine, because the mass of old growth surrounding the fruit prevents it from getting adequate light and air circulation.

After crop regulation, the second most important reason to prune and train grapes is to make the vine manageable and the fruit accessible. You can train or guide grapevines to grow in a greater variety of forms, sizes, and situations than any type of fruit tree or bush. Grown in pots, grape vines can be compact, bearing only one or two clusters of fruit per year. At other end of the scale, at the University of California at Davis, a vine of the Mission variety of *Vitis vinifera* covers a massive trellis that extends over one-tenth of an acre, and it produces at least a half-ton of fruit per year. A Mission grape vine planted in 1842 in Carpenteria, California, produced eight tons of fruit in 1893 and had a trunk circumference of 9 feet. In England, the "Hampton Court" vine, a *V. vinifera* variety named Black Hamburg, has attained amazing size and production in a greenhouse, often yielding 2,500 clusters a year.

The form of a vine can be anything the grower dictates, from a single trunk growing in one direction (as the English sometimes use for greenhouse grapes) to multiple trunks fanning out to all points of the compass on an arbor. Vines can be trained vertically to grow many feet high, or flat on the ground to take advantage of heat radiated from soil and rocks. Training vines horizontally both protects the vines from late frost and allows them to receive enough heat to ripen in cold northern summers. Other training schemes range from using the vine's own shade to protect the fruit from sun in hot climates, to spreading systems used in high latitudes where sunlight has low intensity and vines need to catch all available light.

Pruning helps the grower adjust the vine to the environment in other ways, too. Proper pruning can improve air circulation in the vine to cut down the likelihood of disease. Vines can be pruned so they will bloom later than usual, to escape frost. The right pruning and training system can help protect vines from winter damage, and can allow vines to produce crops reliably even in harsh climates. In short, pruning and training control the size and form of the vine, both for the convenience of the grower and for the sake of the vine, to best adapt it to its environment.

SYSTEMS *of* PRUNING *and* TRAINING

One serious misconception is that there is a single "one-size-fits-all" system of pruning and training for all grapes in all situations. While some principles apply to the pruning and training of all grapes, trying to make one system fit every variety in every situation is a sure way to fail.

How a vine is best pruned depends on two main factors: The system used to train the vine, and the variety of grape. Each factor has an effect on the other. The one thing all pruning and training systems have in common is that they all use one or the other (or rarely, both) of the vine's basic structures—canes or spurs—to carry the fruit buds.

Fruiting canes may have from five to as many as fifteen buds, with ten to twelve the most common number. A fruiting spur is generally recognized as a cane that has been shortened so it has from one to four buds, with two to three being the most common number.

The difference between spur-pruning and cane-pruning systems is largely a matter of how long the spurs or canes are and how they are positioned, in relation to both the vine and to the trellis. The spurs or canes are replaced every year, while the older wood of the vine is basically unchanged, once it has been trained into its permanent form early in the vine's life.

Spur Pruning

Spur pruning is done on a vine that is trained to a permanent framework of two-year or older wood with the fruit-bearing wood—spurs with one to four buds each on them—spaced along the framework. The buds on the spurs produce the fruit-bearing shoots every summer. In turn, most of those shoots are removed every winter, with one of the lowest shoots on the old spur being cut back to become a new spur (see illustrations). Spur pruning is probably the easiest system for the novice to learn. Once the spur positions have been established, pruning involves little more than the removal of unwanted canes, plus cutting back of the remaining shoots at the spur positions. The old spurs help serve as a guide, and you just repeat what has been done the year before.

The common training systems using spur pruning are head-trained, spur-pruned vines (HTSP) and cordon-trained vines. A HTSP vine is nothing more than a vertical trunk, usually tied to a post, with spurs radiating from the top one-half to one-third of the trunk, making the vine look

1. Unpruned spur on vine of "Cayuga."

2. Growth removed above shoot, which will become the new spur.

3. Shoot cut back to two buds.

3a (close-up, left.) Depending on variety, the spur could have as many as 4 buds.

tangle of growth reduces air circulation, which makes the vines both more prone to disease and more difficult to spray.

In the past, HTSP vines were common in the wine vineyards of California, but the system lost favor because of difficulties in caring for the vine and harvesting fruit. The system is only suited to low- to moderate-vigor wine grapes with an open growth habit. Table grapes grown with this system may have poor appearance due to difficulty controlling disease. Tangling of the clusters in the vine can crush and deform berries and make it difficult to pick them without damage.

The other important system using fruiting spurs is the cordon system. In this method, fruit spurs are carried on permanent, horizontal arms extending outward from the top of the trunk. Usually there are two arms, giving the vine a "T" shape, though other arrangements are possible.

A head-trained, spur-pruned vine.

something like a bush or a dwarf tree. The system is easy and cheap to establish because untreated wooden posts can be used as supports; by the time the wood rots away, the vine's trunk has become rigid enough to support itself. However, vines trained this way tend to yield less because they are restrained to a smaller size than they are capable of reaching. The clusters are all produced near the trunk and tend to get tangled in the shoots, making them harder to pick and more prone to damage. The dense

Each arm is usually 3 to 4 feet long and has up to six spur positions. While each position may start out with only one spur, as the vine matures and gains vigor, it may be possible to add additional spurs at each position to increase overall production capacity.

Vines trained to cordons need full trellising, with wires, posts, and wire anchors, while HTSP vines need only untreated wood posts for initial support. However, the difference in production and fruit quality, especially with table grapes, makes cordon training worthwhile. On cordon-trained vines, clusters are spaced evenly and regularly, usually hanging just below the cordon arms, where they are easy to harvest and protected by the foliage from sunburn. Growth is spread evenly along the wires, so air can circulate through the vine well and spray can penetrate more uniformly than with HTSP vines. A vine properly trained to cordons is very easy to prune, even for novice pruners.

In cold climates, one variation of the cordon-trained vine is a straight trunk trained diagonally, with spurs on the upper half of the trunk. A diagonally trained vine is easier to lower to the ground and cover up for winter protection. (See chapter 12 for more information.)

Cane Pruning

Cane pruning, as the name indicates, relies on canes rather than spurs to produce the fruit. Canes may have as few as five buds to as many as fifteen. Cane systems often require more wires or other supports than spur systems, and pruning them takes more

Row pruned to cordons.

After pruning.

Note extra spurs left at each spur location.

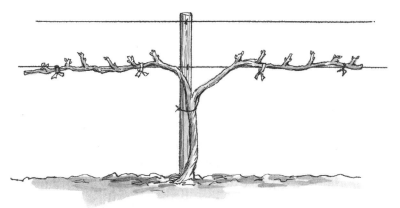

Cordon-trained vine with spurs.

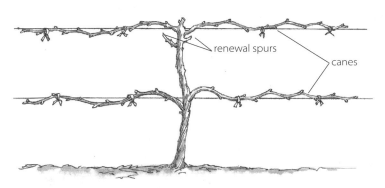

renewal spurs

canes

Cane-trained vine.

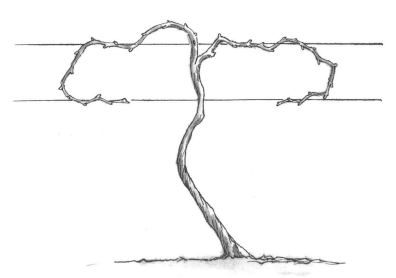

Cone-trained vine—"umbrella" Kniffen.

experience and decision making. However, cane pruning is a more flexible system than spur pruning, and canes allow more year-to-year variation in the amount of fruit buds left on the vine. If you want to increase the number of fruit buds on spurs for a greater crop, you can usually only add twelve or so per season. With cane pruning, you can add as many buds as there are canes available, possibly even doubling the amount of fruit buds over the previous year.

The main difficulty with cane pruning is that it takes more experience to learn how to choose which canes to cut back to become the replacement spurs and which to leave as fruiting canes, as well as deciding how many canes to leave. New growers often fail to remove enough wood, letting the vine overcrop. Around 90 to 95 percent of the previous season's growth should be removed in proper pruning.

Various forms of cane pruning are used extensively in modern commercial wine vineyards (these are discussed on page 42). The version of cane pruning that most home growers will recognize is the old Kniffen system, both the two-cane "umbrella" Kniffen and the four-cane Kniffen.

PRUNING *and* TRAINING TECHNIQUES

This section covers the techniques involved in pruning and training grape vines. It will show you how to develop the main structure of a vine to suit the purpose and location of the vine. This will include vines on standard trellises, on arbors, and in several other, unusual locations. You will learn how to train a young vine, or prune and re-train an old vine that needs repair or rejuvenation.

Tools for Pruning

To prune most grape vines, you will need just one tool, a good pair of pruners or secaturs (hand-held pruning shears). Invest in a reputable brand, not just a cheap knock-off from the local discount center. If possible, order from a professional nursery supply company. My personal favorite is Felco. The advantages of Felco pruners are:

- They cut with a blade sliding past an opposing surface. When the blade is sharp, it slices cleanly without creating ragged or crushed ends, such as can happen with pruners of the type where a blade strikes an anvil.
- All parts are replaceable, and the blade can be taken off for easier sharpening. Also, the steel is hard enough to hold an edge well.
- Felco has several styles, including one for left-handed people. My personal favorite is the type with a rotating handle, which reduces the strain on your wrist and lessens the likelihood of carpal tunnel syndrome.

When larger cuts are needed, use a short pair of lopping shears or a small pruning saw. I use commercial-type, wooden-handled lopping shears because they are lighter than all metal types, and if the handles are damaged, then can be replaced much more easily than metal ones. I use a Japanese saw purchased from a nursery supply store. It has a much tougher blade than any other I have tried and it stays sharp a very long time.

Training Young Vines

In northern climates, it is usually best to let grape vines grow without training or pruning the first season after planting to allow them to re-establish their roots. In southern climates, where the growing season is longer, it may be possible to begin training vines the same year as they are planted, as long as you can keep them well watered. Also, vines planted as newly rooted cuttings can be trained the same year they are planted.

Basic training. During the planting year, you will have put individual stakes in place on which to train the young shoots (for details on this, see chapter 2). Training begins in early spring in the first year after planting. Here is the basic technique:

1. In early spring, prune the vine back to two buds.
2. When the buds sprout and grow, observe them to see which is the stronger shoot. You will train the stronger shoot to grow up the training stake. Don't remove the second shoot entirely, but pinch it back to retard its growth. It is your replacement in case something happens to the stronger shoot.
3. When the shoot is about one foot long, tie it *loosely* to the stake, using sisal bailing twine or plastic tape. This support is important to keep the stem straight and prevent it from breaking off. (Straight shoots are desirable because they produce the fewest suckers when older.)

Basic training.

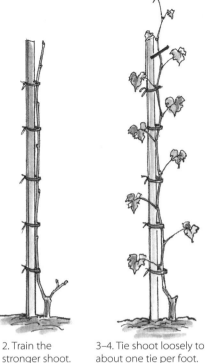

1. Early spring, pruned to two buds.

2. Train the stronger shoot.

3–4. Tie shoot loosely to stake, about one tie per foot.

4. As the shoot continues to grow, add more ties, about one per foot.
5. When the shoot has grown at least 18 inches above the support wire on which the canes or cordons will be trained, cut the shoot off just below the wire. This will cause two or more lateral buds to break, producing the shoots that will become cordons or fruiting canes.

This technique will produce one main trunk. If you want to train a vine to two or more trunks, you will want to leave more than two buds when you first cut the vine in early spring.

The shoot may only extend as high as the support wire the first year; this is fine. When the shoot breaks bud in the spring, more than one bud will send out shoots, and you can continue training from there. If the shoot doesn't make it up to the wire

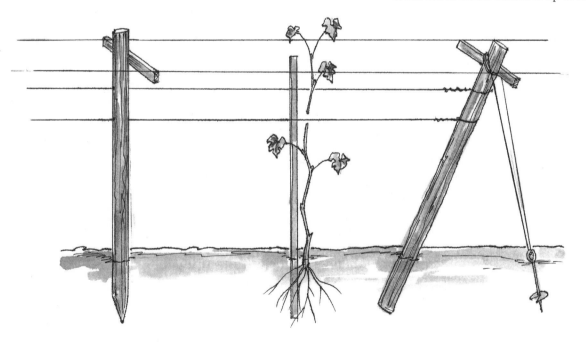

5. When shoot is 18 inches above support wire, cut just below wire to produce lateral buds.

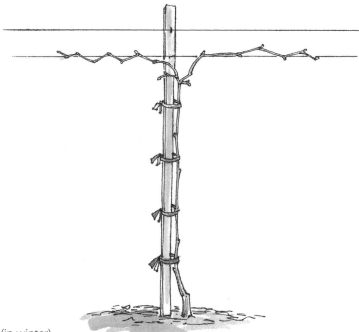

Dormant vine (in winter).

the first season, cut the shoot back to two buds in winter and start over the next spring. Trying to train a shoot that only went half-way will leave a kink in the trunk that will always produce unwanted suckers. Cutting the short shoot off and starting over will ensure a straight trunk that will be less likely to produce watersprouts.

Another way to prevent future watersprouts on the trunk is to remove unwanted buds. You can do this in the spring, when the buds that were at the bases of the leaves on the shoots will still be visible. Use a sharp knife to nick off the buds, or a wire brush to scrub off the buds, in all but locations where you want shoots. Be sure to get all of the bud at each location. If you miss a secondary or tertiary bud, they will remain in the wood, able to grow into watersprouts in some future year.

There is one drawback to removing these buds. In cold climates, if a vine suffers win-ter damage, and it has no buds left, it will not be able to produce replacement canes from the disbudded area.

Establishing fruiting canes and cordons. When training side shoots to become cordons, always use shoots that start slightly below the wire and bring them up to the wire. Using a shoot that is as little as 1 inch above the wire will result in a "hump" on the cordon arm that will always throw excessively vigorous shoots. By training the cordon arms as close to horizontal as possible, you will help distribute the vigor more evenly among the spurs.

If the side shoots don't grow enough the first year to become full-size cordon arms, cut them back to one or two bud spurs on the trunk and start over.

Let the side shoots get as long as they can during the growing season. They can be wrapped once or twice around the wire,

1. Using lopping shears, work your way along the row, cutting out anything you *know* should be removed: Watersprouts on the trunk, suckers from the base, the upper shoot on a spur that you know will be removed, and dead wood. Be sure to look for suckers at the base of the vine: They can come out right at or slightly below soil line and may be hidden in grass or soil. Miss one, and it can layer and put up new growth away from the main trunk, redirecting energy away from the trunk.

   As you work, pull the prunings out into the aisle, out of the way.

2. Now you can see what is left. For a cane-pruned vine, look for large, healthy canes. Because these canes will be removed after they bear, the fruiting canes don't have to be growing directly from the trunk; if need be, you can select canes that are growing out of the lower quarter of an old fruiting cane. Avoid leaving bull canes—extra long, large-diameter canes that are noticeably more vigorous than most of the canes—as these are usually unfruitful. Bull canes can be cut back for replacement spurs, though. The number of canes you select will depend on the variety, the age of the vine, and its health and vigor.

   Cut each cane back to ten to fifteen buds, leaving one extra internode beyond your last fruit bud. Cut through the node at the end of that section diagonally to remove the bud, but leave a small "knob" on the end.

3. Choose at least one shoot to be a spur for every cane you leave. It doesn't matter if the shoot is small in diameter, so long as it is healthy and is as close to the trunk as possible. You can leave a second spur if you wish, to give you more canes to choose from the following year. The spur should point in the direction you want the new cane to grow, so avoid making a spur that points out, away from the wires. Prune the spur to two buds, with the top bud pointing where you want the future cane to grow.

4. You will now have just the fruiting canes and the replacement spurs left on the vine. Wrap the canes once around the wire and tie each at the end of the cane. This is where the "knob" left on the end is used. The end of the cane can be tied tightly to the wire, and the knob prevents the twine from slipping off the end. With two vines side by side on the same trellis, the ends of the canes can often be overlapped and tied at the same time.

   Tie with twine or plastic tape or use a tape gun.

5. With spur-pruned vines, cut off the upper part of the old spurs and the shoots attached to them, leaving just one shoot as low on the spur as possible. Sometimes a watersprout will sprout at the base of the spur, and this can be used as a complete replacement for the spur. Take advantage of this to keep the spurs close to the old wood of the trunk or cordon arm. Cut the shoot back to the correct number of buds. You should now have a vine with the permanent wood and the spurs only.

   Above all, *do not be afraid to prune.* You will do more harm by underpruning than by overpruning. You will learn, but you'll never get there without experience.

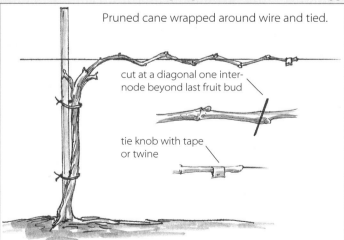

Pruned cane wrapped around wire and tied.

cut at a diagonal one inter-node beyond last fruit bud

tie knob with tape or twine

Spurs Up or Spurs Down?

HOW SHOULD ONE POSITION the spurs on a grapevine trained to a cordon system? When the shoots that become the "arms" of a cordon system are first trained out on the wires, half the buds point down and half the buds point up. When I went to school, it was believed that spurs should only point up, so all shoots coming from the downward-pointing buds were removed. But often the weight of the new growth would twist the arms, so that the spurs would wind up pointing down anyway. We had to tie the shoots up to keep the arm from turning. This meant the system had to include extra wires above the cordon to provide something to which the shoots could be tied.

Later research showed that exposing the base of the shoot to maximum sunlight made the buds in that area much more fruitful, increasing the potential crop for the following year. And what system provides the most light to the base of the shoot? One in which the spurs point downward, and the shoots tend to grow down in a curtain.

As with so many things, the system that works best is a compromise according to where the grapes are to be grown. In areas with high sunlight and high summer heat, it is usually better to use a system with the spurs pointing up, so there will be an overhead canopy of foliage to help protect the developing fruit from damage by the sun. In northern areas with low light, the downward-pointing spurs catch more light to help ensure the fruitfulness of the following year's buds, and to let leaves catch as much light as possible for producing the food needed to ripen fruit and harden off the growth for winter.

My vineyard is fairly far north, but summers can be hot enough that I use upright-pointing spurs.

There are systems for wine grapes that use a combination of up- and down-pointing spurs. One of the more notable involves training alternating vines differently; one with shoots up, the next with shoots down. That is, one vine has cordon arms only a short distance above the ground, and all the shoots are trained up in a vertical curtain. The next vine has the cordon arms high, with spurs that point down to allow shoots to be trained down. With this system, the base of the shoots are exposed to maximum light to increase the fruitfulness of the buds for the following year.

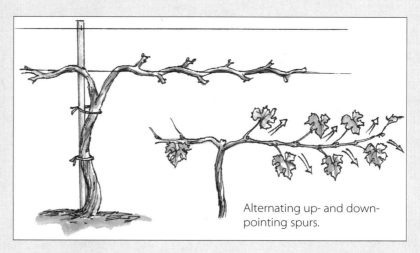

Alternating up- and down-pointing spurs.

or fastened loosely in place with twine or with a Max Tapener tape gun. The Max Tapener tape gun puts a loop of (nonsticky) tape around the shoot and wire, staples the ends together, and cuts the loop free of the roll. You can leave the shoots wrapped and they will grow around the wire as they get older, embedding the wire in the wood. This won't harm the vine, but it can make it difficult to remove the wire.

If the shoots are longer than you need for cordon arms, don't cut them back until dormant pruning season. When they are cut back, they should be at least 3 feet long and have a minimum of twelve buds on them, if not more. If the vine is being trained to a cordon system, you need at least six buds on each arm in the locations where you want fruiting spurs, but half of the buds on a shoot will be pointing down and half will be pointing up. This means only half the buds will be pointing in the direction you want the fruiting spurs, so twice as many buds are needed to wind up with the right number in the right places. If the shoots were vigorous, there may already be lateral shoots from the axillary buds that can be cut back as one-bud spurs.

In the winter, when you cut back the canes, don't cut them back right to the last bud. Leave one extra internode past the end bud. Then, make a diagonal cut through the swollen node so that the bud is removed, but part of the swollen area is left. This leaves a knob on the end of the cane that will not slip free after the cane has been tied.

If you are going to train a vine to canes, the length of the side shoots is less important, as long as the cane you leave at dormant pruning time is healthy, well-matured wood. Since the canes will be cut off and renewed each year anyway, it won't matter if the first set of canes are short.

The next growing season after the canes have been trained out to be fruiting canes or new cordon arms, the vine will start bearing. At this stage, the vine still needs to spend more energy on getting established than on fruiting. However, recent evidence suggests that allowing a young vine to bear crop will help it reach full bearing faster. So when the vine starts to bloom and set fruit, rather than take all the fruit off, just reduce the crop load by clipping off some of the clusters after set. Unless the vine is quite weak, it should be possible to leave a cluster at each spur position, or about half that many clusters on cane-pruned vines. As a general average, a healthy young vine should be able to handle up to 5 pounds of fruit the first year.

Pruning Established Vines

For cordon training, at the next dormant season after the first bearing year, you should now have canes at each location where you want spurs. These can now be cut back to become the first set of spurs. If you want to avoid having to thin the crop the next year, you can prune most varieties to create one-bud spurs, which should reduce the crop size enough to eliminate the need for hand-thinning. At the next pruning, more buds per spur can be left, gradually increasing each year as the vine matures and increases in productivity.

Remember, when pruning spurs, prune weak spurs heavily, and vigorous ones very little—just the opposite of how you would prune most fruit trees. Try not to leave large wounds. Vines don't heal like fruit trees can so disease can enter large wounds

Spur, showing where buds grow.

Next winter, prune to create a new spur.

Leave two spurs to increase crop.

more readily. It's sometimes better to leave stubs sticking out (which may eventually rot) than to cut off a cordon arm or large spur flush with the old wood and leave a big wound that won't heal.

Here's how to add a new spur. When pruning spurs, there are usually at least two shoots coming out of the previous year's spur, assuming it was a two-bud spur. If you were pruning the regular way, you would cut off the upper half of the old spur, and the attached shoot, then make a new spur by cutting back the remaining shoot to two buds. To add an additional spur, simply leave both shoots, and cut each one back to become a new spur. Or, if you are lucky, there are often suckers near the base of the old spur and one of those can be cut back to become a new spur itself.

Don't be in a hurry to add new spurs at every location: It's usually better to add only three or four spurs to the vine at first, then wait and see how it performs. If the vine carries the new crop load well with no sign of overcropping, more spurs can be left during the next pruning season. Eventually, instead of a row of straight spurs lined up on the cordon arms, there may be two spurs at each location, arranged in a "V" shape.

With cane-pruned vines, the canes that have borne crop should be cut off and new bearing canes and replacement spurs chosen from the shoots near the trunk.

Specialized Training Systems

There are several variations of the cordon system, including the Geneva Double Curtain, and forms that have up to four arms vertically. The Geneva Double Curtain (see illustration, facing page) is an extremely productive system, though it has some disadvantages. If the variety is a vigorous one, the double "curtains" may be so dense as to create a dead air space between them where air circulation is restricted and spray doesn't penetrate readily.

So many different training systems have been developed for commercial wine vineyards that it isn't possible to cover all of them here. Each is designed to make best use of light, help develop fruit buds, help ripen fruit, and/or give better air circulation for disease control in a specific climate, site, and situation. Because of that, a would-be commercial grower should seek out advice about training systems from others who have similar climate and site. A good place to start is to find out if your state has a grape grower's association. Ask at extension offices or at your state's land-grant college (state universities, such as Oregon State University, Iowa State University, etc.)

Systems such as the Geneva Double Curtain are very efficient at producing large crop loads because the system allows the new shoots to hang downward, exposing the bases of the shoots to full sun, which increases the fruitfulness of developing fruit buds.

The drawback of the Geneva Double Curtain, as noted earlier, is the dead air space in the center of the vine that fosters disease. Use of the system in Oregon with vigorous vinifera wine grapes increased yield, but powdery mildew became rampant and the accompanying decrease in fruit quality offset any gain in crop size.

Balanced Pruning

Several techniques have been developed to help growers determine whether they have removed enough wood at pruning time.

Geneva Double Curtain

One method is to weigh the wood removed from the vine, a technique known as balanced pruning. It is used to determine the fruiting capacity of a vine for the coming season. This technique is best tried only by experienced growers.

A common balanced pruning formula for *Vitis vinifera* is to leave twenty buds for the first pound of prunings, plus another twenty buds for each additional pound of prunings, up to a maximum of sixty buds. For French or American hybrids, leave twenty buds for the first pound of prunings, plus another ten buds for each additional pound of prunings, up to a maximum of fifty buds. For Native American varieties, the formula is thirty buds for the first pound of prunings, plus another ten buds for each additional pound of prunings, up to a maximum of sixty buds.

Practicing balanced pruning by counting the number of fruiting buds is by far the easier method for home growers or anyone who closely observes their vines. When you have followed a vine through training and into bearing, you get to know it well enough to tell if you have left too many buds, or not enough, by the quality of the fruit and how the vine grows.

How many buds *should* you leave? It depends on your climate, soil, the age of the vine, and the variety of the grape(s) you are growing. Here are some basic rules:

- First bearing year: Leave twenty-four buds (two cordon arms with six spurs each, or two canes with twelve buds each) for the first bearing year, and remove at least half the crop, just after fruit set.
- Second bearing year: Still leave twenty-four buds, but leave the full crop.
- Third bearing year: Leave thirty-six buds (three canes or an extra bud at each spur on the cordon), and so on. In other words, if the vine is growing well, ripening its crop well, and seems healthy, add

another twelve buds each pruning season, up to a maximum of about sixty.

The two main exceptions to the sixty-bud limit is (1) if the variety is extremely vigorous and clearly can carry more crop; or (2) if the clusters of the variety are small, and the only way to produce a reasonable crop is to leave more buds to get more clusters. Some of the French Hybrid wine grapes, such as Marechal Foch, often have small clusters, and the only way to get a reasonable crop is to leave as many as six canes with twelve to fifteen buds each per vine. Even in this case, the vines must be on fertile soil. Vines on poor soil may not be able to carry large crops, or the fruit quality may be lowered if the crop is too large.

It should be noted that, while poor fruit quality is a sign of overcropping, it is possible to decrease the quality of wine grapes by overcropping, without actually overloading the vine. That is, the fruit may ripen well and on time, but subtleties of flavor and character in the wine can be lost. A friend of mine with a vineyard did an experiment in which he left three canes on some vines and two canes on others. The fruit on all vines ripened well and on time, but the wine from the two-cane vines had flavor that was more intense, with extra subtle undertones to it. These are the sorts of results that are personal, and each grower must try different crop levels to find what is best in a given area, and what suits a particular taste.

Pruning to Escape Frost

While you are at the mercy of nature with respect to frost on most fruit-bearing plants, the right pruning method can give you considerable leeway with grapes.

If a grape cane is left unpruned, the buds at the ends will start to expand and open before the ones farther down. Hormones released by the upper buds will delay the opening of the lower buds by a few days to one week or longer. Taking advantage of this situation is just a matter of timing your pruning correctly. Here's how to do it:

1. At the usual winter pruning time, remove only those canes that will not be used for fruiting or as a source of spurs such as suckers and undersized canes. Leave everything else unpruned.
2. In the spring, when buds are starting to swell, wait until the buds on the ends of the canes are swelling enough so that the new leaves are just visible, opening out from the buds. Now is the time to prune these shoots back to fruiting canes or spurs.

Compare these late-pruned vines to ones pruned at the usual time in winter, and you will see that the buds on the winter-pruned vines are visibly farther along, at least one week ahead of the buds on the spring-pruned vines. Thus the buds on the spring-pruned vines are still tight enough to be able to withstand frost that can kill the unfurling buds on the winter-pruned vines. And though the spring-pruned vines will open their buds later, they will ripen their crop at the same time as vines that were pruned in winter.

Pruning Neglected or Overgrown Vines

At least once, expect to have to prune a neglected arbor, vines that weren't trained correctly to start with, or vines that have been left unpruned for a long time. There will be a mass of dead and tangled shoots, and most of the new growth will be too small or poorly placed to be of use as new fruiting canes or fruiting spurs. The arbor or trellis will need work as well. What are your options?

If a useable vine structure or at least a good trunk is visible under the over growth, it *might* be worth saving. Usually, however, the time spent cutting out masses of old growth while hunting for the few shoots usable as new fruiting wood is a waste of time.

If the trunk of the vine is straight, or is otherwise healthy, you may be able to shortcut the process by cutting everything back to the head of the trunk. You will have no crop that season, but you can easily train the new shoots that emerge as canes or new cordons to bear a full crop the following year.

More often, the vine will be such a mess of old growth and oversized wood combined with twisted, multiple trunks that the simplest way to prune it is with one quick cut, through the base of the trunk(s), right at ground level.

Kill the vine? No! Almost without fail, the vine will bounce back and refill the arbor or trellis in one season, because it has the full vigor of a large, established root system behind the new growth. The newly regrown vine should resume full production the very next year.

With the vine cut off, you can repair the arbor or trellis, and you can train the vine up in a better form than it had to begin with, as though you were training a new vine (which is essentially what you now have, at least from the ground up).

The only time this method may present a problem is if the vine was grafted to a rootstock, but the odds of this are small. Grafted vines are usually encountered only in commercial vineyards. Further, the vines in a commercial vineyard, even when neglected, will very likely have a good basic structure. They can be brought back to fruitfulness without having to resort to the "hack 'em off" method.

After cutting an own-rooted vine to the ground, mound soil around the base of the shoots during the winter. (Wait until winter because green shoots may rot if covered with soil.) Because grapes are not able to heal large cuts by growing new bark over the wound, a large cut-off stump may rot out in a few years. By putting earth over the base of the new trunk(s), they can root and establish a separate root system long before the stump rots down into the old roots.

A final word of advice: If you are restoring an overgrown vine that belongs to someone else, explain your strategy in advance, or they'll think you *must* be killing the vine when they watch you hack it off next to the ground.

Summer Pruning

Home grape growers often ask me, "The shoots on my vines grow where I don't want them in the summer. Can I cut them off?"

I answer that I prefer not to remove any green shoots unless absolutely necessary. Green leaves and green shoots produce the food that the vine needs to ripen its fruit and to mature its new wood for winter. Further, cutting the shoots may stimulate buds at the end of the cut cane to start growing, which keeps the vine active late in the season when it should be preparing for cold weather. In general, the only shoots that should be cut or removed from a vine are suckers from the trunk, which should be taken off as early as possible.

If a vine is growing so vigorously late into the summer that it produces an excessive mass of green growth, then you should suspect that the vine is receiving water and fertilizer later in the season than it should. It's better to stop watering and fertilizing to make the vine slow down rather than to prune it.

Finally, if you prune shoots in the summer too much, you may find yourself short of long canes at dormant pruning time: You will have shortened them prematurely.

Of course, there *are* times when a vine is just too big, either because it's a very vigorous variety, or because you have no control over the moisture or fertility of the location where it is growing. In these cases, you have to do something to keep the vine from overrunning its space.

One compromise is to cut green shoots back only to the point on the shoot where the leaves are half of mature size. Until a leaf reaches half size, it isn't producing food for the vine, so it will be missed less than mature leaves that are feeding the vine.

One school of thought says to cut the shoots off beyond the clusters to make the vine put energy in the clusters. Not so. This only reduces the amount of foliage that the vine would use to make food for the clusters. Further, if cutting the shoot stimulates new growth, that growth may divert food from the cluster.

Removing leaves (known as "leaf pulling") in summer from the area around fruits cluster to expose them to light can improve ripening. This is an accepted practice in many commercial wine vineyards, especially in northern climates, although it is only done when the clusters are approaching maturity. In hotter climates, leaf pulling is not as necessary and can expose the fruit to sunburn.

Disposal of Prunings

If you have a small home vineyard, collect prunings and chip or shred and compost them, especially if the vines suffered from disease during the growing season. Proper composting kills the disease spores, and you can use the compost in your vineyard.

In my vineyard, I find it easiest to leave the prunings in the aisles and go over them with a flail mower. At a low speed, the mower completely grinds up most canes. By early summer, there is little or nothing left. If you grow only a few vines, you can use hand pruners to cut the canes into short pieces and leave the pieces in the row to break down.

BIGGER SEEDLESS GRAPES

Very often, the first time home growers try growing seedless grapes, they are disappointed in the small size of the berries. Having bought seedless grapes in the grocery store, the home growers think that all seedless grapes should be just as large.

Commercially grown seedless grapes are usually girdled or treated with a plant hormone called gibberellic acid as a means of increasing the berry size. Without the treatments, the berries would be as small as homegrown.

Girdling is a process of removing a ring of bark from the trunk, or from the canes between the fruit and the trunk. A special double-bladed tool, called girdling pliers, is used to cut a strip of bark 3/16-inch wide all the way around the trunk or cane. Girdling doesn't kill the vine, because when a vine is girdled, the phloem cells are cut, but the xylem stays intact. Water can still move from the roots to the top of the vine and keep it alive while the cambium heals the wound.

If the girdle is clean, all the way to the xylem, the wood showing in the cut will be white. If any cambium is left, it quickly oxidizes and shows as brown. While the wound is still open, the food that would have moved down through the phloem is stored in the fruit, and this extra food is what causes the increase in berry size in girdled vines. If you watch a girdled vine heal, the callus always grows faster from the top of the wound down, as it is using freshly made food, while the lower callus is drawing on stored food from the roots, which is mobilized more slowly.

After a couple of weeks, the girdled strip heals and the vine resumes sending carbohydrates to the roots.

The current preferred method of increasing berry size commercially is to spray the vines with gibberellic acid (GA) at or just after bloom. Gardeners often use this plant hormone without realizing it; it is the main ingredient in the products used to stimulate fruit set in tomatoes.

For home growers, however, neither girdling or GA is the answer if you want to have larger seedless berries. It's not always easy to girdle a vine correctly. Using GA is even riskier because it's very tempting to spray too much of it and overcrop your vine. Some years back, however, I found a method that is safe and effective for home growers. It is based on the same principle as girdling, but is accomplished differently. Here is the method:

When you prune your vines in the winter, leave twice as many fruit buds on each vine as usual. For example, if you usually leave 40 fruit buds, leave 80 fruit buds instead. Each bud will put out at least one shoot with one or more clusters (again, for convenience, let's call it one cluster per shoot, or 80 total clusters).

From here, there are two ways to proceed.

With loose clustered-varieties (Himrod is one), go through the vineyard *before* bloom time and remove 60 of the 80 clusters. You will end up with half the number of clusters you ordinarily would, but the remaining clusters will set more and the berries will be larger. The clusters will be fuller, and the total crop will weigh as much as the crop on a vine that was simply pruned the normal way and had nothing else done to it.

With tight-clustered varieties (like Canadice), remove the 60 clusters immediately *after* bloom. The vine will have tried to set more fruit than usual, so the clusters won't set as many berries. After you remove clusters, though, the vine's energy goes into the remaining clusters and the remaining berries get larger. The finished clusters are big, but not excessively tight, because there aren't as many total berries per cluster. If they had been thinned before bloom, the increase in berry size combined with tight clustering would have made the clusters too tight, and there would have been berry splitting.

I ran across this method by accident when I was gathering pollen of Himrod to use in breeding. I left many more fruit buds than usual so I could collect lots of pollen and wound up thinning the crop the way I have described here. When harvest time came, the remaining clusters of Himrod were more than twice as long as normal and the berries were easily twice as big, and more. Further, the clusters were so well-filled and handsome, some of them weighed 3 and 4 pounds each, if not more.

ARBORS *and* OTHER UNUSUAL PLACES *for* GRAPES

If I wanted a large quantity of fruit without having to plant a lot of vines, I'd build an arbor. An arbor, or similar trellising techniques, can help you produce high- quality grapes in a wider range of conditions, and on a smaller amount of ground than you might think. It all hinges on the fact that the trunk of a grapevine takes up only a few square feet of ground, as long as the soil is fertile and well-drained. The trick is where you put the top of the vine.

Types of Supports

Arbors can be free-standing or attached to an existing building. In the latter case, the leafy vine can shade a patio area in summer, while a bare, pruned vine in winter will let most of the light through.

Where summers are short or cool, or there is no yard space for an arbor, training a grape vine up the side of a building on a trellis can give the fruit the extra heat needed for ripening in cool climates, as well as providing the vertical equivalent of the space the vine would cover on a large arbor. The ideal wall for grapes is brick, cement,

or stone. You can anchor supports directly into these types of walls, and they hold and release heat, maintaining a more constant temperature for the vine. Wooden walls should have trellising supported away from the wall so that excessive humidity isn't held near the wood, which would encourage rot problems.

Getting Started

A sunny, well-drained location is basic for growing grapes, but you have some latitude in how the site gets sun. You can position an arbor between two single-story buildings where it is shady at ground level, as long as plenty of sun will reach the canopy of leaves at the top of the arbor. To be sure, it will take longer for the vine to grow up through the shade to the sunny level, but the vine will thrive once it reaches the top of the arbor in full sun.

If you don't have a site that is sunny all day, try for a spot that receives morning sun and is shaded in the afternoon, rather than the other way around. Morning sun warms the vine, dries off dew, and gets the vine's metabolism going sooner. The vine handles shade in the afternoon better, when the warmer air temperature offsets some of the effects of reduced light. A vine that is shaded part of the day may ripen its crop a week or more later than one in full sun, so allow for that when you choose the variety.

Grapes will prosper when planted in a hole in an area paved with cement, as long as the hole is at least 1 yard square (3 feet by 3 feet) and the soil is well drained and deep, extending under the paving, if possible. In some cases, this type of site is better than open ground, because the

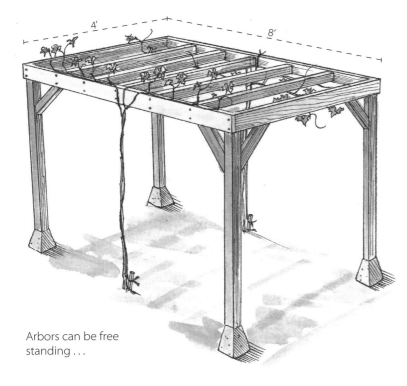

Arbors can be free standing . . .

. . . or attached to a building.

pavement will store and release heat, helping the grapes to ripen earlier, as well as protecting the vine from frost. I've seen photos of a Niagara vine in such a location, growing three stories up the side of a brick building, producing close to a half-ton of fruit.

Do *not* plant vines in areas paved with asphalt. The asphalt will give off substances that can harm or kill the vine, and even if it doesn't, the vine and fruit may absorb hydrocarbons that are not safe to eat.

Arbor Materials

Wood is the easiest material to use for an arbor, though such things as iron pipes will serve if appearance doesn't matter. If you use pressure-treated wood, only the legs should be treated, as they don't come in direct contact with the grapes, and the preservative should be a relatively non-toxic type such as zinc napthenate. Other preservatives can harm the vines—grapes are very sensitive to herbicides, and some wood treatments include herbicides that volatilize in hot weather.

The simplest arbor uses posts set in the ground with untreated, rot-resistant wood, such as cedar, for the overhead parts. If you want to avoid treated wood altogether, use concrete footings with brackets set in them, to which untreated corner posts can be anchored.

If available, black locust wood is ideal for arbors as it is naturally rot resistant. As long as the wood doesn't come in contact with soil, it will probably last as long as you need. If you attach one side of the arbor to a house, using joist hangers, you can attach the support posts to patio or deck-type footings. Any paint the vine might come in contact with should be a nontoxic latex type.

You can also use metal pipes for the corner posts and bolt the top to them, but in some soils, pipes rust as fast as wood will rot, so you have to decide if pipes will serve well in your location.

When you build the top of the arbor, be sure to use sufficiently strong stock such as 2 x 4s; 2 x 2s could bow under the load of a crop of grapes and develop a serious sag after a few years. Construct the horizontal "platform" on the top as you would the wall for a house. You can set the studs 24 inches apart instead of 16 inches. The studs won't be the only support for the vine, however.

To support the vine properly, stretch 9-gauge, high-tensile, galvanized wire across the frame to support the vine as it grows. That is, if the studs run east and west, the wires will run north and south. Space the wires 18 inches apart, so that when you look up, you will see a series of rectangles. Using wire has several advantages: It weighs less than wood, it's easier to tie grape shoots to wire, and it's much easier to reach through wire than wooden beams to pick fruit or work on the vine. Additionally, wire blocks less sunlight in winter.

The height of the arbor should be sufficient to allow the fruit to hang down and still leave head room. You will want the grapes to be within reach. Usually a height of 7 feet from the underside of the top to ground level works well. Anything lower will let vines hang down in your face when you try to go under the arbor. Remember, it is easier to use a stool or short ladder to pick the fruit and work on the vine than to have an arbor that is so uncomfortably low that you feel claustrophobic when you're

under it. I like arbors at least 8 feet tall, but I'm tall. If you build your arbor high and strong, you can hang pots of shade-loving plants such as begonias from the studs for a decorative touch. The same applies to the legs: nice 4 x 4 posts will support brackets for hanging pots or for small plant stands.

How big should an arbor be? We've seen that a healthy vine can cover a large area, given care and time. The *minimum* size of an arbor for one vine of average vigor, such as Concord, should be 32 square feet—outside dimensions of 4-by-8 feet. The vine will easily cover an arbor of this size and hang over the sides in a few years. If not kept regularly pruned, both summer and winter, the vine will spread over twice that area and still hang over the sides. Very vigorous varieties like Niagara can easily take more than twice that basic area, and then some.

This is where patience can pay off. If you don't mind waiting an extra couple of years, starting with one vine on an 8-by-8-foot arbor is a good idea. It may take longer for the vine to fill the space, but it will be easier to keep the vine in bounds and make the space under the arbor more airy and pleasant. Plant a vigorous grape on a too-small arbor, and between the dense foliage on top and the heavy curtain of shoots hanging off the sides in midsummer, the space underneath is more suited for mushrooms than people. The decrease in air circulation under such a dense arbor also encourages disease more than beneath an open arbor.

Plan a large arbor in multiples of the basic 4-by-8-foot spacings; 8-by-8 for two vines, 8-by-16 for four vines. If you are planning for a super arbor like the Winkler vine, your arbor could be as large as 40-by-40 feet for a single vine.

Training a Vine on an Arbor

For one vine on an arbor, the best place to plant the vine is in the center of the arbor. You only need to support the growing vine until it reaches the top, so you can use an untreated wooden post as the support for the trunk. An alternative is to drive a short stake next to the vine and tie a piece of heavy plastic baling twine from it up to the arbor, and use that twine as the support.

Train the vine as you would any other grapevine. If the trunk doesn't reach the top of the arbor in the first year, cut it back and start over until a single shoot grows all the way to the top in one season. When the vine reaches the top, depending on the variety, you can train canes out radially over the top of the arbor, or develop up to four cordon arms radiating around the top. Be sure to remove part of the crop every year until you are sure the vine can handle it, since you will be leaving more spurs or canes initially than you would be with a vine on a regular trellis. And don't think you can skip a year: dealing with an unpruned vine on an arbor is not fun, and the quality of the fruit suffers.

For two vines on an 8-by-8-foot arbor, you will get the best distribution of the vine over the top if you plant a vine at each end, *between* the end posts, and train to the middle. If you plant vines at the corner posts, plant them diagonally opposite each other.

Growing Vines on a Wall

A south-facing wall is best for grapes, to ensure full sun for the vine. You can choose almost any type of trellis to support the vine—just be sure it is strong. The weight of a vine spread out on a vertical trellis is distributed differently than on an arbor, and a trellis made of 2 x 2s can be sufficiently strong.

Attach the trellis to the wall using brackets that hold the trellis at least 1 foot away from the wall. This will help keep moisture (which can promote wood rot) away from wooden walls. Also, the fruit will stay in better shape if it doesn't rub the walls, and the vine will have fewer disease problems if air circulates through and behind it well. A space behind the trellis often creates a "chimney" effect that can cool that area of the house, as well as shade it.

Be *sure* to anchor the trellis *well*: A large crop of fruit on heavy vines can pull brackets and siding right off a house. Use concrete anchors on brick or cement walls and long lag screws on wooden ones, and make sure they go into the studs.

Since you are trying for a pleasing appearance, you may find it more aesthetic to train multiple trunks on the trellis. You can prune the trunks as vertical cordons: Just keep track of the number of fruit buds to regulate the crop and avoid overloading the vine. As the vine matures, you can extend extra shoots out and leave more spurs. Beyond that, the pruning and training can be more creative than with an arbor, as long as you don't overcrop the vine.

Greenhouse Growing of Grapes

Greenhouse growing of grapes isn't practiced much in the United States, but it is an art in parts of Europe, especially the United Kingdom. In Victorian times, greenhouses were used to produce grapes out of season, to grow varieties that required more heat than was possible outdoors, and for ornamental purposes.

For very early grapes, growers might have raised vines in pots outdoors or in an unheated stone or brick building, and brought the vines into a heated greenhouse in late January. Forced into growth at that time, a very early-ripening variety such as Chasselas D'Or might produce ripe fruit by May. In addition to being grown for off-season fruit, potted vines were also used as special table decorations, with guests able to pick their own dessert right at the banquet table.

Some varieties would be grown directly in the ground in a greenhouse; often planted in brick-lined trenches in the dirt floor in specially enriched soil. During winter, the greenhouses were left open to satisfy the vines' cold requirement for dormancy. Closing up the greenhouse in early spring was usually enough to stimulate the vines to grow, though coal or wood-burning stoves might be used to get the vines growing faster. In midsummer, the greenhouses were opened again when the weather was warm enough, then closed in the fall to finish ripening the fruit when the weather outdoors cooled. By these methods, English gardeners were able to ripen varieties such as Muscat of Alexandria, which is late to ripen outdoors even in the warm climate of southern California.

The vines were usually trained as low cordons, along the sides of the greenhouse, so the shoots and foliage could be trained up to the roof as they grew. This method gave the vines maximum exposure to sun, and left the inside floor space clear for other types of plants, usually shade-tolerant types. Every shoot was carefully trained, guided, or clipped to keep a neat appearance, to maintain as much air circulation through the vine as possible, and to keep the vines from being in the way. Shoots had to be grown on guy wires or other supports to keep the foliage from touching the glass, where condensation might cause disease. Special lead clips or anchors were usually set in the brick walls of the greenhouse, below the glass, to help anchor and guide the vines' trunks.

The Royal Horticultural Society in Great Britain published a book on growing grapes in greenhouses as recently as the late 1980s, so it would seem the art is still alive and well.

Greenhouse problems. Growing grapes in a greenhouse can present special problems. For one thing, grapes are mostly wind-pollinated, but in a greenhouse there often isn't enough air movement to dislodge the pollen from the anthers, making it necessary at bloom time to shake the clusters gently to ensure pollination. This is usually done every day for one week or longer, until all of the flower clusters have finished blooming.

While it would seem that grapes in a greenhouse would be protected from pests, disease spores usually find a way in. The warmth and constant humidity in a greenhouse provide an ideal atmosphere for fungal pests. The same is true for insects: When a pest invades a greenhouse, odds are there won't be any predators in the greenhouse to keep the pests under control. Also, vines in a greenhouse can be attacked by pests such as scale that normally don't trouble grapes outdoors in most climates. So it's important that your greenhouse be clean to start with, and that you cover all openings with extra fine screen to keep insects out. Serious growers can equip the greenhouse with two sets of doors with an "airlock" between, so that the first is closed before the second is opened. Also, before you bring other plants into your greenhouse, check them carefully for any pests or diseases that could spread to the grapes.

It's important to be extra diligent in watching for the first signs of disease or insects on greenhouse grapes. If you catch the problem early, it's usually possible simply to dispose of a diseased plant part or remove a small colony of insects, without having to resort to chemicals or other treatments. A "Big Power" vacuum cleaner (see page 86) might be used as an air filter in a tight greenhouse to remove spores from the air before they can cause trouble.

Most traditional greenhouse grapes are varieties of *Vitis vinifera*, such as Black Hamburg, Muscat of Alexandria, and Canon Hall Muscat (a giant form of Muscat of Alexandria). However, there is no reason why other varieties, even Concord, can't be grown in a greenhouse. Some varieties of grapes have traits that make them unsuited for greenhouse culture, though. Extra-vigorous types like Flame Seedless and Niagara would require extra work to keep them contained. Thompson Seedless needs high light intensity for good fruitfulness, which may not be available in a greenhouse, unless supplemental lighting is used.

Overwintering a grape in a greenhouse doesn't necessarily mean keeping it heated. Even *V. vinifera* grapes are hardy to at least 0°F (−17.8°C), and a well-built greenhouse can usually stay a good deal warmer than the outside air, so maintaining a sufficient minimum temperature shouldn't be that hard. If anything, it might be necessary to open the greenhouse on warm winter days to prevent the vine from becoming active (and cold-tender) too early in the spring.

The avid home gardener will have to do some experimenting: North America has too many different climates to set standards for greenhouse growing for the whole country.

Still, the limits on where grapes can be grown in greenhouses are whatever you want to put into them. You can construct a double- or triple-pane greenhouse to hold out extreme cold. If you combine supplemental high-intensity, full-spectrum lighting and extra heat, it ought to be possible to grow greenhouse grapes even in the Arctic. Grapes are a splendid fruit and well worth the effort.

4 *GROWING GRAPES ORGANICALLY*

I<small>T *IS* POSSIBLE</small> to grow grapes organically, that is, without using toxic chemicals to control pests and diseases. There are several strategies for doing it, but no single approach is right for every grower. In this chapter, I will cover the main categories of strategies and point the reader to many good methods. However, organic grape growing is a new field, and it is developing rapidly. New substances and methods for disease and insect control are being developed at an amazing rate, so fast that, in many cases, I can only report on a fraction of them. Some are rather anecdotal: They seem to work for some growers, but there were no reports of controlled tests to verify them. You, the grower, must be the ultimate judge of what works best for you.

First, to help you understand what is involved, let's start with some background.

For thousands of years, grape growers had few disease problems to contend with in their vineyards. *Vitis vinifera* grapes evolved with resistance to diseases in the areas where humans first found grapes. Humans carried grapevines with them to new lands, but the movement was slow enough to allow the grapes to adapt to the pests and diseases encountered along the way. In some cases, *V. vinifera* probably hybridized with local grapes, producing new varieties that were better adapted to the local climates.

When colonists tried to grow Old World grapes in America, the New World diseases and insects, not to mention the cold, soon laid low the vines. Fungal diseases—black rot, anthracnose, downy mildew, and powdery mildew—attacked the fruit and leaves, while phylloxera (a soil-dwelling insect pest) attacked the roots. In the Southeast, a bacterial disease (later named Pierce's disease) killed vines outright. After repeated attempts to grow European grapes in North America, people finally turned to growing native species.

NATIVE AMERICAN GRAPES

In the beginning, when colonists first found that *V. vinifera* couldn't survive in its new home, they began to use the native species to make wine. *Vitis labrusca* made poor, coarse, low-alcohol wines, so it eventually fell by the wayside for that purpose. It did, however, have large, showy berries that were bred into table grapes, of a sort. Those early types would taste harsh to our modern palates, but the colonists continued to grow them for food. Many, if not most, American table grapes contain at least some *V. labrusca* in their ancestry.

Other species, however, are probably fairly close in quality to the original forms of *V. vinifera,* and have good potential for wine. The variety Norton, derived from *V. aestivalis*, not only has very good resistance to disease, it also makes a red wine equal in many ways to vinifera wines. *V. riparia* has high enough sugar to make wine, but also has very high acidity. However, there is enough variation in the species that superior types could be selected. In fact, a private breeder in Minnesota has selected forms of *V. riparia* that have a sugar-and-acid balance sufficiently good to make acceptable wines.

In short, native American grape species have potential to be bred and selected into good wine and even table grapes. Yet even with careful, intense breeding and selection, it would likely take several decades to achieve these selections. Varieties selected only from native species would have the best chance to be well adapted to local conditions and should need the least pro-tection from disease and pests. This kind of selection not only *can* be done, it *has* been done with muscadine grapes (*Muscadinia rotundifolia*). This species was transformed from a wild species to one with numerous cultivated varieties in only forty years or so.

So the first (and essentially ultimate) strategy for growing grapes organically would be to breed new grapes from local species instead of depending on imported species, which are out of their element and need so much work to protect.

Breeding Resistance

This brings us to the next strategy: transferring the fruit quality of *V. vinifera* into vines that have the toughness and disease resistance of the American grapes.

More work has already been done on this strategy than almost any other method of adapting grapes to difficult environments. At present, it still appears to be the best option for producing grapes organically, demanding the least amount of work on the part of the grower over the long term.

The French were the first to breed Hybrid Direct Producers, also called French Hybrids. These vines produce good fruit, and do not need to be grafted to resistant rootstocks for protection from the phylloxera. In the process, they also produced vines with generally greater disease resistance and cold hardiness than *V. vinifera*. Ironically, they succeeded too well: The vines needed so much less care than the classic pure vinifera grapes that the French government eventually outlawed the commercial growing of the Hybrid Direct Pro-

Overcoming Resistance

IN MANY CASES, it isn't difficult to breed plants (or animals) with resistance to specific diseases or insects, but very often such resistance lasts only a few years, or a few generations at best. Then the pest becomes as virulent as before. How can a plant suddenly lose its resistance to a disease or an insect?

The common notion is that the resistant plant somehow "creates" the resistant pest. That's sort of true, but not entirely.

Let's consider a specific case. Suppose you breed a plant containing a gene for resistance to a bacterium (this is old-fashioned breeding, not genetic engineering). In this case, the resistance works because the resistant plant has a slight change in its cell membranes that stops the bacteria from being able to enter, because the bacterium's enzymes cannot eat through the altered cell membrane. But the bacterial population is very big, and there are a few individual bacteria that produce a different form of the enzyme. Up until now, the different form of the enzyme didn't help the bacteria, because it took more energy to make than the "old" form of the enzyme. Now, however, only the bacteria with the "new" form of the enzyme can successfully attack the resistant plant. Within a short time, the bacteria with the "new" enzyme has outreproduced the "old" form and there is enough of the new form to attack the resistant plants like mad.

This sequence of events doesn't necessarily happen quickly. The "new" bacteria may be so rare that it takes time before a resistant plant and the new bacteria meet, but once they do, the contest is over for that round. If all the resistant plants disappeared, however, the "old" form of the bacteria would become common again, because Nature prefers types that use the least amount of energy, and the "new" bacteria is less energy-efficient (in the absence of resistant plants) than the "old" form is.

But this is only one kind of resistance: single gene resistance. Other types of resistance are created in different ways, and involve more than one gene, and these types, called multigenic resistance, are much more stable and long-lasting. They also usually don't involve total resistance to disease, but instead make the plant able to tolerate the pest without serious harm. Muscadine grapes, for example, have multigenic resistance to the Pierce's disease bacterium. Varieties of muscadines can, and often do, show some symptoms of the disease, but the disease doesn't stop them from growing more or less normally and bearing useful crops of fruit.

In the case of grape rootstocks in California, which are being overcome by phylloxera after years of resisting that pest, the root stocks affected have *V. vinifera* in their parentage. *V. Vinifera* has no resistance to phylloxera, but it does tolerate alkaline soil and some nematodes. Breeders crossed *V. vinifera* with other, phylloxera-resistant species to create rootstocks with resistance to nematodes, alkalinity, and phylloxera. But the crossbred rootstocks had fewer genes for resistance to phylloxera, making it possible for a resistant phylloxera to overcome the rootstock. The solution is to return to rootstocks that have only the most phylloxera-resistant American species in their parentage. The Germans foresaw this problem decades ago and have long since produced stocks with better, more complete phylloxera resistance, the type that won't be overcome soon, if ever.

ducers, as they were afraid growers would flood the market with cheap wine. One old book also suggested that the hybrids were outlawed at least partly because they would have put the vine grafters out of work.

What made French Hybrids different from most American varieties was that the French breeders used the species *V. rupestris, V. riparia,* and *V. aestivalis* in breeding their varieties, at a time when most American grapes were based on *V. labrusca.* Ironically, coinciding with the time at which the French experimented with the Hybrid Direct Producers, the Germans outlawed the planting of anything but pure vinifera grapes for many years. Later, the French outlawed the use of interspecies hybrids, and, not many years after that, the Germans began breeding new varieties using the French Hybrids, as a source of disease resistance and cold hardiness. However, the Germans have used a different strategy in their breeding so that they have created selections that have kept almost none of the genes from the American species except those for the specific trait sought: hardiness, disease resistance, and resistance to phylloxera. They have been so successful that wines from such selections test identical to pure vinifera wine, using such methods as gas chromatography.

Resistance to disease in the French Hybrids varies considerably with varieties and with the climate the vines are grown in. For example, while the variety Marechal Foch can be grown without spray in much of the North and Northeast, as it moves farther south, it develops disease. Increasing disease susceptibility as the variety goes south is probably a moot point with this variety, since Foch usually does not pro-duce good-quality wines in areas where the climate is warm enough to make disease a serious problem. Known disease resistance of other varieties will be mentioned in chapter 10 on varieties.

But varieties with very high resistance or tolerance to disease are not the complete solution to organic grape growing. Under cultivation, grapes are put in conditions that are often not natural to them, which can set up the plants for lots of problems. For example, when large numbers of a single variety or type are planted in one area, it can set up conditions for a pest to produce a form that is able to overcome the plant's natural resistance and attack the monocrop planting en masse. This has already happened in California, where the root pest phylloxera has produced a form that is able to attack several rootstocks that were formerly resistant to it.

Part of the problem is that we have been relying on the grape to do all the work of resisting pests, when really it should be a cooperative effort.

The COMPLEX WEB of LIFE

When I was a boy in the late 1950s, our family always had an organic garden. This was a time when chemical fertilizers were fashionable, and people who didn't use them were considered strange. It's almost a wonder to me to see how much organic growing of plants has developed in the intervening years: new products such as pheromone lures for trapping insects, nontoxic soap-based substances to literally clean disease off of plants, and so much more. Yet for all the advances, the basis of organic growing still comes back to maintaining healthy soil life. The only difference now is that we understand the process more and know more about how to help it along.

At a young age, I knew compost was the basis of organic gardening, because it helped worms and other soil life. Yet I didn't even start to learn the importance of soil life until I was asked to write an article on mycorrhizal fungi and I interviewed Dr. Robert Linderman, one of the leaders in the field of soil microbiology. Not only was I amazed to learn how the fungi interacted so intimately and beneficially with the roots of plants, but even better, that selected forms of this fungi had been isolated and cultured and the inoculum was available commercially. I connected with one of the dealers of the inoculum, Don Chapman, president of Bio-Organics, and began trying the fungi.

About this time, I also began to hear of the work of Dr. Elaine Ingham at Oregon State University. Ingham was studying the relationship of all soil life to plant growth. Mycorrhizal fungi are one of the key building blocks of the soil, and the way the fungi interact with other life forms is not only fascinating, but also explained why gardening organically works so well.

In healthy, well-balanced soil, an amazing, complex web of life is working constantly, creating a series of chemical and physical events on which plant life depends.

While vines need water and a number of nutrients to survive and thrive, growers commonly think that applying fertilizers, minerals, and micronutrients is all that the vines need in order to grow well.

But, according to Ingham, it is ultimately a multi-organism delivery system in the soil that provides plants with nutrients when needed and in a form the plants can digest. Some of the organisms in the so-called "soil food web" prey on each other. Others form symbiotic partnerships, exchanging complementary forms of nutrition with one another. Certain fungi, largely the mycorrhizal fungi, barter their ability to obtain nutrients not otherwise available to the plant in exchange for complex sugars and other substances produced by plant roots. In this metropolis of microbes beneath the vineyard floor, organisms in the soil live their lives, eat their meals, eliminate waste, mate, raise their offspring, and eventually die and decompose. They create a web of life in the soil.

A Feeding Chain: Fungi, Bacteria, Mites and "Bugs"

In healthy soils, mycorrhizal fungi set up a symbiotic relationship with plant roots, producing fungal threads called *hyphae* that form an interconnecting network among plants—even plants of different species. Dig a fresh root out of healthy soil and many of the fine hair-like structures you will see on the root are largely comprised of a network of mycorrhizal fungi. Mycorrhizal fungi interlace and penetrate the roots, receiving sugars and other complex molecules in return for making essential plant nutrients available to the roots. Indeed, it has been shown that plants growing in phosphorus-poor soil that contained mycorrhizal fungi did better than plants in soils with a normal amount of phosphorus but no fungi. (There is reason to believe this may hold true with other nutrients.) The fungi also provide a substrate for bacteria, which grow around the hyphae, helping take up and convert nutrients into forms the fungi use. Microarthropods such as mites travel along the fungal hyphae, moving nutrients from points away from the plants into the root zone. In the process of working with the soil life, the fungi also set up conditions that prevent plant-damaging bacteria or root-eating nematodes from growing in the root zone. For example, the fungi produce antibiotic and inhibitory compounds that prevent the disease-causing or pest organisms from being able to grow.

While some annual plants can grow without mycorrhizal fungi, grapevines and many other perennials do best in fungal-dominated soil, for the following reasons:

- Fungi produce organic acids, which help maintain soil pH between 5.5 and 7.0.
- Fungi are eaten by fungal-feeding nematodes, plus species of large amoebae and microarthropods. These fungal predators release nitrogen in the form of ammonium, which the plant can use.
- Because fungi maintain soil pH on the acidic side, nitrifying bacteria (bacteria that convert ammonium to nitrate and nitrite) are excluded from the food web. So the majority of nitrogen in fungal-dominated soils is present as ammonium, not nitrate. Grapevines grow more efficiently when using ammonium instead of nitrate.

Research at the School of Enology at the University of California at Davis (U.C. Davis) has shown a relationship between sluggish, stuck fermentation and nitrogen-deficient grape juice. Further, off aromas can often be produced in fermentation of nitrogen-deficient musts. The common method of correcting such problems is usually to apply more nitrogen to the soil.

However, diversity of soil microorganisms may be a more effective way to help vines get the type of nutrition they need, when they need it. Soil organisms in healthy soil produce the form of nitrogen (and other nutrients) most usable to the plant (ammonium, again) right in the vicinity of the roots, where it can be taken up and used most efficiently. So improving vine nutrition might be better served by boosting the levels of beneficial fungi, nematodes, and microarthropods in the soil. The two best ways to accomplish this are inoculation with mycorrhizal fungi and use of compost.

While there are native mycorrhizal fungi in all soils, inoculum levels may be low, especially if soils have been abused. Adding inoculum ensures that there is plenty of this important first link in the soil food web. Research has isolated and cultured strains of the most effective species of mycorrhizal fungi, which can help get the rebuilding of the soil food web off to a better start.

The next step is to provide food for the soil food web, in the form of compost.

The Importance of Compost

Wineries reap one excellent material for compost as a byproduct of winemaking: pomace, which is the stems, skins, and seeds remaining from the grapes after the juice, or *must,* has been extracted. Additional material could include chipped and shredded wood from commercial pruning operations, which will often dump this material for free when the vineyard is close to a work site. The vineyardist might also save and chip vine prunings to add to the mix. Properly made with thorough turning and aeration, the compost should heat sufficiently—to about 135°F (57°C)—during the initial stages, which will kill most weed seeds, human pathogens, plant pathogens, and root-feeding nematodes.

Spreading one to two inches of this finished compost under the vines before midsummer can go a long way to fostering the soil food web. While compost can be added any time, applying it fairly early in the growing season allows time for the soil organisms to interact with it and begin releasing the nutrients the vine needs most during its spring burst of growth. It can also be added in the fall, after harvest, to give the vine additional nutrients to improve its health to better withstand winter. The soil food web seems to recognize that the plants require less nitrogen and adjusts the nutrients provided to the plants accordingly so as not to cause new growth at the time the plant should be going dormant.

Protecting Soil Structure

Another part of developing and maintaining the soil food web involves reducing or eliminating activities that disturb soil structure. As microfauna feed on the fungi and the creatures that feed on the fungi, some create holes or compartments in the soil for themselves. This adds pores to the soil structure that provide spaces for further development of soil life. When the soil is cultivated, these areas are destroyed or compacted. In the process of compaction, oxygen in the soil is used up, and the nitrogen may be volatilized by anaerobic processes that release nitrogen as ammonia gas. Initially, this causes a burst of growth by plants, mostly weeds, but afterward, very little new ammonium is created because the soil food web has been disrupted. Alternatively, when soil is disturbed, bacterial growth is enhanced. If compaction also occurs, this may result in the growth of nitrifying bacteria, which produce nitrate, changing the dominant form of nitrogen in the soil to one that promotes vegetative growth.

To summarize, then, the ideal system for the vineyard is one that leaves the soil intact to allow the soil food web to continue to improve and refine the structure of the soil, for its own benefit and for the plants, year after year.

Rebuilding the Web

Knowing that a healthy vineyard depends upon a diverse set of microorganisms in the soil, a wise grower will reduce or eliminate the use of pesticides and herbicides that could destroy soil microbes, thus throwing the soil food web out of balance. The alternative course of building proper soil microbial diversity seems more hopeful. With a healthy vineyard soil, use of industrial sprays and chemical fertilizers can be greatly reduced. Those applications that are made will be smaller doses that are consumed efficiently by the vines and decomposed by soil bacteria.

A healthy soil microbe population goes far beyond simply breaking down applied chemicals. A diverse population of bacteria, fungi, and other organisms is also essential for preventing plant diseases and pests from gaining an advantage in the field. As soon as this diversity is weakened or destroyed, the opportunistic disease organisms quickly take over, leading to all the plant diseases and stress growers have come to know so well. "The only way out of this downward spiral," according to Ingham, "is for growers to reestablish the once abundant, diverse microorganism populations that thrived in their croplands."

In a healthy soil, there are almost no disease organisms at all: They are literally crowded out by the symbiotic life there. Additionally, many of them produce substances that inhibit or are deadly to disease organisms.

Dr. Ingham's work indicates that spraying compost tea on crops fosters high levels of beneficial microorganisms that can actually block the sites where disease organisms could enter.

One of the most attention-getting results of rebuilding the soil food web that Ingham has observed is that phylloxera never reach high populations in soil with good compost levels (or organic matter levels above 2.5 percent) and good microbial life. Given how much expense goes into protecting grapes from phylloxera, this is an exciting revelation.

An effect of mycorrhizal fungi that could bear on the control of phylloxera is the ability of the fungi to stimulate root development. As a test, I grew currant and gooseberry bushes with and without mycorrhizal fungi. Then I dug up one plant from each group; the plant with the fungi had masses of fine roots, while the untreated plant of the same variety was almost totally lacking in small roots. Since phylloxera harms the vines by killing or stunting roots they feed on, stimulating the vine to produce many new roots could help offset the harm of these sucking insects. An additional benefit of a healthy web of life in the soil is that

it can help foster the types of soil fungi that attack and kill harmful, plant-eating nematodes, while providing conditions that lead to an increase in the populations of "killer" nematodes—types that attack and kill harmful soil insects and arthropods.

Interestingly, the value of fostering microlife to aid in the health of plants is being verified by conventional scientists who weren't particularly researching organic methods. Gregory English-Loeb, an assistant professor of entomology at Cornell University's New York State Agricultural Experiment Station in Geneva, New York, learned that tydeid mites feed on powdery mildew of grapes. In studying wild grape vines, English-Loeb wondered what ecological role these tydeid mites might play on the grape leaf. They did not appear to feed on the leaf tissue and, interestingly, he did not find much powdery mildew fungus on plants where the mites were abundant. This led to his discovery that the mites were eating the fungi.

In other experiments, it has been found that spraying apples with yeast-sugar solutions significantly reduces the incidence of fruit rots. It seems that the yeast cells simply outnumber the rot organisms and block the entry points where the rot would ordinarily enter the fruit.

The work of Ingham and others like her is being confirmed bit by bit by researchers in different areas. It all ties together.

It's also interesting to note that accepted practices for older types of organic (or at least low-spray) culture of grapes sometimes run counter to these new discoveries. For instance, one of the most common recommendations is cultivation. Cultivate to turn under diseased material so disease spores aren't released and cultivate to destroy overwintering stages of insects in the soil. But the new information suggests that this kind of soil cultivation is harmful, because it constantly disrupts the soil food web, which could keep the plants truly healthy and reduce the incidence of disease if left undisturbed.

GROUNDCOVERS
and WEEDS

Weeds, while often called "plants out of place," are, in fact, "plants with a mission." Weeds are really healers of the soil. To understand this idea, let's follow some cycles of plant growth.

Start with soil freshly disturbed either by cultivation or a natural cause. Bare soil is open to drying, to being washed away, to being lost. Whole communities of microlife have been disrupted or even destroyed. But within days, seeds of fast-growing annuals that have been dormant in the soil for decades or longer begin to grow, including pigweed, lamb's-quarters, and purslane. These are pioneer plants that grow fast and thickly to anchor the soil and provide organic matter. They tend to produce large amounts of seed to "refill the bank," as it could be decades before those new seeds get a chance to grow.

As these first, fast-growing annuals develop, they provide shade, hold moisture, and cool the soil a bit, creating conditions that allow other types of plants to sprout. so that other seeds can start to grow. These others are usually a combination of annuals that fill in around the taller, spindlier plants, plus the sprouts of longer-lived plants. Where I live, for example, white clover will start to grow among the bases of the faster growing weeds, but will expand little the first year, especially when starting in midsummer or later. By fall, the first pioneer plants have died and become a source of organic matter to start rebuilding the soil.

By the second season, there is little or no exposed soil left, and very few of the first, fast-growing annuals reappear. White clover and similar biennials and perennials spread and fill in as grasses increase, and still more plants begin to appear. The succession continues to shrubs, first-generation trees, and finally the climax vegetation. In many areas, especially where native grapes grow, the climax vegetation is a forest. And in many forests, the floor has comparatively few plants, but large amounts of organic matter. As the plant life changes, reaching this climax stage, the soil life changes with it. How does this help us understand the weeds?

Most of the weeds we deal with are plants of the first round, the colonists, because we keep stirring up the soil, bringing up more seed. But beyond that, we keep the soil in a very unnatural state by continually disturbing the web of life in the soil.

Most fast-growing annual weeds grow without associated mycorrhizal fungi, at least partly because their life cycle is too short—they grow and die before the fungi would have a chance to sporulate.

In connection with this, it is interesting to note that several growers have told me that when they inoculate their perennial plants with mycorrhizal fungi, especially if they use compost to keep the organic matter in the soil high, they have a lot fewer annual weeds.

Most likely, the presence of the fungi is at least part of the "signal" that keeps the annuals from sprouting. As long as there is a web of life in the soil, it gives off substances that help keep the seeds dormant, waiting for when they are needed. Or, if the weeds are already present, they receive a signal to finish their cycle.

Mixed populations of plants also mean that few species ever become numerous. Quackgrass is a constant nuisance in regularly cultivated areas where I live. However, in fields that are only mowed, never cultivated, quackgrass plants are few. Only when the soil is cultivated and the "competition" removed does the quackgrass manage to send out its long rhizomes and spread quickly, to become an invasive "weed."

What this means is that if we avoid the disruption of the soil that breaks up the web of soil life and sends the signal that starts the "weeds" growing, we will have a lot fewer "weeds." Instead of cultivating the soil back to "Stage One," we need to learn to keep or rebuild it to a later stage—one that resembles the forest where there are comparatively few plants, and most of those are perennials. In many ways, this is simply giving the grapevine what it wants, as many grape species grow in such a "climax forest," with a soil microenvironment that is covered with organic leaf litter, constantly cool and moist, and full of soil life.

The ideal care of the vineyard would then be to avoid all cultivation, and find other ways of dealing with weeds.

In my vineyard, I simply mow the native grasses and allow them to grow right up to the vines. This is possible because the soil is deep and the grapes have put their roots down deep, so they aren't in competition with the grasses. With this system, all organic matter goes right back into the soil web, and it is disturbed very little. The soil is held in place and water is absorbed and doesn't splash back on the vines.

Use of the local mixed native grasses and plants also agrees with findings of a study of several groundcover plants conducted at Oregon State University. Researchers tested several species as vineyard groundcovers and found that just allowing native grasses to grow worked as well as other groundcovers. By this definition, I don't have any weeds, only groundcover.

If we go back to the wild grapes, with their layer of leaf litter on the forest floor, it would seem that the ideal situation, from the grapes' viewpoint, would be year-round mulch. A test of such a system was conducted at Cornell, and vineyards of Concord that were mulched instead of having groundcover had the second-best moisture retention through the season, as well as the second-largest yield (in both crop weight and number of clusters). However, the grapes had lower sugar than did grapes grown with other systems. The system with the best results had rye planted in the fall, which was killed by applying Roundup in the spring and left on the ground as a mulch.

Mulch has other values, besides just keeping the soil moist. At a cool-climate grape-growing symposium held in Rochester, Minnesota, one presentation showed that bud break in mulched vineyards could be delayed by as much as seven days. This could be an advantage in frost protection, or a problem if ripening were similarly delayed. The type of mulch could have an effect, though. A rock mulch would hold heat to help keep the soil more uniformly warm and help speed ripening, as well as protecting vines from early and late ground frosts. The drawback would be that rocks don't add organic matter to the soil and require considerable labor to place. They would be suited best to small plantings. In my area, rocks would have the drawback of creating protected areas where gophers could tunnel.

A layer of properly made compost would solve most of the problems created by other mulches. Compost is dark enough that it would warm up as well as bare soil, would add organic matter and support the soil microlife well, and wouldn't attract rodents or other burrowing animals.

Several other types of groundcovers were tried in the Cornell study, including live annual rye, orchard grass, bluegrass, crownvetch, and red clover. Most of the information on groundcovers is done on plantings of only one species used as the groundcover, not a mixed planting such as the native plants that were used in the Oregon State University trials.

To build the soil's web of life, it is likely that a mix of plants is needed; the different species become tied together by the microlife in the soil, and the effects are shared among all the plants, including the grapes. In some ways, the ground cover has to make up for the other plants that would be present if the grapes were growing in the wild, among trees and other perennials. From this perspective, it makes sense that a mixed groundcover would be more useful than a monocrop groundcover.

One thing that should be apparent is that even straight mulch would be preferable to clean-cultivated soil in a vineyard. Clean ground would seem to have several disadvantages, including:

- erosion of soil;
- puddling and compaction of soil;
- more splashback of rain onto vines from bare soil, which help spread diseases, especially ones like downy mildew;
- more rapid fluctuation of soil temperatures without an insulating layer of vegetation or organic matter on it;
- no plants other than grapes to help support microlife in the soil.

A grower in Minnesota once told about how he kept his vineyard cultivated to bare soil to keep the vineyard warmer. When he used grass as a groundcover, he could actually feel the coolness of the vineyard and the grapes ripened almost a week later than the ones in the bare soil. However, what would a bare-soil vineyard be like in a few years, with nothing to hold the soil every growing season? And doesn't bare soil increase reflected heat on the vines and increase the likelihood of scalding, which can in turn lead to problems like crown gall? Keep in mind, this isn't just when the entire vineyard is cultivated; it also happens on a lesser scale when the area under the vines is kept bare of plants.

Ultimately, each grower has to decide what works best in his area, but clean cultivation should be the last choice on the list. If water conservation is a consideration, there are plants like subterranean clover that bloom in spring, seed themselves by pushing seed into the soil, then die off in the summer, when water is less available.

The dead plants are there to hold the soil, but without using water. In fall, when the rains resume, the seed germinates and the cover crop comes back.

As for annual weeds, you'll see that most such plants disappear once the soil is not being disturbed regularly, so adjusting your system to one of maintaining a ground-cover of plants and/or mulch can reduce or eliminate the need to "control" weeds.

One problem with attempting to build the soil web of life when you first plant a vineyard is that it takes longer to get the vines into bearing. At first, the young vines are competing with the vegetation of the groundcover, and they have to work harder to send their roots down to the levels where they are no longer in competition with the groundcover plants. Use of drip irrigation can help, as it not only concentrates the moisture where the vine needs it, but waters deeply, encouraging the vine to send roots down for water, rather than spreading out near the surface.

Recognizing that planting a vineyard is an artificial situation, most growers will find it necessary to treat weeds by conventional methods, at least for the first few years. After about the third year, the effect of competition from weeds decreases as vines become established, and shading from the vineyard canopy reduces weed growth. Before that time, weeds must be controlled at least in the strip under the vines to reduce competition until vines are established.

The following is a mix of weed-control methods, derived and adapted from a discussion of more conventional methods of establishing a vineyard collected from various sources.

Chemical Herbicides

In most vineyards, herbicides are used only on a narrow strip of soil centered on the vineyard row; thus, the area treated with herbicides in these vineyards is 15 to 30 percent of the total vineyard area.

For treatment of small areas, especially for perennial weeds, a backpack sprayer or low-volume controlled droplet applicator can be used.

Pre-emergent herbicides. Pre-emergent herbicides are active in the soil against germinating weed seedlings. These herbicides are applied to bare soil and are leached into the soil with rain or irrigation. If herbicides remain on the soil surface without incorporation, some will degrade rapidly from sunlight. Weeds that emerge while the herbicide is on the surface, before it is activated by rain or irrigation, will not be controlled. Also, large weed seeds, such as wild oat, may germinate in the soil below the herbicide zone and still be able to emerge.

Post-emergent herbicides. Post-emergent herbicides are applied to control weeds already growing in the vineyard. They can be combined with pre-emergent herbicides or applied as spot treatments during the growing season. In newly planted vineyards, selective post-emergent herbicides are available for the control of most annual and perennial grasses, but not broadleaf weeds. Young vines need to be protected from contact by some post-emergent sprays. Be sure to check and follow individual label instructions. Specific herbicides acceptable for use by organic growers are covered later in this chapter.

In conjunction with the use of herbicides in the vine row, mow the weeds between the rows. Mowing may be required four to eight times during spring and summer, whenever weeds are 6 to 8 inches high.

Reducing herbicide and pesticide damage. Even with organically grown grapes, herbicide damage is a possibility because grapes are very susceptible to several herbicide compounds that can drift surprising distances. In the Midwest, where corn and soybeans are grown extensively, vineyards two to three miles away from sprayed fields are routinely affected. The University of Minnesota grape-breeding program even includes a test plot near commercial fields of corn and soybeans so that the grape selections can be tested for herbicide susceptibility from drifting spray.

Roundup is less of a problem than other types of herbicide because it is a heavier, more oily material and doesn't drift far. However, any spray containing 2,4-D, or similar types of compounds can affect grapes from surprising distances, up to several miles, especially if the wind is blowing toward the vineyard.

When herbicides first came into use, vineyardists panicked, because several herbicides cause symptoms on grapes that are very similar to fanleaf, a viral disease. Grape growers thought there was an epidemic of virus and some began uprooting their vineyards before the real cause was found. The symptoms included leaves pulled into a small fan shape, leaves with missing lobes, with veins radiating from the base, an irregular bumpy surface, and white streaks and patches in the leaves. Roundup causes

downward cupping of the leaves, which could be mistaken for leafroll. All types of herbicides slow or stop growth of the vine, depending on how severe the exposure is, up to and including defoliation and death of the vine.

You may be able to help vines damaged by spray drift. Try applying mycorrhizal fungi to the roots (punch holes in the soil around the vine and put in the powdered inoculant), mulching with composted organic matter at least 2 or 3 inches thick, and watering at least 1 to 2 inches per week. Remove all fruit clusters so the vine can direct its energy entirely to recovery.

Feeding an herbicide-damaged vine chemical nitrogen has little effect most of the time and might, in fact, shock the plant beyond recovery. Fertilizer should be mild and balanced, such as fish, either liquid emulsion or in pelleted form.

Even at that, there may not be any visible change in the vine the first year. If you have been successful, though, the vine will break bud and grow normally the following year. Watch for any signs that herbicide is still in the plant, such as leaf distortions or slow growth. If the vine shows such symptoms, it hasn't fully recovered and should not be allowed to bear a crop that year. Continue the compost treatment, though no more applications of mycorrhizal fungi will be needed.

If for some reason you *must* use herbicide in your vineyard, such as when there is a particularly stubborn perennial weed that has been hard to control any other way, use the following guidelines:

1. Try nontoxic sprays first, such as white vinegar to burn succulent weeds, or

some of the stearic acid (soap-like) weed killers such as Scythe. A propane weed-burning wand may work in some cases. Use toxic commercial herbicides only as a very last resort.

2. Spray only when vines are dormant. Leaf-less vines are less likely to be able to take up herbicide and be harmed by it. Do *not* use pre-emergent herbicides around grapes: These substances can kill roots and disrupt soil life seriously.

3. Protect the vines' trunks with grow tubes or similar protection. Small vines can be covered with plastic buckets.

4. Use a hand sprayer set to low pressure, and don't use ultra-fine nozzles, which can break the spray into extremely fine mist that drifts more readily.

5. Spray in early morning or at sunset, when there is little wind to blow the spray around.

Nonchemical Controls

One effective method of controlling weeds before planting vines is to cultivate, then irrigate to germinate new weeds, and cultivate again to destroy seedling weeds. Frequent cultivation lowers weed seed reserves in the soil, thus reducing weed growth. At least two cycles of cultivation/irrigation/shallow cultivation are needed for a marked reduction in weed seedlings. This method is not effective on established perennial weeds.

Soil solarization is a nonpesticidal method of controlling soil-borne pests by placing clear plastic sheets on moist soil during periods of high ambient temperature. The plastic sheets allow the sun's radiant energy to be trapped in the soil, heating the upper levels. Solarization during the hot summer months can increase the soil temperature to levels that kill many disease-causing organisms (pathogens), nematodes, and weed seedlings. It leaves no toxic residues and can be easily used on a small or large scale. For more information on solarization, see pages 15 to 16.

Mulches. Weeds in the vine row can be controlled using mulches. Organic mulches (cereal straw, green waste, composted wood chips) can be used around young vines. Always apply mulches when the soil surface is free of weeds. Mulches prevent the growth of weed seedlings by blocking light and preventing it from reaching the soil surface. Mulches create more uniform moisture conditions, which in turn promotes development of soil flora and helps young vine growth. Mulches do not control perennial weed growth unless all light can be excluded. Woven fabric mulches seem to offer long-term weed control, but there have been problems with woven fabric mulch beyond the high cost of purchase and installation.

Weed fabric is a heavy, black, cloth-like material woven from plastic. The theory is fine: The weave lets air and water, plus water-soluble fertilizer, through to the plant, but blocks light so weeds can't grow. I tried using weed fabric and for the first year it seemed to work as promised. However, the fabric blocks organic matter from reaching the soil, and earthworms soon stop working under the fabric. At the same time, the fabric warms the soil and lets moisture evaporate through the weave, instead of holding moisture as conventional mulches would. Before long, the soil under the fabric becomes quite hard and dry. At the same time, the fabric offers a perfect shelter for gophers and mice, which burrow directly under the fabric. Further, weed seeds that land on the fabric can push roots through the material and grow, so the fabric soon has weeds on it anyway, unless it is covered with something such as wood chips. Between the cost and these problems, I found little advantage to using this material instead of an organic mulch.

Cultivation. During the first two or three years of the vine's life, mulching is preferable to cultivation, because mulching helps rebuild the soil food web. If you don't have a supply of mulch materials, however, you can control weeds with shallow cultivation (less than 2 inches deep), such as hoeing using weed knives around vines several times during spring and summer, as well as cultivating or mowing between vine rows.

Cultivate when weeds are still seedlings; when weeds grow large, cultivation becomes harder. Use hand tools close to the vine to reduce risk of injury to the trunk. Mechanical cultivators for use in the vine row include weed knives, spyder cultivators, and rotary tillers. Rotary tillers such as a Weed Badger, Kimco, or Clements Hoe are most effective on loose soil that is not rocky. Hand-held mechanical flails (Weed Eaters) may be used, but can injure vine trunks. Disks, tillers, or mowers can be used between the rows. Mechanical control of weeds must be done repeatedly when weeds are immature. The equipment should be set to cut shallowly, to minimize damage to vine roots. When using any mechanical equipment around vines, be careful not to injure the grapevine feeder roots or trunk.

Cover crops. Planted cover crops reduce weed populations between vine rows by making the "weeds" unnecessary, as discussed earlier. With cover crops, the species selected and management will differ from one area to another. Ideally, one would want to use a mix of different species, to balance each other and add diversity to the soil web.

One idea of what to look for can be seen in a mix that, while not developed for use in vineyards, illustrates the idea nicely. There are a series of "ecology lawn mixes" sold that contain a mixture of plants that support each other and create a lawn that needs little or no fertilizer, requires no supplemental watering, and needs mowing much less than standard lawns. The mixes vary according to where they are to be grown, but one mix formulated for the western United States contains such plants as baby blue-eyes, to act as a support plant for the grasses, disappearing after the first year; Dutch clover to provide nitrogen for the grass; yarrow to help give drought tolerance; several species of grass; and English lawn daisies. After a year's time to let it establish itself, you will have a low-growing lawn that, if not golf-green perfect, is quite serviceable and needs essentially no care beyond a couple of mowings per summer. It remains for a good organic agronomist to assemble something on the same order as cover crops for grapes in different areas.

What I am describing is surely going to be considered radical or unworkable in many areas, because it "goes against what everyone knows." Established belief in many West Coast vineyards, especially California, says that ground under vines has to be kept clean to conserve water. In response to that, I can only describe an experience I once had with a peach grower in Merced, California. He showed me his standard orchard, with bare soil under it, and a section with vegetation on the ground that had been that way for three years. He told how, when the water was let into the irrigation trenches in the bare soil, they had to shut the water off when it reached halfway down the trench. Water soaked in so little that it would still run all the way to the end of the trench. In the area with groundcover, the water was allowed to run to the end of the trench before being shut off, and it soaked in twice as fast. The trees in that area were nearly twice as tall, with 5 and 6 feet of new growth versus about 2 feet on the bare-soil trees. Further, while the trees on bare soil bore an adequate crop, the trees in vegetated soil had limb braces everywhere to support the crop and they still had to thin twice per season.

Would these same results apply to grapes? I suspect they would. However, this system won't work everywhere or for everyone. For example, in climates where vines have to be buried for winter, the areas under the vines need to be left bare to allow a place to do the burying. But perhaps this is an indication that hardier vines should be planted so the vineyard *can* have complete groundcover and a fully developed web of life.

Organic Herbicides

In a mature vineyard, weeds can usually be controlled by mulching and mowing, but there are often conditions under which some weeds need direct control. A few weeds can be removed by hand, but large numbers either require cultivation, which

we are trying to avoid in pursuit of rebuilding the soil structure, or they have to be killed with herbicide. Fortunately, there are now some effective new substances that are nontoxic or low toxic to animal life and don't remain in the environment. Below is a sampler of some of them.

New products come out so fast that some of these may be replaced or renamed after this book is published. One Web site to check is www.biconet.com.

WeedBAN. The active ingredient of Weed-BAN (formerly sold as WeedzSTOP) is corn gluten. Researchers don't fully understand which compounds in corn gluten actually control seed germination. However, corn gluten is extremely effective when applied twice a year, in the spring and fall, when weed seeds germinate. In areas where WeedBAN is applied, seedlings never develop secondary feeder roots, thus the weeds cannot develop and live.

This product is effective against crabgrass, dandelions, clover, foxtail, purslane, lamb's-quarters, creeping bentgrass, smartweed, redroot pigweed, and bermudagrass.

WeedBAN was once registered as an herbicide. However, it is so safe that registration is no longer required.

Additional fertilizer may be applied two to three weeks after WeedBAN's application. At that time, a low-nitrogen fertilizer may be applied. Six to eight weeks after WeedBAN's application, a high-nitrogen fertilizer may be applied. Tests at Iowa State University have shown that WeedBAN, applied twice yearly over a three-year period on a heavily crabgrass-infested lawn, can reduce crabgrass by as much as 91 percent.

The application rate is 20 pounds per 1,000 square feet. It should be deeply watered in after application and then allow the soil to dry.

For lawns or grassy vineyard aisles, use a drop-type spreader. Do not use on newly seeded or overseeded lawns. Wait until after the first mowing. Use WeedBAN Granular in rotary spreaders.

Scythe Herbicide. Scythe is a fatty-acid-based, non-selective contact herbicide. Formulated as a liquid, Scythe readily mixes with water to be applied as a foliar spray for the control or suppression of annual weeds and grasses, and for top-kill of perennial species. It effectively controls both annual broadleaf and grass weeds that are less than 6 inches tall. It suppresses biennial and perennial weeds by destroying green foliage. Visible effect on most weeds usually occurs within hours.

Scythe disrupts normal membrane permeability and cellular physiology resulting in cell leakage and death of all contacted tissues. Results are usually visible within minutes after treatment. Depending on plant size and species, some re-growth may occur and require additional treatment.

Because Scythe is rapidly degraded into the environment, treated areas can be sown or transplanted into as soon as desirable levels of weed control are obtained. Scythe may be applied for post-emergent control of weeds in areas that have been seeded, or planted with bulbs or other underground propagation parts, provided that the desirable plants have not yet emerged.

For most rapid kill, apply in warm, sunny weather. Avoid applications when rainfall is imminent. A rain-free period of one to two hours following application is usually sufficient for effective kill. Avoid cold temperatures. Applications made when temperatures are below 70°F (21°C) slows the rate of kill and reduces the visual effect of the herbicide even though weeds may still die.

Burnout. Made of vinegar and lemon juice plus other ingredients, this product works faster than harsh chemicals. It kills weeds in three hours and grass overnight. A second shot kills unwanted plants right down to their roots. Yet this material won't harm the environment, animals, or humans.

Burnout is intended for non-selective control of herbaceous broadleaf and grass weeds. It can be used safely around grapevines.

Bioherbicides for the Future

Agricultural Research Service (ARS) scientists have recently found a new bioherbicide that shows promise as an alternative to methyl bromide for controlling weeds in tomatoes, and other field crops. This research was part of an agency fast-track study to look for alternatives to methyl bromide, a widely used fumigant and ozone-depletor. Worldwide, seventy-two thousand tons of methyl bromide are used in preplant and postplant applications and fumigations.

Common purslane, horse purslane, ground spurge, and spotted spurge are serious weed pests in commercially grown tomatoes. Tomato crops have the highest consumption of methyl bromide of all crop uses. Tomato crops account for 23 percent of pre-plant methyl bromide use. About 3,773 tons are applied annually to the crop to control nematodes, insects, and weeds.

Methyl bromide has been used to fumigate vineyard sites, especially ones where grapes have been grown in the past, to kill phylloxera and armillaria, among other things. However, methyl bromide is highly toxic, destroys ozone in the atmosphere, and is not a permanent solution—some of the pests almost always survive to infect new vines. Further, it almost totally disrupts or destroys the web of life in the soil, which usually means the pests come back with nothing to keep them in check. Methyl bromide is scheduled to be banned in the United States in 2005, and worldwide by 2015.

The bioherbicide *Myrothecium verrucaria* comes from the sicklepod plant, which is found primarily in the southeastern United States. ARS scientists have reported that the fungus controls kudzu, a problematic weed in the South.

Researchers C. Douglas Boyette and Hamed K. Abbas at the ARS Southern Weed Science Research Unit in Stoneville, Mississippi, treated plots with natural infestations of these weeds with *Myrothecium* before planting Beefsteak tomato seedlings. *Myrothecium* eliminated these weeds in several field tests.

Myrothecium was applied in place of methyl bromide. After fourteen days, no weeds were found and the tomatoes prospered.

The researchers are also examining several other possible natural alternatives to methyl bromide for controlling weeds, including *Fusarium solani* and *Colletotrichum truncatum*.

The
ORGANIC VINEYARD

Given all this information, here are the first, basic methods for establishing the ideal organic vineyard.

- Choose varieties with high resistance to disease for your area.
- In place of cultivation, plant permanent cover crops in the vineyard. Inoculate the cover crop with mycorrhizal fungi. If the vines have not been inoculated, the fungi can move from the cover crop to the grapes, given a chance. Mow cover crops, but do not cultivate the soil, so that the soil food web can develop.
- Replace cultivation and the application of herbicide in the area under the vines with a weed-suppressing mulch of compost or other organic matter.
- Spray vines with regular applications of compost tea made from piles that have been built correctly to heat up well (to 135°F [57°C]) over a short period of time. Compost tea will increase proper microflora, which can block or inhibit pathogens.
- Remove any diseased plant part that *does* show up and compost it in a compost pile that is properly made to heat up sufficiently to destroy the disease organisms. If that isn't possible, burn the diseased material.

This is only intended as a basic plan, to give you a starting point. In much of the country, many other elements will have to be added. For instance, in the western part of the United States, with its dry, low-humidity summers, organic growing of grapes is simplified, as most of the diseases common in the eastern United States do not grow under such conditions. Further, western growers have fewer and different insect pests to deal with in many cases than their eastern counterparts. The ease of organic culture in the West is apparent by the greater number of large-scale organic grape growers in that part of the country.

In all parts of the country, managers of established vineyards may have more work to do than managers of new vineyards to attain the "ideal" condition. Soils in established vineyards will have residues from spray, and will lack organic matter. Strong reservoirs of disease and insect pests will have built up. Varieties may be less than the best for organic purposes. There is hope, though. There are many new innovations in pest control, as well as substances that are safer for the user and the environment than traditional pesticides, so that a diligent grower can make the transition with a lot less difficulty than one even ten years ago.

I have also seen a fair amount of evidence that leads me to recommend that anyone interested in organic growing of grapes should look into biodynamics carefully. When I first encountered biodynamics, I did not understand the methods. Much of it seemed to involve concocting arcane brews. But new evidence suggests that the biodynamic system is closely allied with the process of building the soil food web. For instance, one formula involves putting manure in a cow's horn and burying it for a prescribed length of time. If done correctly, the material will turn purple, and it is then ready to use.

That description *does* sound mysterious. However, I met a man from Australia who told me that a contemporary of his had analyzed the purple material and found it to contain a very dense population of fungi that are very important in soil health. Taken in that context, it shows that at least some of the methods of biodynamics are designed to stimulate a good diversity of healthy soil life.

Further, a commercial company in California that is using biodynamic methods claims it has been able to cure Pierce's disease and restore virus-infected vines to productivity, which is not supposed to be possible by current methods.

Biodynamics is not a recent development, having been around for most of a century, so there is a considerable amount of literature on the subject, too much to cover here at this time. For those who want to go further with it, see the Resources section.

Nutrient Disorders

Nutrient disorders in grapes are uncommon when vines are growing in healthy soil. The soil microlife makes nutrients available to the plants, so that deficiencies rarely occur. However, since deficiencies are possible, especially in soils that are out of balance, it helps to know what the symptoms of nutrient imbalance look like, especially since some of the symptoms could be mistaken for those of diseases.

The nutrients most likely to show deficiency are nitrogen (N), potassium (K), magnesium (Mg) and boron (B). Less-common deficiencies include sulfur (S), phosphorus (P), manganese (Mn), zinc (Zn), and iron (Fe). Deficiencies of calcium (Ca), copper (Cu), and molybdenum (Mo) are not likely to be observed. Likely toxicities include aluminum (Al) and manganese (Mn) on acid soils, and boron (B).

Nitrogen. Symptoms associated with nitrogen deficiency include foliage is pale green to yellow-green. Typically, young leaves near the shoot tips are yellow and internodes are short. Yields can be greatly reduced with severe deficiency. Nitrogen deficiency is more common on light-textured soils, where soil organic matter is low, or where the vineyard inter-row area is grassed down (that is, where grass serves as a groundcover in the vineyard aisles).

Potassium. Potassium deficiency symptoms become obvious in early summer. Yellow areas appear at the leaf margin and progress into the area between the main veins. Leaves are characteristically shiny. Flower clusters may shatter, with most of the flowers falling off, so the resulting cluster is straggly, with only a few berries. The yellow leaf areas can turn bronze or red (for colored fruit varieties) and marginal burning and leaf curling also occurs. Potassium deficiency also may show up as "black leaf," where blue-black flecks appear in midseason on the upper leaf surface. This symptom commonly occurs on native American (*V. labrusca*) grapes. With severe deficiency, shoot growth is reduced and leaves may drop early. The lower part of the bunch stem may collapse, causing berry raisining. Potassium deficiency can be confused with symptoms of leaf roll virus.

Magnesium. Magnesium deficiency results in chlorosis (yellowing) of margins of basal leaves in midseason. The chlorosis moves inward between primary and secondary veins, and may become creamy white in color for white varieties. Leaf margin burn may subsequently develop. For red-fruited varieties, a red interveinal coloring develops, possibly even coloring most of the leaf, if water stress is associated with it. Magnesium deficiency is commonly found on sandy soils, especially where heavy potassium applications have been made. It is also commonly found on vines grafted to certain phylloxera-resistant rootstocks, such as SO4.

Boron. Foliar symptoms of boron deficiency appear in early summer. Young leaves show a mottled fading between the veins, which can develop as a severe interveinal chlorosis. When severe, older leaves will show interveinal necrosis. The shoot tip commonly dies, and lateral growth develops. Tendrils and internodes near the shoot tip show black bands when held up against the light. Root extension is reduced, and the root tips are swollen and stubby. Fruit set is much reduced, and small seedless berries are commonly found along with normal-sized ones. Boron deficiency's effects on leaf deformation and fruit set can be confused with symptoms of fan leaf virus. Similarly, longitudinal cracks in the shoots can resemble symptoms of acute boron deficiency and corky bark virus. Boron deficiency is commonly found on sandy, gravelly soils, particularly those with low pH. Temporary deficiency is often associated with drought.

The margin between boron sufficiency and toxicity is very narrow for grapes. Extreme care should therefore be taken when applying boron fertilizers. The first sign of boron toxicity is dark brown to black spots around the inside of the leaf margin, which can also develop inward towards the center of the leaf between the veins. Young leaves typically show cupping. When severe, defoliation of all but the youngest leaves is seen. Boron toxicity can be due to irrigation water with a high boron concentration or excessive application of boron fertilizer.

Other nutrients. Sulfur and iron deficiencies both show varying forms of chlorosis, while lack of zinc is commonly called "little leaf" disease, because it is characterized by shoots with leaves that are much smaller than normal. In California vineyards, the common remedy for zinc deficiency is to have a worker follow along behind the pruners, swabbing all fresh pruning wounds with a rag soaked in zinc solution. Enough zinc enters the vine in this way to alleviate the deficiency.

Manganese toxicity is to be expected on acid soils, especially where waterlogging is a frequent occurrence. Among the most consistent symptoms of high manganese content of leaves is the development of black stripes along the conducting tissues (shoots and petioles); the leaf is rolled, marginal necrosis is common, and leaf fall is frequent. Yield can be severely reduced.

There are no characteristic foliar symptoms associated with aluminum toxicity, although root growth is restricted and young plants may die. Both manganese toxicity and aluminum toxicity can be overcome by raising the soil pH above 6.0.

In the Northwest, the most commonly deficient elements are potassium and boron, due to leaching of those elements in winter rains. An easy remedy for these and other mineral deficiencies is to sprinkle a cup of wood ashes at the base of each vine at budbreak. If boron is needed, sprinkle one *level* teaspoon of laundry borax under each vine every second or third year. Applying borax too often can result in boron toxicity.

Applying wood ashes also ensures good mineral availability in most areas. If wood ashes are not available, rock and mineral dusts may be of value, according to their mineral content.

It's good to know the pH of the soil and the nature of your water before adding nutrients, however. In some soils, minerals may be present but unavailable to plants due to soil pH. In Davis, California, for example, it is common for many plants to show iron deficiency. The soil has adequate iron, but the local water is so hard that it makes the soil too alkaline, and iron is unavailable to plants in alkaline soil. Plants that are mulched to conserve moisture instead of being watered frequently do better, because they get less of the alkaline water that causes nutrients to be unavailable.

In such cases, the grower may have to resort to foliar sprays to get the needed nutrient to the plant until the soil becomes balanced enough that the plant is able to get it through the roots.

An ORGANIC GROWER in OREGON

I first met Lars Nordstrom about 1988 when he came to me looking for grape vines to plant. Lars, a Swedish immigrant, and his American wife, Cynthia, owned a few acres in the northeastern Willamette Valley of Oregon, and were interested in growing organic wine grapes. At the time, they already had a couple of acres of Pinot Noir, and they were looking for other varieties to try. Lars finally decided on the French Hybrid Marechal Foch and a collection of table grape varieties.

At that time, there was a very strong bias against everything except traditional European wine varieties (Pinot Noir, Reisling, etc.) in Oregon. It was a little surprising to have someone take an interest in hybrid grapes.

One winery, Serendipity Cellars, was making wine from Foch at that time and had done respectably well with it. As important was the fact that they had much lower expenses in growing it. In the Oregon climate, Foch didn't suffer from any disease, it ripened early, and always had good sugar levels. In most years, it could be picked before the fall flights of birds came through. It required very little care other than pruning and picking.

Lars soon found that Foch had other advantages for him. His site was at a higher altitude than other growers even a short distance away, and his grapes ripened later. Foch, however, ripened early enough that he had no trouble harvesting before frost, while the Pinot Noir vines were touch-and-go some years.

One winter, cold wind caused quite a bit of damage to the Pinot Noir vines. Temperatures fell to 15°F to 20°F (–9°C to –7°C) and the vines had dead buds, areas of injured canes, and more. But the Foch vines came through unscathed.

The final straw came during an early, wet fall when no one escaped mildew, rot, or disease in their vinifera grapes—even the growers who used traditional chemicals. But the Foch was clean and healthy without any spray. After that, Lars took out his Pinot Noir and planted more Foch. He continued experimenting with hybrids and is finding them much more to his liking. And his grapes are to the liking of organic wineries, which pay him top price for them.

As important as the varieties is the system that Lars has developed for growing them. All aisles are left in native grass groundcover, while the spaces under the vines are mulched with wood chips from a local tree trimmer. There is enough leaf matter in the chips that they break down well, but not so fast that they would drain the soil of nitrogen. Lars also adds mineral supplements, including wood ashes, and some nitrogen for young vines. He uses drip irrigation on young vines; his established vines don't need it.

Lars is attempting to reduce the use of equipment in the vineyard to a minimum so that the soil structure will be at its best. He even wants to eliminate mowing. To accomplish *that*, he is experimenting with sheep in the vineyard. He has trained the vines high, and once the trunks are woody, the sheep (a short-legged breed) can graze on the vineyard groundcovers with no restriction. They are too short to reach the vines, except for very long shoots that hang down far enough for them to nibble, and then they can only nip the ends. They help the vines further by producing manure with high potassium, an element needed in the soils of the Northwest.

He hasn't achieved the perfect system yet, but he is obviously having some success: the winemakers rave over the complexity and quality of his grapes. His first Foch vineyard—though it doesn't have sheep in it yet—is over eleven years old and continues to show small but measurable increases in yield every year. Since vines are usually considered fully mature at seven years old, Lars is definitely treating his vines the way they like to be treated. At present, his yields on Foch are around 2½ tons per acre.

If you're intrigued by this description of Lars's vineyard, you may want to read *Making It Home* (Prescott Street Press), his very poignant memoir of his experiences coming to America, building his home, and starting his vineyard.

ORGANIC CONTROL METHODS

One of the most significant changes brought about by the relatively new science of Integrated Pest Management (IPM) is a change in attitude—growers no longer freak out at the first sign of an insect pest. Nature very often brings problems under control, if we give it half a chance. The appearance of a pest insect is never a solitary occurrence: there are always counterbalances, usually in the form of predators. Leave small populations of the pest alone and the predator has something to feed on so that it can begin to build its population. Many species of predator insects are now raised and sold commercially. One of the important instructions for using predators is not to apply the predators until the pest population is large enough to support them. Otherwise the predators starve for lack of prey, or move out of the area looking for food.

So if you find pest insects on your grapes, the first thing to ask yourself is: "Are they really doing harm, or just a little cosmetic damage?" Watchful waiting should be your first line of defense.

Even when it becomes apparent that the pest population is increasing so rapidly that nature isn't going to handle it entirely, be sure you know the pest and know that it *needs* control. I have seen people get upset at finding ladybugs on their vines, thinking they were a pest, simply because they didn't know any better.

And there are certain "pests" that aren't. In the Eastern United States, the grape plume moth will emerge early, web some leaves together without eating enough to harm the vine, and disappear by June. No harm done to the vine or fruit; no need to treat it at all.

The ideal vineyard—with a soil full of life and organic matter and predators in balance with pests—would be nice, but it is a rarity, at least for now. First, the vineyardist who is just converting from conventional to organic systems will have several years of having to deal with shifting pest populations—some pests may flare up for reasons beyond the grower's control, and some will continually move in from other areas. The grower who is surrounded by nonorganic areas or other areas that act as reservoirs of pests will have to fight the insects and diseases that move into his area, even if his own area is in balance. This means the grower needs nontoxic ways to deal with the pests, at least until the situation is corrected.

In this section, I describe control methods to deal with pests without using chemicals toxic to grower, plants, or soil. In addition to methods already proven for grapes, some are included that haven't been used much with grapes yet, but have shown promise on other crops and are worth experimentation. And there are a few "wild cards" that have to be considered "try and see" approaches.

At best, this is only a sampling. There are now a healthy number of businesses developing and selling all sorts of biological and/or nontoxic insect and disease controls. Fortunately, the Internet has simplified life for organic growers seeking these new products by making them readily accessible to anyone who can use a computer. One of the best sources of information on products is the Organic Materials Review Institute (OMRI). Their Web site (www.omri.org) has lists of all approved organic products and their producers/suppliers.

Disease Control Products

In developing nontoxic materials to control plant diseases, researchers and developers have come up with an interesting array of approaches. Some form a physical barrier, some are biological agents that actually attack the disease, and some are materials that, while mildly poisonous (such as copper) are acceptable for organic use when properly handled.

In many cases, the products and methods have turned out to be effective in stopping insects as well as diseases. Because some of the products in this list are useful against disease *and* insects, they may be described under "Controls for Insects" but are listed here to show that they have applications against disease as well.

Surround WP. See page 84.

Envirepel. See page 84.

SoilGard. SoilGard, a fungicide which is itself a fungus, *Gliocladium virens*. In the soil, it produces natural antibiotics that control damping off and several types of root rots (pythium, rhizoctonia, sclerotinia, and fusarium). Mainly for commercial use.

Mycostop Fungicide. This environmentally safe product contains live strains of soil bacteria (*Streptomyces griseoviridis*) that colonize plant roots to provide preventive biological protection against fusarium, alternaria, phomopsis, botrytis, phytophthora, and pythium. Mycostop is labeled for use on vegetables, herbs, and ornamentals. Since this is a preventive treatment, it must be used at the time of seeding or transplanting. For seed inoculating, use $14/100$ of an ounce per pound of seed; for soil drenching or foliar spraying, use $18/100$ of an ounce per 1.3 gallons of water. Do not mix with pesticides or fertilizer solutions.

AQ-10. AQ-10 (*Ampelomyces quisqualis*) is a natural parasite of powdery mildew being sold by the Ecogen company as a biological control for different species of powdery mildew, including grapes.

A. quisqualis can penetrate the cell walls of powdery mildew cells and use a host to reproduce more *A. quisqualis* spores. the parasite can spread throughout a mildew colony in seven to ten days. Within two to four days afterward, the mildew colony is destroyed and the *A. quisqualis* assumes a dormant "waiting" form, "lying in wait" for another rainstorm.

With grapes, timing is vital, as the AQ-10 must have mildew to feed on, but not so much that it can't overcome it all. So a grower must apply AQ-10 when there is no more than 2 to 3 percent infection in

Where's the Grapes?

To me, grapes seem like the foolproof fruit. They have an amazing ability to bounce back from frost, odd training, poor soil, and many other problems and still produce a crop. So it surprises me how often novice home growers report they aren't getting any fruit on their grapevines. Sometimes the reasons are unique, like the gas line under a vine that is leaking just enough to weaken the vine without killing it. However, more often, one of the following problems causes poor fruit set.

Overfertilizing

Too much nitrogen will make grapes grow lush and vigorously, but the flower clusters will shatter—shed most of their flowers and even parts of the cluster stem—leaving the vine to produce only a few straggly clusters. In a reasonably fertile soil, grapevines don't need fertilizing. A mulch of wood chips or well-rotted compost is often all that's needed.

Even if you think you aren't applying fertilizer to the vines, they may be getting more than you think. Once a fellow told me all about his overvigorous, nonproductive Interlaken vine. It sounded like a classic case of excess nitrogen, but he swore he didn't fertilize the vine at all. I asked him to describe his yard near the vine and found out he had a collection of roses just up a slight slope from the grape. "You give your roses the best of care, don't you—including lots of fertilizer?" I asked.

I didn't have to say more: He realized that the fertilizer from the roses was moving through the soil to the grape, giving it nitrogen overload.

If you think your vine is suffering from overfertilizing, remove as much of the fertilizer as possible. If it's already in the soil, repeated heavy watering to flush it away from the vine may help. Or, you might try applying of 2 or 3 inches of fresh sawdust, which takes up nitrogen as it breaks down. You won't know if you have removed enough nitrogen until the vine starts to grow the next season. If it bears a normal crop, you have succeeded. If it is still overvigorous and not bearing much, try again.

Potassium Deficiency

Potassium deficiency is another cause of poor set. Although few varieties show no obvious symptoms of this deficiency other than straggly clusters, most grapes will show enough other symptoms to cue you that something is really wrong. Sprinkling a cup of wood ashes around the vine just before bud break in the spring provides enough potassium to prevent deficiency in most cases.

Light Levels

Grapes need sunlight to initiate the development of flower clusters in the new buds. All grapes are more fruitful in full sun. A vine growing in a shady spot is likely to bear less fruit than it would in the open. With most varieties, it's unlikely that they would fail to have any fruit at all when grown in the shade. However, some grapes are more sensitive to low light levels than others. A friend in England growing Delight, Fiesta, and Flame Seedless in a greenhouse reported that they were unproductive when pruned to spurs, but when pruned to canes, they produced good crops. In California, all three varieties are fruitful when pruned to spurs. Apparently these varieties need high light to develop flower clusters in the buds at the base of the shoots. Since light levels are lower in England than California, especially during the early part of the growing season, the lower buds were not fruitful. However, the buds that developed later in the season received enough light to develop flower buds, so when the varieties were pruned to canes, they were able to set fruit. Most American varieties are less sensitive to lack of light than these vinifera varieties, but growers in the northern parts of North America should try pruning their vines to canes instead of spurs as a means to increase the size of the vine's crop.

One possible method to get more light to developing shoots is to grow the vines facing south, with a reflective background behind them. Another involves a type of reflective, metallic plastic that is sometimes put under fruit trees to get more light into the interior for better fruit color. Such material might also be spread under vines to help reflect more light into the interior, which should help developing buds become more fruitful.

Incorrect Pruning

Incorrect pruning can reduce or eliminate fruit in some grapes. For example, Himrod and Seneca are two varieties that must be pruned to canes. If the fruiting wood of those varieties is cut back to spurs, they have little or no crop (this is explained in more detail in chapter 3). And there are overzealous growers who remove *all* the previous season's growth, which leaves no buds at all for fruit.

Disease

Botrytis is a fungal disease that can attack flower buds and reduce or in some cases eliminate set. Virus diseases such as fan leaf and leaf roll will drastically reduce the set and quality of fruit.

Varieties and Environment

Some grapes have difficulty setting good crops in cool, wet conditions during bloom time. Heavy rain may wash away pollen and thus affect set, but some types of grapes may have reduced set simply if there is heavy dew and cold, moist air around the flowers. I've seen Swenson Red trained so that the clusters were no more than 2 or 3 feet from the ground, with long grass under the vine that held a layer of cold, most air around the clusters. As a result, the caps of the flowers tended to stick, interfering with set. When the vines were retrained higher, the clusters hung above the layer of cold, wet air, and fruit set improved dramatically.

Male Vines

This one shows up as a problem most often when someone buys an older home that has an established vine, usually trained on an arbor, that is apparently healthy, but nonfruitful. Male vines, particularly *Vitis riparia,* are sometimes planted where an arbor is wanted, but the home owner doesn't want to deal with fruit. Such vines are beautiful, and the male flowers are very sweetly scented when in bloom, but they set no fruit.

the vineyard, but may not get control if the infection is greater than that. At present, AQ-10 is only available for commercial use, mostly because the rate of application is hard to scale down for home use (i.e., $1/100$ of an ounce for a 1-gallon sprayer).

Serenade. Serenade is a biocontrol agent, a select strain of *Bacillus subtilis*. It attacks and "eats" the following pathogens: powdery mildew, downy mildew, Cercospora leaf spot, early blight, late blight, brown rot, fire blight, and others. Besides grapes, it can be used on a range of other fruits and crops. It comes as a wettable powder than can be sprayed on.

Supresivit. Like Serenade, this is a biocontrol agent. It is *Trichoderma harzianum*. The manufacturer doesn't indicate everything it attacks, but I would expect it to be able to attack a range of diseases similar to Trichodex (next item). The manufacturer/distributor is Borregaard and Reitzel, Denmark, or Fytovita, Czech Republic.

Trichodex. A selection of *Trichoderma harzianum* that attacks primarily *Botrytis cinerea,* but also *Collectotrichum* spp., *Fulvia fulva, Monilia laxa, Plasmopara viticola, Pseudoperonospora cubensis, Rhizopus stolonifer,* and *Sclerotinia sclerotiorum.* In addition to grapes, it can be used on cucumber, nectarine, soybean, strawberry, sunflower, and tomato. It is a wettable powder that is mixed with liquid and sprayed on the plants.

Lawn Sweeper/Lawn Mower. Many diseases and insects of grapes have a stage that overwinters in debris under the vines. Standard practice calls for cultivating the soil to bury or destroy the organisms. A better option is to pick up the debris using a lawn sweeper, or even a riding mower. The gathered material can then be composted in a hot pile to destroy the pests and later returned to the soil.

Copper, Sulfur, and Lime Sprays

An organic grower should avoid using copper, sulfur, and lime sprays exclusively. While these products are allowable under most organic programs, they are mineral elements and do not degrade, but can build up in the soil. In the amounts used in most sprays, accumulation would take years, but depending on the soil, they can eventually build up enough to adversely affect both soil microlife and soil pH.

Copper sulfate, Bluestone. This old-fashioned source of copper sulfate is often mixed with hydrated lime to make Bordeaux mixture. It is used against black rot, anthracnose, downy mildew, and more.

Basic copper sulfate 50%. This mixture contains no less than 50 percent metallic copper. It is registered for use on most crops and proven against a wide variety of fungus problems, including brown rot, shothole, anthracnose, rusts, leaf spot, leaf curl, downy mildew, fire blight, bacterial blight, and other blights. Apply at 2 to 5 pounds per 100 gallons of water according to the label.

Hydrated lime. Though most commonly used with copper sulfate to make a Bordeaux mixture, hydrated lime may also be applied alone to combat some fungal and bacterial problems, and as a soluble source of nutritional foliar calcium. Rates vary, to a maximum of 20 pounds per 100 gallons of water.

Microcop-Sta-Stuk M Twin Pack. Microcop contains 50 percent copper (equivalent to 95 percent micronized tribasic copper sulfate) and 50 percent inert ingredients. It comes with Sta-Stuk M, a spreader/sticker specially formulated to adhere Microcop to bark and leaves, which increases its effectiveness and extends its activity in wet weather. A twin pack contains 8 ounces of each product. This micronized form of copper sulfate is used against black rot, downy mildew, anthracnose, and other diseases. Mix and apply at 1½ to 2 tablespoons per gallon of water.

Black Leaf Bordeaux Powder. Use this Bordeaux copper fungicide in your orchard or garden to control blight on potatoes and tomatoes, anthracnose on tomatoes, and downy mildew on grapes. Mix the powder with liquid and spray according to package directions.

Black Leaf Dusting Sulfur. This product contains 92 percent sulfur. Use this sulfur for the control of powdery mildew, black spot, citrus thrips, and spider mites on specified ornamentals, fruit and nut trees, citrus, flowers, vegetables, and roses. General rates are 2 to 3 tablespoons per gallon of water; check the label for specific instructions.

Top Cop with Sulfur. Top Cop is a combined liquid copper and sulfur formulation labeled for use on over fifty crops and for over twenty diseases. It contains 8.4 percent tribasic copper sulfate and 50 percent sulfur. For 1 acre, apply 2 to 4 quarts per 100 gallons of water.

Safer Garden Fungicide. This liquid, all-natural sulfur fungicide has the advantages of convenience and good adherence and distribution. It leaves no unsightly residue. It is used on fruits, vegetables, flowering plants, and ornamentals, to control mites as well as fungal problems, such as powdery mildew, blackspot, scab, brown rot, brown canker, leaf spot, and rust. Use up to the day of harvest. Follow package directions.

Concern Copper Soap Fungicide. Concern Copper Soap Fungicide is a patented, fixed copper fungicide, made by combining a soluble copper fertilizer with a naturally occurring fatty acid. The copper and the fatty acid combine to form a copper salt of the fatty acid, known technically as a *true soap*. The copper soap fungicide controls many common diseases using low concentrations of copper, down as low as 90 parts per million. The net result is an excellent vegetable, fruit, and ornamental fungicide. Concern Copper Soap Fungicide is suited for use in domestic circumstances, both indoors and outdoors. Treats fungal diseases. Apply according to package instructions.

Lime Sulfur Fungicide. Lime sulfur contains 29 percent calcium polysulfide. It is one of the least toxic, but most effective, controls for peach leaf curl, brown rot, and other fungus problems. It is also used for control of pear blister mite, caneblight, and scab. It may be applied with water or mixed with oils for use as a dormant spray. Use at 4 to 16 tablespoons per gallon of water and 8 to 12 gallons per acre. Consult the product label for specific application rates and directions.

Kocide 101 Micronized Copper. This product is registered for all major fungus problems on most crops and is also registered for frost control. It contains 77 percent cupric hydroxide (metallic copper equivalent: 50 percent). The micronizing process reduces particle size, which dramatically increases coverage and control.

Each pound of Kocide contains over 125 trillion particles specially formulated to adhere to waxy leaves as well as coarse bark surfaces. Kocide mixes and stays in suspension better than traditional coppers. Use at ½ to 10 pounds per acre, according to the label.

Kocide 2000. Kocide 2000 is an advanced copper product. It utilizes a patented formulation to improve copper bio-availablity in order to optimize performance at lower usage rates. Kocide 2000 is dry flowable and disperses well in solution. It is as effective as other copper products, however, the volume of copper needed is reduced by up to 25 percent. Kocide contains 53.8 percent cupric hydroxide (metallic copper equivalent: 35 percent).

The following is from a grower I know: "I have used Kocide on grapes for years, and I have learned that it is sometimes difficult to predict which hybrid selections are sensitive to copper. For example, the variety Kay Gray is not sensitive to Kocide, but the hybrid of Kay Gray with Veeblanc is extremely sensitive. (I learned this the hard way.) I mix in an equal part of hydrated lime with the Kocide, which eliminates any phytotoxity problems. Keep in mind that the longer Kocide stays wet on the foliage, the longer the period of phytotoxity risk. The quicker it dries, the lower the risk. For example, don't spray Kocide in the morning when there is dew on the leaves and the air is still and heavy.

"I really like Kocide for protecting grapes against black rot and downy mildew. I have not been real impressed with its ability to protect against powdery mildew especially in seasons with a lot of environmental disease pressure."

Micronized Wettable Sulfur. This product contains 90 percent sulfur, 10 percent inert ingredients, and a wetting agent. It may be used as a dust or spray. Ultrafine "micronized" particles, maximize coverage, adhesion, and disease control, and minimize the risk of sulfur burn. (However, sulfur should not be used on melons, cucumbers, or apricots without testing on a small area first.) Use at 1 to 3 tablespoons per gallon or 2 to 7 pounds per acre according to label.

Stylet-Oil. See page 88.

Other Control Substances

These are all unconventional (some are relatively new) substances that will kill fungal diseases.

Kaligreen. Kaligreen is a contact-type fungicide for the control of powdery mildew. However, I have been hearing from growers who say it also controls downy mildew. It is new enough to be worth testing on all the fungal diseases of grapes.

The active ingredient is potassium bicarbonate. Direct contact with the fungus is absolutely necessary for control. Kaligreen breaks down the potassium ion balance in the fungus cell; cell walls collapse, shrinking the cells and destroying the fungus. Mix thoroughly with water and add a spreader-sticker (such as Therm X70) and agitate. Do not apply through irrigation systems. Do not mix with highly acidic materials since Kaligreen is a weak alkaline material and decomposes in highly acidic conditions. Labeled for grapes, cucumbers, strawberries, tobacco, and roses. Because it contains 30 percent potassium, it also acts as a fertilizer for your plants.

Apply at a rate of 2 to 3 pounds per acre.

Fungastop. Citric acid and mint oil are the broad-spectrum antifungal and anti-bacterial compounds in Fungastop. The mode of action upon fungi and bacteria involves the alteration of cell membranes and the inhibition of cellular respiration. Use this product on fungi such as phytophthora, sclerotinia, and botrytis as well as bacteria like pseudomonas, salmonella, listeria, and streptococcus. Other ingredients include citrus pulp, fish oil, glycerol, vitamin C, and water. Mix 1 part Fungastop with 50 parts water. It is labeled for all food crops, pre- and post-harvest, as well as ornamentals and turf. Apply when disease conditions are favorable for outbreaks, at seven- to fifteen-day intervals, depending upon disease pressure and environmental conditions.

Jungle Rain. Jungle Rain contains pure Castile soap and volatile oils of citrus (mainly orange). The mixture is about 75 to 100 parts soap to 1 part volatile oils.

This product is an organic foliage cleaner that removes mildew, fungus, spores, black sooty mold, insects, and chemical residue. It is nontoxic and biodegradable, and can be used both inside and outside the house for many pests as well, such as ants.

Jungle Rain controls insects, aphids, scale, mealybugs, ants, and whiteflies by means of suffocation and or dehydration. Use of this product does not lead to the destruction of beneficial insects if used only on a specific pest or plant.

OxiDate. OxiDate is a highly refined peroxide containing patented additives that prevent the peroxide from breaking down on exposure to ultra-violet light. OxiDate is used to control powdery mildew. This product utilizes a peroxygen chemistry formulation that is specifically labeled for agricultural field crops as well as greenhouse productions and post-harvest storages.

OxiDate should be considered a curative rather than a preventative product. A grower in the northern Willamette Valley of Oregon reported good results in curing a serious infection of powdery mildew. Other growers have found that results are not always as good as with traditional chemical fungicides. The difference seems to be connected with difficulties ensuring good coverage.

Advantages of this material include an absence of toxicity to humans, a lack of harmful residues, plus a very short re-entry time.

Improved sprayer. ARS scientists recently evaluated a superior sprayer that saves growers time and money when they apply pesticides in their orchards.

Plant pathologist Charles C. Reilly with the ARS Southeastern Fruit and Tree Nut Research Laboratory in Byron, Georgia, studied the effectiveness of the Proptec nozzle-less sprayer in cooperation with Michigan State University engineers who developed the sprayer.

The sprayer uses about 20 percent less chemicals per acre and cuts spraying time in half while still providing superior coverage to fruit trees. Current air-blast equipment sprays about 50 gallons per acre, one row at a time, shooting the spray into the air, and not fully covering the pest-ridden trees.

The new sprayer looks like the letter "T." It travels above the tree, rising and lowering (from 5 feet to 17 feet) to accommodate the tree height. It sprays low-volume, uniform droplets directly down and into the tree. It can spray two rows at once, applying 25 gallons per acre. Another bonus is that the Proptec sprayer reduces soil compaction, because it is relatively lightweight and does not go down every row. A grower can easily alternate which rows the sprayer travels to minimize soil compaction. California growers are evaluating the sprayer for grapes, blueberries, and stone fruits.

Controls for Insects

This is a collection of methods and materials that a grower will find useful to control insects without resorting to toxic materials. Many are pest-specific and don't affect predators or other types of insects. A few have been used only a short time and should be explored to find their full potential. Additionally, as noted earlier, some of these treatments, such as Stylet-Oil and Surround, also work on diseases.

Surround WP. Surround contains microscopic particles of kaolin clay. When this material dries after application, it forms a barrier film on the plant surface that allows light to pass through, but repels and irritates insects. The film can also help prevent sunburn of the fruit and can reduce heat stress.

Fruit sprayed with Surround appears dusty or to have an extra-heavy "bloom." This is a drawback to applying Surround on table grapes, though it can be washed off. If Surround is as chemically neutral as it is reported to be, it should be no problem on wine grapes.

Pests that Surround can control or at least suppress include plum curculio, apple maggot, leafhoppers, pear psylla, first-generation codling moth, and Japanese beetles. Tests have shown that Surround deters the glassy-winged sharpshooter leafhopper, which has become a serious problem in California due to its ability to spread Pierce's disease. Because this product is so new, it will need to be tested further to find all its uses and limitations.

Surround WP is now listed by the Organic Materials Review Institute (OMRI) for use in organic production.

Envirepel. There are several garlic juice products on the market, but after studying them, I've concluded that Envirepel appears best by a wide margin. Envirepel is an excellent all-purpose organic "pesticide," if that is the word for a substance that doesn't kill the pests, but still keeps them off the crops.

All other garlic products are essentially cooked, strained garlic juice. Envirepel, however, is uncooked and processed with an organic acid to stabilize it. Cooked garlic products contain two main ingredients, a sulfur compound and a natural form of dimethyl sulfoxide (DMSO), which is what makes garlic juice an effective systemic pesticide. DMSO has been used as a carrier for many substances as it readily penetrates all sorts of tissues.

Envirepel contains DMSO and the sulfur compound and twenty-three other substances all of which contribute to its effectiveness. Envirepel is not only a repellent: it can be mixed with other pesticides, natural or not, to increase their effectiveness. Envirepel is registered to repel ants, aphids, beetles, borers, cambium miners, chafers, curculios, cutworms, earwigs, fruitworms, grubs, leafminers, leafhoppers, leafrollers, maggots, mealybugs, mites, phylloxera, plant bugs, rootworms, sawflies, scale, slugs, spittlebugs, stem girdlers, thrips, tree crickets, tortrix, weevils, whiteflies, white grubs, and wireworms. In addition to its uses against fungi and insects, Envirepel will also repel deer.

Not just a surface spray, Envirepel is actually taken up by the plant and becomes a systemic. However, the compounds that make Envirepel smell like garlic are not carried along, at least in the form we recognize, so you won't wind up with garlic-flavored grapes. The plant actually incorporates the compounds in such a way that it subtly alters the chemistry of the plant. The standard chemical feeding cues that plants give off to insects are changed, so that the plants no longer attract pest insects.

Envirepel by itself works best as a repellent, so it should be started before insects begin to build up on the crop. The product isn't harmful to predatory insects, and because it doesn't actually kill the pests, populations of beneficial insects will increase and help with overall control.

Application depends on the crop, but two to five sprays per season are usually sufficient to control most pests. Spraying should begin at very early stages of plant growth to enhance the buildup of effectiveness.

Beneficial Nematodes

While nematodes are thought of as attackers of plants, many species are predators of insects and soil microflora. Some of these types have been isolated and cultured and are available commercially. The one most commonly sold is *Steinernema feltiae*.

These "killer" nematodes attack a wide range of the soil-dwelling phase of many insects, such as the larva of root weevils, junebugs, Japanese beetles, and more. Research indicates they can destroy more than 230 different pests including fleas, fungus gnats, black vine weevils, and white grubs. Naturally occurring, they are not harmful to people, pets, plants, or earthworms, and will continue working for 18 months. They can even be used to treat insects that bore into wood.

They are applied by suspending them in water or a nutrient solution and drenching the soil with the material. They can be applied any time that the soil is not frozen.

One pint contains 7 million nematodes and treats 200 to 400 square feet.

Parasitic wasps. Trichogramma wasp (*Trichogramma minutum*), mini wasp (*Trichogramma platneri*), and moth larvae parasite (*Trichogramma pretiosum*) are parasitic wasps that lay eggs on the caterpillars of various species of moths and butterflies. When the eggs hatch, the wasp grubs burrow into the caterpillar, eating as they go until the caterpillar dies. The species here are largely host-specific for grape berry moth and grape leaf roller. They don't give one hundred percent control, which is as Nature intended, since they would starve without some of the moths to feed on.

Milk as Fungicide

RESEARCHERS IN BRAZIL found that, under greenhouse conditions, a 50 percent mix of raw cow's milk and water was more effective than a chemical fungicide against zucchini squash powdery mildew (*Sphaerotheca fuliginea*). In connection with this, the Dutch government has put milk on their approved fungicide list. This is an anecdotal item, but one that is worth putting to the test in home trials.

However, they can keep the damage the pests cause down to tolerable levels. It is usually necessary to leave areas of the vineyard unmowed to allow them safe areas to overwinter.

Dipel. Dipel is a Bt (*Bacillus thuringiensis*) product. Bt is a fairly wide-spectrum bacteria able to attack many species of moths and butterflies. It can kill 90 percent or more of the caterpillars when properly applied as a powder. Caterpillars do not die immediately, but usually stop feeding within hours. Dipel is labeled for grape berry moth at the rate of ½ to 1 pound per acre.

Yellow sticky cards. Many species of insects are attracted to certain wavelengths of light given off by plants, with yellow being one of the main ones. Yellow apparently indicates that a plant is under stress, or at least is of interest to the insects. This yellow coloration isn't apparent to our human eyes. Yellow sticky cards have been used with success in greenhouses and small gardens for years, though their use in multi-acre plots would be prohibitive in terms of the labor and time needed to put the cards out and service them. They are effective against a range of insects, usually sucking or chewing types, including aphids, leafhoppers, and flea beetles. Larger insects may be attracted, but can often pull free of the stickum.

Commercial sticky cards are often waterproof, which makes them last longer. For small-scale use, bright yellow posterboard can work. Simply wrap it in a clear plastic bag and coat the bag with a sticky material such as the commercial "Tanglefoot" and hang the cards from the vines. Two to four per vine is usually enough. Check the boards regularly to make sure they are working and trapping target insects. If not, you may wish to change to a different shade of yellow. Depending on the concentration of pests, you may need to change the plastic bag and put on a new coat of Tanglefoot every one to two weeks.

Sticky tape. Sticky tape is similar in action to the yellow sticky cards and works against the same types of pests. This is a continuous tape that can act as an unbroken barrier to insects, especially those that must move up from the soil into the vine. Commercially available, this is a one-use product, to be replaced as needed.

Reflective foil under vines. This relatively new product consists of a plastic sheeting material with a metallic surface that is highly reflective. When reflective foil is unrolled under grapevines, the metallic surface reflects the full spectrum of sunlight. Any yellow wavelengths emitted by the plants that might attract insect pests are washed out and masked by the reflected sunlight. Home growers can lay aluminum foil under their vines to get a similar effect. The reflective surface should come out at least to the drip line of the vine, if not a little farther.

This technique appears effective against a wide range of pests, but it should be started before the insects get into the vines as ones already there are not affected as much.

An additional benefit of using reflective foil is that extra sunlight reaches parts of the vine that would otherwise be shaded, getting more sun to fruit and developing fruit buds.

Bug vacuum. In California, there have been experiments with riding-type vacuum devices that literally suck pests off of row crops such as strawberries. While such a unit has not been developed for commercial use in grapes, I have found a type of vacuum cleaner that will work for home growers. The "Big Power" vacuum cleaner works well for this purpose because, instead of a bag, it circulates the air intake through a tank of water. The value of this is that when a leaf covers the opening entirely, the machine doesn't tear it to pieces or suck it in as an ordinary vacuum cleaner would. Instead, the water acts like a safety valve to allow the air to "churn" until the passage is open again. At the same time, the actual inflow is very strong and will suck up insects that might escape an ordinary vacuum.

The device has a further use in greenhouses or in a house as an air filter. With the hose removed, the vacuum can be allowed to run (it is much quieter than an ordinary vacuum) and it will filter the entire volume of air in a large house in less than thirty minutes. Because the water tank is clear, the results of cleaning are visible. At the start, the water is clear. After the machine has run for twenty minutes or so the water will be distinctly gray and cloudy. In a closed greenhouse, such a device could be used to remove disease spores from the air.

With a long extension cord attached, this type of vacuum cleaner could be a good tool for removing insects the size of Japanese beetles (or possibly larger) from an average backyard vineyard.

Diatomaceous earth. A direct-contact insecticide, diatomaceous earth is made up of microscopic silica particles from the fossilized shells of diatoms. The sharp crystals cut the cuticle of the insect; fluids leak out and the insect desiccates. Diatomaceous earth is approved for wide-spectrum use, but must be applied carefully. While not directly toxic to humans, workers should use means to avoid breathing it, as the tiny sharp particles can physically irritate lungs. Use only "natural" grade diatomaceous earth for insect control; do not use swimming pool filter grade.

Pheromone lures and traps. These work in two ways. One way is to flood the area with mating scent so that male insects are unable to find actual females. The females go unfertilized and lay sterile eggs. The second way is to lure males to traps where they can be disposed of. The advantages of pheromone lures are that they are host specific, that is, they only act on one species. However, in most cases they don't totally get rid of the pest species and some infestations can still occur. Rates of success can vary depending on factors such as humidity, wind circulation, and timing of placement.

Species for which there are lures/traps available include black cutworm, California red scale, European grape berry moth, European grape vine moth, grape berry moth, gypsy moth, raisin moth, San Jose scale, aphids, thrips, whiteflies, and Japanese beetles.

Neem and Azadirachtin. Neem, a tropical tree native to India, has been used for centuries as a fungicide and pesticide, as well as in health care products for people. The active insect-killing substance, azadirachtin, has been extracted from neem seed oil and is sold by itself.

Azadirachtin mimics insect juvenile hormone, causing immature insects to develop incorrectly and eventually die. Most predators present near pest insects are usually adults, so azadirachtin doesn't affect most of them. Ladybugs are an exception, with the voracious larvae often feeding on aphids and other pests alongside the adult beetles. Azadirachtin does have an affect on adult aphids because aphids give birth to live young. Treated adults produce young that are legless or otherwise incomplete, which die. In spite of this drastic effect on insects, neem has no record of any adverse effects on humans, having been used in India for centuries, even to the extent of using the twigs as toothbrushes.

Several companies produce neem products. If you don't see neem in the list of ingredients, look for azadirachtin. One commercial product is Neemix, which contains 0.25 percent azadirachtin. It is registered for a wide variety of pests on row crops, fruit and nut trees, herbs, berries and grapes, cotton and more, but not ornamentals. Rates vary from ½ to 2 gallons per acre, according to the severity of the pest population.

Stylet-Oil. Several friends told me of the excellent results they had controlling both mildew and mites with this product, so I looked up the product in the Internet, and here is what I found.

Stylet-Oil is a highly refined mineral oil with its own emulsification system. It is labeled for use simultaneously as a fungicide, insecticide, and to control certain aphid-transmitted viruses. The oil is colorless, tasteless, and odorless. It has no residue tolerance and is said to be biodegradable and safe to the environment.

Stylet-Oil is used to control fungal diseases such as powdery mildew and botrytis bunch rot. Stylet-Oil will kill powdery mildew on contact as well as prevent development of mildew for ten to fourteen days, depending on the use rate. The oil also controls insect pests such as mites, whitefly, and leafminer. In addition, the oil will control aphid-transmitted virus diseases, such as potato virus Y, tobacco etch virus, and cucumber mosaic virus, by blocking the feeding of aphids carrying the disease.

Stylet-Oil controls fungi by interfering either with respiration or attachment of the organism to its host. Stylet-Oil controls insect pests primarily by modifying insect feeding and egg-laying behaviors and by suffocation.

Plant-feeding insects use tiny hairs called *sensillae* to detect special chemicals in plants that identify the plant as a host or non-host. Contact with these plant chemicals can trigger critical insect behaviors such as feeding and egg-laying. Stylet-Oil can plug the hollow pore on the end of the sensillae, thus shutting down the insect's ability to communicate with its environment. Beneficial insects are minimally affected by Stylet-Oil application because they use different host-sensing mechanisms than plant-feeding insects. However, if enough oil contacts a beneficial insect, the beneficial insect will die.

Concern Pesticidal Spray Oil. Canola oil is the active ingredient in Concern pesticidal spray oil, which is for use during the dormant and growing seasons, as well as indoors and in greenhouses. This oil spray controls aphids, mites, scale, and other pest insects. It kills all stages of insects, including eggs, by suffocation or smothering, and acts as a repellent. The general use rate is 4 teaspoons per quart of water.

Naturalis-L. Naturalis-L contains a selected strain of the fungus *Beauveria bassiana*. Naturalis-L is for food crops. Sprayed on, its spores germinate only in contact with an insect. A hypha (fungal thread) pierces the insect's shell, causing fluid loss and death, after which the fungus digests the body. It affects mainly pests, largely leaving predators such as ladybugs and parasitic wasps unharmed, due to differences in body form and behavior. Most insect pests sit close to the surface of the leaf for easier feeding access. This means that the insects often actually sit on spores, which then stick to their bodies and start germinating. Predators, on the other hand, straddle the insects on which they feed, so they stand away from the leaf surface. Thus predatory insects rarely contact the spores closely enough to allow the spores to stick and grow. Naturalis-L is effective on a wide range of pests, including whiteflies, aphids, thrips, mites, and weevils.

Sugar esters. Sugar esters have been tested by the ARS and by university entomologists around the country and found to be lethal to mites and soft-bodied insects—whiteflies, aphids, thrips, and pear psylla—almost instantly after contact. The esters soon degrade into harmless sugars and fatty acids. They do little harm to insect predators and are completely nontoxic to animals and people. In fact, some are approved as food-grade safe.

AVA Chemical Ventures of Portsmouth, New Hampshire, and ARS have applied for a patent on the sugar esters. AVA hopes to have the first of these compounds on the market by the time this book is in print.

The sugar esters can kill up to 100 percent of the soft-bodied insects and mites they contact. Insects are not expected to develop resistance any time soon because of the way the esters work, according to ARS entomologist Gary Puterka at the agency's Appalachian Fruit Research Station in Kearneysville, West Virginia. Puterka coordinated the studies nationwide and is co-inventor on the new patent.

During four years of tests, the sugar esters have been proven as (or more) effective as conventional insecticides against mites and aphids in apple orchards; psylla in pear orchards; whiteflies, thrips, and mites on vegetables; and whiteflies on cotton.

One drawback: The esters must come into contact with insects to be effective, and the esters don't kill insect eggs. Like insecticidal soaps, sugar esters kill insects by either suffocating them or by dissolving the waxy coating that protects them from drying environments.

5 DISEASES of GRAPES

OF THE PROBLEMS that plague grapes, disease can require more constant effort to combat than anything else. At the same time, there are more ways of dealing with disease than anything else a grower has to contend with. In this chapter, I have attempted to cover, or at least touch on, any diseases a grower is apt to encounter, and as many strategies for dealing with it as possible.

Where management programs mention using fungicides, a number of possible alternate methods or nontoxic fungicides are covered. Since many of these alternates and nontoxic types will work with more than one disease, or need further trial on more diseases, some should be tried for several of these diseases. See chapter 4 for detailed information on disease control products.

DISEASES of HUMID REGIONS

These are mostly fungal diseases that require both heat and humidity to grow and cause problems. They are commonly found where there is regular summer rainfall, such as in eastern North America.

Black Rot

Black rot (*Guignardia bidwellii*) is one of the most serious fungal diseases of grapes in the eastern United States. While it can attack all parts of the vine, the most serious effect is on the fruit. In warm, humid regions, black rot can cause complete loss of crop on susceptible varieties if left uncontrolled.

Symptoms. Leaves are susceptible for about one week after they unfold. Reddish brown, usually circular leaf spots first appear on the upper leaf surface. After a few days, a tan to light brown area appears in the center of the spot, followed by small, black, pimplelike bodies (pycnidia) in the center of the spot, usually in a loose ring just inside the dark brown edges of the spot. Leaves may wilt due to black, elongated blotches on the petioles. The same lesions on green shoots may weaken them, so that they break easily in wind.

Berries, susceptible from bloom until veraison, first turn brown; then may drop off or hang on the cluster; and finally turn into a shriveled, dark brown or black "mummy" with black pycnidia developing on the surface.

Disease cycle. Mummified berries, either on the ground or hanging on the vine, are the main overwintering form of black rot, though some of the cane lesions may overwinter. Spring rains release the spores, infecting tender new growth, though old cane lesions can start the process even before bud break. Spores of the fungus are produced within the diseased fruit and canes and released during spring rains, infecting leaves, blossoms, succulent shoots, and young fruit. Mature leaves and ripe fruit are not susceptible. Very few fruit or leaves are infected after late July, and none are infected after the end of August. Black rot infections depend on temperature and the length of time susceptible tissues remain wet. At 45°F (7°C), the fungus is unable to infect, while the optimum temperature is 80°F (27°C), at which point infection can take place in six hours on wet leaves.

Disease management. For organic growers, the first line of defense is planting varieties resistant to the disease. This should be accompanied by practices that keep the vines open to allow best air circulation for fast drying off of the vines. Careful observation and removal of infected berries and leaves as they arise can help minimize spread.

Where susceptible varieties are being grown, fungicides should be applied early, to block infection before it can start. Infected prunings and mummified berries should be removed and composted or buried before growth begins. One way to deal with fallen mummies on the floor of the vineyard without disturbing the soil is to apply a layer of mulch, such as compost, to bury the mummies and block spore release.

Start protectant fungicide applications when shoots are 3 to 5 inches long, with variations according to weather and how bad the disease was the previous year. Continue the fungicide application every ten to fourteen days, until the berries are about ¼ inch in diameter. At this point, management can end if the disease has been controlled well.

Recommended organic fungicides. Lime sulfur, copper sprays.

Grape Anthracnose

Anthracnose (*Elsinoe ampelina Shear*), a fungus sometimes called "bird's-eye rot," may cause extensive losses, but it is easy to control.

Symptoms. The appearance of anthracnose on fruit, stems, and leaves is fairly distinctive and not readily confused with other diseases. The shoots, berries, and leaves are all attacked, but symptoms on shoots and berries are easiest to recognize.

Fruit infections appear as a "bird's-eye" effect, having light gray centers and reddish brown or purple borders. Berry infection often cracks the fruit skin, which leads to decay of the berry.

Stem lesions are similar in color, sunken, with slightly raised borders. Anthracnose can kill the tips of many new shoots by girdling them.

Affected leaves have sunken spots with dark brown to black margins and light gray centers, especially on newer growth. Later, the center of the lesion drops out, to create a "shot-hole" effect that gives the leaf a ragged look overall. Young leaves are most susceptible. Severely infected leaves become distorted and curl down from the margins, because the disease damages part but not all of the expanding leaf blade.

Disease cycle. Anthracnose overwinters on infected canes. It spreads to all new growth during wet periods in early spring.

Disease management. Plant resistant varieties. During dormant pruning, cut out and remove all affected wood if possible. A delayed dormant spray of liquid lime sulfur applied just before bud break will greatly reduce the threat. During the growing season, use a program of preventive fungicide sprays at two-week intervals from bud break until veraison. Prune out damaged shoots and clusters, remove the prunings from the vineyard, and rake the ground under the plants in fall to remove all fallen berries.

Recommended organic fungicides. Lime sulfur, copper sprays.

Downy Mildew of Grapes

Downy mildew (*Plasmopara viticola*) is a native American fungus of grapes, which was accidentally introduced into Europe in the 1870s. Today downy mildew can be found anywhere that is sufficiently warm and wet during the growing season. Resistance ranges widely, with *Vitis vinifera* being the most susceptible species. *Muscadinia rotundifolia* and some forms of *V. aestivalis* have the greatest resistance.

Symptoms. All green parts of the vine are attacked by the fungus, which enters through mature stomata. Yellowish green lesions appear on the leaf surfaces seven to twelve days after infection. As the lesions grow, they become brown, dry, or mottled. At the same time, the white "downy" sporulation of the fungus appears on the lower surface of the leaf, matching the boundaries of the lesion on the top. Severely infected leaves may curl and drop off the vine. This type of defoliation is serious because it can affect the overwintering buds, making them more susceptible to winter injury. Lesions on older leaves in late summer are sometimes oily, somewhat angular, and are located between the veins. Eventually, all lesions become brown and dead with age.

Young, infected shoots and cluster stems may become distorted and curl. They are frequently covered with a white, sporulating fungal mass. Berries on these clusters turn brown and eventually shrivel. Severely infected parts of the vine may shrivel and die. When infected young, berries may be entirely covered with white, fuzzy fungal growth. This may resemble powdery mildew, particularly when weather is wet, or when dew is present. After berries are old enough that the stomata no longer function, no new infections or sporulation occur, but existing infections will continue to spread into healthy tissue. Later in the season, berries remain hard and turn dull green to reddish purple. Infected berries remain firm and are easily detached from the stem, leaving a dry stem scar.

Disease cycle. The downy mildew fungus overwinters as dormant spores (called oospores) in dead leaves on the vineyard floor. In the spring, the oospores become active two to three weeks before bloom. They germinate in water to form sporangia, which release small swimming spores, called zoospores, if there is standing water present. Rain splashes these zoospores onto grape tissues, where they swim to the vicinity of stomata and form cysts.

Epidemic disease development can result from repeated cycles of secondary spread, which is caused by new spores that are produced within the white fungal growth on infected tissues. These spores are produced only at night when the relative humidity is greater than 95 percent. They can be blown relatively long distances and cause infection when they land on susceptible wet tissues.

Disease spread is most severe during periods when humid nights with moderate to warm temperatures are followed by rain. These conditions allow spores to germinate and cause new infections. Frequency of rain and duration of wet periods correlate with the number of additional infections during the growing season. Downy mildew infection can become a severe problem when a wet winter is followed by a wet spring and a warm summer with a lot of rainfall.

Disease management. Rain and humidity promote downy mildew more than any other factors, so the first line of defense should be cultural practices that improve soil drainage and good airflow through the vineyard and the individual vines. Developing the soil structure by organic practices such as applying compost and inoculation with mycorrhizal fungi will greatly reduce standing water on the vineyard floor, as well as generally promote vine health. Early spring application of sufficient compost as mulch will bury inoculum to further reduce early-season disease incidence.

Some type of fungicide is still likely to be needed on all but the most highly resistant cultivars, especially in vineyards making the transition to organic. On vinifera grapes and other highly susceptible cultivars, apply fungicide sprays as early as two to three weeks before bloom, during bloom (if bloom is slow), after bloom, ten to fourteen days later, and at ten- to fourteen-day intervals until veraison. On less susceptible varieties, spraying can be started just before bloom. Ultimately, you should base the use of fungicide on weather conditions. If the weather is favorable (dry and not conducive to the disease), treatments may be timed farther apart.

Recommended organic fungicides. ZeroTol, Serenade, Trichodex, basic copper sulfate 50 percent, black leaf Bordeaux powder, copper sprays such as Kocide.

Angular Leaf Scorch

Angular leaf scorch (*Pseudopezicula tetraspora*) is a fungal disease first identified in 1985. It is similar to a European disease, rotbrenner, and the two are closely related species.

Symptoms. The main part of the vine affected is the leaves, which develop faint chlorotic spots. Veins within the spots look brownish when viewed against strong light. As the lesions enlarge, they turn brown and the center area usually dies, leaving a yellow border, except on red wine grapes like Cabernet and Pinot Noir, in which the borders are red. Labrusca-type cultivars like Concord may not show much of any border. The infections usually occur between veins, creating a sharply delineated, wedge-shaped area. Infected leaves usually fall off the vine well before normal leaf fall.

Disease cycle. The fungus overwinters on dead leaves in the vineyard. In spring, small fruiting bodies (apothecia) form, which discharge spores when they have dried down after several rains. The spores land on leaves and start the infection cycle. There is usually only one cycle of infection per year, but if there is enough rain, some of the fungi on the new leaves can mature enough to produce apothecia and release spores, also.

Disease management. There is a lot of variation in resistance to this disease among cultivars. Surprisingly, the resistance is not all in American varieties. A number of vinifera grapes are resistant, and several French Hybrids and American grapes are not. Choose resistant varieties when possible.

As with other fungal diseases, an open vineyard, with vines trained to open canopies, and good sanitation of the vineyard before bud break are recommended. Fungicide treatment consists of applying the material when shoots are 3 inches long and maintaining protection through fruit set.

Recommended organic fungicides. Several of the wide-spectrum fungicides should be effective for preventing angular leaf scorch.

DISEASES FOUND *in* ALL CLIMATES

This section covers diseases that either do not require hot, humid conditions in which to grow, or can become established and grow in a wide range of conditions. As a result, many can be found wherever grapes are grown.

Eutypa Dieback

Eutypa dieback (*Eutypa lata),* more commonly known as "dead arm disease," attacks the woody parts of the vine. A very widespread disease, it can attack at least eighty species in twenty-seven different families. One important host besides grapes is the apricot.

Symptoms. Cankers forming around pruning wounds are usually the first sign of the disease, though these cankers may be hard to observe, as they often form under old bark. Instead of the actual canker, you may see an area of bark where the wood looks somewhat flattened. Cutting through the affected area may show a wedge-shaped section of dark wood, like a piece of pie with the point in the very center of the wood. Unfortunately, the grower often isn't aware of the symptoms of Eutypa dieback until after the canker stage is well established, as much as two to four years after the original infection of the pruning wound.

New shoots that grow above an infected area are often stunted and the internodes are short. Infected leaves are small, yellow, and crinkly. Often, it is easy to miss the symptoms until at least late spring, because healthy foliage usually masks the infected leaves. There may be a mixture of large and small berries in the clusters on infected shoots. The symptoms in the affected area become more pronounced each year until eventually the diseased arm stops all growth.

Disease cycle. At one time, dead arm was thought to be a form of Phomopsis cane blight, leaf spot, and fruit rot.

In winter or early spring, during cool, wet weather, rainfall or snow melt washes spores from fruiting structures on dead, infected wood. The spores are spread by wind and infect grapes when they encounter fresh, wet pruning wounds. As wounds dry and heal, they lose susceptibility to the disease. Two weeks of dry weather during and after pruning usually reduces infection nearly to zero. Dead arm develops slowly on grapes, so that it usually isn't seen until the third or fourth season, when cankers and affected foliage are noticed. The vine deterioration continues several more years until the trunk or arm is finally killed.

Disease management. Sanitize the vineyard by removing and destroying any large infected trunk or cordon piece. Large cuts should be protected by painting or spraying with a solution of the fungicide Benlate. One California grower has reported that Ivory dish detergent was as effective as Benlate in stemming the spread of the disease. Consequently, the grower taught the pruning crew to carry spray bottles of Ivory on their belts; they sprayed each pruning cut that was larger than a pencil size.

A few grape varieties are believed to resist the disease (see Table 10-13). The best time to remove diseased wood is in late spring, when the weather is apt to be dry and foliage symptoms make it easier to locate the disease. Also, it is usually still early enough to allow time for a shoot to be trained to replace the part that has been removed. The fungus can occur in cherry orchards, which may be reservoirs of the fungus for grapes. Old grape trunks and cordons can also be sources.

To avoid problems with dead arm disease, make big cuts when two to four weeks of dry weather are expected. Or, make most of the cuts in winter, let the fungus infect the cuts, and come back during the dry summer months and remove the rest of the wood. However, this involves double cutting, which you may forget to do.

Organic control method. Spray Ivory dish soap on pruning wounds, as noted.

Phomopsis Cane, Leaf Spot, and Fruit Rot

Phomopsis cane, leaf spot, and fruit rot (*Phomopsis viticola*), can be found in most of the world where grapes are grown, but it is not common. It only causes crop loss when disease pressure is intense during periods of very cool, wet weather, when there is much splashing in the vineyard.

Symptoms. Phomopsis appears early in the spring, usually showing up when the green shoots and berry cluster develop black, elongated lesions or splits in the green tissue. If there are a lot of lesions, the surface of the area will have a blackened, scabby appearance. On the leaves, the infections are black or brown and have black, pimple-like fruiting bodies that show up in late summer. The disease can make cluster stems brittle and break off, so that the fruit is lost. In severe infections, fruit is also affected and turns brown, shrivels, and falls off. Sometimes fruiting bodies will also form on the fruit.

Disease cycle. The fungus overwinters mostly in the lesions on the bark. Spores are released in spring and splash onto newly developing shoots. The shoots are usually infected between bud break and the time the shoots reach 6 to 8 inches long. Shoot and leaf lesions appear within three to four weeks after infection, but do not form new spores until the following year. Cluster stems are susceptible from the time they first become visible until after the fruit is pea-size. Fruit infections occur primarily from bloom through shatter. If the infection rate at bloom time was severe, cool, wet weather near harvest time can reactivate the disease, leading to fruit rot.

Disease management. The first line of defense is to choose a planting site with good air drainage, with the rows arranged so that air movement after rain is maximized. Any cultural practices that improve air drainage will help, as will establishing good ground cover in rows and mulching under vines to reduce splashing as much as possible. In winter, learn to identify infected canes and remove and destroy all infected wood by burning, burying, or discing the material in before spores are released.

Because inoculum remains viable in canes for several years, hedged vineyards are more at risk of suffering loss of yield due to phomopsis.

This disease is easily controlled by one or two early fungicide sprays. This could include copper spray, which is acceptable for most organic growers. Careful sanitation should be sufficient in most cases if the other lines of defense have been followed.

Organic control methods. Use careful sanitation first. No specific fungicide recommendations, but copper types are probably most effective.

Botrytis Bunch Rot

Botrytis bunch rot, also called gray mold (*Botrytis cinerea*), is a fungus with worldwide distribution. Causing decay of ripe or nearly ripe fruit, as well as damage to flowers, botrytis bunch rot affects *V. vinifera* and some French Hybrids the most. Many American varieties can tolerate or resist the disease. Ironically, the same disease, under the right conditions, can also make for some of the world's most sought-after wines, when it becomes the "noble rot."

Continued cool, wet weather is necessary for the disease to cause serious damage. Once weather warms and dries, the disease slows or stops activity. If the fungus invades the fruit cluster, it can reactivate when weather becomes cool and wet again.

Symptoms. In early spring, infected buds turn brown and dry. Large, reddish brown patches develop on leaves. After bloom, the fungus develops as a saprophyte on aborted berries in the fruit clusters. These become a source of inoculum to infect ripe berries. Moisture on the inside of tight-clustered bunches can reactivate the fungus, and the fungus can enter any wound or break in the skin of the fruit. This is one of the more serious side effects of wasps attacking the fruit: breaks in the berry skin caused by the wasps allow entry of the fungus. Eventually, the whole cluster becomes moldy and covered with gray masses of spores. In dry climates, the disease can progress undetected inside tight clusters. The outside of the cluster looks normal, but when picked, the cluster collapses into a moldy mess.

"Noble rot" develops when mornings are cool and dewy, which allows botrytis to start growing, but afternoons are warm and dry, which stops the growth of the fungus. At this stage, the fungal growth has made the skin of the grape permeable to moisture, allowing the warm afternoon to draw moisture out. This concentrates the flavor elements and leaves those flavor elements intact, so the grape doesn't oxidize and simply become a raisin.

Disease cycle. Botrytis overwinters in debris in the vineyard as a saprophyte (able to live on dead material), under the bark of vines and on wild alternate hosts, of which there are many. The fungus produces small, dark, hard fruiting bodies called sclerotia that are resistant to weather. In spring, the sclerotia produce conidia (spores) that spread the disease. Botrytis usually starts by infecting dead tissue, before moving on to green shoots and flower clusters. Tissue injured by hail, animals, birds, or other mechanical means are all open to infection by botrytis.

Cool temperatures, from 55°F to 77°F (13°C to 25°C), and moisture in the form of fog or dew allow spore germination, which can start in only one to four hours, depending on specific temperature.

Varieties whose berries are tightly packed in the cluster are often prone to botrytis, because internal pressure causes berries to split or loosens berries from their brushes (attachment point to the stem). Berries that have been attacked and split by powdery mildew are very often infected by botrytis as well, so that it can be hard to tell that two diseases are present, not just one.

Disease management. Botrytis is best controlled by proper cultural practices and selection of resistant varieties. As with other fungal diseases, it helps if the vineyard is situated for maximum air circulation for rapid drying of the vines. Vines should be pruned and trained to allow maximum air flow though the canopy. This should prove effective, along with good sanitation of the vineyard to remove inoculum sources, such as infected mummified berries and dead leaves. Avoid applying excess nitrogen to the vines, as lush, tender growth is more vulnerable to the disease. It can also be useful to apply growth regulators to lengthen the rachis, which spaces the berries out so that the clusters are loose instead of compact. This will prevent the disease from spreading within clusters.

If fungicide is used, it is most important to apply it to the inside of the cluster before the cluster "closes" (berries grow to the size that keeps the inside of the cluster from being accessible) to halt any botrytis that might otherwise form inside the cluster. Fruit may be further helped by selective leaf removal to allow more air and light to reach the clusters so they will dry faster after dew, rain, or fog.

Recommended Organic Fungicides. Mycostop, Fungastop, Trichodex.

Powdery Mildew

Powdery mildew (*Uncinula necator*) is an American grape disease that has spread to

European grape-growing regions. This fungus affects all green parts of the vine, but is most noticeable first on leaves, spreading to other parts of the vine later.

Symptoms. Infection on leaves appears conspicuously on the upper surface as white or grayish, powdery patches. Later, the entire leaf surface may be covered with the fungus. Severe leaf infection can result in cupping of leaves. Diseased leaves will scorch or turn brown and fall.

Affected berries have a dull, darkened appearance and are usually covered with powdery growth. New fruit infection ceases as the sugar content reaches 8 degrees Brix in most fruit. When grape cluster stems become covered with the fungus, the stems shrivel and considerable losses from shelling of the fruit may occur. Overwintering spore-forming bodies appear as black specks in the older affected areas. Cluster infections at bloom time may lead to poor fruit set, while infection slightly later can cause berry splitting, as the fungus prevents the berry skin from expanding and the skin bursts under pressure from the developing flesh. Fruit infection reduces wine quality, leaving a "musty" taste in the wine.

Resistance varies between different cultivars, not only in the severity, but also in the location of the infection. For example, in the Pacific Northwest, Himrod will often develop small colonies of mildew on shoots, just sufficient to make discolored blotches, but will suffer no symptoms on the fruit or leaves.

Resistance also affects the size of colonies on the leaves. Immune varieties will have no disease at all. Very resistant varieties may show only a tiny spot where the fungus germinated, but never increased in size. Colonies range all the way from limited, small colonies that grow slowly and barely sporulate, up to colonies that cover the entire leaf surface. Even then, some varieties can have entire leaves infected and still not show many symptoms on the vine as a whole. As before, it seems to be a matter of how well the vine can block the initial colony's ability to sporulate and produce secondary infections.

Disease cycle. The powdery mildew fungus overwinters inside dormant buds and on the bark of the vine as tiny black fruiting bodies (cleistothecia). Spores (ascospores) contained in the cleistothecia are released during rains from the time of bud break until shortly after bloom. They are wind-dispersed to emerging leaves and clusters, and can infect wet or dry tissue at temperatures of 50°F (10°C) or higher. Infection usually starts soon after the blossom period and will continue on the foliage through the growing season.

Powdery mildew is the only fungal disease that can germinate and grow in low-humidity conditions. Thus, it is a problem in California, while the other American fungal diseases, which require rainfall and humidity, are essentially nonexistent there. In California, powdery mildew becomes inactive when the temperature exceeds 90°F (32°C) for more than a few hours. Above approximately 95°F (35°C), the fungus begins to die after five or six hours. Unfortunately, even if some of the fungi die from the heat, there are usually enough in the protected interior of the vine to begin reinfection once the temperature drops, so heat waves can't be counted on to do more than slow the progress of the disease.

Mildew colonies produce masses of white, powdery secondary spores (conidia). Conidia are wind-dispersed throughout the vineyard and do not require rain for release or infection. New colonies that result from these secondary infections produce additional conidia, which can continue to spread the disease. This repeating cycle of infection, spore production, spore dispersal, and reinfection can continue to recur in as little as five to seven days. Thus, in the East, powdery mildew epidemics can suddenly explode when temperatures are favorable, unless the disease is managed efficiently. In the West, mildew increase is steady, but commonly does not go into explosive sudden jumps.

Recent studies have demonstrated that berries are highly susceptible to infection from the immediate pre-bloom stage until about two weeks after fruit set. Berries of Concord become almost completely resistant to infection after this time. The rachises of Concord grapes remain susceptible until harvest, but the economic importance of mid- or late-summer rachis infections on processing fruit is questionable. Extensive splitting of berries and severe fruit damage are almost always the result of infections that occurred during the period from pre-bloom through fruit set, when berries are most susceptible.

Disease management. Multiple rains (four or more) at a time when the fruit is most susceptible can make powdery mildew particularly difficult to deal with in the East. Management programs should be at their peak from pre-bloom through fruit set, especially if weather is wet. After the fruit-set period, leaf infections are much less serious on Concord and other American labrusca type cultivars than on *V. vinifera* and susceptible hybrids. Concord crop yield or quality is essentially unaffected. In the drier West, most hybrids don't require treatment for mildew if proper cultural practices such as maintaining open vines and choosing sites where air circulation is good are practiced.

On *V. vinifera* and highly susceptible hybrid cultivars, continued suppression of foliar mildew generally is required at least until veraison to avoid early defoliation.

Good management of late-season leaf infection also reduces disease pressure the following year, by limiting the number of fungal fruiting structures that overwinter and become sources of infection in the spring. For effective management of powdery mildew, sprays may be required as early as the time when 1 to 2 inches of shoot growth show on vinifera cultivars (depending on rain and temperature) and should not be delayed beyond the immediate pre-bloom stage on any cultivar. In the West, control measures are usually sufficient applied every 6 inches of shoot growth.

High disease levels the previous year increase early-season disease pressure and consequently the importance of early-season sprays. Keep up protection at least through veraison to ensure maximum fruit quality on *V. vinifera* and susceptible hybrid cultivars, and to help avoid premature defoliation, which might prevent the vine from fully preparing for winter.

An additional tool to help commercial growers with powdery mildew is the U.C. Davis Powdery Mildew Risk Index, a computer forecasting model, which provides daily disease-tracking information to growers. It uses temperature, moisture, and time parameters to allow the grower to predict how severe the disease will be in the near future and can determine which fungicides will be most effective and how long the grower can wait between applications. With this tool, growers can often eliminate two or three fungicide applications during a season and still achieve equal or better control of the disease than previously.

To summarize, cultural practices that can reduce the severity of powdery mildew in the East, and often prevent it altogether in the West, include:

- planting in sites with good air circulation and sun exposure;
- use of a training system that allows good air movement through the vine and prevents excess shading;
- planting hybrid cultivars that have resistance to mildew.

More organic growers in the West are turning to the French Hybrids or similar types in preference to vinifera varieties, because they can grow the French hybrids with so much less attention to managing mildew and other disease problems. With these hybrids, in many cases, vine care simply is a matter of pruning and picking.

Recommended organic fungicides. ZeroTol, OxiDate, M-Pede (fatty acid soap), Serenade, Black Leaf Dusting Sulfur, Safer Garden Fungicide, AQ-10 Biofungicide, JMS Stylet-Oil, Kaligreen.

If you are using only sulfur products (dust, wettable, flowable, or micronized) to control powdery mildew, begin treatment from budbreak to 2-inch shoot growth.

Reapply at seven-day intervals if treating every other middle or at ten-day intervals if treating every middle. A "middle" is the strip between rows. Spraying every other middle means taking the sprayer down alternate strips, blowing spray on the vines on either side of the strip. With this method, the grower is relying on the sprayer to blow the spray completely through the vines to the other side of them. However, the far side of the vines will receive less spray than the near side. Spraying in every middle means that both sides of each row of vines are thoroughly covered with spray.

Reapply if sulfur is washed off by rain or irrigation.

Treatments may be discontinued for wine and raisin grapes when fruit reaches 12 degrees Brix, but should be continued to harvest for table grapes.

JMS Stylet-Oil may be alternated prebloom with sterol inhibitors. It is extremely important not to apply this material within ten days of a sulfur treatment. Insecticidal soap and potassium bicarbonate may also be alternated with the sterol inhibitors; do not apply soap within three days of a sulfur application.

JMS Stylet-Oil may be used as an eradicant anytime in the season as long as there is no sulfur residue present (at least two weeks after a sulfur treatment). Apply it on a fourteen- to seventeen-day interval.

AQ-10 Biofungicide (*Ampelomyces quisqualis*) is a biological control agent that selectively controls the powdery mildew fungus. It has a restricted entry interval of four hours. For early season control, begin making applications at bud break, and continue applications on a fourteen-day interval for four applications, at which time switch to a strobilurin, sterol inhibitor, oil, or sulfur program. (Strobilurin is a fungicide derived from a species of wood fungi, only recommended for commercial use as it should be alternated with other spray substances to prevent the target disease from developing resistance to it. Sterol inhibitors are a class of substances used as fungicides, some of which are accepted by organic programs, while others are not.) For late-season control, begin applications near harvest in regions where cleistothecia function in the disease cycle (see page 98). Continue applications on a two-week interval for three to four applications. Apply as a tank mix with 1 percent JMS Stylet-Oil.

Kaligreen (potassium bicarbonate) is an inorganic fungicide with a restricted entry interval of four hours. Apply by ground only in sufficient water (25 gal/acre minimum) to ensure complete and thorough coverage of foliage and crop. Use as a protectant on a seven-day interval. Contact of the disease organism is essential for control. Use of non-acidifying spreader/sticker or nonphytotoxic crop oil is recommended.

JMS Stylet-Oil (narrow range oil) has a restricted entry interval of four hours. Never mix oil and sulfur or apply one within two weeks of the other. Can be used as a protectant or eradicant. As a protectant, alternate it pre-bloom with the sterol inhibitors. At the 2 percent rate, this oil is an excellent eradicant and can be used at any time during the season (except within two weeks of a sulfur treatment); good coverage is essential. Apply at fourteen- to eighteen-day interval. Do not use on table grapes after berry set.

M-Pede is an insecticidal soap with a restricted entry interval of twelve hours. Alternate use with one of the sterol inhibitors. Apply in water 100 to 150 gallons per acre. Complete coverage of upper and lower leaf surfaces, as well as grape clusters, is essential for control. Apply every seven to ten days. Do not combine with sulfur or apply within three days of a sulfur application.

Crown Gall of Grapes

Crown gall (*Agrobacterium tumefaciens*) is a bacterial disease that occurs worldwide on over six hundred species of plants. There are different variations or biovars of it, with biovar 3 being the one found most commonly in grapes. *V. vinifera* is the grape species most susceptible to the disease, with varying levels of susceptibility or resistance in American and French Hybrid grapes. The disease is characterized by rough galls or overgrowths on the roots, trunk, and arms of grape vines; most of the galls are usually found on the lower trunk, close to the soil line. In some cases, galls can form rapidly and even girdle a young trunk in one season. Root galls can interrupt the movement of water and nutrients into the vine and can result in poor growth, dieback, and, on occasion, death of a vine. Galls are most common in conditions where injury to the wood can occur, such as in cold climates where trunks may be damaged by cold, or where vineyard workers are careless about cultivation and wound the vines.

I have seen nursery stock mulched with sawdust that reflected and concentrated heat at the point where the trunk of the young vines came in contact with the mulch, such that nearly every vine in some rows was damaged and had galls.

Symptoms. The obvious symptom of crown gall is the brown, rough galls. Most galls occur near the soil line, in the crown of the vine, but they can also appear on upper shoots or on roots. Root galls may only be evidenced by slow, weak shoot growth. If a gall girdles the trunk, the vine may die above that point. If the vine is own-rooted, it can usually be saved by training a new shoot up from below the galled area.

Disease cycle. New galls may be white and fleshy in early summer, turning brown, dry, and corky by fall. The bacterium that causes crown gall is commonly present in the tissue of healthy-looking vines but doesn't cause disease unless the vine is injured. It can also cause necrotic decay spots on roots, with or without gall formation. The bacterium can be detected in the sap of infected vines, and it commonly concentrates at nodes. The bacterium also lives in soil, and can survive for long periods without a host.

Biovar 3 causes galls by attaching to plant cells, where it injects a portion of its DNA that directs the host cells to overproduce growth hormone, causing rapid cell division and gall formation.

Disease management. Biovar 3 is the only type regularly found in grapes, and the disease can be avoided by planting clean stock in soil that has not held grapes previously. The bacterium can't be controlled by chemicals because it lives in the soil.

When planting new vineyards, discard any vines with galls. In established vineyards, cut vines off below the gall, if possible.

Budding and grafting often result in development of galls, especially in field-grafted vines where the trunk is cut to bleed out the sap so the vine can't push out the graft. Interestingly, in many cases, growers report that galls produced on such wounds tend to be sloughed off by the vine.

Cold injury is by far the most important factor in the northern part of the country, though sunburn on lower trunks may be as serious in southern areas. In northern areas, use management practices that reduce possible cold injury (see chapter 12 for more information on these practices).

Some growers have reported success by painting turpentine on existing galls to dry them up.

At present, only one biological control is available, *Agrobacterium radiobacter*, strain 84, sold as Galltrol. When used as a dip on cuttings before rooting, control of gall has been as high as 90 percent, while the results of using it as a curative are irregular.

This is also an area in which proper building of the soil food web (see pages 57–62) should have definite benefits, certainly in keeping the bacterium from entering the plant, and possibly also in allowing natural "inoculation" by *A. radiobacter*.

The Germans use a special hot water dip to clean up stock of crown gall bacteria; however this technique is rather exacting and doesn't protect the vines from reinfection once they are planted in the field.

Oak Root Fungus

Oak root fungus, also called armillaria root rot or shoestring root rot (*Armillaria mellea* Vahl:Fr.), can survive on diseased or dead wood and roots below ground for many years. Healthy plant roots can become infected when they come in contact with inoculum from the preceding orchard crop or nearby oak trees. Flood waters sometimes help spread infection in a vineyard. The fungus is favored by soil that is continually damp. Although the pathogen produces mushrooms, they are not considered significant in disease spread.

Symptoms. Infected vines become nonproductive and often die within two to four years. Adjacent vines develop weak, shorter shoots as they are infected by the pathogen. White mycelial mats can be found under the bark at the soil line. Dark, rootlike structures called rhizomorphs originate from the vine's root and grow into the soil after symptoms develop on vines.

Disease cycle. There is no disease cycle as such with *Armillaria*. Infection is mainly a matter of the fungus being present in the soil on roots, either those of grapes, or alternate hosts whose roots remain in the ground when the land is cleared for vineyard.

Disease management. The standard commercial control method is soil fumigation. There are no known experiments with organic controls, thought it seems likely this condition would respond to rebuilding of the soil life by applying compost and avoiding tillage to recreate a healthy soil food web that could combat the fungus.

Although it isn't specifically recommended for this disease, Thermo Triology's SoilGard parasitic fungus might be effective against *A. mellea*.

Pierce's Disease

Pierce's disease *(Xylella fastidiosa),* or PD, is a serious bacterial disease that is native to the southeastern United States. The bacteria itself is not limited to grapes, but also causes disease in citrus and peaches and is widespread in other plants, often without causing obvious symptoms. Originally known as Anaheim Disease, it wiped out thousands of acres of vineyards in Southern California in the 1880s. It was later named after Newton B. Pierce, California's first professionally trained plant pathologist, who was the first to attempt to isolate the cause of the disease.

Symptoms. Depending on the susceptibility of the grape cultivar, symptoms vary from sudden collapse and death of the vine to virtually no effect. General symptoms include chlorotic spots on leaves, which appear and spread as the center of the spots dry out and become brittle. Concentric zones develop, and eventually leaves fall prematurely. Fruit set is reduced and berries dry up. Wood fails to mature. Bud break is delayed in the following season. Suckers can develop from the base of chronically affected vines.

In severe cases, vines die within days or weeks, with leaves and foliage appearing as though they had been severely sunburned or scorched and dried. In lesser cases, some shoots show the scorching, with the vine going into gradual decline over three or more years, until it dies or reaches a state in which it is still alive, but so stunted and lacking in vigor as to be worthless.

Muscadine grapes have the greatest resistance, with some vines showing no effects at all, even though the sap tests positive for the bacteria. In some cultivars, leaf margins will show scorching, but there will not be any serious effect on the vines or reduction in yield. Southern forms of *V. aestivalis* show strong tolerance to the disease, though tolerance varies with the origin of the form: types from Florida have the greatest tolerance, equal to that of muscadine grapes.

Disease cycle. The bacterium can survive in many alternate hosts, but is not a threat without a vector to carry it to grapes. Leafhoppers are the most common vectors of the disease. In California, most native leafhopper species do not travel far or feed very vigorously, so that in the past, the disease never spread far. Affected vines could be easily controlled by removing a circle of vines around the affected area, followed by replanting with new vines. In the 1990s, the glassy-winged sharpshooter (GSS) leafhopper reached California from the southeastern United States and greatly intensified the problem, because this species feeds vigorously and flies farther and faster than other leafhoppers. Where other species might infect a few dozen vines in a vineyard, the GSS can spread the disease to entire vineyards in a matter of weeks.

Once in the plant, the bacteria multiply and clog the vascular system of the plant, so the tissues literally are starved of water and nutrients. In susceptible varieties, such as most vinifera vines, this usually kills or reduces the vine to uselessness.

Climate appears to have an effect on the severity of the disease, in that varieties that can tolerate PD in the central South may be seriously hurt by it in the Deep South, down into Florida. For example, the variety Norton is able to tolerate PD with no ill effects in Arkansas, even when testing positive for the bacteria. But along the Gulf Coast, where disease pressure is much stronger, Norton may decline from the disease after a few years. There is anecdotal evidence that suggests the bacterium is affected by cold and that vines in central Southern areas tolerate it better because winter cold clears much of the bacteria from the vine's system, or reduces the bacteria's rate of reproduction, whereas vines in the Deep South experience little cold. No conclusive research has been done on this at present.

There is evidence that some seriously affected grapes can recover to some degree from PD. One grower in Florida, who grows northern grapes by using a rigorous spray program to control leafhoppers, finds that infected vines are often able to put out healthy new growth and show reasonable recovery if protected from the leafhoppers.

One thing to keep in mind is that the disease is only a serious problem if the GSS or a comparable vector is around to spread it. At the same time, the presence of the GSS is not serious if it has none of the PD bacteria to spread. In fact, the GSS is believed to shed PD bacteria each time it molts (many insects shed the lining of their gut when they molt, which would shed the bacteria) and must then reacquire the PD.

Disease management. In the past, PD was considered incurable. Vines were replaced, if possible, or only resistant types were planted in the first place, depending on the situation. When vines are removed, it is necessary to remove a circle of vines around the ones with obvious symptoms: By the time a vine shows symptoms, several vines around it will likely have the disease also. The old rule was to remove a circle about three vines wide around a diseased vine, but with the coming of the GSS, that rule is useless. By the time one plant shows the disease, a half-acre of vines could be infected.

With the serious threat to California viticulture from the rapid spread of PD by the GSS, several people have been exploring different avenues to deal with both the disease and the GSS. More than one option looks promising.

In Texas, a researcher has found that the native Mustang grape, *V. mustangensis* (also called *V. candicans*), which is resistant to PD, is apparently able to transfer that resistance to varieties grafted onto it. Vinifera grapes on Mustang rootstocks have survived for eleven years in an area where PD has killed all other susceptible grapes not grafted on *V. mustangensis.*

In some areas, it may be possible to test for the PD bacteria in surrounding vegetation and remove any that is infected, so the GSS would be no threat. Elderberry, for example, has been found to be a reservoir for the bacteria. This kind of large-scale testing it not generally practical, as it could take considerable time and resources to test all the perennial plants in an area; but, in some isolated cases, it could work.

A commercial biodynamics company, Agri-Synthesis, reports successfully treating infected vines and restoring them to normal fruitfulness with biodynamic methods (see page 72).

If all else fails, many grape varieties are already resistant to PD, in addition to muscadine grapes. Many PD-resistant bunch grapes have been bred in the South and Southeast to be able to cope with the longstanding PD situation there. Some of these will be covered in chapter 10.

Viral Diseases

Viral diseases are often difficult to quantify in grapes. Some viruses can infect vines apparently without harming or even affecting the plants, producing symptoms only when the infected variety is grafted to a second type that is more sensitive to the virus. Other virus-infected plants may be very vigorous but have reduced yield.

For at least a century, it was believed that the only way viruses could spread was when new plants were grown from cuttings taken from infected plants. Now it is known that nematodes and some sucking insects can spread viruses, usually at a slow rate. However, the rate of spread isn't fast, so the presence of a diseased vine in the area isn't cause for serious concern, though it should be destroyed if possible to prevent it being used as a source of cuttings, or to keep virus from being carried from it to healthy vines.

The best "cure" at the present time is to start with material that is known to be virus-free, or at least free of any symptoms and able to produce good crops.

Most viruses are not common enough that the average grower will encounter them, but the following are some that you should be aware of.

Grapevine leaf roll. Yellowing (chlorosis) between the leaf veins of white varieties, reddening in red varieties, and rolled margins of basal leaves are typical symptoms of leaf roll. Symptoms are easier to identify in red than white varieties because the yellowing in white varieties is often not obvious.

Symptoms are first seen midseason, especially on leaves that are low on the shoots. Although the leaf turns yellow or red, there is a thin strip of tissue along the veins that remains green. This is often termed the "Christmas tree" effect.

Severely infected vines produce a reduced crop and maturity is delayed. Often fruit set is poor in infected vines, with a lot of variation in berry size; with red varieties, the fruit show reduced color. Leaf roll was common in the old red table grape variety Emperor, and infected vines produced fruit without color, leading grapevine leaf roll to be nicknamed "white emperor disease."

Traditionally it was thought that leaf roll could only be spread through the use of infected cuttings, scion buds, or rootstocks. However, in time, leaf roll can spread within a vineyard. One or two vines adjacent to infected vines can become infected each year. Nematodes are believed to be the vectors of this disease.

Fan leaf. Typically, plants suffering from fan leaf produce leaves with open sinuses (the region where the petiole attaches to the leaf) and shortened main veins. Hence, the leaf takes on the shape of a fan. These symptoms are seen throughout the season. Sometimes the leaves can be more yellow than healthy leaves. Multiple branching and fasciation (flattened stems and shoots) often occur with this disease. Other symptoms include yellow spots or patches on leaves, shoots, tendrils, and/or flowers. Also, veins on leaves can develop yellow bands.

When encountering symptoms of what appears to be fan leaf, be aware that some herbicides will cause symptoms that are very similar. However, herbicide damage will usually include white patches and a very rough, bumpy look to the leaf. Also, herbicide damage may be accompanied by the stopping of growth, while fan leaf vines will keep growing. Be suspicious of herbicide if symptoms appear suddenly on a vine that has been free of them for several seasons.

Fan leaf is spread mostly through the use of infected cuttings, scion buds, or rootstocks. However, fan leaf can spread within a vineyard by the nematode *Xiphinema index*.

To control fan leaf, collect propagation wood only from vines known to be free of fan leaf, preferably from certified virus-free stock. At the least, propagate from vines that have been observed as being free of disease symptoms for one year.

Corky bark. Leaf symptoms of corky bark are similar to those of leaf roll, and it is now thought that corky bark is associated with type 11 leaf roll. The leaves tend to become uniformly red or yellow, rather than just in the areas between the veins. Also, the leaves remain on the vine longer than healthy leaves.

True "corky bark" is only seen on a limited range of varieties (eg., LN 33, Rupestris Saint George, and Richter 110). These rootstocks are so sensitive to the virus that scions that carry the disease, even without showing symptoms, will not graft successfully to the rootstocks. The virus causes graft failure.

Most commercial stock is free of corky bark. It is not known to be spread by any method other than using infected cuttings.

Rupestris stem pitting. Some vines infected with Rupestris stem pitting (RSP) decline slowly, though many varieties show no symptoms at all, especially if grown on their own roots. In some cases, however, if a variety is carrying the disease, and it is grafted onto the rootstock 3309, it can be fatal. In other cases, when infected scions are grafted on to Rupestris Saint George rootstock, pitting of the trunk results, but it is not fatal.

There is no proven vector for the virus, and the only way to spread it is by using cuttings from infected vines. There has been considerable debate about this virus in the United States, as plant material from other countries is often prevented from entering if it is found to carry RSP. Yet, the virus causes symptoms in so few varieties that many growers feel there should be no restriction on plants carrying the virus. Canada now allows material with RSP as a "virus without consequence" (similar to "fleck" virus, which causes small flecks on leaves of some varieties, but no other damage).

Peach rosette mosaic virus (PRMV). Concord, Catawba, and Niagara grapevines are infected with peach rosette mosaic virus (PRMV) in a large percentage of vineyards in Michigan, and it may be of concern to growers in all of the eastern United States. This virus is soil borne and is spread from plant to plant by the root-feeding dagger nematode *(Xiphinema americanum)*. Dandelion, curly dock, and Carolina horsenettle are weed hosts for the virus.

Where the disease exists, there are "holes" in the vineyard, that is, gaps due to missing vines. Infected vines are usually umbrella-shaped, because the virus causes the canes to grow somewhat crookedly. Internodes are shorter than normal, and leaves are distorted. Berry cluster shelling will occur on vines that have been infected for several years. The virus is seed-borne in grapes (whereas most viruses are not carried into the seeds). The practice of spreading fresh grape pomace in the vineyard should be halted in areas where PRMV is known to exist, because this can reintroduce the virus into the vineyard. The dagger nematode will spread the virus from infected grape seedlings to healthy vines. If the pomace is composted properly first, the seed will be killed by the heating of the pile, and no seedlings will result. Delaware grapevines are less susceptible to PRMV than are Concord, Catawba, and Niagara varieties.

Commercial control of the disease calls for soil fumigation with methyl bromide or a similar chemical before planting to kill the dagger nematodes. The appropriate organic response would be to build the soil with compost for a year or so before planting, to help balance the soil life and reduce the nematode population—large populations of such pests usually only exist in soil where the soil food web is out of balance.

If a grower is dealing with diseased vines in an established, nonorganic vineyard, the infected vines should be removed and the soil rebuilt for one year with a program of compost and nontillage to restore the soil life before replanting.

Tomato ringspot and tobacco ringspot. French Hybrid grapevines (especially blue-fruited varieties) are susceptible to infection by these two viruses. The symptoms are the same regardless of which virus causes the disease. Tomato ringspot is more prevalent than tobacco ringspot virus.

Leaves on infected canes are yellow and smaller than normal, vines appear stunted, and internodes are abnormally shortened. Vines lose vigor and will often die of winter injury if infected with either virus. The dagger nematode, *Xiphinema americanum,* spreads this disease by feeding on the roots of infected weeds (chickweed, dandelion, plantain, and others) or grapevines, and then feeding on the roots of healthy vines.

Control is similar to that for peach rosette mosaic virus (see page 107).

Producing Virus-Free Grapevines

One problem with old grape varieties is that the longer they have been around, the more likely they are to have contracted viruses. Once in the plant, a virus is there to stay. The virus is carried along every time a new vine is started from cuttings of an infected parent plant.

There *is* a way to get "clean" plants, though it is usually left to professionals. The National Clonal Germplasm Repository (NCGR) has several branches in the United States where collections of different perennial fruit and nut crops are gathered. Institutions such as NCGR use a process of heat-treating to ensure they have only clean, virus-free stock in their collections, since material from those collections may be sent all over the world. Their ability to remove virus from vines is often vital, since those institutions may only be able to obtain an old or rare variety from one source, which may be virus-infected..

The first step in the treatment process is to identify any virus in the plant material. Originally, that meant using "indicator" plants—plants that react strongly to

certain diseases and develop very clear symptoms. Material from the potentially infected plant might be grafted onto the indicator plant, or ground up, and the juices rubbed into the leaves of the sensitive indicator. If the indicator came down with the disease, the plant under scrutiny was known to carry the disease. It was a tedious process, because the tests had to be repeated several times to be sure that no mistakes were made.

More recently, antibody/antigen tests make the process much faster and more certain. If a known virus is injected into a lab animal, that animal's blood makes antibodies against the virus. Blood can be drawn, and the antibodies removed and purified. Then, if the virus is introduced into a solution with those antibodies, there will be a visible reaction within minutes or hours. This makes it possible to screen plants for virus in a matter of days, instead of weeks to months.

Plants infected with virus are put into growth chambers where heat and light are controlled. When grown in conditions of 100°F to 105°F (38°C to 41°C), viruses are inactivated or slowed down drastically, allowing the shoot tips of the infected plants to "outgrow" the virus. These shoot tips are harvested and new plants are grown from them. Since the tips are usually only a fraction of an inch long, they are grown using methods such as tissue culture. When the new plant is growing well, it is again tested for virus. If it tests clean for all known viruses, several new plants are started from it to become "mother" plants for virus-free stock for growers. The now "clean" plant is put into a specially protected screen house to prevent insects from reinfecting the plant. Some cells of each treated variety may also be kept in tissue culture as a backup, in case something happens to the plant in the screen house.

Some viticulturists feel that heat-treating creates genetic instability in vines and causes them to produce sports and variant types not identical to the original variety. German viticulturists, for example, avoid heat-treated stock whenever possible, or conduct a process of repeated testing and selection of heat-treated vines to ensure that the plant material is stable and won't produce vines of lesser quality. From what I have observed, this testing is justified, at least for wine grapes, where seemingly small differences can affect wine quality. Growers who use heat-treated stock should observe their vines carefully for possible differences in the quality of the fruit.

This is less of a problem with table grapes, of course, as long as the basic character of the fresh fruit doesn't change and the vines are as productive as their progenitors. It might even be an advantage, if a sport arises that is an improvement, such as better size, different color, or higher productivity.

Ironically, it has been found that a total lack of virus in a plant may not be good for it, from a producer's standpoint. When all viruses are absent from some fruit crops, the plants become more vegetative and less productive. Apparently, some symptomless viruses stress the plant just enough to stimulate it to put more energy into bearing than it would if no virus were present.

Regional Grape Diseases

The following are a few regionally important diseases of grapes. There are many other diseases and pests that can attack the vines and fruit of grapes, but most growers will never encounter them. In just about all cases, measures used to control the more common problems will take care of these less well known diseases.

Fungal diseases. Anthracnose and bird's-eye rot (*Elsinoe ampelina* shear) is a common pest of grapes in the eastern United States. It causes characteristic "bull's eye" marks on fruit and leaves. It was once considered a major pest of grapes. However, since the use of fungicides, it is much less of a problem since it is controlled by the same materials used on diseases such as black rot and downy mildew. Also, it causes less overall damage to the crop than other fungal diseases.

Phymatotrichum root rot or cotton root rot (*Phymatotrichopsis omnivora* [Duggar] Hennebert) is a serious disease of grapes in parts of Texas, particularly in the "black waxy" soils. In areas where it exists the only way to grow grapes is to plant resistant varieties or graft susceptible ones to resistant rootstocks. The main grape species resistant to it are *Vitis mustangensis* and forms of *V. berlandieri*.

Leaf blight or Isariopsis leaf spot (*Mycosphaerella personata* Higgins) is a pest of grapes in Florida, mentioned here because "Orlando Seedless" is reported as being susceptible to this disease.

Berry rots and raisin molds. Several of these are particularly troublesome in the Southeastern United States. The best treatment is varieties able to resist fruit rots.

6 INSECTS of GRAPES

A SURROUNDING NUMBER OF different insects feed on the fruit or vines of grapes. Fortunately, they don't all occur in the same parts of the United States, and few of the insects found in any given area attack at the same time. Growers usually have to deal with only one or a few species at a time. Knowing the life cycles of pest insects can help growers find safe, easy ways to minimize insect problems.

I have used complete life cycle descriptions in some cases, though in other cases the information is less formal. First, in the less formal descriptions, knowing the exact timing of the life cycle is less necessary for control. That is, treatment of some insects can be applied at several times in their life cycles. Further, I have not had personal experience with some of the insects, so life cycle information was gathered from other sources in those case. Where I have personal experience, or hands-on experience from growers, I have tried to include that to make it as directly useful as possible.

In this chapter, I will describe the major insect pests of grapes, the areas where they are most likely to be found, and organic control methods. For detailed information on insect control products, see chapter 4.

Life cycle information and some of the control methods for grape Berry moth, grape cane gallmaker, grape cane girdler, grape flea beetle, grape leafhopper, grape rootworm, and grape tumid gallmaker are from information published by the New York State Agricultural Experiment Station, Geneva, authored by E. F. Taschenberg and H. Riedl; T.J. Dennehy and L.G. Clark; and L. Clark and T. Dennehy (www.nysaes.cornell.edu:80/ipmnet/ny/fruits/grapes/grapesfs/).

Grape Berry Moth

The grape berry moth (*Endopiza viteana* Clemens), a major pest of cultivated grapes, is native to eastern North America, where it originally occurred on wild grapes. Its present range of distribution is the territory east of the Rocky Mountains, wherever its wild or cultivated hosts occur. The grape berry moth feeds only on grapes and has one and a half or two generations per year.

The adults. The adult moths begin to emerge from overwintering pupae in mid- to late May, before the blossom period of the widely planted Concord variety. Emergence of the overwintering generation peaks in mid-June and continues until mid-July. First-generation adults begin to fly in late July, peak in early August, and continue to emerge until early September. The adult grape berry moth is small and has an inconspicuous brownish appearance. When resting it is about 1/4 inch long. Its wingspread is up to 1/2 inch. The forewings are gray-blue at the base and become cream-colored with brown patches toward the tips. The smaller, smoky brown hindwings are hidden underneath the forewings when the moth is at rest. The body color is brown. During most of the day, moths rest on the vines. Around mid- or late afternoon they become active, and their rapid, zigzag flight can be observed until after dusk.

The eggs. In early spring, eggs are laid singly on buds, stems, or newly formed berries. Later, most eggs are deposited directly on the grape berries. Depending on temperature, eggs hatch after four to eight days. The speck-sized, opaque white eggs are oval and scale-like.

The larvae. The newly hatched larva is creamy white with a dark brown head and thoracic shield. As the larva grows, its body becomes greenish and eventually turns purple. The head of the mature larva is light brown but the thoracic shield remains dark-colored. The mature larva is 3/8 inch long.

The first larvae in the spring feed on tender stems, blossom buds, and newly set berries. Often they feed inside large protective webbings, which can envelop the entire grape cluster. When berries have reached about 1/8 inch in diameter, larvae begin to burrow into them. Second-generation larvae feed only on the berries. They usually enter where berries touch each other or where the berry is joined to the stem. Once inside the fruit, larvae feed just below the skin, but eventually the inside of the berry is attacked. Often larvae feed successively on two to three berries. Up to seven berries can be destroyed by a single larva. Mature first-generation larvae move to a leaf, where they cut out a circular flap to construct a pupation chamber. Also, some larvae pupate in the fruit cluster where they have fed. Most fully developed second-generation larvae spin down to the ground, where they construct overwintering pupal cells in fallen leaves.

The pupae. The grape berry moth overwinters in the pupal stage. The pupa is less than 1/4 inch long and is either light brown with a green shade on the abdomen or entirely dark green.

Injury. The damage done by early first-generation larvae can be quite serious; a single larva can destroy a dozen or so potential berries. Often a reddish spot surrounds the point of larval entry. This discoloration can extend over half of the surface of an otherwise green berry. Injured berries ripen prematurely, split open, and shrivel. Webbing produced by the larvae prevents injured berries from dropping to the ground. Larval feeding directly reduces yield and contaminates the crop. More importantly, feeding by grape berry moth lar-

TABLE 6-1

Guide to Stages: Grape Berry Moth

Stage	Timing	Where to Look
Adults (1st flight)	Late May (before bloom) until mid-July	Pheromone traps
Adults (2nd flight)	Late July until early September	Pheromone traps
Eggs (1st generation)	Late May until mid-July	On stems, blossom buds, or newly set berries; later only on berries
Eggs (2nd generation)	Late July until early September	On berries
Larvae (1st generation)	Early June until late July	First on stems, blossom buds, or newly set berries; later only in berries
Larvae (2nd generation)	Early August until end of September	In berries
Pupae (1st generation)	Late June until August	On leaves on the vine
Pupae (overwintering)	August until late May of following year	On fallen leaves on the ground

vae creates infection sites for rot organisms and invites attack by *Drosophila* fruit flies. Infestations by the grape berry moth can vary greatly from year to year and are often very uneven in a vineyard.

Control. In light infestations, injured berries can be removed by hand. Several cultural methods have been used in the past to reduce the overwintering grape berry moth population. A measure of control can be achieved by gathering the leaves in the fall and destroying them. Covering leaves containing cocoons under the row with 1 inch of compact soil will prevent emergence. This must be completed fifteen days ahead of the bloom period.

Where the grape berry moth is an annual problem, postbloom sprays with insecticides may be necessary if the problem is severe. Consult your nearest Cooperative Extension office for control recommen-

dations. Sex pheromone traps have been used to monitor emergence and activity of male moths. Use of these traps may be helpful to improve timing and determine the need for control measures against this grape pest.

Organic controls. Dipel (*Bacillus thuringiensis*), pheromone strips to disrupt mating, and hand removal of affected clusters or parts may all be helpful.

Grape Cane Gallmaker

The grape cane gallmaker (*Ampeloglypter sesostris* LeConte) is one of two *Ampeloglypter* species that can damage new shoot growth in the spring. This small snout beetle is apparently present throughout eastern and midwestern North America and has caused considerable injury in some areas during recent years. It has only one generation per year.

Grape berry moth.

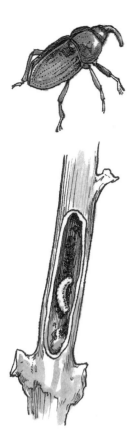

Grape cane gallmaker, adult (top) and larva (below).

The adults. The reddish brown adults are small, 1/4-inch-long weevils with a distinctive curved snout. Except for their color, they look similar to the shiny black adults of the grape cane girdler, (*A. ater* LeConte). The grape cane gallmaker overwinters in the adult stage in debris on the ground. Egg laying begins in May or June when shoots are 10 to 20 inches long. In selecting an egg-laying site, the female tends to avoid shoot nodes that will produce fruit clusters. In midsummer, adults begin to emerge from infested canes. Adult emergence continues through September.

The eggs. The female hollows out a small cavity just above a node. After placing a single egg into the cavity, she fills it with frass. Then she proceeds to hollow out from eight to fourteen additional cavities in a straight line up the cane. Only the first hole contains an egg. The specklike egg is yellowish white and oval. The egg hatches after seven to ten days.

The larvae. The cane swells in the area of the egg-laying injury. The young larva feeds on tissue surrounding the egg cavity.

Later it feeds along the center of the shoot in the pith above or below the gall. The mature larva is about 3/8 inch long, legless, and yellowish white. It has a light brown head with dark mouthparts.

The pupae. The larva pupates within the gall. The pupa, which resembles the adult beetle (with legs and snout clearly discernible) is light colored but becomes dark just before it changes to an adult. The pupal stage lasts about two weeks.

Injury. The gall-like swelling on the cane is caused by the egg-laying injury and reaches full size after six to eight weeks. Galls are usually twice as thick as the cane and 1 to 1 1/2 inches long. They are found just above the nodes and are of uniform shape except for a deep longitudinal scar on the side of the gall where the female made the egg cavity. On galls where beetles successfully completed development and emerged, a round exit hole can be found near the longitudinal scar.

On varieties that produce dark-colored fruit, the bark and wood surrounding the injury turn reddish purple. On varieties

TABLE 6-2

Guide to Stages: Grape Cane Gallmaker

Stage	Timing	Where to Look
Adults (summer)	Early August until September	Emerging from shoot galls
Adults (overwintering)	September until May of following year	Under fallen leaves and debris
Adults (spring)	Spring when temperatures rise above 60°F (15.5°C)	On the shoots
Egg	Late May through June	Above terminal vegetative node in small cavity
Larvae	June through early August	In shoot gall around egg-laying injury
Pupae	Mid-July through August	In shoot gall

with white or green fruit, this discoloration does not occur.

Galls apparently have little effect on vigor and growth of the vine, but they can weaken the mechanical strength of the cane and cause breakage.

Control. Except in some localized areas, the grape cane gallmaker is usually a minor problem. Since primarily vegetative nodes above the terminal fruit clusters are attacked, it is possible to prune out galls without affecting the crop. This will reduce the overwintering population, provided the galls are pruned out and destroyed before the adults emerge in August. In heavy infestations, it may be necessary to spray against the adults before they begin laying eggs in the spring. Materials recommended for control of the grape cane girdler are also effective against the grape cane gallmaker. Timing of sprays is similar for both species since adults are active at about the same time in the spring.

Grape Cane Girdler

The grape cane girdler (*Ampeloglypter ater* LeConte) is one of two *Ampeloglypter* species that can attack new shoot growth in the spring. It has been reported throughout the midwestern and eastern United States. Originally this species was described as feeding primarily on Virginia creeper (*Parthenocissus quinquefolia*), but apparently it has adapted quite well to cultivated grapes. It has only one generation per year.

The adults. The shiny black adults are small, 1/8-inch-long weevils with a characteristic curved snout. Except for their color, they resemble the reddish brown adults of the grape cane gallmaker (*A. sesostris* LeConte). The adult beetles emerge from infested canes during August and subsequently overwinter in vineyard trash on the ground. In May of the following year, the adults leave their overwintering sites. When grape shoots are 12 to 20 inches long, usually in late May before bloom, the female begins to lay her eggs and girdle new canes. Egg laying continues for about one month.

The eggs. The female hollows out a small cavity in the shoot, places a single egg into it, and fills the egg cavity with frass. Then she proceeds to girdle the cane at two places: just below the egg cavity and several inches above. The speck-sized egg is elliptical and off-white. It takes about ten days for the egg to hatch.

The larvae. The fully-grown larva is white with a brown head, legless, and about 3/8 inches long. It burrows in the center of the shoot on either side of the egg cavity. Larval development takes over one month. The shoot in which the larva feeds either breaks off at the girdled point or dies back to the first node below the egg cavity and drops to the ground.

The pupae. The pupa forms within the dead shoot on the vine or on the ground. Development to the adult stage is completed after about two weeks. The pupa is light colored but becomes darker just prior to emergence. Some of the adult features such as legs and snout are already clearly visible in the pupal stage.

Injury. The girdling by the female causes the terminal growth of the new shoots to bend over above the upper girdle and drop to the ground. Later, the whole infested shoot dies back to the lower girdle and falls from the vine. Vines "pruned" by the grape cane girdler have a ragged ap-

TABLE 6-3

Guide to Stages: Grape Cane Girdler

Stage	Timing	Where to Look
Adults (summer)	August	Emerging from infested shoots
Adults (overwintering)	September to May	In fallen leaves and debris in or near vineyard
Adults (spring)	May through June	On shoots
Eggs	In June before bloom	In egg cavity between two girdles on terminal shoot growth; note bent and dying terminals
Larvae	June through July	Inside dying shoot terminals
Pupae	Late July	Inside dead shoots on the vine or on the ground

Grape cane girdler, adult (top) and larva (below).

pearance suggesting serious injury to the plant. However, the actual damage is usually minor. Girdling of the terminal growth has little or no effect on the crop unless fruit-producing nodes are close to attacked shoot tips.

Control. Shoots injured by the grape cane girdler are quite conspicuous early in the season. Cutting off infested shoots below the lower girdle before the adults emerge in the summer and destroying them may help reduce the overwintering population. In severe infestations, grape cane girdler adults should be controlled with special sprays before they begin laying eggs in the spring. Sprays applied against the grape flea beetle when the buds are swelling should also be helpful against the grape cane girdler.

Grape Fleabeetle

The grape fleabeetle (*Altica chalybea* Illiger), also known as the steely beetle, is a native insect and occurs in most states east of the Rocky Mountains and in Canada. It has been found in all grape-growing areas of New York. At the turn of the century, the grape fleabeetle reportedly was the most serious grape insect pest in the Lake Erie district.

This insect primarily attacks buds of wild and cultivated grapevines and Virginia creeper (*Parthenocissus quinquefolia*). A number of other plants have been listed as food plants, but all are doubtful hosts.

The grape fleabeetle is one of the first insect pests to appear in vineyards in the spring. There is only one generation per year. Overwintering adults become active and migrate to the grapevines at about the time grape buds begin to swell. Usually infestations are localized. However, in plantings located near favorable hibernating quarters such as wasteland, woodland, and abandoned vineyards, feeding can be severe, especially in border rows.

The adults. The grape fleabeetle overwinters as an adult. Its body is somewhat oval, a metallic, shining blue, and less than 1/4 inch long. The antennae are threadlike and about half as long as the body. The thighs of the hind legs are enlarged, enabling the adult to jump quickly when disturbed. The grape fleabeetle derives its name from its ability to jump.

The eggs. The speck-sized eggs vary from yellow to orange in color. They are cylindrical and rounded on the ends. Some eggs are placed on the hardened scales surrounding the buds, but most are laid under the loose bark of the canes and near the buds. As foliage develops, some eggs are laid on the upper side of the leaves, but none are deposited on the underside.

The larvae. Newly hatched larvae are dark brown, but as they grow their color lightens. By the time the larvae reach maturity they are light brown and between $1/4$ and $3/8$ inch long. The larval body is covered with black, circular and rectangular plates of various sizes, which give the larvae a spotted appearance. These plates become more prominent as the larva matures and its body becomes lighter in color.

The pupae. The grape fleabeetle passes through the pupal stage in a cell prepared in the soil by the larva at a depth of $1/2$ to $2 1/2$ inches. The pupae are bright yellow, up to $1/4$ inch long, and have conspicuous, reddish brown eyes. Wings and legs are off-white.

Injury. Overwintering adults attack the swelling buds by boring into them and hollowing out the inside. In contrast, the larvae and summer adults feed on the tender leaf tissues but avoid the leaf veins. Feeding on the primary buds is by far the more serious damage, causing yield loss and stunted growth from secondary or tertiary buds. No fruit develops on canes where the primary and secondary buds were destroyed. The various climbing cutworms that can occur in vineyards can do similar damage to primary buds in the spring. The amount of injury varies from year to year. It is more serious in years when bud development is prolonged by unfavorable climatic conditions. Under favorable growing conditions, the bud passes rapidly through the stage when it is susceptible to attack. As the small shoots appear, the adults and young larvae feed on the expanding leaves.

Grape fleabeetle, adult (top) and larva (below)

TABLE 6-4

Guide to Stages: Grape Fleabeetle

Stage	Timing	Where to Look
Adults (overwintering)	Late April through June	Migrating to grapevines as buds begin to swell
Adults (summer)	Latter part of July and early August	Feeding on leaves and seeking hibernating quarters in dry leaves and dead plant material, wood, and wastelands
Eggs	Late April to mid-June	Near buds and under loose bark on canes
Larvae	June to late July	Upper surface of grape leaves
Pupae	Late June to late July; sometimes into early August	In soil in an earthen cell, beneath vines

Control. Wherever possible, it is advisable to clean up wasteland and woodland located near cultivated vineyards. This eliminates or reduces hibernating sites. Frequent discing to control weeds between grape rows can also break the pupal cells in the soil. This exposes the delicate pupa and it dries up. However, some adults can still emerge from the undisturbed band of soil beneath the trellis, which was not touched by the discing operation. To prevent bud-feeding, treatment with a broad-spectrum insecticide is effective against adults migrating to grapevines from their hibernation sites, but timing is very critical.

At the time larvae and beetles are feeding on the upper surface of grape leaves, they are easily controlled by spraying. The insecticide treatments applied post-bloom against the grape berry moth will also help reduce grape flea beetle populations.

Pyrethrum may be applied as a dust or sprayed as a wettable powder, according to package instructions.

Diatomaceous earth may be applied as a dust to kill the fleabeetles. Thorough coverage is necessary, and it may be necessary to reapply, especially after rain.

Some growers have reported using a band of yellow sticky tape stretched along the row near the base of the vines. As the beetles emerge from the soil and begin to move toward the vines, they are attracted to the tape and get stuck on it.

Grape Leafhopper

Three leafhopper species can be found feeding on grapes in the Northeast: commonly known as the grape leafhopper (*Erythroneura comes* Say), the three-banded leafhopper (*E. tricincta* Fitch), and the po-tato leafhopper (*Empoasca fabae* Harris). Of the two *Erythroneura* species, *E. comes* is the dominant species in most areas of the Northeast. In contrast to the green leafhopper (GLH) and the three-banded leafhopper, the potato leafhopper does not overwinter in this area. It is an annual migrant from the South and usually appears around mid-June in this region. In some years, the potato leafhopper can be more destructive than the GLH.

The GLH has one and a half to two generations per year. It overwinters as an adult in noncultivated areas adjacent to vineyards, preferring dry, elevated, sheltered sites with accumulations of plant debris. Wide fluctuations in abundance between localities and from year to year are common.

The adults. As spring temperatures in May reach about 65°F (18°C), the overwintering adults emerge from hibernation and begin feeding on plants such as strawberry (*Fragaria* spp), berry bushes, catnip, Virginia creeper (*Parthenocissus*), burdock, beech (*Fagus*), and sugar maple (*Acer saccarum*). The leafhoppers mate but don't reproduce on these plants. They remain there until new growth develops in the vineyard. In western New York, migration to the grapevines begins in late May and continues through mid-July.

Generally, the 1/8-inch-long adults emerge from hibernation with a reddish orange coloring that changes to yellow when they begin feeding. The summer form of the GLH adult is pale yellow with three black spots and some zigzag lines of deeper yellow on the forewings. As the season continues, the markings darken and, just prior to hibernation, the insect becomes salmon-colored overall, with red eyes.

The GLH is found in the vineyard into the fall. Migration to overwintering sites begins the latter part of October and continues into December.

The eggs. The eggs of the GLH are laid singly just beneath the epidermis on the underside of the grape leaf, producing a slight blister. They are tiny, colorless, and slightly bean-shaped. Egg-laying usually begins during mid- to late June.

The nymphs. The first nymphs appear in late June and reach the adult stage by late July. The second-generation nymphs and adults are found in late August. There are five nymphal instars. A few days before hatch, a dark eye-spot can be seen in the egg. Newly hatched nymphs are semi-transparent with conspicuous red eyes. The eye color of second instar nymphs is less intense, and their thorax turns yellow and shows small lateral wing pads. With successive molts, the markings on the thorax become more prominent and the wing pads become larger. After the fifth molt, the fully formed wings appear, extending beyond the tip of the abdomen.

Nymphs as well as adults are very active, especially on hot dry days, and are easily disturbed. During the summer, all stages and the cast nymphal skins can be found on the lower leaf surface.

Injury. Adults as well as immature leafhoppers feed on the underside of leaves by sucking out the liquid cell contents. The tissue surrounding the feeding puncture turns pale white and eventually dies. Feeding injury shows up first along the veins, but later the whole leaf is affected. Feeding is limited initially to the lower leaves.

Grapevines can tolerate populations of up to fifteen hoppers per leaf with little or no economic damage. However, heavy leafhopper feeding can result in premature leaf drop, lowered sugar content, increased acid, and poor color of the fruit. Ripening fruit is often smutted or stained by the sticky excrement ("honeydew") of the hoppers, which affects appearance and sup-

Grape leafhopper, adult (top) and nymph (below)

TABLE 6-5

Guide to Stages: Grape Leafhopper

Stage	Timing	Where to Look
Adults (overwintering)	Late October until May of the following year	Under fallen leaves and debris in dry, sheltered areas in or adjacent to vineyard
Adults (spring)	In May when temperatures reach 65°F (18°C)	On spring food sources; on vines when leaf growth begins; found on underside of basal leaves
Adults (summer)	Late July through November	On underside of grape leaves
Eggs	Mid-June through mid-August	Beneath epidermis on underside of grape leaves
Nymphs	Early July through October	On underside of grape leaves

ports the growth of sooty molds. Also, severely infested vines may be unable to produce sufficient wood the following season. Damage to the vine can be serious if infestations are allowed to persist unchecked for two or more years.

Control. The GLH has few natural enemies. Cold and wet weather conditions in spring and fall are damaging to leafhopper populations, as are wet winters. Fall cultivation and cleanup of adjacent weedy land will eliminate favorable overwintering sites in and near a vineyard.

When the GLH appears in high numbers, the application of a contact insecticide may become necessary. For good GLH control, it is important to obtain complete spray coverage of the undersides of the leaves. Coverage of the fruit clusters is of secondary importance.

The organic controls for California leafhoppers described in the next section also apply to GLH, three-banded leafhopper, and potato leafhopper.

Other Leafhoppers
(California and the West Coast)

The grape leafhopper is a pest of grapes north of the Tehachapi Mountains, especially in the San Joaquin, Sacramento, and Napa valleys. It is also occasionally a problem in coastal valleys. The variegated leafhopper is the major pest of grapes in southern California and in the Central Valley as far north as San Joaquin County.

Description. Leafhoppers overwinter as adults, and are found in spring on basal grape leaves and weeds. The adult grape leafhopper is light to pale yellow with distinct dark brown and reddish markings. Eggs of the first brood are laid in epidermal tissue in the leaves in April and May and appear as a bean-shaped, blisterlike protuberance.

Although similar in size to the grape leafhopper, about ⅛ inch long, the variegated leafhopper is darker in color and distinctly mottled brown, green, and white, with a reddish tinge. The nymphs are almost transparent when first emerged, becoming orange-brown to yellow-brown, in contrast to the white nymphs of the grape leafhopper. Eggs are similar in appearance to those of the grape leafhopper but laid deeper within the leaf tissue. This latter characteristic reduces the effectiveness of the egg parasite against variegated leafhopper.

Damage. Feeding from nymphs and adults of both species causes pale yellow leaf stippling. Loss of leaf efficiency and leaf drop can occur when leafhopper densities are extremely high. This can result in fruit sunburn and can weaken the vine for the following season. Feeding can also result in low berry sugar and excrement spotting of fruit. Adult leafhoppers are also a nuisance to workers when populations are high at harvest time.

Biological control. Egg parasites, including the parasitic wasps *Anagrus epos* and other *Anagrus* species, are commonly found in vineyards during part of the season. These parasites may be more abundant in vineyards that are adjacent to alternate hosts for leafhoppers such as prune, plum, and almond orchards, and riparian areas. After a leafhopper egg is parasitized, it becomes visibly red. This parasite is not as effective on variegated leafhopper eggs as it is on those of the grape leafhopper.

General predators of grape leafhoppers include green lacewings (*Chrysopa* spp.), minute pirate bugs (*Orius* spp.), lady beetles (*Hippodamia* spp.), and predaceous spiders and mites. The predaceous mite *Anystis agilis*, is an important predator of first instar nymphs, especially in the Napa Valley. Although many growers have experimented with releases of lacewings for leafhoppers, control of economic populations has not been achieved in university field trials.

Cultural controls. Remove weeds in vineyards and surrounding areas before vines start to grow in spring to reduce leafhopper populations that might disperse to new grape foliage. The use of a flail mower before budbreak is particularly effective in controlling overwintering adults if mowing occurs during early morning hours before temperatures warm up to above the flight threshold. Removing basal leaves during berry set and the two-week period following (before adult leafhoppers emerge) will normally reduce peak leafhopper populations during the season by 30 to 50 percent. Also, leaf removal will improve coverage and efficacy of pesticides. In warmer growing areas, be careful not to remove excessive numbers of leaves, which can lead to sunburned fruit. Maintaining a low-growing, summer cover crop to encourage populations of beneficial insects will also help reduce leafhopper populations. Preventing overly vigorous vine growth will also help suppress leafhoppers.

Organically acceptable sprays. Although leafhoppers infest most vineyards in California, they may not require chemical treatment because vines can tolerate fairly high populations without harm. If chemical control of leafhopper is necessary, wait until the second (summer) generation, whenever possible, before treating.

Monitor leafhoppers by counting the number of nymphs or utilizing the presence/absence sampling method described in *Grape Pest Management*, 2nd edition, UC/DANR Publication 3343 (see Bibliography). Examine leaves for the presence of parasitized (red) leafhopper eggs at the same time. Even a minimal level of parasite activity on eggs of the first generation may result in economic control of the grape leafhopper during the second and third generations. If the leafhopper population is made up primarily of the variegated leafhopper, economic control by the parasite is less likely. However, a combination of parasite and predator activity can be effective.

Treatment is not necessary if twenty or fewer nymphs per leaf of first generation grape leafhoppers are found on Thompson Seedless grown for wine or raisins. If *Anagrus* parasitic wasps are active on eggs of the first generation, it is best not to treat unless leafhopper numbers are well above the treatment threshold. If you have to treat, wait until more than half of the nymphs are in the fourth instar; this allows sufficient time for most eggs to have hatched. Remove basal leaves to allow better spray coverage and thus improve the efficacy of the pesticide.

The treatment level for Thompson Seedless wine or raisin grapes in the second or third generation is an average of fifteen to twenty nymphs per leaf; lower populations do not need treatment. Vigorously growing vines can support higher populations.

The leafhopper treatment level is lower for table grapes because they need better fruit protection; it should not exceed fifteen leafhopper nymphs per leaf in the first generation. In the second and third gen-

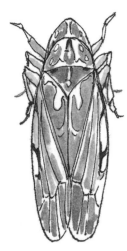

Glassywinged
sharpshooter
leafhopper

erations, early varieties (Flame Seedless) should not exceed ten nymphs per leaf; midseason varieties (Thompson), five to ten nymphs per leaf; and late varieties (Emperor), five to eight nymphs per leaf. Vine vigor and length of high leafhopper activity are factors that could alter treatment levels.

One of the most exciting new products for use against leafhoppers is Surround. In trials in 2000 and 2001 in California, Surround effectively blocked the glassy-winged sharpshooter leafhopper, the most serious vector of Pierce's disease, from feeding on grapes. Its only serious drawback is that it affects the appearance of table fruit. Home growers can carefully wash the fruit, but this is more difficult for commercial growers.

Leafhopper resistance to the materials listed below may be a problem, but the materials are useful in a limited way. Field studies continue to evaluate insecticidal soaps, applied alone or in combination with pyrethrin, and foliar oils.

Pyrethrin and piperonyl butoxide (usually sold as Pyrenone Crop Spray). Spray the plants with a mix of one pint Pyrenone per 150 gallons of water. It can be applied by itself or in combination with a narrow-range oil. In fact, you should use it in combination with a narrow-range oil when spraying the first-generation leafhoppers, except on table grapes. But do not use oil on later generations. Wait at least 12 hours before going back into the vineyard.

Insecticidal soaps and narrow range oil. While insecticidal soap works to some degree on leafhoppers, it works better when combined with low rate of oil. This combination is partially effective on low leafhopper populations if it is applied when nymphs are small. The mixture must be used carefully as both products can spot the waxy bloom on the berry, which would mar table grapes.

Grape Rootworm

The grape rootworm (*Fidia viticida* Walsh), or GR, is a native species of leaf beetle that occurs from the Atlantic Seaboard states to North Dakota, Nebraska, Kansas, and Texas. The wild hosts of this pest are grapes (*Vitis* spp.), Virginia creeper (*Parthenocissus quinquefolia*), and redbud (*Cercis canadensis*). Feeding by GR larvae (grubs) on the root system of vines can seriously damage commercial vineyards.

The grape rootworm produces only one generation per year. Eggs are deposited under the bark of grape vines by an adult females. Immature grubs spend nine to ten months in the soil feeding on roots. Adults feed on grape foliage and lay eggs for about one month. The GR requires at least one year to complete its life cycle.

The adults. Though the leaf-feeding adult stage of grape rootworm inflicts little damage to vines, control of GR is most easily achieved by insecticide treatments carefully timed to kill the adult stage. Adult beetles begin to emerge from the soil sometime between late May and early to mid-July, depending upon yearly variations in soil temperatures. Mating of adults takes place within approximately seven days after emergence. The life span of adults is highly variable, ranging from one to seven weeks in the laboratory.

Adult GR are approximately $5/16$ to $3/8$ inches long and are grayish brown or chestnut-colored with fine, light-colored hair covering the thorax and elytra (wing covers). Initially, the beetles seem to concentrate their feeding among the leaves of sucker growth and the lower canopy. When present in high densities, GR beetles have been found feeding on the leaves of the upper canopy and on grape berries. There seems to be a peak in activity of rootworms around mid- to late morning.

The eggs. Mature females produce their first eggs three to seven days following mating, generally between early June and late July. Egg laying peaks between late June and late July, but can continue into September. GR eggs may be found in infested vineyards during this period by carefully peeling off strips of bark from the vine and examining the underside of the strips for egg clusters. Eggs are laid in tight crevices between layers of the bark of canes and stems. The creamy yellow to white, oblong eggs are about 1/20 inch long, are deposited in clusters, and hatch in ten to fifteen days.

The larvae. The larvae of GR are creamy white with a dark brown head capsule. They move from the hatching site under the bark to the soil, where all further larval development takes place. Development through the five larval stages progresses as the larvae feed on grape roots throughout the growing season. It is this feeding that is detrimental to vine health. Though most larvae complete development through all five larval stages during a single growing season, some larvae do not complete larval development before the onset of winter and must continue developing the following season. Upon completion of larval development in the following growing season, these "two-year larvae" remain in the soil for the duration of their second season. They pupate and emerge as adults the following spring. While actively feeding on roots, most GR remain within the upper 12 inches of soil. In late fall, they move deeper into the soil and form overwintering cells. The following spring, they move back toward the surface to pupate or to complete larval development.

The pupae. After overwintering, fifth-instar larvae construct a chamber in which pupation takes place. Pupation occurs in the upper 6 inches of soil and is completed in

Grape rootworm

TABLE 6-6

Guide to Stages: Grape Rootworm

Stage	Timing	Where to look
Adults	Late May to early Aug.	Surfaces of trunk, canes, and leaves
Eggs	Early June to mid-Aug.	Under bark of trunk and canes
Larvae (1st–3rd instars)	Late June to late Aug.	Top 12 inches of soil within 18 to 24 inches of trunk
Larvae (4th–5th instars)	Throughout year, but most common in early to late May and late July to mid-October	Top 12 inches of soil within 18 to 24 inches of trunk, and deeper in overwintering cells during winter
Pupae	Mid-May to late July	Pupal cells in upper 6 inches of soil

about fourteen days. Pupae are ³/₁₆ to ¼ inch long and are initially pearly white, but the body becomes increasingly brown in color and the eyes progressively darken. The newly hatched adults remain in the pupal cell several days before emerging from the soil.

Injury. The most serious damage that grape rootworm causes to grapevines is that caused by larvae feeding on the roots. However, the most noticeable damage is the characteristic chainlike feeding pattern caused by the adults on the leaves. In heavy infestations, the beetles have been observed to feed on immature berries in addition to leaves. Vine damage by adults is relatively inconsequential.

The damage to the grape root system resulting from high densities of GR larvae can stunt and, in some cases, even kill grapevines. Larvae are thought to prefer small, tender roots, but in heavy infestations they have been observed to channel along the inner bark of older, larger roots. In some vineyards, marked reductions in vigor and production have been observed in as little as three years. Because dispersal of GR is generally slow, infestations are often spotty within a region and within a particular vineyard.

Control. Control of the grape rootworm is most easily accomplished through treatments directed at the adult stage. The key to effective control of adult GR is proper timing of treatments. Treatments applied too early may not persist long enough to kill rootworm adults during the three- to four-week period when most emerge from the soil. Treatments applied too late will allow some eggs to hatch and the larvae to enter the soil unharmed. Treatments should

be made when the first beetles are observed in vineyards. This period will vary from late May to mid-July, depending upon location. Growers should carefully check their vineyards each week following application of treatments. A second application should be made if any adult rootworms are detected.

Predatory nematodes should be tried, at least on an experimental basis, applied to the soil in late summer or early fall. Experiments in North Carolina suggest that a heavy mulch applied just as the larvae are about to enter the soil could block or smother them.

Grape Tumid Gallmaker

Grape tumid galls, also called grape tomato galls, are caused by larvae of a small fly known as the grape tumid gallmaker (*Janetiella brevicauda* Felt) or GTG. This pest is native to the northeastern United States and southeastern Canada. It infests only wild and cultivated grapes (*Vitis* spp.). Infestations are generally spotty both within vineyards and within infested vines. In the past, tumid galls were attributed to as many as five species of flies, but it is now thought that the single species *J. brevicauda* accounts for almost all of the damage seen in northeastern vineyards.

Life cycle overview. Midges (adults) produce from one to three generations per year. The actual number of generations produced in a given year depends upon weather conditions and the location of the vineyard. The life cycle begins with an egg laid within the unfolding bud or shoot tip. Maggot-like larvae hatch from these eggs and enter the vine tissue. As the larvae feed, a small reddish gall forms around them.

When the larvae have fully developed, they leave the gall and drop to the soil. There they form a cocoon for pupation within 1 to 2 inches of the soil surface. Depending on the time of year, the larvae will either pupate and produce emerging midges within two to three weeks, or will overwinter in the soil and continue development to adulthood the following spring.

The adults. Tumid gallmaker adults are small, measuring about 1/10 of an inch long. They are dark brown to reddish, fragile flies with plume-like antennae and only one pair of wings. It is difficult to identify the adults because of the large number of similar gall midges in North America.

The adult is very short-lived; most only live one day. It is reported that adults do not feed. Female midges apparently attract males with an odor emitted from the ovipositor. Egg-laying begins within forty minutes of mating. There is some indication that females prefer to lay egg masses on grape shoots close to the ground.

Adults developing from the overwintered larvae begin to emerge in early to mid-May; emergence of this "spring" generation peaks sometime around mid-June. Most of the adults emerge between 7:00 A.M. and 10:00 A.M. Emergence does not occur if air temperature is below 66°F (19°C).

The spring emergence of midges can include individuals that overwintered as either first-, second-, or third-generation larvae from the previous year. The "first" (first complete) generation of the season emerges from approximately the first week of June until the third week of July. The second generation emerges from mid-July to the third week of August, and the third generation emerges from mid-August to mid-September.

Because adult midges live only a short time, and because they are so small, they are difficult to detect in the vineyard. Adults cling to the undersides of grape leaves or rest in the ground cover during inactive periods. They are thought to be inactive at night and during windy and rainy periods.

The eggs. Grape tumid gallmaker females lay their eggs in masses between developing tissues at the bud or shoot tips from early May to mid-September. The microscopic eggs are pale to bright orange and hatch in four to six days. Females each deposit an average of more than two hundred eggs.

The larvae. The larval stage of the midge causes the highly visible galls on the grapevine. Upon hatching from the egg, the larvae of GTG bore into the tissue at the shoot tip (mid-May to late September). The boring leaves a whitish, circular scar on the vine that is still visible after the gall forms. Larvae are orange, about 1/8 inch long, and lack appendages. It is uncertain how many distinct instars form but, upon reaching maturity within the gall, larvae exit through the same hole formed on entering the plant tissue. They then drop to the ground and form a cocoon 1/2 to 2 inches below the soil surface. Late-season larvae will overwinter in these cocoons and continue their development the following spring. Early and mid-season larvae will pupate immediately and then emerge as adults to continue the life cycle.

The pupae. Pupae are about 1/16 inch long and vary in color from pale to dark orange. Pupation occurs in the silky co-coons located less than 2 inches below the soil surface. The overwintered larvae of the spring generation pupate from late April to mid-May. The first complete generation of the season pupates from mid-June to mid-July, and the second generation from late July to mid-August. Pupation occurs one to two weeks after larvae enter the soil, depending on soil conditions. Adults emerge within one to two weeks following pupation. For overwintering larvae, which can be from the first, second, or third generation, pupation does not occur until the following spring.

Injury. Grape tumid gall was originally called grape tomato gall because the round, reddish, succulent galls resembled tomatoes. However, grape tumid gall, ("tumid" meaning swollen or distended), is now the encouraged name because it avoids confusion with the tomato plant. The galls, which measure ⅛ to ¼ inch in diameter, are typically located on leaves, petioles, and flower clusters. In heavy infestations, the galling may reduce vine vigor and can cause shoot breakage, but, in most instances, galling is of little economic importance. Galling on flower clusters, however, can result in poorly shaped fruit clusters or the complete loss of clusters.

Of greatest concern is the overwintered generation, because the offspring of these individuals can severely damage the developing foliage and flower clusters early in the season.

Control. Pesticide applications for GTG are not economically prudent unless the infestation is heavy or the vineyard has a history of tumid gall problems. Treatment, when economically justified, should be timed to kill adults of the overwintered generation as they emerge. In view of the difficulty in detecting the adults, it may be most feasible to base control measures on the first sign of larval entrance into vine tissues—the small white scar—or on the first indication of gall formation.

Several parasitic and predatory species of insects attack the larvae of grape tumid gall midges. Growers might also consider burying the pupae by mounding soil up under the vines early in the season (late April). This form of cultural control might prevent adults from reaching the soil surface.

Green June Beetle

The green June beetle (*Cotinis nitida* Linnaeus) occurs in the eastern United States westward to Kansas and Texas. I first saw June beetles in Arkansas in 1989. They were large, colorful, metallic-looking beetles that swarmed over the grape clusters, reducing them to a few stems and bits of skin in a short time. When disturbed, they would sometimes drop, but more often flew away with a loud clacking, buzzing sound. They also defecated as they flew, giving off a strong odor in the process. The frightening thing about them was that the grapes had been sprayed with an insecticide having a recommended re-entry time of seven days, yet even with piles of dead beetles under the vines, there were hoards of beetles back feeding within two days, with no apparent mortality. Obviously, pesticide was and is not the answer.

Life cycle. Like Japanese beetles, green June beetles require only one year to complete their life cycle. This pest overwinters

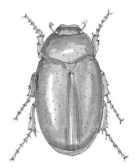
Green June beetle.

Japanese beetle.
Note size difference
—Japanese beetles
are smaller than
Green June beetles.

as larvae that may become active on warm winter days. The larvae are up to 1½ inches long and are whitish with a brownish black head and conspicuous brown spiracles (breathing spores) along the sides of the body.

Larvae increase their activity in the spring, and pupate in June in earthen cells a few inches below the soil surface. The pupae are brown, approximately the same shape as adult beetles, and about ⅝ inch long. The pupal stage lasts about 18 days. The pupae turn metallic green just before the adult emerges in July and August. The adult beetles are about ½ to ⅞ inch long with dull, velvety green wings. The head, legs and underside are shiny green, and the sides are brownish yellow.

In midsummer, adults lay eggs underground in earthen balls. Each female lays sixty to seventy-five eggs over a span of about two weeks. The tiny eggs are pearly white and elliptical, and gradually become more spherical as the larva develops inside. About eighteen days after egg laying, the eggs hatch into small, white grubs. The larvae molt twice before winter. The third larval stage lasts nearly nine months, after which pupation occurs. At night, the larvae may be found on the ground crawling on their backs. This curious form of location is peculiar to green June beetle larvae.

Injury. Green June beetle adults prefer ripening fruits of many plants. The larvae feed on decaying organic matter in the thatch and root zone of many grasses, as well as on the underground portions of other plants such as sweet potatoes and carrots.

Adult and larval feeding on economic crops causes some financial loss; however,

the larvae's tunneling for feed and the adults' burrowing into the soil each night cause more serious destruction. The tunneling uproots young plants. The many exit holes of the adults and larvae resemble ant hills and mar lawns and golf course greens.

Control. Survey for the grubs in the same manner as for Japanese beetle grubs. If the density is ten grubs per square foot, control is needed.

To treat grubs in the soil, apply killer nematodes such as *Heterorhabditis bacteriophora* (the nematode recommended for Japanese beetles). Milky spore disease, *Bacillus popilliae,* though effective on Japanese beetle larvae, has not been fully tested on June beetle larvae.

Other controls include Surround, diatomaceous dust, pyrethrins, and resistant grapes. Because the adults feed on fruit, rather than leaves, there are no really resistant grapes, though they do prefer aromatic, labrusca types to nonaromatic grapes and will go to those first.

Japanese Beetle

Both as adults and as grubs, Japanese beetles (*Popillia japonica* Newman) are destructive plant pests. Adults feed on foliage and fruit, skeletonizing the leaves and damaging or destroying the fruit. The grubs develop in the soil, feeding on roots.

Life cycle. The adult is a little less than ½ inch long, has a shiny, metallic green body, bronze-colored outer wings, and six small tufts of white hair along the sides and back of its body under the edges of its wings. The males usually are slightly smaller than the females. Adults are usually seen in late spring or early summer.

Females intermittently leave plants, burrow about 3 inches into the ground—usually into turf—and lay a few eggs, repeating this until forty to sixty eggs total have been laid.

Eggs hatch in midsummer into white, six-legged grubs with dark heads. The grubs feed on grass roots until reaching 1 inch long. In late autumn, they burrow 4 to 8 inches into the soil and remain inactive all winter.

In early spring, the grubs return to feeding on roots until late spring, when they change into pupae, taking about two weeks to metamorphose into adults. Adult beetles emerge almost a year after the egg was laid.

Control. To survey adults, trap adult beetles using a combination of a pheromone, or sex attractant, and a floral lure to attract both male and female beetles to the trap, which is essentially a one-way funnel connected to a collecting bag.

When beetles are flying, if your traps fill in a day, you have a Japanese beetle infestation that requires attention. If the bottom of the trap is only just covered after a week, there is likely little or no local population, mostly beetles from other areas, since they can fly a mile or more in looking for new feeding grounds.

To assess grub populations, sample in late summer (August to October) and late spring (April to June). Cut an 8-by-8- inch square of turf 3 inches deep near the edge of brown or dead areas in your lawn, which are likely infested with the grubs. Turn the sod over on newspaper and search the roots and soil in the hole for grubs. Return the turf and water it back in. Repeat in several areas to get an average. Multiply the resulting average by 2.25 to determine the number of grubs per square foot. If more than ten grubs per square foot are present, treatment should be done.

Biological control methods. To treat grubs in the soil, apply parasitic nematodes. *Heterorhabditis bacteriophora* is a commercially available type that feeds on the grubs. When feeding, the nematodes release a strain of bacteria into the grub, which feeds on it, and the nematodes in turn feed on the bacteria, killing the grub.

Bacillus thuringiensis (Bt) is registered for Japanese beetle control at the grub stage only. Bt is a stomach poison and must be ingested to be effective.

Milky Spore (*Bacillus popillae*) has been registered for use on Japanese beetle grubs since 1948. When the grub eats the spores, they germinate in the grub's gut and enter the bloodstream. Spore buildup in the blood causes the characteristic milky appearance.

Milky spore disease builds up over two to four years as grubs die, each releasing one to two billion spores back into the soil. Milky spore disease can suppress the development of large beetle populations.

Two parasites of the Japanese beetle have been brought to the United States from Asia: *Tiphia vernalis,* a parasite of the grub, and *Istocheta aldrichi,* a parasite of the adult. They have been successfully established in some areas, but are not yet commercially available. Contact your cooperative extension agent to see if they are established in your area. If so, planting the appropriate food plants will attract these parasites and increase the rates of parasitization, and thus help control the Japanese beetle population on your property.

Tiphia vernalis is a small, parasitic wasp of Japanese beetle grubs that resembles a large, black, winged ant. Its current distribution is believed to be throughout the northeastern United States and south to North Carolina. The female wasp digs into the soil, paralyzes grubs by stinging, and lays an egg on the grub. The egg hatches and the wasp larva consumes the grub.

Adult wasps of this species feed on the honeydew of aphids associated with the leaves of maple, cherry, and elm trees as well as peonies. In North Carolina, they feed on the nectar of tulip poplars as well.

Istocheta aldrichi is a solitary fly that lays eggs on the thorax of female beetles; the maggot burrows into the beetle's body. The female flies can lay up to one hundred eggs in about two weeks. The maggot usually kills the beetle before it can reproduce, greatly helping to reduce the beetle population.

Adult *I. aldrichi* feed on aphid nectar of Japanese knotweed (*Polygonum cuspidatum*), a persistent perennial weed native to Japan.

Mechanical traps with pheromone and floral attractants capture about 75 percent of beetles that approach the traps. The traps actually attract more beetles than they capture, so position traps away from plants that the beetles may damage. Traps are most effective when many of them are spread over an entire community.

Other controls. Japanese beetles tend to prefer smooth-leaved grapes, such as certain French Hybrids like Aurore. Coarse-leaved types with heavy pubescence, such as some of the labrusca grapes, are usually not attacked unless there is nothing else available. Some growers have had reasonably good success planting susceptible varieties at one side of the vineyard to draw the beetles into a smaller area for easier treatment.

Spraying the vines with Surround (discussed in chapter 4) will deter the beetles.

Dusting the beetles with diatomaceous earth to kill them is only effective if the dust actually contacts the beetles, and the dust must be reapplied after rain.

Spraying or dusting with pyrethrins is also effective. Since this is a poison, the beetles could develop resistance if it is used too often, so alternate it with other controls.

Grape Phylloxera

Grape phylloxera (*Daktulosphaira vitifoliae*) feeds on the roots of *V. vinifera*, stunting growth of vines or killing them. This pest prefers heavy, clay soils. It is not a pest on sandy soils.

Life cycle. In the West, most grape phylloxera adults are wingless females, usually oval in shape, although egg-laying females are pear-shaped. They are tiny and vary in color from yellow, yellowish green, or olive green to light brown, brown, or orange. Newly deposited eggs are yellow, oval, and about twice as long as wide. Nymphs resemble adults except they are smaller.

Grape phylloxera overwinter as small nymphs on roots. In spring, when soil temperatures exceed 60°F (15.5°C), they start feeding and growing. First instar nymphs are active crawlers and may move from plant to plant in the ground, on the soil surface, or by blowing in the wind. This is part of the reason phylloxera prefer heavy soils, which crack when dry, allowing them easy routes to the surface or to other roots.

Phylloxera can be moved between vineyards on cuttings, boots, or equipment—

any object that has soil (which may contain the insects) clinging to it.

In the eastern United States, winged females are produced that leave the soil and fly off to establish new colonies. These new colonies may either be soil-dwelling forms or leaf-dwelling types, which form rough, rounded, spiky galls on the surfaces of leaves of susceptible grape species. Species such as *V. vinifera* that are susceptible to the root form are generally resistant to the leaf form, while species with high root-resistance, such as *V. riparia,* are susceptible to infestation with leaf galls. While most individuals of the leaf gall type remain as such, they can also produce nymphs toward the end of the season that drop to the soil and move to roots. Occasionally, winged phylloxera are seen in vinifera vineyards in California, but they are believed to be sterile under California conditions.

Once established on a root, phylloxera feed externally in groups. In fall, when soil temperatures fall below 60°F (15.5°C), all life stages die except the small nymphs. There are three to five generations each year.

Damage. Grape phylloxera damage the root systems of grapevines by feeding on the root; either on growing rootlets, which then swell and turn yellowish, or on mature hardened roots, where the swellings are often hard to see. Necrotic spots (areas of dead tissue) develop at the feeding sites on the roots. The necrotic spots are a result of secondary fungal infections that can girdle roots, killing large sections of the root system. Such root injury causes vines to become stunted and produce less fruit.

Severity of infestation will differ with the vigor of the grapevine as well as with soil texture and drainage.

Biological controls. A potential method is to rebuild the soil food web so that there are fungi present that are antagonistic to phylloxera, as well as fungi that the pest may actually prefer to feed on. Building up soil life also increases populations of microfauna that will prey on the phylloxera.

Cultural control. Planting vines with resistant rootstocks is the main means for phylloxera control in the most severely affected areas. Avoid rootstocks that have *V. vinifera* in their parentage, because these have incomplete resistance and use of them can select the phylloxera for more virulent biotypes. This has already happened in many counties in California, where the resistance of rootstock AXR#1 has broken down under the new biotype B phylloxera. It is necessary to use rootstocks that have strong resistance and no *V. vinifera* parentage for durable protection against phylloxera.

If you are replanting in a previously infested vineyard, there are nonchemical options to reduce phylloxera.

One strategy is to grow annual crops for at least four years, using organic methods to build the soil in the process. Grape roots can remain alive in the soil, supporting phylloxera, for up to four years. Because they are very host-specific to grapes, the phylloxera populations will be greatly reduced, if not eliminated, by this procedure.

Another approach is to flood the area in winter for more than six weeks, suffocating much of the phylloxera population.

In California's Central Valley, phylloxera damage may be reduced by good water management, fertilization, and other cultural practices that help limit plant stress.

Monitoring and when to treat. Initial infestations of grape phylloxera appear as a few weakened vines. These insects are difficult to detect in an apparently healthy vineyard. Therefore, monitor vines in an area of the vineyard that has consistently displayed weaker growth. Grape phylloxera are more readily identified on vines growing in poor soils, because their impact shows up better on these vines than on vigorously growing vines.

In some vineyards, infected vines may initially exhibit potassium deficiency symptoms. The infested area expands concentrically at a rate of twofold to fourfold per year. Secondary infestations frequently establish downwind from larger infested areas. When searching for phylloxera, be aware that populations die out on declining vines. Therefore, concentrate monitoring efforts on the periphery of declining areas, where damage symptoms are still minimal. Dig around the trunk of vines and look for whitish-yellow, hooked feeder roots that are galled. Examine the galls with a hand lens for the presence of phylloxera.

Pesticide treatments will not eradicate phylloxera populations; chemicals cannot easily penetrate the heavy soils that this pest prefers. Also, effectiveness of a treatment is difficult to evaluate because, although many phylloxera may be killed, populations can rebound rapidly and resume feeding on the vines. Because it may take years of insecticide treatments to reverse severe damage, treatments to prevent damage may be a better strategy than curative treatments.

Treatment. The first line of defense is always to plant resistant rootstocks. Beyond that, rebuilding the soil food web looks like the best method to decrease, if not eliminate phylloxera.

Strawberry Root Weevil

The strawberry root weevil, *Otiorhynchus ovatus,* occurs over much of North America, though they don't often cause serious damage. Usually the first sign of them is the lacework look to the edges of leaves where the adults have been feeding. This is only cosmetic—damage done by the larva is the real problem.

Life cycle. Adult strawberry root weevils are brown to black, blunt-snouted weevils that are about 1/3 inch long. The wing covers are marked by many rows of small pits. The adult strawberry root weevil cannot fly. Larvae are thick-bodied, white, comma-shaped, legless grubs that reach approximately 1/4 inch in length.

Root weevil adults lay eggs throughout the summer, with each female depositing one hundred and fifty to two hundred eggs in the soil. Eggs hatch in about ten days, and larvae burrow through the soil to feed on roots until they mature or until cold temperatures cause a suspension of their activity.

The strawberry root weevil overwinters as a full-grown larva, pupa, or adult in soil, or as an adult in plant debris or other protective habitat. Larvae and pupae complete development in the spring, emerging as adults in May or June; overwintered adults become active in strawberries in May.

Injury. Strawberry root weevils are a minor pest of grapes in vineyards, unless there is a very large population and the vineyard is young. However, in confined areas, such as pots, these weevils can devastate plants. I have had potted grape plants go into winter in good shape, but fail to grow in spring because a single lava had shorn all roots and even bark on underground portions of the vines.

Control. Application of parasitic nematodes to soil will provide control that lasts several years. I treated soil with the nematodes and then kept up with applying compost and mycorrhizal fungi, and the weevils never reappeared.

Other Insect Pests of Grapes

Other types of pest insects are occasionally found on grapes; however most are local in nature and either do not cause severe damage or will be controlled by methods already recommended for other pests. In many cases, the damage they cause is mainly cosmetic, and simply leaving them alone will allow natural predators to take care of them.

Many species of aphids, mites, and scale insects can be pests of grapevines, but in a healthy vineyard, they rarely build to any level that is problematic. Spider mites, for example, generally are kept in check by natural predators, and cause not more than minor cosmetic damage. Likewise, a healthy vineyard that includes a few strips of uncultivated grass and weeds will generally harbor enough aphid predators to prevent aphids from causing damage.

Achemon sphinx
moth larva.

Queen Anne's lace (*Daucus carota*) is a wildflower that is especially attractive to beneficial predator insects.

If problems with aphids, mites, or scale insects should occur, you can choose from a range of products to control them, including Envirepel, Naturalis-L, neem, and light horticultural oil (to smother winter stages). Releasing ladybugs, lacewings, or predatory mites (mainly to control pest mites) can also be effective.

In the West, the grape erineum mite (*Colomerus vitis*) sometimes causes blisterlike galls, the undersides of which appear to be lined with white felty material, on grape leaves. These mites are invariably controlled by predator mites, or by sulfur used to treat powdery mildew. Grape erineum mites rarely cause more than minor cosmetic damage to a few leaves on any vine.

The Achemon sphinx moth (*Pholus achemon*) is a large moth the size of a hummingbird whose adult caterpillar can reach 4 inches long. A large caterpillar can eat nine leaves of a grapevine in twenty-four hours. This species is found mainly in California. It is mentioned here mostly because people occasionally find them and believe that tomato hornworms, which these caterpillars resemble, are feeding on their grapes. The caterpillars can be controlled by hand-picking, or with Dipel (*Bacillus thuringiensis*).

7 ANIMAL and BIRD PESTS

HUMANS AREN'T THE ONLY warm-blooded beings that enjoy grapes: Many animals enjoy not only the fruit, but other parts of the vine as well. As a grower, you will have to deal with some types of animal pests, no matter where you live. Fortunately, there are ways to outwit or prepare for many of them in advance.

DEER

The proliferation of deer in North America due to the "Bambi syndrome" has made them the top animal pest. Anyone who has seen the movie *Bambi* and thinks that deer are sweet little creatures to be preserved at all costs should live in a suburban home and try to grow any sort of garden. First, they'll see deer in the yard, and wonder in amazement that "such beautiful wild creatures would come right into the yard." However, after a few months of unwittingly feeding the deer with everything they try

to plant, most such homeowners would go to *Bambi* to root for the hunters.

Tender young grape shoots rate high on the list of favorite foods of deer. One hungry deer can strip a lot of vines in a single day (or night, since most deer are nocturnal feeders, especially in the presence of humans). It wouldn't be too bad if deer nipped only the tip ends of shoots, but this isn't the case. Deer will devour young shoots right down to the wood, removing the flower clusters (and your crop) at the same time.

Whatever your feelings about deer, you must keep them out of your vineyard if you expect to have any crop. (See page 12 for tips on locating the vineyard away from deer routes).

Since most deer can't jump more than 8 feet high, the ultimate deer prevention device is a 10-foot-high fence around the vineyard. However, since building such a fence isn't always financially possible, I include other options below. Deer in different regions may have different behavior patterns that affect how well some of these methods work, so don't expect any single tactic to be the perfect solution without testing it. There is too much material on deer control to offer more than an overview here. Fortunately, there are several good websites that cover deer control, such as www.deerbusters.com.

Here are a few deer control strategies that have worked for me and for other fruit growers.

Fencing. As mentioned, erecting a tall fence is the only way to keep deer reliably out of an area. However, there are new materials available that can greatly reduce the cost of fencing, such as various types of plastic or nylon mesh. One grower whose vineyard was close to the ocean and a fishing community reported good results with used fishing nets.

The single-strand electric fence. Compared to the cost of conventional fence material, this is a less expensive way to keep out deer. One strand of wire 3 to 4 feet above ground level is supported with fiberglass fence stakes. Attach flags of bright tape to the wire to make it visible, and dab peanut butter on metal tabs and attach the tabs to the wire at regular intervals. Deer are curious. The peanut butter will attract them to investigate, and they'll receive a shock from the wire. After that, they will avoid the wire even though they could easily go over or under it.

The Virginia slanting multi-wire electric fence. Only 5 feet tall, this fence slants outward, confusing the deer with its three-dimensional effect. They could jump over it, but the angle confuses them, and when they try to push through, they contact the electric wires, and receive a shock.

Monofilament fishing line. Elwyn Meader, long-time vegetable breeder at the University of New Hampshire, kept deer out of his garden with a single strand of monofilament fishing line strung from posts at about 2 feet above the ground. The deer couldn't see it and when they ran into it, it would spook them so much they avoided the area. The line often gets broken a few times in the early season until all the deer learn about it, and it may not stop high concentrations of really determined deer, but it works for small areas.

Egg spray. This is something I use with good results. The recipe is to put four to six eggs in a blender with water. After blending, pour the mixture into a 3-gallon sprayer and fill the rest of the way with water. When sprayed on plants, this mixture dries and humans can't see or smell it. It can last up to six weeks, but should be reapplied after three heavy rains or after the plants have been sprayed with irrigation water three times. Also, in areas where the deer populations are concentrated, the deer will often feed on shoots that have grown 6 inches or more beyond the sprayed part of the plant.

A wildlife biologist once explained to me that eggs contain a sulfur compound that is chemically close to the deer alarm scent, so they avoid anything with that odor on it. The first time I learned of the method I had just purchased some mail-order deer

*Mark
Hart's
Wisdom*

ALL DEER-REPELLING METHODS have some limitations, however. The following is some sound advice from vineyardist Mark Hart in Wisconsin, whose experiences sum up the situation for many growers.

"At my vineyard in northern Wisconsin, deer have been the biggest detriment: more than disease, winter damage, and nutrient problems combined. Deer definitely prefer fertilized grapes over native vegetation or nonfertilized plants. They will *mow* fertilized grapes down to stubs.

"I've hung soap; used predator urine; set up speakers to broadcast the sound of barking dogs; and sprayed Hinder, Deer Away, Bobbex, and more. Most of these strategies work to some degree, but deer adapt very quickly and constantly test to see if these barriers are a real threat. When the deer discover they are not, each successive technique becomes useless. The sprays work, but are expensive and need to be applied constantly (very expensive in the "time is money" sense).

"I have never used penned dogs. I don't live on the property and don't like the idea of keeping my own dog in a corral.

"I finally settled on a 6-foot, eight-wire, high-tensile electric fence. It is working, but it has taken me a while to deer-proof the fence, with many errors along the way. Here is what does (or does not) work in my experience.

- Anything that deer learn is not a real threat to them, including wimpy or inadequate fences, will not work for long.
- The deer tore down a barricade made of nylon bird netting.
- Any non-electrified fence that deer can push through, they will. Non-electrified, high-tensile fences will not work unless you have spacer battens every 3 to 6 feet so the deer can't push the wires apart to get through. *Electrify the fence!* Eight-foot-high or taller woven-wire or chain-link fences are excellent, but incredibly expensive.
- Galvanized wire will corrode very quickly if it contacts other types of metals, so use nonconductive (nonmetallic) battens and/or insulators.
- Fence construction must be sturdy enough to allow for good tension on the wires, so that wire spacing is maintained. End posts and corners should be solid and well built to handle the tension.
- Although my fence is only 6 feet high, the deer have never jumped over it, to my knowledge. Before I had a good charger, they went through the fence, and under it. Now when they breach the fence, they go underneath, due to uneven ground, but I am closing those holes.
- You must have a reliable, low-impedance (or wide) fence charger. You must maintain at least 5,000 volts on the fence. You need an electric fence tester that gives accurate strength readings. Claims by most fence companies are inaccurate; 100 miles of fence equals less than 10 miles (of wire) in reality. The output should be at least 4 joules, and preferably 6 joules for small commercial vineyards, and at least 6 joules for larger vineyards. Be suspicious of a fence installer who does not mention a joules rating (or a voltage at a

specified resistance)—they may be trying to sell you equipment that isn't up to the job. Output joules are usually 70-80 percent of stored joules, so take that into account in the equipment.

- A good grounding system for the charger is essential, usually three to four 6-foot rods set into moist soil. Test the ground for any shock while charger is on, and add more rods if there is a charge.
- Deer hair and hooves have a high electrical resistance (deer are not well grounded, thus the rarity of lightning-fried venison). The best fences have alternating hot and grounded wires to a height of at least 36 to 40 inches. The bottom wire must *always* be hot or the deer will go underneath. Wires must be no more than 8 inches apart with this system, so the deer will contact both alternate wires in front of the eyes/ears. Baygard makes a charger (5000 Twin Power) especially for alternate wire fences that has a positive voltage on one set of wires and a negative on the others, so the voltage differential is even greater between alternate wires with one set grounded.
- Extremely few solar- or battery-powered chargers are up to the task for deer. The cheapest that make the cut start at $350 ($450 solar), or about $300 for AC electric chargers. I tried six chargers on my fence before I woke up to reality.
- I do not believe that you can effectively reduce the deer herd with a gun where deer populations are high, unless you employ a full-time sharpshooter. More deer just fill in during the next week."

repellent. I found it was formulated from egg solids with a bit of dye added. Nothing more. When making your homemade egg spray, though, adding some predator urine can double its impact. (Humans, being meat eaters, definitely qualify as deer predators.)

Garlic juice. The effect is similar to the egg spray, as the garlic also contains sulfur compounds that resemble deer alarm scent. (See chapter 4, page 84 for more information on garlic juice products).

Chicken wire. This barrier is laid flat on (or slightly above) the ground around the perimeter of your vineyard. A Canadian grower recommends this method. Deer hate to walk on something that catches on their feet; in many cases, they move on after they encounter the chicken wire. You'll have to "lift" this wire several times a year so that it keeps slightly suspended above the ground in order to keep its effectiveness.

Some people have found that two strands of wire about 3 feet off the ground and about 3 to 4 feet apart work well. Deer almost walk over the first row, then they hit another. Apparently this second wire confuses them and they depart.

Dogs. Here is a creative solution, sent by a friend.

"Jennie, at Chrysalis Vineyards in Virginia, has a really neat answer to the deer problem—a 'two-bird, one missile' solution. She goes to the Humane Society and picks out some nice used dogs. Her vineyard is 'electronic fenced' and the dogs wear the collar receivers. They run as a friendly pack every evening. No deer.

"They're the cutest motley crew of beasties you've ever seen! Jennie obviously chose them because they were sweeties, and not because they acted like vicious guard dogs."

"However, in the final analysis, deer that become wise to a good fence do have to be converted to venison."

BURROWING ANIMALS

Gophers are a problem in some areas, burrowing under vines and gnawing roots. Sometimes you don't know they are there until a vine suddenly wilts and collapses. Old, established vines are almost never killed by gopher damage. (More often, one of the main roots is severed, slowing the growth of the vine for a year or so until the root regrows.) Trapping a gopher is possible, but it may be hard with a wary old-timer, and it is a slow, time-consuming process. The most effective method I have found is gassing, not with gopher bombs—which almost never produce enough gas to be effective—but with a propane weed torch.

To use a propane weed torch in this way, find a fresh mound and open the tunnel nearest it. Put in a handful of sulfur flakes (sold as "sugar sulfur" in farm and agricultural supply houses) and play the flame of the torch on the sulfur, igniting it and forcing the fumes down into the tunnels. After a few minutes you should see yellow fumes puff out of the ground as much as 20 feet away as the sulfur dioxide reaches the other end of the tunnel. Continue for another five minutes or so, then close the tunnel. The sulfur and the fumes oxidize and are harmless to the soil, and you can be sure any

gopher in that tunnel is a deceased gopher.

This method doesn't work with all burrowers, because some, such as rabbits, usually have an open exit that allows them to escape. Gophers rely more on hidden chambers and fast digging for safety and don't usually have a second opening to the tunnel.

Some growers have reported being able to flush rabbits and groundhogs out of their tunnels with water, with the grower waiting nearby with a good dog or a gun.

RABBITS *and* OTHER SMALL HERBIVORES

Most small animals such as rabbits, squirrels, and groundhogs that feed aboveground are mainly a problem in the first year or two of establishing a vineyard. Once the vines are trained up and the trunk is woody, these types of animals leave them alone, except for shoot tips that hang down where the animals can reach to nibble on them.

There are repellents such as "Scoot," a paint-on product, but the simplest method is the use of grow tubes. These are plastic tubes that encircle the vines, not only protecting them from rabbits, but also blocking spray from reaching the plants at ground level. In addition, these tubes form a mini-greenhouse effect that speeds vine growth. The size and type of tubes you use is important, however. The first ones I tried were translucent, so I thought the plants would be fine. However, the tubes I used were too tall, and the type of plastic blocked too much of the necessary light wavelengths the vines needed, so they became thin and spindly. The type of tube known as "BlueX" seems to transmit more of the right light wavelengths, so the vines grow up better and less spindly, and they are protected from rabbits and other nibblers.

FRUIT-EATING ANIMALS

Raccoons and possums are the main subjects here. Both *love* grapes, and even show preference in varieties. I can always tell when there is a raccoon in the area when Reliance grapes are ripe because the little stinker goes for that variety first. After that, any labrusca grape is fair game: Raccoons like the aroma, apparently.

Live traps are an option, though one must be diligent, and often start well before the grapes ripen. The trap *must* be big enough for the animal to go all the way in to get the bait. If not, the door may be held open when it bumps the back of the animal, and the animal can just back out.

When we first started trapping raccoons and possums, the bait tended to attract cats as well. The cats weren't harmed. However, if you trap a feral cat, getting it out of the trap can be like sticking your hands into a buzz saw. Then we found the right bait for raccoons: marshmallows. The odor lures the raccoons in and the marshmallow sticks to the bait holder so they can't help but set it off. Dispose of captured animals in accordance with your state's game laws.

Foxes and coyotes will eat grapes, especially American labrusca types. Stinging these animals with an air rifle a few times will do the trick on one or a few, but if a pack of coyotes visits your vineyard, you may have to have them trapped or shot.

Squirrels and chipmunks will eat green grapes, and the damage is usually noticeable as half-chewed grapes. The damage may or may not be serious, depending on the size of the animal population. My research has not turned up any definite solution. Hot pepper spray works, but it may affect the flavor of the grapes. Providing something else for the squirrels and chipmunks to eat, such as nuts, can backfire by attracting more animals to the area. Live traps have worked for some growers, but not always: The little rodents learn quickly.

BIRD CONTROL

Birds are probably the most universal pest of grapes. In every climate there are avian fruit-lovers ready to have a meal of grapes, or sometimes, grape seeds. (Cedar waxwings will often peck into a grape to get the seeds, and may or may not eat the fruit.) An amazing number of methods for dealing with the little feathered (fill in appropriate term) have been devised.

Covering vines with netting was the first method I tried to foil birds. It works, but it has to be pegged down perfectly. Otherwise, birds will find their way through any hole that is available. If you have cats, a bird caught under the net can be a cause for hilarity or a serious problem. That is, a cat will try to catch the bird, which is probably too scared to find its way back to the entry point. The cat may grab the bird through the net, but the cat may instead get tangled in the net and can be strangled.

Drawbacks of nets are expense and labor. Cost to cover large areas of grapes with netting can be high. It usually takes at least two people to install a net over a row of grapes, and two to remove it. It also takes time to make sure the net is fitted in place so nothing can get under it. The presence of nets can slow harvesting, as the pickers usually must open the net to pick.

At least part of the drawbacks of netting have been solved by the use of disposable, one-time nets. These are made to be ripped off the vines for picking, then gathered and recycled, saving the time-consuming jobs of rerolling and storing.

At the moment, I know of only one brand of disposable netting, called Bird Ban. For most grape rows, the best size to use is 24 feet wide. In 1999, one roll of netting 24 feet by 830 feet cost $75. The Kansas State Horticulture Research Center in Wichita has used it for several years. They put the net on right before veraison and remove and dispose of it before harvest. According to the research center, the netting is very effective if put on before the birds start feeding on the grapes. Also, the extra shading from the netting doesn't seem to adversely affect the grapes.

The second most effective bird-protection method I have found is bird scare-away line. This technique is based on an old method used in the Middle East. There, long strips of cloth are stretched over the rows. The cloth vibrates in the wind and makes an ultrasonic sound that birds can hear, but not people. The modern equivalent is a clear plastic tape that does the same thing. The first time I tried it, a flock of starlings flew high over the vineyard, split in two when they reached the area above the plastic tape, then reformed after they had passed the area. No birds reached the grapes under the tape, and the effect was good for at least 3 rows on either side.

Your choice of grape varieties and how you plant them can help foil some birds. Birds start eating small, blue or black berries first, then move to other colors and sizes later. However, birds don't always recognize red or white grapes as being ripe unless they are around long enough to start tasting them. Plant red and white grapes away from blue or black grapes with small berries that ripen early, to give the red and white types a better chance to escape birds. Migratory birds are less likely to stay around long enough to sample the grapes and find out that they are ripe, and just move on without eating them. It isn't a perfect bird solution, but it may help in some areas. Also, many birds won't bother with a grape that is too big to get their beaks around, so that large-berried types (larger than Concord, if possible), especially if they have tough skin, will have a certain amount of bird resistance. Very late grapes may not suffer bird damage because they don't ripen until after migratory birds have passed in the fall. This assumes, of course, that your growing season is long enough to permit these varieties to ripen.

Following is a collection of other bird-control methods, all of which have worked for at least some growers.

Bird Against Bird

One of the most interesting bird-control methods I've heard of involved using other birds, namely, wrens. A blueberry grower told me that he kept wren houses at each corner of his acre of bushes. Wrens, which are insect (not fruit) eaters, are very territorial, and they would drive all other birds away from their area, which pretty much kept the field clear of fruit-eating birds. The method might not work with grapes, as they ripen later than blueberries and the wrens might have moved on by the time the grapes ripen.

Repellents

Giving the birds an unpleasant experience in the vineyard can deter a lot of species. One method is to use a very sticky compound such as Tangletrap on horizontal poles installed around the vineyard, creating sticky "roosts" there. Birds land there to look the place over, get sticky stuff on their feathers, and fly off leaving a few feathers behind. Put the roosts up before veraison, but don't apply the sticky stuff until after veraison has started. Take the "roosts" down after harvest.

Scare Devices

Bird scare flash tape is a tape that is silvery on one side and red on the other. When it moves in a breeze, it is supposed to resemble fire, which scares the birds. It can be hung in strips, or one long piece can be strung along the top of a row.

The Peaceful Pyramid is a device that looks like a small pyramid covered with mirrors. It rotates and the flashes of light reflecting from the mirrors are supposed to scare birds for miles.

Devices for commercial vineyards include propane cannons, which set off a loud explosion at intervals to scare the birds; electronically broadcast bird alarm sounds; and bird scare eyes. These last are inflatable plastic balls with a huge eye-like design. When hung over the vines, they are supposed to fool birds into thinking a predator is present. There are plastic owls, rubber snakes, hawk silhouettes, and more,

which are supposed to do the same. All of these are used only after veraison starts, so that the birds don't have enough time to lose their fear of the device.

I have also heard of home growers who created their own scare sounds by setting radios in the vineyard, usually with a loud talk show on.

The biggest problem with any device that relies on scaring birds is that, if they are used too much, the birds learn not to fear them, and they lose their effectiveness. Also, scare methods are more effective with birds that flock: scare one starling and the whole flock takes off. Scare one robin and the rest stay there and keep eating unless you scare each one.

Chemical Repellents

Chemicals to make fruit unappealing to birds have been tried. Measurol was one of the most promising, but it was banned after fears of harm to human health. A new product called Bird Shield, made from Concord grapes, is promising on table grapes, but may taint wine grapes with off flavors, especially if used too close to harvest.

A recent piece of research suggests that sucrose (plain table sugar) might be the key to deterring many birds. The research was conducted on blueberries, but it should be relevant for grapes and other fruits as well. The study found that bird damage was at least 50 percent less when a sucrose solution was sprayed onto the fruit. Researchers theorize that because most birds lack the enzyme to digest sucrose, ingesting sucrose gives them severe digestive upset, and they quickly learn to avoid treated fruit.

This is an inexpensive method of bird control. If 230 pounds of sugar per acre needs to be applied each of four times during the fruiting season, the per season costs for bird control would be about $200 per acre. At a price of $.50 per pound for grapes, one would only need to "save" 400 pounds of fruit per acre to recoup the materials cost (assuming 100 percent control). That's only a 2 percent bird loss (at 10 tons per acre); surveys in Oregon estimated an average of 10 percent loss to birds.[*]

Trapping

This is a somewhat controversial subject, but trapping doesn't have to mean the birds will be harmed. Plans are available on the Internet for one type of cage that has a top that hinges down in a "V." Birds land on the top and are let into the cage, where they are caught. My grandfather used a smaller version of such a cage to catch sparrows, so I know they work. A large version of such a cage could be used just before harvest to trap and hold a fair-sized flock of birds alive until after harvest, when they could be released again.

In many areas, there may be both local, resident birds, and migratory flocks of the same species of birds. In Oregon, this is the case with starlings. Often, the local population shows the migratory flocks where the food is located. If there are no locals of that species, the migratory flocks may bypass an area. Thus, trapping the locals may keep the migratory flocks from finding the fruit quite as rapidly.

I will add that in Italy songbirds are a popular food. The usual method of use is to skin the birds and pickle them whole.

Most nongame birds are protected by state and federal law. Be sure to check with your state fish and game department before hunting or trapping songbirds.

Baits

In New Zealand, a product called Alpha-Chloralose is being used to bait birds without harming them. Alpha-chloralose is a hypnotic and anesthetizes the brain. Essential bodily functions are unaffected, the bird is merely stupefied. Drugged birds can be collected and nonprotected birds disposed of. Protected or nonpest birds can be revived quickly in a warm, dark place and then released. This is acceptable in New Zealand because the main pest species of birds are all non-native introduced species. Destroying pest birds is considered desirable as it helps reduce competition with the native species.

[*]A. M. Socci, M.P. Pritts, and M.J. Kelly. 1997. Potential use of sucrose as a feeding deterrent for frugivorous birds. *HortTechnology,* 7:250–253

8 *PROPAGATION*

OLD AUNT MARTHA had an ancient gnarled grapevine that you played under as a kid. You've never found grapes as delicious as the ones it bore and you'd love to have a vine of the same kind for your home. But try as you might, you can't find anything like it in a nursery. Well, the good news is, if Aunt Martha's vine is still growing, you have your solution in hand.

Most grapes are so simple to grow from dormant cuttings that you can start as many "copies" of that old vine as you want. And if it's one of the few types that don't grow easily from dormant cuttings, there are still other ways to start new vines. In this chapter, I'll cover propagation techniques that have worked well for me in a wide range of situations.

One caution: Many private and university grape breeders patent their varieties in hopes of making some sort of return on their work. Many of these people get very little money to help them with their work, so be kind and don't propagate patented (usually labeled "PVP") grapes without permission or without paying the royalty.[*]

GROWING HARDWOOD *or* DORMANT CUTTINGS

Grapes are most commonly propagated from dormant hardwood cuttings, and most varieties will root just by sticking cuttings in the ground, in warm, moist soil.

But though a grape cutting just pushed into the ground will often take root, using additional measures and proper care results in larger plants with better roots, in less time. Done right, it is even possible to have vines ready to bear a small crop the year after the cuttings are started.

*Brooks and Olmo's *The Register of New Fruit and Nut Varieties,* 3rd edition (Alexandria, Va.: ASHS Press, 1997) is a good reference to check on varieties that have current patents on them.

Selecting Plant Material

Preparation for taking dormant cuttings should start at least a year in advance. If at all possible, observe the "parent" vine for a full growing season beforehand to be certain it is healthy and true to type—that is, that it grows and bears fruit that is typical of that particular species or variety of grape. There are several ways to evaluate the vine.

First, see if the vine resists, or at least tolerates, insects and fungal diseases. Be sure the vine bears full, regular crops, because some viral diseases, such as fan leaf and leaf roll, will reduce fruit bearing even though the vine grows vigorously. If you select vines in winter, having never seen them in summer, be aware that some virus-infected vines could seem healthy, with larger, heavier canes than non-infected ones. But cuttings of infected vines only grow into more diseased, poorly bearing vines.

There are ways to produce vines free of virus, but they usually aren't practical for the average grower. Fortunately, commercial growers and reputable nurseries use stock that is virus-free or at least is productive, with no outward signs of disease, so virus-infected vines are not as common now as they were in the past.

While virus-infected vines should be avoided or destroyed, vines affected with fungal diseases such as mildew or black rot can be used for cuttings as long as the fungus wasn't so severe during the growing season that the canes weren't able to harden off well. Cuttings from such vines should be disinfected before rooting, to reduce spread of fungus in the new nursery or vineyard.

Another disease to avoid is bacterial canker, sometimes known as crown gall, which usually manifests as warty, misshapen growths, most often on the trunk near or at the ground line. In serious cases, the growths can girdle a vine, killing it, or causing it to die back. The bacteria causing these growths often stays in the tissues of the cuttings where disinfectants can't reach them, increasing the odds that vines grown from the cuttings will also develop the disease. Also, the presence of the disease suggests that the variety may be more susceptible to it to begin with. Unless you have no other source of the variety, avoid taking cuttings from vines that have crown gall.

Timing

Hardwood cuttings can be taken anytime after the vine has gone dormant and lost its leaves, but there are several reasons to wait if you can. First, several good freezes will kill incompletely ripened shoots. Cuttings of half-ripe wood are more prone to rot or die back in storage, so let nature weed out the weak wood before you take cuttings. Additionally, cuttings taken too early in the season still contain natural inhibitors that help the vine stay dormant. After a while, these built-in chemical inhibitors break down and only cold weather keeps the vine from growing. At this point, the vine and the cuttings taken from it are ready to grow as soon as the weather warms.

In experiments in California, cuttings taken before late December were slower to root and produced fewer roots than cuttings taken after the first of January, when the natural growth inhibitors in the wood had mostly disappeared. This timetable would vary in colder climates.

Cuttings taken early in the season can lose a fair amount of dormancy if held properly in cold storage, so if you must take cuttings before the "ideal" time, you can still expect reasonably good results if you hold the cuttings in cold storage for several weeks before rooting them.

There is evidence that rain helps wash the inhibitors out of the vines, so that vines in areas with dry winters need more cold to help them break dormancy than ones where winters are rainy or foggy. This suggests that it could be possible to help vines in dry areas break dormancy by spraying them with water during the winter. However, no research has been done to verify this or establish how much spraying would be needed.

Making Cuttings

Well-matured cutting with small pith.

The best cuttings are from the first 1 to 2 feet of the new wood. Buds or nodes in that section of the cane are situated closer together than ones located farther out on the cane. This is important because most roots arise from the nodes, so the more nodes, the more areas there are to give rise to roots. Also, the section of the cane closest to the old wood will be the most mature and contain the most stored food. The extra stored food helps the new plant until it is capable of producing food for itself. However, wood farther out on the shoot is acceptable, if it is healthy and well-matured.

Ideal thickness of cuttings ranges from pencil diameter to about ¾ inch thick. Thicker canes do work, but may be hard to handle. Some varieties, especially American ones, may have naturally small-diameter canes, in which case it is better to select on the basis of health and maturity of the wood

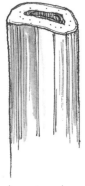

Poorly matured cutting with large pith, flattened or oval outline.

rather than size. For example, canes of Valiant that are about the diameter of a round toothpick can still be healthy and able to grow. Avoid shoots with wood that is soft and spongy and has proportionally large and/or oval pith. The best wood is light green inside and has round pith that is no more than half the diameter of the cutting. After you have cut a few canes, you will get a "feel" for mature, healthy wood just by the way the pruning shears cut through it: the sound they make and the amount of pressure it takes to cut will tell how good the cutting is.

Over the centuries, many methods of making and growing grape cuttings have been devised. One old system was to coil up a long cane and bury it with a single bud left exposed. The reasoning was that the extra plant material provided more food to get the new vine off to a better start. In England in Victorian times, grapes were often started from short pieces of cane having only one bud, planted in pots or flats like seeds. These methods must have worked well enough, or they wouldn't have been recommended by the authors of old texts on grape culture.

For me, the best cuttings are a minimum of 12 inches long, with 18 inches the maximum length that can be handled easily. Shorter cuttings can work, but whatever the length, there should be at least three buds on the cutting, with more being better for improved rooting. Make the cuttings with the top cut at least 1 inch above the bud and the bottom cut ¼ inch or less below the bud. It is useful to make the top cut on a slant, which makes it easy to orient the cutting properly in the bundle for storage, and at planting time. Some growers prefer the reverse, with the bottom cut at a slant. However, having the bottom cut flat instead of slanted makes it easier to tamp the bundles so the cuttings are even, when handling large quantities of cuttings.

Bundling cuttings for storage

Cuttings should be tied in bundles with non-rotting plastic twine or wire and tagged with waterproof tags, either plastic marked with permanent ink, or metal tags. If you have just a few cuttings, you can tie them with twist ties, but be sure to watch for rusting or breaking of the twist tie wire. If you can procure some, the individual color-coded wires inside telephone lines (such as those your house is wired with) are some of the best wire for bundling grapes and tying tags.

Large amounts—twenty or more cuttings of a single variety—can be bundled tightly using the "nurseryman's knot" (see illustration). Use plastic baling twine for this knot, as the twine grips itself and prevents the knot from slipping. To start, tie a square knot at the end of the twine. Loop the twine around the bundle and tie it around itself using a square knot, so the twine can slip through the knot. Leave about 2 inches of the knotted end beyond where the twine is tied around itself. Now you can pull the twine tight and the knot will grip the twine. Tighten it gently, then tap the bottom of the bundle on a smooth, hard surface to get all the cuttings even. Hold the bundle with one hand and pull the twine towards yourself, as tight as possible, by repeated jerking to take out slack. Roll the bundle slightly to shift the cuttings as you tighten so they will settle into the most compact position. The knot on the

end of the twine will prevent the end from being pulled through the knot below it. Now tie a half-hitch around the short piece above the knot, and cut the twine loose from the roll. Use the same technique to make a second knot at the other end of the bundle to keep all the cuttings straight.

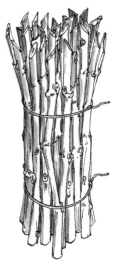

Bundled cuttings.

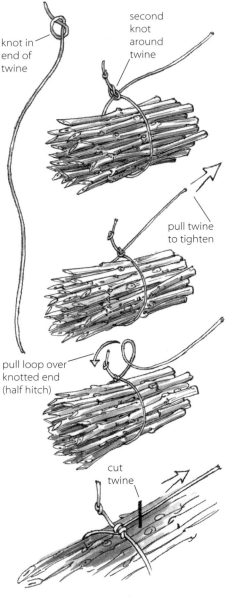

knot in end of twine

second knot around twine

pull twine to tighten

pull loop over knotted end (half hitch)

cut twine

Tying cuttings in a bundle.

Storage

Before storing cuttings, some growers prefer to disinfect the cuttings to kill any spores or fungus that might cause damage in storage or infect young plants when the cuttings start to grow. A 5 percent solution of liquid chlorine bleach in water does the job. Dip the cuttings, swish them around for *no more* than five seconds, and *rinse thoroughly* in clean water to remove the solution, which could cause damage if allowed to remain on the cuttings. You don't have to disinfect cuttings if you know they were taken from healthy, well-matured vines, as such wood is generally safe in storage. A white mold may form on cuttings in storage, but in my experience it only grows on the dead outer layer of bark and has no effect on healthy cuttings.

Another cutting disinfectant is Chinosol, a chemical used in medicine as a topical antiseptic and tissue disinfectant. Its use on plants was pioneered in Germany, where it was shown to provide excellent control against bacterial and fungal pests on stored cuttings. Growers who use it report rooting and graft take is higher with the Chinosol-treated material.

Chinosol is usually applied as a dip solution, with the material kept submerged in the solution for varying periods of time. One grower reports using 1 teaspoon Chinosol per gallon of water for a 24-hour dip, with 2 teaspoons per gallon (0.25 percent) for 8 hours used by others. Don't go above 0.25 percent though; this can inhibit bud break and subsequent growth.

The preferred method seems to be to treat cuttings before they are put into storage, though treatment can be done anytime before rooting or grafting. Soaking cuttings for eight to twenty-four hours takes the place of regular pre-callusing hydration (see page 147).

Small amounts of cuttings (up to one hundred) can be stored in closed plastic bags with damp paper or moist peat moss to provide moisture. Peat has natural fungicidal properties and can itself reduce mold formation. Storage temperatures should be between 32°F and 36°F (0°C and 2°C), if possible. An unheated building will serve in many cases. Some references note that cuttings should not be stored in a refrigerator with fruits and vegetables, because the produce emits substances such as ethylene gas that can harm the buds. However, I have stored cuttings in a walk-in cooler, in plastic bags, where fruit was present, and I have not noted any problems with my cuttings. This could be due to the circulating fan in the cooler, which might have kept any harmful gasses from settling on the cuttings. Properly disinfected cuttings stored in humid conditions (a minimum of 60 to 70 percent humidity) at 32°F to 34°F (0°C to 1°C) will keep for over a year.

One low-tech storage method used for large quantities of cuttings in times past was to bury the bundles upside down in a pit of sand in a well-drained location on the north side of a building. Six to eighteen inches of sand was put over the cuttings, depending on the severity of the expected winter, topped with boards and tarps if more protection was needed. In spring, the covering and some of the sand was removed so that the bottoms of the cuttings would begin to warm first, to allow root callus to form before the tops of the cuttings (which were in deeper, cooler sand) started to grow.

Callusing the Cuttings

Callusing is the formation of lumpy or grainy-looking, white, undifferentiated tissues in grape cuttings. The cutting has to form such tissue before rooting can occur, as the roots arise from the callus. Most often, callus will show as a ring on the bottom of the cutting, but it will also appear as lumps under the bark of the cutting. In some cases, callus may only show as slight bumpiness on the bottom and sides of a cutting before roots appear. Most callus is produced close to buds, but it can appear anywhere on the cutting in the right conditions. Some varieties produce more callus before rooting than others.

Stimulating the formation of callus on the bottoms and lower nodes of grape cuttings is one of the most important steps in rooting and growing them. If the cuttings are not callused before planting, they will not start to form roots until soil warms enough to allow callus to form. Further, since the soil is apt to be warmer near the surface than in the root zone, upper buds may sprout. The resulting shoot growth will drain the cutting of its stored reserves, which can weaken or kill the cutting. By callusing the cutting before it is planted, roots can grow right away, since roots can grow at temperatures lower than those needed for callus formation. With roots moving out into the soil right away, the cutting has means to feed itself within a short time after planting and can begin shoot growth weeks ahead of an unrooted, uncallused cutting. Callusing should not be done until mid-spring, or approximately one to two weeks before it is time to plant the cuttings.

If the cuttings are to be planted directly into open ground, wait until frost danger

Ring of callus on end of cutting.

Roots forming from callus.

Starting Cuttings: The Short Form

1. Stand cuttings in water for several hours or overnight to allow them to imbibe as much as possible.
2. Dip in medium-strength rooting hormone—a five-second dip if using liquid type (such as Dip'n'Grow).
3. Dip in powdered Endomycorrhizal fungi.
4. Fill 6-inch-tall plastic or open-bottomed paper pots with light potting soil or a mix of perlite and peat (3 parts perlite to 1 part peat). Set the pots in a flat and place the flat on a heat mat. Punch a hole in the mix in each pot. Insert cuttings into the hole, to within 1 inch of the bottom of the pot (to ensure that the bottom of the cutting is close to the heated area). Tamp soil around the cuttings and water them well.
5. Keep mat and flat in a cool area, out of direct sun. The plants don't need light until the buds break.
6. Keep soil moist, but water as little as possible: water cools the root zone and slows rooting until the area warms up again.
7. When plants are rooted (in two to four weeks), they can be planted out in a nursery bed, a permanent location, or in pots—one plant per 1-gallon pot.

**Go
Soak
Your
... Cuttings**

How thirsty can a grape cutting get, even in good storage? Enough to make a difference in how well they will grow.

While working for a large wholesale berry nursery, I noted that one of the grapes they grew, the old Catawba, was never included on the price list. Even though five thousand cuttings were planted every spring, only about one thousand to fifteen hundred plants were obtained, just about enough for one regular wholesale customer, leaving none left over.

The grape cuttings used to grow the nursery stock were packed in moist wood shavings, inside plastic bags, and held in a cooler for three to four months until it was time to plant. The nursery owner thought they stayed moist enough that way, and anyway, they were watered in the rooting bench.

I suspected otherwise.

The day before the cuttings were to be put out in the rooting beds to be callused in preparation for planting, I arranged to have the bundles of cuttings stood up in water in big stock tanks overnight. They stood in just a couple of inches of water, enough to ensure that all the bottom ends were submerged.

The cuttings surely had life, because many of them began oozing sticky material from the top ends, and, when I nicked the bark, the inside was definitely juicier than it had been.

That fall, over forty-five hundred good Catawba vines were dug, and the owner had an embarrassment of riches without planting any additional cuttings, from 25 percent rooting to over 90 percent. This improvement was all from letting the cuttings stand in water overnight, so they finally had enough moisture to make lots of juicy callus tissue necessary for producing good, healthy roots.

is past. The soil should be as warm as it would be for setting out garden crops such as tomatoes.

While grape cuttings can be callused directly out of storage, a much higher percentage of cuttings will root well if some preparations are followed.

Hydrating cuttings. First, callus tissue is very tender and juicy; a cutting that contains sufficient water can produce callus more easily than a dry cutting. Cuttings benefit greatly from being soaked in water for several hours, or even overnight, prior to being callused. A nursery that had rarely had more than 20 percent usable plants from its Catawba cuttings saw an improvement to over 90 percent the first time the cuttings were soaked before callusing.

Stand bundles of cuttings in water deep enough to ensure that the bottoms of all cuttings are submerged—usually 3 or 4 inches of water. You can use a pail, a livestock watering pan, a molded plastic wading pool, or a box lined with several sheets of heavy plastic film as a container. One nurseryman lines the back of his pickup truck with plastic and uses that.

After cuttings soak for several hours, some of them may exude gummy material from the top ends. This varies with variety and is not harmful.

Rooting hormone. Next, while most grapes root naturally, the number of roots and the speed of rooting is enhanced by adding rooting hormone. A dip in liquid rooting hormone generally works better than rooting powders. Most liquid types contain fungicides to inhibit rot and have carriers such as dimethyl sulfoxide (DMSO) that ensure penetration of the hormone quickly into the cuttings' tissues. A five-second dip is sufficient with brands such as Dip'n'Grow. The hormone should be no more than medium strength, as too high a concentration of rooting hormone can make the cutting go all to callus and it won't root well. The exception would be some of the types that are difficult to root. Most American grapes need only light- to medium-strength rooting hormone.

At the time of this writing, I had started another experiment in rooting cuttings that had great initial results. Instead of applying rooting hormone, I wetted individual cuttings, dipped them in Endomycorrhizal Inoculant from Bio-Organics, and placed

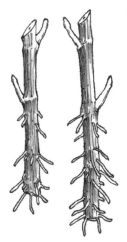

Cuttings, showing roots and white shoots pushing.

them in holes pre-punched in the soil of individual pots placed on a heat mat. (I pre-punched the holes in the soil to prevent the fungal powder from being scraped off when I pushed the cuttings into the soil.) I firmed the soil around the cuttings and watered them in. Within seventeen days, there were large, thick roots showing in the bottom of almost half the pots, which is at least one to two weeks before cuttings with rooting hormone usually show roots. Not long after, I heard of two other people who had tried the same sort of experiment with similar results. From this, it appears that mycorrhizal fungi are, in some conditions at least, able to promote root formation on unrooted grape cuttings.

Callusing methods that need no special equipment. Home growers can callus small amounts of cuttings by putting them in a black plastic trash bag along with some moist paper or peat moss and placing the bag where it can be kept at 80°F to 85°F (27°C to 29°C). The top of a refrigerator is often a good place, especially if the machine is in its own "nook" between cupboards with a low cupboard or ceiling close to the top of it. Heat constantly rises from the condensing unit in the back and collects around the top of the refrigerator, and the cuttings will callus in as little as a week. If small white shoots form, try not to break them off, as the cutting would have to use its reserves to produce more shoots when it is planted.

Another low-tech callusing method for a few cuttings is to plant them in a mix of three parts perlite and one part peat in a 1-gallon black plastic pot. Set the pot in a

---

When and How Does Callus Form?

CALLUS DOES NOT FORM over winter in stored cuttings. Cuttings require warmth for callus to form.

At 70°F, callusing will take about a month. Spring cuttings don't root any more slowly than winter ones, but you have to take them before the buds have swollen. Once they swell, the shoots will try to grow, and drain the cutting before it roots.

Rooting bench with heat mat in bottom.

warm, sunny area such as a greenhouse or cold frame. The black plastic pot warms and heats the root zone, stimulating callous formation and rooting. Anything larger than a 1-gallon pot holds too large a volume of planting material to heat evenly. If the pot can be kept constantly warm, rooting will take place in two to three weeks, though it can be as long as six weeks if temperatures fluctuate.

Heat mats and other aids. Most garden centers sell heat mats or small heat cables to put in the bottom of flats for the purpose of stimulating seed germination. These mats can provide a constant source of heat for efficient callusing of grape cuttings, too. However, while heat mats are not excessively expensive, they are enough of an investment that I don't recommend buying them unless you have other uses for them besides rooting cuttings.

If you do use a type with an adjustable thermostat, be sure to put a heat probe or thermometer with the temperature-sensing end at the same depth as the bottom of the cuttings, where callusing will occur. Simply setting the thermostat is not enough, as heat is lost as it travels up through the rooting medium. A setting of 80°F (27°C) at the thermostat might show up as 75°F (24°C) or cooler in the zone where the heat is needed. And while the loss of 5°F (3°C) may not seem significant, it can add an extra week to two weeks time to the callusing of the cuttings.

A method that has been successful for a grower I know is to prepare a bed outdoors and cover it with black plastic. (Prepare and water the soil before spreading the plastic.) Cuttings are then planted directly through holes punched in the plastic. It would seem to be a viable system, as the plastic would warm the soil enough to stimulate callusing and should speed growth of the plants once roots have formed.

Handling large quantities of cuttings. The storage of cuttings in sand pits, as mentioned earlier, was also a way to callus the cuttings before planting. While it worked fairly well, the grower had less control over the cuttings than with other methods. Disease and insects could invade the cuttings in the sand, and, since the grower had no control over the weather, the cuttings might callus earlier or later than desired, and might not callus uniformly.

Another method for callusing large quantities was the "sweat box." Cuttings were packed into very large wooden boxes with a layer of moist, baked, coarse sawdust around them, and the boxes were placed in thermostatically controlled rooms at 80°F (27°C). Within a week, the cuttings would be thoroughly callused and ready to plant. Often, so much callus formed all over the cuttings that the cuttings actually grew together in the bundles. cuttings also tended to push out many white shoots, which would break off in handling and cause the loss of some of the Cuttings. And with so much tender callus tissue formed, the cuttings had to be planted immediately on removal from the sweat box.

One large-scale method I've used is a rooting bench with a heat cable in the bottom.

The planting bench is a big, flat box with 12-inch-high sides made out of 2 x 6s. It was constructed in sections, with each section 4 feet from front to back and 8 feet long. The legs of the bench were 4 x 4s. The inside of the bench was treated with a horticulture-grade wood preservative that is nontoxic to plants, such as copper or zinc napthenate. It could also be painted with nontoxic latex paint, though this is not vital if the wood is well-preserved.

If the bench is located outdoors, it should have a low roof to keep the cuttings shaded, and, if possible, should be located on the north side of a building or wall. Some growers put such a bench in a walk-in cooler, where the cold air will retard bud break more efficiently than simply trusting to weather outdoors. In a cooler, cuttings callus with virtually no bud break at all. This makes the rooted cuttings much easier to handle, because they have no shoots that might drain the reserves of the cuttings before rooting occurs, or that might be broken during handling.

In the past, bottom heat in a bench was provided by an elaborate system of cables that were tedious to install and had to be protected from damage to prevent danger of electric shock. At that, such cables lasted for only a few seasons before they had to be replaced.

Now there are heat mats: sealed, rubberized mats with heat cables inside them. Requiring no installation, they can simply be laid where they are to be used and connected to a source of electricity. These are available in several sizes and work well for home growers. Some of the smaller mats available from Hydrofarm are just large enough for two flats of pots. Once the cuttings have been rooted, the mats can be used to start seeds, to provide heat under terrariums, and more.

The Monarch Company offers a system of collapsible flats and tall paper pots (the Zipset System) that make it easy to root grape cuttings on a heat mat. I've tried them and found that two of their flats fit neatly on the larger rubberized heat mat sold by Hydrofarm. Depending on the size of the pot you use, this setup can allow you to

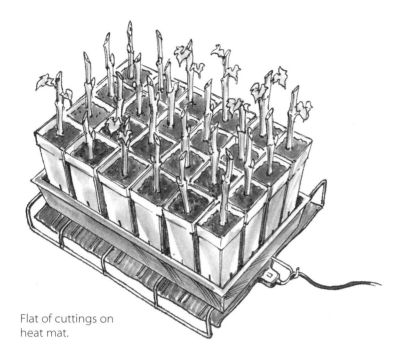

Flat of cuttings on heat mat.

root over one hundred cuttings in a small area. After the cuttings have rooted, they can be set out in the vineyards right in the pots, as the paper will disintegrate over time.

For bulk rooting, bundles of cuttings are loaded in the bench by standing them up, with the bottoms on the perlite, packing them as close together as possible, but with 2 or more inches of space between them and the wall of the bench. When all the cuttings are packed, perlite is poured in to one-half to three-quarters of the depth of the cuttings and watered to settle it in place. It is possible to store cuttings in the perlite for a few weeks before starting the heat, if necessary, providing the weather is not severe. Set the thermostat on the water heater at a temperature of 100°F to 110°F (38°C to 43°C) but check the temperature in the rooting zone (the area around the bottoms of the cuttings) with a probe thermometer

to be sure the temperature there is between 80°F and 85°F (27°C and 29°C). The benches usually need to be watered once a day, though this varies with outdoor benches. Use of peat with the perlite, at three or four parts perlite to one part peat, can improve water-holding capacity and reduce the need for watering.

Within five days, start checking the bundles of cuttings for callus. Most of the cuttings should be ready to plant within seven to ten days of starting the heat. Ideally, cuttings should have a ring of callus on the base, with roots just starting to show at planting time. Once callus is showing well, turn off the heat to slow excessive root production before the cuttings can be planted. If roots are too long, they will anchor in the bench and break when the bundles are removed, as well as breaking more easily when the cuttings are planted.

An alternate method is to plant the cuttings one to a pot, in flats, then put the flats on heat mats. Using 2 x 2 x 6-inch pots, fifty cuttings can be planted per flat. When the cuttings have rooted, they can be left in the pots for a while, if needed. If started in late winter (February in the Northern Hemisphere), such plants are usually of good size by May and can be planted out in their permanent location. It is necessary to ensure a good water supply for the young plants—1 to 2 inches per week, at least— but, with care, the vines can be trained the same season and should bear a cluster or two of fruit the following year.

Planting Cuttings

Because grape cuttings can be callused and ready to plant in a relatively short time, callusing should not be started until the planting site is ready to receive them, or can at least be tilled and prepared in time. Cuttings may either be planted in a nursery, in which case they are allowed to grow for a season, then dug as dormant vines the following winter and planted in their permanent locations, or they can be planted directly in their permanent locations. Both methods have advantages, as will be seen.

In a nursery, grape cuttings should be planted to at least half the depth of the cutting. In hot, dry climates, such as central and southern California, 18-inch cuttings are preferred and these are often planted to almost their full depth, with only the top bud exposed. Further, loose soil is hilled over the top of the cutting to protect it until the bud pushes and grows. In such cases, the soil must be kept cultivated and loose so it will not crust over the cutting. In cooler climates, shorter cuttings are planted more shallowly and soil is hilled around them to create a warmer rooting zone.

If you mulch cuttings, be sure to use dark materials. I have seen cuttings mulched with sawdust that was so light in color that

Clonal Selection

You would think that if plants are grown from cuttings, all the plants produced this way would be identical to the parent plant. In fact, they are not. Every day of its life, a plant is bombarded with ultraviolet light, cosmic rays, unknown chemicals from the environment, and more, all of which can cause mutations—sudden, heritable changes in the genes. Most of these are never seen, or cause changes that make no difference to the vine. But sometimes a cell that has a mutated gene is in position to grow and become the basis for a bud, which in turn grows into a new shoot. And all, or most, of the cells in that shoot will have the new mutation in them. If that shoot is then used as a cutting, the vine that grows from it will be genetically different from the vine it came from originally. It will most likely be recognized as the same variety, but it can differ in productivity, ripening time, color of fruit, differences in wine quality, and other characteristics. Usually it takes analysis such as careful measurement of the yield or testing of the fruit to determine the differences. The older a variety is, the more of these mutations that have developed in it, and the more there are to find if an observer knows what to look for.

This is the theory behind clonal selection, and the reason that there are many different selections of wine grapes. Researchers and growers have found different strains of varieties, such as Pinot Noir (for example) that perform differently from others. Some are better adapted to certain climates or soils than others. Some have enough differences in chemistry to affect the wine made from them. Some are more productive. So many clonal selections, as they are called, have been found in the classic varieties that it is impossible to say which is the original form.

While clonal selections are most often found in very large plantings of a single variety, they could show up anywhere. I once found a clone of Interlaken (a seedless variety) that had normal seeds. Such a grape would be very useful to breeders. Unfortunately, I lost my "find" to poor growing conditions, but there could be others.

So keep an eye on your own grapes. You might be surprised at what you find.

it created a zone of reflected heat at the point where the cutting met the mulch. At that point, tissues were killed, weakening the cuttings and very often resulting in a spot where crown gall entered and formed a large gall around the cutting.

Cuttings can be planted in a trench or cut made by a spade or plow, or in a strip cultivated and watered to create a soft mud into which the cuttings can simply be pushed. In such conditions, some roots may break off, but as long as the callus is intact, the cutting should be able to produce more of them. Cuttings in a nursery row should be spaced 6 inches apart, with rows 2 feet or more apart. By mid-season, the vines have usually grown enough to form a solid canopy over the row that blocks further weed growth and greatly reduces, if not eliminates, the need for cultivation for the rest of the season.

Cuttings should receive at least 1 inch of water per week, more in hot climates, so that the soil never dries out between waterings. Fertilize every week to two weeks with a balanced fertilizer, such as 16-16-16, or liquid fish emulsion (for the organic or home grower). Fertilizing should not be started until the cutting has 3 to 4 inches of shoot growth, as the new roots aren't able to take up fertilizer well before then.

Stop fertilizing in midsummer, or at least two months before frost, so the vine can slow its growth and begin to harden off. Watering should be stopped later, but at least one month before frost. If first frost can be severe in your location, it is better to stop applying water and fertilizer earlier and have smaller vines that are more thoroughly hardened than to keep encouraging big, lush vines that could be killed back by frost.

The advantage of growing plants in a nursery is that cultivation and care can be concentrated in a smaller area, so that one person can tend many vines. Also, dormant, nursery-grown vines are tougher and able to withstand more abuse during planting than tender, newly callused cuttings.

But transplanted dormant vines usually need a year to reestablish their roots, plus another year to have a trunk trained up, before they are ready to bear. Thus, at least three years must pass before nursery-grown vines start bearing fruit.

Callused cuttings planted in place, then watered and fertilized by drip irrigation, can establish their roots directly in place. They can often put on enough growth to allow the grower to train a shoot up as a trunk in the same season they are planted. The vine will be ready to bear one or two clusters of grapes the very next season after the cutting was started. Careful growers using this method have reported that 9 feet of growth from a new cutting was not uncommon. Bearing can start a full two years before a nursery-grown vine.

GREEN SOFTWOOD CUTTINGS *of* GRAPES

While all grapes can be grown from green cuttings, the method has special applications not suited to dormant cuttings.

For rapid propagation. With proper care, green cuttings can be rooted in as little as one week, potted in a greenhouse, and forced to grow quickly to generate more green cuttings. It is possible to start with one cutting and create several thousand in only a few months.

To save time. With green cuttings, vines can be started in summer and, properly handled, the vines can be planted out by early fall. Roots can establish themselves sufficiently during the fall, and the new vines can be ready to start training the following season, along with, or only slightly behind, the first planting.

To save varieties. If you only have one vine of a particular variety, and it is damaged in the middle of the growing year, you can take green cuttings to start a new one, saving the variety, if not the original vine.

To root difficult varieties. This is one of the most important reasons for growing grapes from green cuttings. Some varieties and species root poorly as dormant cuttings. Only green cuttings yield an adequate percentage of rooted vines to be commercially feasible. Muscadine grapes had to be propagated mainly by layering until the technique of taking green cuttings was developed. Many of the varieties produced by American grape breeder T. V. Munson had *Vitis lincecumii* in their parentage, which is hard to root from dormant cuttings, and many of the varieties inherited this trait. Almost certainly, some of his varieties were lost because nurserymen of the late nineteenth century and early twentieth century had too much trouble propagating them from dormant cuttings and discarded them as unprofitable.

Green cuttings can be made from any vigorously growing shoot on a vine. They should be taken early, usually no later than bloom time, to give the new vines time to grow and harden well, unless they can be held in a greenhouse over the winter. Avoid shoots that are not growing and have started to harden off (ones that have turned from green to brown). Cuttings should be about 6 inches long with two to three nodes. Only the top leaf is left attached, and if full size, it is cut in half to reduce transpiration. Don't remove all the leaves, as leafless cuttings don't root. Dip cuttings in liquid rooting hormone (see page 148) and plant in a mixture of three parts perlite and one part peat in a mist bench with 80°F to 85°F (27°C to 29°C) bottom heat in the root zone. A mist bench is the same arrangement as the rooting bench described on page 150, but with the addition of an overhead watering system to spray the cuttings at regular intervals, preventing desiccation. Such a bench is usually placed in a greenhouse or similar shelter, though in the southern United States, it may be set up outdoors in the summer, in a shaded, wind-sheltered location.

If a mist bench isn't available, use a flat with a heat mat in the bottom. Mist the flat by hand several times per day, or enclose it in a plastic tent to maintain humidity. Misting is preferable to a plastic tent in some cases, because the tent can get too hot and the lack of air circulation in it is more conducive to disease.

For small quantities of cuttings, you can use a black plastic pot with a clear plastic bag supported by sticks or wire over it. The bag shouldn't touch the cuttings, or rot may set in where moisture condenses. Place the pot in a bright, wind-sheltered location, though not in full sun. The black pot draws heat to the root zone. Any container larger than a 1-gallon pot usually doesn't heat evenly. While green cuttings will root in as little as seven to ten days with controlled, steady heat at 85°F (29°C) in the rooting zone, cuttings in plastic pots can take up to six weeks because of temperature fluctuations.

Once roots form, pot up the cuttings, then hold them in high humidity for another week, either under mist or in a plastic bag. Gradually wean the cuttings from high humidity. After that, grow them in a shade house, or at least out of direct sun for another two weeks or so. At this point, set the plants in the field, as long as you can water and fertilize regularly.

When setting rooted cuttings in the field, shade them to prevent sun scald. One method is to put an open milk carton around them, with the bottom of the carton partly surrounded with soil to hold it in place. Leave this protective container in place for a few weeks. Scorching may either kill the plant or cause it to lose its leaves, slowing its growth until it can push new leaves and resume growth. If you believe scorch may be a serious problem, hold the plants in pots protected from the sun until they are dormant, then plant them as normal dormant plants. As pot-grown plants, they will suffer less root disturbance than nursery-grown plants that have been dug, and will establish themselves in the field faster than nursery-grown vines.

Start small quanties of cuttings in a black plastic pot with a clear plastic bag supported by sticks or wire over it.

TROUBLE-SHOOTING GRAPE CUTTINGS

Are the cuttings dead or alive? To find out, scrape a small area of the bark off with a sharp knife. If the tissues under the bark are brown, the cutting is dead. If the cutting is still alive, there will be green under the bark.

Possible causes of dead cuttings

1. *Cuttings stored too wet.* Storing or shipping cuttings in soggy media will encourage rot, especially at room temperatures. The paper, peat, or other materials with the cuttings may have been too wet. If you can squeeze more than a very small amount of water out of the material, it is too moist.

2. *Cuttings stored too warm and/or too dry.* Cuttings left unprotected in warm temperatures will dry up and die very quickly. Prevent by sealing cuttings in plastic with only enough moisture-holding material to keep the inside of the bag humid—one sheet of moist paper towel is enough with a 1-gallon ziplock bag of cuttings.

3. *Cuttings shipped unprotected.* People sometimes ship cuttings in a plain envelope with nothing to keep them moist. In such conditions, after two days in the mail, the cuttings are just dead, dry sticks. Prevent by shipping cuttings with moist paper, inside a plastic bag to prevent drying.

4. *Disease.* Rarely, rot can infect an otherwise properly handled cutting and kill it. This is not common. More often it happens because cuttings are kept too wet when being rooted in pots, especially with a peat-based soil mix that stays very wet. Prevent by using a light, fast-draining mix.

5. *Incorrect disinfection.* Cuttings may have been treated to get rid of disease organisms, but disinfectant was either too strong or wasn't used properly. For example, a 5 percent solution of chlorine bleach can be used as a disinfectant, but

if it isn't rinsed off completely after the treatment, it will continue to act on the cutting and may burn or kill tissues.

Possible problems with live cuttings

1. *Cutting is callused and has roots, but the shoots aren't growing.* Cuttings were exposed to very cold temperatures that killed the buds. This can happen either before cuttings are taken from the vine, or when they are in transit. To check, slice into a bud with a very sharp knife or razor blade. If the bud is dead, it will be dark and brown inside. If there is any green showing, even around the edge of the bud, there is a chance the secondary or tertiary bud is alive and can still grow, though it may be slow to do so.

2. *Buds have broken and started to grow, but there are no roots.* The air temperature is too high, or the temperature in the rooting zone is too low. The ideal temperature to start the rooting process is 80°F to 85°F (27°C to 29°C) *in the root zone.* If the air is too warm, the buds break before the roots form, and the cutting may collapse when food runs out. Try to raise the temperature in the root zone.

3. *Cuttings take a long time to callus and root.*

a. Temperature in the root zone is too low, or cuttings are being callused at too low a temperature. At 85°F (24°C), cuttings will callus in seven days. At 75°F (24°C), it may take as long as three weeks. At 70°F (21°C), callusing may take over one month.

b. Temperature is not constant. If the temperature fluctuates between day and night, callusing and rooting will be slower than if it can be held steady, or with no more than 5°F (3°C) difference between night and day.

4. *Some varieties have rooted while others are not showing activity.*

a. Different varieties vary in how fast and how well they will root. This is especially true of American and French Hybrid varieties, because they often have more than one species in their ancestry, and some species are harder to root than others. For example, varieties with *Vitis lincecumii* or *V. aestivalis* in their background are often hard to root. Solution: Be sure conditions are as close to ideal as possible and be patient.

5. *Cuttings started to root, but roots withered and there seem to be little worms eating the roots.* Soil/rooting media was too wet and rot (damping-off fungus) has attacked the plant through the roots. White worms are the larvae of fungus gnats, which are feeding on the fungus in the soil: They aren't responsible for the death of the cuttings, but arrived after the rot got started in the soil.

LAYERING

The actual process of layering is simple. In one method, a dormant cane is bent to the ground and a section about 1 foot long is held down in a hole with pegs or a rock and covered with 2 to 4 inches of soil. All buds on the cane should be trimmed off, from the point where the cane is buried back to its point of origin. This prevents unwanted shoots from taking energy from the section that is to root and become the new vine. One foot or more of the end of the vine should extend beyond the hole.

During the growing season, the section in the ground roots, and by the following dormant season, the vine is generally rooted enough that it can be cut free from the parent plant and handled like an ordinary, nursery-produced vine. Some grapes, such as muscadines, may be left buried for an extra season to ensure a good root system.

An alternate method that produces more vines is to peg the entire length of the cane to the ground in a shallow trench 2 inches deep. The vine may or may not be nicked or cut near each node to encourage rooting. As the shoots grow, the cane is covered with soil or moist sawdust, and the cane tends to produce roots at each node. During the dormant season, the cane is uncovered, and each rooted shoot can be cut from the cane to become a new plant. Layering takes more labor than rooting cuttings, and the amount of plants produced per parent vine is lower, making commercial production by layering more expensive.

Air Layering

Another variation is air layering, in which a shoot is layered in a container of soil or rooting media away from the ground. I've never used air layering with grapes, but some southern breeders and grape growers have used it to propagate muscadine and muscadine hybrids as a means of producing plants with no soil pests on the rooted plant.

I have air-layered other plants though, and have found an easy method. Cut a large

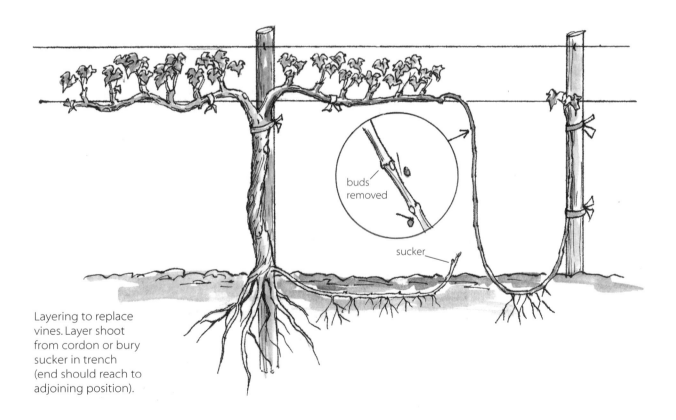

buds
removed

sucker

Layering to replace vines. Layer shoot from cordon or bury sucker in trench (end should reach to adjoining position).

Air layering a green shoot.

plastic freezer bag (quart size is usually large enough) open into a single sheet of plastic. If the bag is a ziplock type, remove the ziplock. Bring the edges together around the stem of the plant and fold them into a double-thick seam along the side, then staple the seam. This creates a tube that surrounds the stem. Now put a twist tie around the stem at the point where you wish to root it, tightening just enough to barely start to pinch into the stem. Apply a little rooting hormone just above the tie. Tie the bottom of the tube shut around the stem and fill the tube from the top with soil, rotted sawdust, or other material. Water the material, and tie the top shut. Support the bag if needed. Keep the tube out of direct sun to prevent baking the contents. Watch for roots to show inside—they'll be visible through the plastic. Once it has rooted, you can cut the new plant loose and pot it up.

Replacing Vines by Layering

Layering has a useful application for vineyardists. When a vine is lost in an established vineyard, a new young vine planted in the empty space may be slow-growing and difficult to bring to bearing because of shade and root competition from surrounding established vines. In such a case, it is faster and more effective to layer a cane from an adjoining vine to the site of the missing vine than to plant a new one. Instead of competing with other vines, a layered vine is supported by the older vine to which it is attached.

Usually, an adjoining, existing vine will have a cane long enough to reach the site where the new vine is wanted. A vigorous cane may be long enough that the end of the cane beyond the layered area can be tied to the post and will reach the first wire, thus automatically becoming the trunk of

Layering vines in vineyards.

the new vine. Cut off all buds on the cane between the point where it comes off the parent vine and the point where it is pegged down and buried. The layered cane roots at the covered area and the new vine often has a few clusters the same year, coming into good production the next year. The new vine is left attached to the old one until the trunk of the new vine is visibly larger in diameter than the portion of the cane between the old vine and the layered area—usually, this takes at least three years. The new vine fills in the gap the same season it is layered, versus three years or more for a newly planted vine to even reach the first wire.

Seen from above, canes radiate from crown.

Layering to propagate difficult varieties.

One peculiarity of layering is that common sense suggests the layered vine would be a parasite, draining the older vine to which it is attached. Oddly, I've often seen the opposite in my vineyard: The layered vine actually "feeds" the older vine.

Layered vines are often large enough the year after layering to have a crop about equal to that of an established solo vine. The parent vine, however, may have a crop that is larger than usual, but only on the side where the layered vine is attached—the other side should bear an average crop. Instead of draining the parent vine, layered vines actually boost them. After a few years, the two seem to balance out, with both bearing good crops.

This observation has obviously been made before, as one old English vineyard system advocated grafting the ends of shoots from adjoining vines together, making each row into one big "super-vine." This seems reasonable, as connected vines could compensate each other for problems like variable soil, with vines in good soil sending energy to ones in poor soil. I have layered vines that are still connected to the parent vine after more than five years, and the connected plants have done better and produced more than neighboring single vines of the same variety. With Himrod and Duchess, both highly vigorous varieties, being connected made the vines do so well I had to cut them loose to *reduce* the vigor. Both the parent and the layered vines had become too vigorous to handle.

Move It!

"THERE'S A HUGE OLD GRAPEVINE in the yard of my [fill in name of older, probably deceased relative] that I want to move. Can I do it?"

Moving a grapevine that is more than two or three years old can be a difficult proposition. Grapes have a large root system that goes a long way, and if you don't get enough of the roots when you move the vine, you are wasting your time. I moved dormant, established vines from one part of my vineyard to another when a road project made it necessary. I had moved dormant fruit trees in the past and, using that as a guide, took as many roots with the old vines as I did when moving the fruit trees. I had moved the trees successfully, but at least half of the vines didn't survive the move, not even to trying to put out new buds anywhere. Three Canadice vines, however, did put out a few shoots less than 6 inches long, but the cordon arms died back to the trunk. It took the vines four years to come back to a condition even close to their condition before the move. At that, all I saved was the trunk. I could have planted a new, young vine and had it trained up in the same amount of time. In fairness, I couldn't keep those transplanted vines watered, which would likely have made a difference, but it does show how difficult it can be to move a big old vine.

In short, unless you have to have *that* particular vine, it makes more sense to propagate a new vine from the old one than it does to try and move it. However, if you *must* move it, consider hiring a tree transplanting service that can use a big clamshell-type digging device that will take a very large ball of soil and roots with the vine. Then be sure to water the newly moved vine religiously and keep it mulched and fertilized with something mild such as fish fertilizer.

GRAFTING GRAPEVINES

Why graft grapes if they are the types that root easily from cuttings? Because many of the best fruiting varieties are not always able to grow in all soils and may be susceptible to diseases or pests of the roots. Additionally, rootstocks can be used that interact with the scion varieties to have such effects as reducing or increasing vigor, delaying or hastening ripening, increasing cold hardiness, and more. This will be discussed more in chapter 9.

Bench Grafting

Bench grafting is probably the most widely practiced type of grafting with grapes. This is simply grafting a dormant, one-bud scion of the desired fruiting variety to a dormant rootstock cutting. Since the cuttings are not rooted when grafted, there is no bleeding to interfere with the grafts, as happens when grafting to established vines. Before the grafting is done, the rootstock cuttings are disbudded—all buds are cut or rubbed off. With small amounts of cuttings, this can be done with a sharp knife. In large quantities, buds are often removed by holding the cuttings against a revolving wire brush. Disbudding is done to prevent suckers from arising from the stock, because grapes cannot produce new buds if there are no pre-existing ones. The stock will still root, but it can't produce shoots.

When bench grafting is done by hand, a standard whip graft, or a whip and tongue graft, is used. However, instead of sealing it with grafting wax or other grafting compound, the graft is left bare. It can be tied with raffia or other biodegradable twine or stapled with a heavy-duty desk stapler to hold it together, but nothing further is needed. Instead, the grafts are bundled and callused (as described on page 148) to heal the scion and stock together. After callusing, however, it is common practice in commercial nurseries to dip the graft and scion in melted wax to keep the tender, newly callused graft from drying out. When the scion bud grows, it easily breaks through the wax coat. Home growers can use a latex-type grafting compound on the graft union—just be sure not to coat the bud itself.

For large-scale production of grafted vines, nurseries commonly use machines to cut the stock and scions. One type of machine cuts matching slots and tabs in the ends of the stock and scion pieces using circular saws with multiple blades. A new type of cutter cuts a rounded tab on one cutting and a matching hole, much like a piece of jigsaw puzzle and its matching slot, so the stock and scion lock together and can't pull apart.

When to Bench Graft. If you want to produce grafted vines to have them actively growing and be able to set them out after frost, figure on grafting six to eight weeks before the time you intend to put them in the field. Once the grafts have been made, they must be callused, which will take about two weeks with good care. Newly callused plants that are starting to root must then be potted and held in a greenhouse or other warm place to get roots well established, which should take at least another month. Mycorrhizal fungi will help develop a larger, more branched root system. Don't be in a hurry to set the plants in

buds removed
from rootstock

Simple whip graft.

the field—plants set out when it is too cool won't gain any advantage over ones that have been held until the weather is warm.

Field Grafting

Anyone who has been growing vines for a while eventually will have an established vine they no longer want, but don't wish to destroy. The obvious solution seems to be to graft a new variety onto the old vine. However, grapes do not respond readily to the same sorts of grafting methods popular with fruit trees, due to problems in grape physiology. In particular, once a vine is active in the spring, grafting wounds bleed profusely. This isn't harmful to the vine, but it makes grafting difficult, as such bleeding will prevent scions from healing to the established vine. There are ways to get around this, and the easiest, most effective techniques will be covered here.

Dormant-to-green grafting. While woody tissues of grapes will bleed profusely, especially in the early part of the growing season, green shoots do not bleed. This can be put to good advantage in grafting. The following method is the most effective I've encountered for changing the variety of an established vine through grafting. It avoids all the problems of cleft grafting or bark grafting of grape vines and gives as close to 100 percent success as any grafter is likely to achieve.

During the dormant season, collect cuttings of the variety you wish to graft onto the old vine and store them. Be sure to take cuttings of several different diameters. In spring, about the time the vines are starting to grow, cut the old vine off within 1 or 2 inches of the ground. This will cause the remaining stump to sprout vigorous new shoots. When several of the new

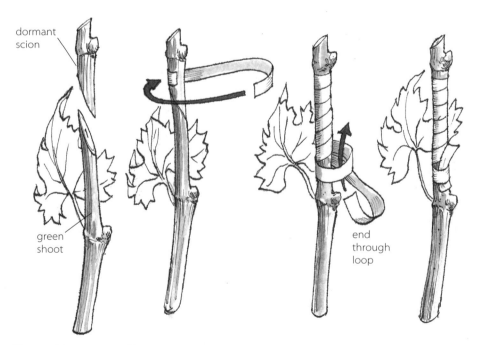

dormant scion

green shoot

end through loop

Dormant-to-green graft.

shoots are 1 to 3 feet long, it is time to graft, as long as the weather is settled and daytime temperatures are consistently 75°F (24°C) or higher.

Compare diameters of the cuttings and the shoots until you find as close to an exact match as possible. Only one bud is needed on the scion to be grafted, and it should be removed from the cutting with as long a clear stretch below it as possible. Make matching long, diagonal cuts on the green shoot and below the bud on the cutting. Practice beforehand until you can make a long diagonal cut with one slice of a very sharp, straight-bladed knife. Using two or more cuts can result in "wavy" surfaces that will not match smoothly. Done correctly, the two diagonal cuts should match. Work quickly to prevent drying of the green shoot, which may cause the cut to seal over and not be able to heal to the scion. It can be helpful to keep a container of water to dip the scions in, to prevent their cut surfaces from drying.

Wrap the grafted area with rubber budding strips or ordinary string. No sealant is necessary, though I found I had better results in a cool year when I wrapped the graft with strips of plastic flagging tape.

Tie the shoot to a stick or other support, because such green shoots easily break loose from their attachment point on the old wood. If the one-bud cutting has been fitted properly, it will heal to the shoot in a few days and the new bud will push and grow within two weeks of grafting.

You may graft more than one shoot, but once one has started to grow and looks healthy, it's best to remove all the other grafted shoots, as well as keeping all other shoots removed. With the full vigor of the established root system behind it, the new bud will produce a whole new vine in one season and should start bearing the very next year. Because the trunk of the old, cut-off vine will eventually rot, it is advisable to mound soil around the new trunk, to encourage it to root on its own so that the rotting out of the old trunk will not harm it. This is the reason the old trunk should be cut as close to the ground as possible, so new shoots will come out low enough to the ground to be easily covered with soil, to root them.

As an alternate form of this method, shoots at the top of the vine may be grafted. In this case, the rest of the vine remains the old variety. If you try this, be sure to tie a large strip of bright flagging tape or other such marker near the graft to make it possible to find the graft later. Otherwise, it can get lost in the foliage of the vine.

Green-to-green grafting. This method is similar to the previous one, except that scions are cut from new, green shoots at the time of grafting. When the stock and scion are matched, the graft can be either tied with string or bound with budding plastic strips or para-film. All leaves are removed from the scions, and the whole graft may need to be covered with a plastic bag for a few days to prevent desiccation. A successful graft will usually start to grow within 1 week on a vigorous vine.

Chip budding. At the time chip budding is usually done, in late summer, the vines will not bleed, which makes it much easier to get the buds to heal in correctly. Chip budding technique is covered in other books and since it is mainly a commercial technique,

I won't describe the full method here. It can either be done on young vines, which were planted that spring, or on shoots from older vines that have been cut back.

The main use of chip building is as a field-grafting technique on rootstocks. All the buds but the top one are removed from the rootstock cutting before it is rooted. Once planted and growing, it is chip-budded in late summer. If the bud is successful, the top is cut off the vine the next spring to both force the scion bud and remove anything from the rootstock itself that could produce suckers. Since grapes can't produce adventitious buds with the top gone, there is nothing left on the rootstock plant except the scion bud that can grow. The drawback is that, if the scion bud fails, the rootstock will die because it can't produce any new shoots.

Nurse grafting for hard-to-root dormant cuttings. There are times when the only way to procure material of a variety is as dormant cuttings. Green cuttings are hard to ship, especially since they often must be sent at times of the year when they will travel through hot weather and arrive in poor shape. If the variety is one of the hard-to-root types, a method is needed to ensure success.

I have used a variation on bench grafting as a way to root such dormant cuttings of hard-to-root varieties or species with almost 100 percent success. Simply stated, just graft a disbudded, one-bud cutting of an easily rooted grape on the *bottom* of the cutting of the hard-to-root grape as a "nurse." Use a heavy-duty stapler to staple it in place and put it directly in to root. Even hard-to-

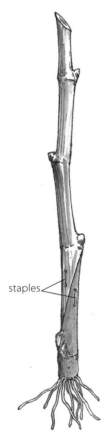

staples

Nurse graft. Note staples to hold graft together.

root grapes will callus enough to heal to the piece of nurse cutting, and the nurse piece will root and support the cutting for as long as it takes for it to root.

Be sure to plant such a vine deep enough to thoroughly cover the graft union, so the variety being "nursed" will root. In some cases, it can help to put a wire, such as a twist tie, just above the graft union. As the vine grows it will be slowly girdled at that site, which helps encourage the nursed vine to root on its own.

GROWING GRAPES *from* SEED

The only way to reproduce selected grapes true to type is to grow cuttings of them. Plant seeds of, for example, Concord, and the odds of getting a seedling that is even similar to Concord are very small. That's because most cultivated grapes contain such a mixture of genes that the seedlings get all sorts of different, new combinations of those genes. So the only times grapes are grown from seed is when the grower is deliberately looking for seedlings that have new combinations of the parent traits, or when vines of pure species are being raised. Within a species, individual vines will resemble each other much more than any two seedlings out of a single cultivated variety, which is something plant collectors rely on when gathering material for breeding or botanical collections. But home growers can grow seedlings for other reasons, such as to be used as ornamentals. Many American grape species not only have handsome, ornamental vines, but the flowers of most are actually quite fragrant.

Get A Grip on Your Grapes

IN AUGUST 1994, I ATTENDED A MEETING of the North American Fruit Explorers in Massachusetts. While there, I was able to accompany Roger Swain on a visit to a man with whom I had corresponded for years, but had never met in person—the late Professor Elwyn Meader. Professor Meader was a vegetable breeder at the University of New Hampshire for many years, and if you've ever had a garden, you have probably come in contact with some of his work at one time or another. But that's another story.

During the visit with Professor Meader at his home in New Hampshire, he referred to a variety of rhubarb he had tested one time and said that it "was hard to get a grip on it." Roger caught my puzzled expression and let me know that "hard to get a grip on" was New England for "had a laxative effect."

That's a very fitting expression for the effect that fresh grapes have on many people: They can't get a grip on them.

That really shouldn't be a surprise, since the aim of a grapevine is to reproduce itself, and the fruit is simply a way that it ensures the process. Birds and animals eat the fruit, then deposit the "remains" some distance away from the parent vine, hopefully in a spot where the new vine can grow with little or no competition. The laxative effect is simply the grape's means of ensuring that the seed doesn't stay in the digestive system long enough to be seriously damaged or killed. The system works so well that most grape seed will germinate better after passing through a digestive tract than if they were never eaten. Digestive juices break down the seed coat somewhat and remove substances that inhibit germination, so the seedling can break through the seed coat more readily. The stimulating effect is strong enough that most birds usually drop the seeds from the grapes they eat no more than 1 or 2 miles from where they ate the fruit.

But if grapes are so well adapted to being eaten by animals, animals are just as well adapted to eating grapes. This *includes* humans. The stimulation of the digestive system helps it expel materials that would ordinarily stagnate and allow the body to absorb toxins back into the system. So powerful is this cleansing action that books have been written about the healing power of grapes. There are even old cancer treatments using grapes. My father was a doctor who used such treatments successfully on occasion. One of my aunts had a pancreatic cancer that went into remission and shrank considerably on the treatment, but she tired of it and quit, allowing the tumor to return.

What it comes down to is that when you eat grapes and find it "hard to get a grip on them," you are actually having a normal reaction to them. If it seems harsh at first, it's because the grapes are pushing old material out ahead of them. Keep eating them for a while and the plumbing opens up and starts running smoothly, if a bit more frequently than you might be used to.

So don't worry: Your reaction to grapes is just what Nature intended.

When growing grapes from seed, the fresher the seed is, the better the rate of germination. If possible, use seed fresh from the fruit, cleaned, but not allowed to dry. Seed which has become completely dry, especially if it has been stored that way for a long time, will usually produce fewer seedlings. Research has shown that such dry seeds aren't necessarily dead, but that dryness puts the seed into a very deep dormancy that is hard to break.

If you are extracting seed from just a few berries, and the grapes aren't too unpleasant to eat, carefully eating the grapes and cleaning the seeds in your mouth is the simple way to go. With some species, such as *V. riparia*, which have high acid, cleaning seeds from more than a few berries this way can make your mouth and tongue sore. In that case, it is better to cut the berries and remove the seeds with the point of a sharp knife, or rub them through a coarse sieve to loosen the flesh, then float the flesh and skins off in water. If the seed has been freed from the flesh, the pulp and skins will float above them in the water. Any seeds that float are generally empty and will not grow; discard them. The percentage of "floaters" will vary with the variety and even the species. Female-flowered grapes that are well pollinated generally produce fewer floaters than perfect-flowered types. Fill the container with water and carefully pour off the pulp and skins. Repeat as needed until the seed has collected at the bottom of the container and there is no remaining pulp.

Stratifying Seed

Grape seed requires stratification, exposure to cold (but not freezing) temperatures in a moist environment in order to break down the substances that keep the seeds dormant, before they will germinate. If the seed is dry, start by soaking it in water for three days, with a change of water every day. This helps start the leaching out of some of the germination inhibitors and rehydrates the dry seed.

Next, mix the seed with moist peat moss, which not only holds the moisture needed for stratification, but has natural germicidal properties that help keep mold and rot from ruining the seed. On the rare occasions mold has appeared in seeds I have stratified, it has either been only surface mold, or the seed was hollow and nonviable to start with. Either way, the mold did no harm. Only a small amount of peat is needed, no more than 1 or 2 tablespoons per hundred seeds, and it should be moist, but not soggy. It should be possible to squeeze only a small amount of water out of the moss, and then only by squeezing fairly hard.

Put the mixture in a small plastic bag. Ziplock types are easiest to use and can be labeled with a permanent pen. Store the seed at temperatures between 35°F and 42°F (0°C and 6°C) for three months to stratify the seed. If the seed stays in stratification longer, it will not be harmed. Seed can be kept refrigerated for up to one year with no ill effects. Some grape species and certain varieties can germinate after as little as one month in stratification, but three months should cover the requirements of all species. In the days before refrigeration, it was common to plant seed directly in the ground in the fall, or in pots or flats that could be stored in an unheated shed for the winter. If you try this, it is wise to protect the seed from rodents by covering the seed rows, pots, or flats with wire screen. For seed rows, bend the screen into a U-shaped tube and press the ends into the soil to provide protection for the seed row and shelter for the emerging seedlings as well.

Germinating Seed

Once stratified, seed may be planted directly out in rows in the ground when soil is warm, or started much earlier, in flats or pots in a greenhouse. Again, use the screen described above to protect outdoor-planted seed from rodents. It also protects seedlings from slugs. Even with protection, this method should only be used with mass-extracted seed where loss of some of the seedlings is not a problem. More valuable seeds, such as those from controlled crosses, should be planted in pots or flats in a cold frame or greenhouse where they can be watched and protected more closely.

Seeds of many grapes appear to respond to day length. In my work, even when temperatures are an ideal 68°F (20°C) at night to 75°F to 80°F (24°C to 27°C) during the day, the greatest amount of germination may not start until the seeds receive fifteen to fifteen and a half hours of daylight, at least for temperate-zone grapes. Tropical species may respond differently. Supplemental light can be used to help augment germination early in the year before natural day length reaches fifteen hours. Once the seedlings come up, they are less dependent on day length for their growth.

Rate and speed of germination varies considerably with different species. *Vitis rupestris*, *V. riparia*, and *V. longii* (more recently known as *V. acerifolia*), as well as

---

The Natural Logic of Seeds

WHEN YOU GROW SEEDS of different grape species, you soon notice that some germinate quickly and almost every seed comes up, while others take their time and only part of them come up in a given year. My own feeling is that this is related to the habitat of the species.

Seeds of *Vitis riparia*, *V. rupestris* and *V. longii* all germinate quickly, and essentially all seedlings come up at once. All three of these species are riverbank species, which suggests that they are adapted to having only one period in the spring when the river floods or otherwise is high enough to provide water for the seedlings to grow, so they must germinate quickly. Further, ungerminated seed would probably either be washed away or in some sort of danger, so all of it germinates at one time, rather than leaving some ungerminated seeds for another year.

Vitis labrusca, *V. aestivalis,* and others are woodland species. They must wait for good conditions of warmth and moisture, so they germinate slowly, to be sure at least some seedlings come up when conditions are ideal. Also, since vines may be scattered farther apart, pollination and fruit set are not guaranteed every year. It is to the vine's advantage for some seed to sit for more than one year before germinating, in case there is a crop failure, and in case conditions one season turn uncertain and kill the first group of seedlings that germinate.

many hybrids with these species in their ancestry, will begin to germinate within two to three weeks, and most all the seed will germinate within a span of one week to two weeks, with very close to 100 percent of the seed sprouting. A number of the French Hybrids, which have *V. rupestris* and *V. riparia* in their ancestry, behave this way. Species such as *V. labrusca* and *V. vinifera* may take more than one month for the first seedling to emerge, with seedlings continuing to come up for another month or longer. As few as 30 percent of the total seeds will sprout. Many American varieties with *V. labrusca* in their parentage follow this pattern. However, with some species that are slow to germinate and have a low percentage germination, much of the ungerminated seed remaining in the soil will germinate after it is stratified a second time. Some growers have even found healthier, stronger plants in the second "crop" of seedlings than in the first, from the same batch of seed. I have taken flats of ungerminated seed left after the seedlings from the germinated seed were removed, put the flat in the cooler in a plastic bag, and after three months, returned the flat to the greenhouse. After that second stratification, half or more of the seed remaining in the soil germinated.

In short, grape propagation is often easier, and certainly is no more difficult, than it is with any other fruit crop, though it may be necessary to use different methods than with other fruits.

9 *ROOTSTOCKS*

W HEN THE AMERICAN grapevine pest phylloxera arrived in France in 1863, it set off a chain reaction that few could have foreseen. Until that time, essentially all grapes were grown on own-rooted vines. Phylloxera readily attacked the roots of *vitus vinifera* grapes, and for a time, it looked as if vinifera grapes could no longer be grown in Europe. However, researchers discovered that the roots of American grape species were resistant to phylloxera, and that vinifera grapes could be grafted onto the American species and survive and produce again.

It soon became evident that different rootstocks gave different results: Some lacked tolerance for the high-lime soils in parts of France; some needed very moist soils to grow well; and others made the varieties grafted on them more vigorous than before. Also, some people felt that the wine from grapes grafted on American rootstocks was not the equal of wines from the same grapes grown on their own roots.

Some French breeders began to crossbreed the American species with vinifera grapes in hopes of creating varieties that wouldn't need to be grafted to rootstocks. Their efforts resulted in the Hybrid Direct Producers, or French Hybrids, as they are known in North America.

Others felt that rootstocks didn't have that much effect on fruit quality and began to crossbreed American species with varying traits in hopes of producing rootstocks that would be reliable in many different situations. For instance, *Vitis riparia* has very good resistance to phylloxera and cold, but doesn't tolerate alkaline soil and isn't always vigorous. In some stocks, *V. riparia* has been crossed with *V. rupestris* to create rootstocks with more tolerance of alkaline (or at least less acid) soils and with more vigor. Note that rootstocks are usually identified only with a number and a breeder's initials or name.

Besides conferring the ability to grow in the presence of phylloxera, rootstocks have other effects as well. Some of these effects include:

- Reducing the vigor of a too-vigorous variety so that it produces more fruit and less growth, which also makes the vines easier to manage.
- Invigorating weak varieties.
- Increasing the cold hardiness of a variety.
- Causing a variety to ripen earlier than it might on its own roots.
- Conferring the ability to grow where there is disease or pests in the soil (besides phylloxera) that might harm the plant if it were growing on its own roots.

Even with the advantages a rootstock can confer on a vine, the majority of vines sold in the United States, at least for home use, are own-rooted. There are several reasons:

- Grafted vines are more expensive, and the average home grower will buy a cheap, own-rooted vine rather than a more expensive grafted one.
- Most American and French Hybrid varieties sold, particularly table grapes, have been bred to grow well (or well enough) on their own roots.
- If a grafted vine is killed back by an extra-cold winter, disease, or injury, it must be replaced, as no regrowth will sprout from the rootstock.
- Producing grafted vines for a mass market is nearly impossible. Different rootstocks need specific climate and soil conditions. A wholesale nursery trying to produce grafted vines for resale by retail outlets around the country would incur far too much expense in grafting

many different rootstocks to the same variety. This could easily triple the price of vines sold to home growers.

Does rootstock *really* affect the variety grafted to it that much? It certainly does, in many ways. As an example, here's what one commercial wine grower in California had to say:

> In my climate, the differences of the rootstocks on timing of budburst and flowering is noticeable.
>
> The first vines to push buds were grafted on stocks of Riparia x Rupestris parentage. These included the rootstocks 101-14 Mgt, 3309 C, and Schwarzman.
>
> The next group to break bud, a week or two later, were on Riparia x Berlandieri rootstocks, including 5C Teleki, SO 4, 5BB Selection Kober, 5A Teleki, and others.
>
> Last, and maybe three weeks or so behind the early rootstocks, are the vines on Berlandieri x Rupestris rootstocks, including 140 R, 1103 P, and 110 R.
>
> Flowering times followed a similar pattern.
>
> If you are in an area of springtime winds and are getting hammered during flowering, the late-flowering rootstocks might be of interest. Last year we got hit by more wind than normal and the varieties on Berlandieri x Rupestris rootstocks set significantly more fruit than any of the other rootstocks.
>
> I can't tell the difference in the juice or wine, but some allegedly can. They claim the 101-14, 3309 imparts earthiness and complexity, whereas SO4, 5C, and others impart fruitiness."

Note the last paragraph above. The difference in the quality of wine made from grapes grafted on rootstocks versus own-rooted vines has long been a bone of contention. There *are* differences, and it doesn't even take an unusual rootstock to cause them. I know a winemaker who showed me how the variety Pinot Gris, when grafted on Reisling (which is the same species as Pinot Gris) would produce wines that always "stuck" with 2 percent residual sugar left and wouldn't ferment to completely dry wine. The chemistry of the Pinot Gris grapes was changed by the Reisling roots enough that it had different winemaking characteristics than when grown on its own roots.

In Germany, the effort has been to create rootstocks that are as similar to the varieties grafted on them as possible, to eliminate many of the influences the rootstock might have on the wine quality. The German breeders do this by crossing the rootstock with the intended variety (we'll say Riesling in this case). From among the seedlings, the breeders select vines that have the desired rootstock quality (phylloxera resistance, cold hardiness, or whatever), but have fruit similar to Riesling. Then that selected seedling is crossed with Riesling (this is what plant breeders call backcrossing), and seedlings from that cross are selected again. The goal is a vine that is as similar as possible to the wine parent in fruit quality, but with the traits desired from the rootstock parent.

The changes made by rootstocks on wine quality aren't necessarily bad. Here's a comment from a grower in the cool northwest part of Washington State.

Our experience in the Puget Sound region has been that we have had smaller, earlier-ripening grapes when grafted on rootstocks. We have the Pommard clone of Pinot Noir on its own roots next to Pommard on 3309 C. The fruit of vines on 3309 C is about a week earlier in reaching ideal levels of sugar and acid. It is visibly riper as well. The greatest boon is the decrease in vegetation. The 3309 C vines look positively "Mediterranean" with their sparse growth and easily visible clusters. The own-rooted vines are a thick mass of vegetation with second- and third-crop fruit set all through them. A nasty job to remove!

Our region has very dry summers compared to the areas east of the Rockies. I wonder if this has any bearing on the different result?

While it may cost more to graft vines on rootstocks, the added expense can be more than offset by the change in the vine's performance. In a study conducted between 1995 and 1998 at the Ohio Agricultural Research & Development Center (OARDC) Grape Farm in Kingsville, Ohio, the performance of vinifera varieties and training systems were compared for White Riesling and Cabernet Franc when grown on their own roots and when grafted on rootstocks. Data from the 1997 harvest showed that total yield of own-rooted vines was 3.47 tons per acre, compared to the average total yield of 6.38 tons per acre for the seven rootstocks tested in the study. For a commercial grower, from a cost/value standpoint, the "savings" from using self-rooted vines is a false economy when one considers the difference in yield—83.9 percent higher!

Do I use rootstocks? No. My climate and soil don't require them, and in my evaluations I want to know how the variety does on its own roots.

If you *do* want to try grafting vines to see if a rootstock will improve them, refer to the techniques described in chapter 8. But which rootstocks should you use? You can try rootstocks recommended in the table below, but it is not necessary to stay with established rootstocks. Some growers needing a rootstock to add cold hardiness have found the fruiting variety Valiant able to increase the hardiness of varieties grafted on it. Other fruiting varieties with exceptional hardiness, vigor, or other useful traits can often double as rootstocks. Baco Noir will invigorate weak varieties grafted on it.

The table below is a generalized list of rootstock varieties and their characteristics that will get you started.

Home growers who live in areas where there are wild grape species might try using cuttings of them as rootstocks. At least two growers I know have started experiments using their local wild grapes as rootstocks in hopes of helping named grapes adapt better to the local conditions. This can be done in one of two ways. One is to cut the vine off and graft directly to the wild root system. This can be a problem if the

TABLE 9-1

Rootstock Characteristics

Characteristics	Rootstock Name
Rootstocks for Cold Climates	
Reduce vigor and/or speed up ripening	SQR or other 100 percent *V. riparia;* possibly 101-14 in soil with low fertility
Enhance vigor/productivity	SO4
Resistance to phylloxera	3309C, SQR, 101-14, S04
Resistance to nematodes	1613 C might work (depending on the type of nematode) but it is not phylloxera-resistant; Borner
Tolerance to alkaline soil	161-49C
Rootstocks for Warm Climates	
Reduce vigor and/or speed up ripening	Pure *V. riparia,* such as 3309 C if irrigation is available
Enhance vigor/productivity	5 BB, 110R
Resistance to phylloxera	Pure *V. riparia,* 5BB, 110R
Resistance to nematodes	Freedom
Tolerant to alkaline soil	41B; Fercal; pure *V. vinifera**

Vitis vinifera, while susceptible to phylloxera, is very tolerant of alkaline soil and resistant to nematodes. Thus, it was used as a parent in a number of rootstocks. AxR, which is Aramon—a vinifera—crossed with *V. rupestris,* had some resistance to phylloxera from the rupestris, but when the new, stronger strains of phylloxera came along, it was susceptible to them.

vine isn't where you want it to grow. The other approach is to take cuttings from the wild vine and bench-graft named varieties to those cuttings (see page 161). In the latter case, it often helps to cut the wild vine back the year before to ensure that there are lots of new long shoots that will make good cuttings.

If your state has a grape-growing association, contact them and find out if they have any local selections that have proven especially good as rootstocks. The Minnesota Grape Growers Association has been testing selections from private breeder Elmer Swenson that have good rootstock potential. His E.S. 15-53 is vigorous, extremely cold hardy (suffering *no* damage at −43°F [−41°C]), adds 10 degrees or more of cold hardiness to varieties grafted on it, and stimulates ripening one week or more earlier than normal. In a region where hardiness and early ripening are essential, this is an excellent "find" as a rootstock. Other states' groups may have similar superior rootstocks among the holdings of their members, as well.

Because this is the barest overview of rootstocks, I am including a list of books on rootstocks in the Bibliography for those who want to pursue the topic further. In addition, it happens that Lucie Morton Garrett, longtime collaborator with French viticultural ampelographer and researcher Pierre Galet, will have a comprehensive new book on rootstocks coming out about the time this book is in print. Look for *Roots for Fine Wine: Rootstock Selection Beyond Phylloxera* by Lucie Morton Garrett. For other books about rootstocks, refer to the Bibliography.

10 *VARIETIES*

M Y FATHER SOMETIMES mentioned my interest in grapes to people he knew, then had to hide his laughter when they said something like, "Oh yes, I have some of the red ones and some of the blue ones." With the estimated number of grape varieties worldwide being between ten thousand and twenty thousand, that's like telling a book salesman, "I already have a book."

What counts is that there are grapes that will grow in nearly every climate and situation. Granted, not all the varieties and species presently available for some climates can equal a good *vinifera* grape, but you can still produce grapes that are entirely pleasant to eat and that yield very decent juice and other products. With the existing varieties, it's possible to grow grapes from the equator to as far north as Sweden and Norway. Not the same variety in all places, of course, though there are varieties with a surprisingly wide range of adaptability.

Variety selection is especially important for the would-be organic grower. There are grapes for almost every climate, but trying to grow a variety where it isn't adapted is asking for trouble. I once visited a very expensive vineyard and winery in Arkansas that had complete state-of-the art equipment for making wine, and they were growing all the classic wine varieties such as Chardonnay and Cabernet. The vinifera grapes were so ill-suited to the area they had to be sprayed twice a week for disease, and they still looked ratty. Between the poorly suited climate and the spray residues, the wine was, as one wag called it, "Chateau Catpisse."

Meanwhile, a few miles away, another, much less pretentious winery was growing the American grape Norton with one spraying per season, yet the wine made from those grapes was the better wine. The difference was that the first place was trying to compete with regions that could properly grow the classic grapes instead of growing better-suited, but less well-known varieties. At that time, Norton was scorned because it wasn't a "classic" variety, but more recently it is finally being appreciated and is more widely planted, with acreage continuing to increase. Ironically, Norton was once a very respected variety when it was tried in France, but lost favor when it was found not to grow in many of the high-lime French soils.

French Hybrids have suffered a similar fate, being looked down upon as "inferior" and as having off tastes, especially by the French. As someone who has tasted many of the French Hybrids (and there are some very good table grapes among them, as well as wine grapes), I could never detect anything about them that was inferior, but I thought perhaps my palate wasn't geared to discern the qualities that the French were looking for. But here is what George Gale, an expert in French Hybrids, had to say about them:

> I made lots and lots and lots of Leon Millot (one of the French Hybrids). Sold every bottle of it I ever made, and at a good price.
>
> Hybrid, schmybrid. The question is one of marketing, and nothing else. Most small wineries make their money from the walk-in trade. And each and every walker-in is amenable to hand-selling. Indeed, that's the *only* way to do it. In the end, if the salesperson is the least bit good at the job, it doesn't matter *what* name is on the label, so long as there is quality *in* the bottle.

If Helmut Becker told me once, he told me a hundred times: "The problems with hybrids are economic and political, *not* enological. Their opponents talk quality, because they're afraid to raise the real issues: With our hybrids, and our production techniques, we'll knock the bottom out of the French table wine market. And they're afraid of that."*

I tasted wines in Becker's cellars that would knock your socks off. In 1982 he secretly entered one in the Rhinegau Landeskammer (a prestigious wine competition). Took first place. And outraged the authorities because hybrids weren't supposed to be entered.

Becker got a huge laugh out of the whole thing.

"Hybrid taste?" Impossible. There's a range of tastes among the species of grapes that fills out an entire spectrum vaster and wider than *vinifera*. The uncountable mixtures then get factored out among the hybrids. To say that there is some one "taste" that links them all together is, quite simply, genetically impossible.

German growers have their new "secret weapons" in the Wine Wars, and, if they have to baptize Regent and the others as *vinifera*, so be it."

The main lesson is to look for grapes that will work in your climate and that don't require heroic measures. If you are in a tough area, take that odd but well-adapted grape and make it your own. And

---

*Dr. Helmut Becker was the grape breeder and a highly respected researcher at the Geisenheim Research Institute in Germany for many years and started the work of crossing German grapes with French Hybrids (at a time when it was illegal to plant anything but pure vinifera grapes in Germany) to create varieties with more cold hardiness and disease resistance. Regent was one of the varieties produced. Technically, such selections would not be "pure" vinifera, but you can see from the quote what Dr. Becker thought of that idea.

if that doesn't suit you, there is always the option of breeding your own new varieties (see chapter 13).

For every variety, there are vintage climates, just as there are vintage years within a climate. Even a grape that grows and bears well in many different climates and soils won't necessarily be the same in all of them. The red seedless grape Reliance has a unique flavor in Arkansas, the place where it was bred. The flavor is similar at Geneva, New York, but for me, in western Oregon, it has never produced that distinctive flavor. I like the flavor of my Reliance grapes, but they never develop the unusual quality it had in the other places I tasted it. Similarly, Kay Gray was very "foxy" with a musky aftertaste in Geneva, New York, while in Minnesota, just a few miles from its place of origin, the flavor was much milder. In both places, the vines were healthy, productive, and seemed to be performing well, but the flavor was noticeably different.

Even the universally grown Concord will vary according to climate. Near Erie, Pennsylvania, thousands of acres of Concord are grown along the shores of Lake Erie for juice. There is regular summer rainfall, and the breezes off the lake often keep day and night temperatures within 10°F (4.5°C) of each other, mostly between about 68°F and 78°F (20°C and 26°C). There, the variety has a much more delicate, aromatic, fruity flavor than at any other place I have tasted it, though the sugar is relatively low: I was told the juice factory would accept the fruit for juice with 16° Brix sugar, while wine grapes usually have to have 19° to 22° Brix, at least.

In eastern Washington State, the other area where large plantings of Concord are grown for juice, summer temperatures are much hotter in the day, often around 90°F (32°C), and may drop 30°F (17°C) at night. There is essentially no summer rainfall, and even the air is drier than in much of the eastern United States In the hot, dry summers of eastern Washington, Concord has higher sugar, often 19° to 20° Brix or

Fall Color Grapes

WHEN I FIRST VISITED the Napa and Sonoma valleys in the fall, it was common to see picturesque vineyards with lots of red and orange, with a few places having only yellow leaves. It wasn't long before I learned that most of the vines with red-colored fall leaves were infected with virus, and that virus-free grapes mostly had yellow fall color. Since then, most of that area has been replanted to virus-free stock, with the result that the colorful vineyards are a rarity now. Virus may have been good for the tourist trade, but it's bad for the productivity of vineyards.

There *are* varieties that have natural red fall color, without being diseased, and most are very decent grapes, as well. If you want to try them for fall ornamental value, choose from: Alden, Schuyler, Steuben, Glenora (seedless), and Venus (seedless).

There is also Brandt, an old American variety that lacks disease resistance and whose fruit quality varies: Some who have tried it dislike it, others rave over it, according to where it is grown. A few obscure French Hybrids also have red fall color.

more, but the flavor is often weaker, and the fruit may be somewhat flat-tasting. In this case, it isn't a problem because the commercial juice producers blend juice from cooler regions to make the final product more balanced.

Similarly, the color of some grapes, especially red ones, may vary. Swenson Red may be light red, dark bluish red, or near white in different years and different climates. Why? Certain pigments in grapes, particularly the reds, are only synthesized at certain nighttime temperatures, with hot nights inhibiting color formation. This is explained in "The Color of a Grape," on page 178. The old vinifera grape Flame Tokay was only grown for table grapes in a few areas of California where the night temperatures were right for the development of the best, brightest red. In other places the color was too pale, or became dark and muddy-looking. Not all varieties vary so distinctly in different areas, but such variation is by no means unusual.

The majority of the following descriptions of varieties reflect my own experience and interests, so the list is heavy with table and juice grapes. There are also a number of varieties I am familiar with or aware of that I felt should be included, but which I either have not grown, or haven't grown long enough to evaluate fully, so I have had to rely on information from other growers. Also, because of the benign climate where I live and the way I grow my grapes, my vines have no disease problems, except in very rare cases, so any disease ratings have come from other sources.

Some grapes are so well known and described so often elsewhere that I felt no need to include them, such as many of the commercial vinifera wine grapes (Pinot Noir, for example).

Also omitted are types that I feel have no real value other than historical interest or otherwise are surpassed by more modern grapes. Rarely, I will include one of these if there is an unusual story behind it.

And while this is a fairly large list, it doesn't even scratch the surface of what it is out there. There are new grapes being developed in breeding programs all over the world. I even have some selections of my own that I hope to release in a few years, but which aren't ready yet.

Finally, don't take these descriptions as "the last word": If you want to try a grape, the experience is always worth it, no matter what the results. You'll never know how a grape will grow for you without trying it yourself. References containing many variety descriptions are included elsewhere.

VARIETY DESCRIPTIONS

To describe varieties, I use a code system to identify the basic traits that all varieties have in common, rather than take a lot of space writing out the same sorts of things for every variety. In addition, the parents of each grape (when known) are included in parenthesis or brackets following its name. For example, the variety "America" is followed by [Jaeger #70 (*Vitis lincecumii* x *V. rupestris*) x Open pollinated]. This means that the variety Jaeger #70, which is itself a cross of *Vitis linceumii* and *V. rupestris,* was left open to whatever happened to pollinate it ("open pollinated"). The resulting seed was planted and the variety "America" was selected from the seedlings.

The Color of a Grape

Customer: "What kind of green grapes are there?"

Me: "Well, there are some that are an opaque gray-green with a dusty look, like the old storage grape Almeria. Then there is a grape that is slightly translucent, grass-green with a touch of white, like Niagara. Or how about yellow-green that can become golden-green with enough sun, like Interlaken. Perlette has a white look over a pale golden. Then there's Himrod, which is closer to a white-green, but can be more yellow in full sun. Of course there are a few "white" grapes that will turn brownish at times. There're more, but is that enough to choose from?"

Okay, so that's nit-picking, but it does show the real range of colors in grapes, and why choosing a color in grapes is more exacting than you think.

Let's try red grapes. There are old red American varieties, such as Caco and Brilliant, that are a dull, brick red that somehow lacks sparkle and pizzazz. Flame Seedless is bright red when raised in some parts of California, but it can be dark red—almost like a Bing cherry, approaching "muddy looking"—when it is grown in cooler climates, even though the fruit is still ripe and delicious. The grape Reliance goes white when it starts to ripen, then begins to turn pink, then fully red. It is not as bright as a good Flame, nor as brick red as Brilliant. But the "red" parent of Reliance, Suffolk Red, is often more of a pink than a real red. Since the other parent of Reliance is Ontario, one of those "white" grapes that shouldn't contribute any color to its offspring, it's as though Reliance inherited more color than either parent had to give.

Then there are "blue" grapes. The old Campbell Early is a slightly dull, essentially black grape. Though if you extract the pigment from either a blue or a black grape, the pigment is the same color. The real difference between a blue and a black grape is the amount of "bloom" on the fruit—the powdery substance that appears to be "dusted" over the surface of the fruit. If there is enough bloom, a black grape will look more blue. If it is lacking, the grape looks more black. Most grapes that are used for making red wine actually have black-looking fruit because the pigment that makes the wine red makes the skin look black. Only when the pigment is released from the skin does the actual red color become apparent.

There are also "in betweeners," grapes that have more than one color, such as Alden, which can have both red and blue.

To further confuse the issue, there are grapes like Swenson Red that are red in some climates, pretty much blue in others, and white in still other climates. In places where the nights are warm, Swenson Red tends to be red. Where the nights are cool, but days are warm, the color leans towards blue. But when days are hot and nights are pretty hot, too, the color doesn't really develop at all and you have a "white" grape (really back to the translucent green).

Why the differences? Because there are different kinds of pigments in grapes with different behaviors. Swenson Red, for instance, has a type of anthocyanin pigment that is dependent on temperature. That is, the plant needs light to make the enzymes that make the pigment. Once dark, the enzymes are no longer being made and the plant can only use the ones that

The author in his vineyard

Einset

Valiant showing forking tendrils

New York Muscat

Reliance

Remaily

Vanessa

Interlaken

Fall color

Mars

Price

Ontario

Canadice

Golden Muscat

Buffalo

St. Croix

'Valiant' flower cluster

Valiant

Suffolk Red

Flame Seedless

Venus

Seneca

Glenora

Cascade

Swenson Red

Cayuga

Lakemont

Steuben

Yates

Venus

Venus showing fall color

Alden

Saturn

Ontario

have already been made. If the night is too warm, the plant breaks down the enzymes and stops making the pigment. Then, in the morning, the plant has to restart manufacturing the necessary enzymes before it can start making pigment again. If the night is cool, however, not all the enzymes break down before morning and the plant doesn't have to start from scratch to begin making pigment again.

So, where nights are very hot, very little pigment is made and accumulates during ripening. The cooler the nights, the more chance there is for pigment to be made, so in cool climates the fruit can accumulate a lot more pigment and can be quite dark. Not all grape pigments are affected by heat in the same way, but this is why wine grapes produce more color in climates where nights are cooler. I once gave a bottle of Marechal Foch wine to a friend in Cincinnati, Ohio. Grown in the Pacific Northwest, the Foch wine was very dark red, almost inky. My friend was excited about it because of the intense color. He wanted to get starts of my Foch because his didn't have enough color in the wine. When I told him my Foch came from the same source as his, he was crestfallen. The difference in color wasn't due to the variety, it was the result of where the grape was grown.

In days gone by, the old Flame Tokay table grape was always grown around Lodi, California, because daytime temperatures were hot, but the cooling sea breeze reached Lodi at just the right time of day. Enough pigment developed to give the fruit the bright red color that made it just right for market without the nights being so cool that the grapes would turn dark and muddy-looking. Nor was it hot enough at night to keep the Tokay from coloring at all.

Not all pigments are as sensitive to heat for proper development, as are certain pigments that have their origin in *Vitis vinifera*. Many of the old American grapes look much the same wherever they are grown, because they get their colors more from *V. labrusca*. But because there are many different pigments, and the proportion of them varies with the cultivar, the exact appearance of any one grape will be different from others of the "same" color.

Nor have we necessarily seen all the colors that will ever exist in grapes. When I was a graduate student working in my professor's lab, testing seedling grapes, one came in that was actually a bright, fluorescent orange. Even the juice appeared fluorescent. Sadly, the grape was supposed to be a wine grape, and because it had such odd chemistry, it wouldn't ferment. Since we couldn't make a wine sample to test, we discarded the grape. Since then, I've found one other "orange" grape, a numbered selection from Vineland, Ontario, Canada. It isn't fluorescent orange. In fact, some of the fruit (for me, at least) is more brown than orange. But a few clusters have fruit that does look orange in the right conditions, and a friend who saw the grape growing at Vineland said it was true orange there. Interestingly, the pedigree of the grape contains some material from the same background as the orange grape I saw in the lab. Maybe there is something else lurking in the heritage of the Vineland grape and, with some grape breeding, the true fluorescent orange grape may yet be seen again.

So, really, is that a "green" grape you are asking for? Or a light green with a touch of white? Or . . .

Following the parentage is the breeder or institution that produced the variety. Why include such information? Because if a variety of certain parentage from a particular breeding program does well for you, knowing of others from the same program or which have the same or similar parents can aid you in finding more varieties right for your conditions.

Type Codes

A = American. These are either hybrids of vinifera grapes with American species, or even entirely American species. May or may not have the flavor of *Vitis labrusca* (Concord-type flavor). Generally hardier and more disease resistant than vinifera, but this varies with the varieties.

V= vinifera. *V. vinifera* is the Old World grape of commerce. Fruit is the standard of quality, but vines are reliably hardy only to about 0°F and are susceptible to all fungal diseases of grapes, requiring heavy spray in many areas.

FH = French Hybrids. Hybrids of *V. vinifera* with American species other than *V. labrusca*, usually with fruit quality closer to *V. vinifera*. Developed in France, the majority of French Hybrids are wine grapes.

Color Codes

WH = white
Y = yellow
G = green
GY = gray or grayish
P = pink
R = red
B = blue
RB = reddish blue
BL = black
O = orange

Uses Codes

T= Table or fresh eating (or for freezing)
J = juice, jam, and jelly
W = may be used for wine
RS = may be used for raisins
LV = leaves suitable for cooking, such as in making Dolmas.

Uses are listed in order of best one first; i.e., "W/J/T" means a variety is first a wine grape, but makes good juice and is good to eat.

Season Codes

VE = very early to ripen, six or more weeks before Concord
E = early, four to five weeks before Concord
EM = early midseason, approximately two weeks before Concord
M = midseason, ripening with or within a few days of Concord
LM = late midseason, ripening one week after Concord
L = late, ripening two weeks after Concord
VL = more than two weeks after Concord

These are based on ripening times in my own material, but should apply well to at least most of the northern half of the United States. In hotter climates, the times between the different ratings are often shorter. Of course, I have not included many southern varieties because they ripen too late for me to test.

Seedlessness

Varieties that are seedless will be noted; otherwise assume that a grape has seeds.

Patents

PVP= Plant Variety Patent; the grape is patented. If a variety has been patented and the patent has not expired, please respect it and don't propagate the grape without permission. The one exception to that is if you are simply planting more vines for your own use. Most breeders will allow a home grower, or even a commercial grower, to start more vines for their own use.

SEEDED AMERICAN *and* FRENCH HYBRID GRAPES

Alden. (ONTARIO X GROSSE GUILLAUME) From the Cornell breeding station at Geneva, New York. Very large berries for an American hybrid. Texture is firm and meaty with a light muscat flavor. The fruit quality is pure vinifera with no foxy flavor at all. The berry skin is tender and prone to cracking. The variety has comparatively low acid, so it tastes sweet at lower sugar than some varieties, or about 16° Brix, which is about as high as the sugar often gets anyway. Extremely productive: 50 pounds from a single vine have been common for me. It should be pruned to two bud spurs to prevent overcropping. Only moderately hardy, to −15°F (−26°C) or so. Not unusually disease-resistant. A, R–RB, T/W/J/EM.

Alwood. (FREDONIA X ATHENS) From Virginia Polytechnic Institute. In appearance, it looks like Concord, but has larger berries. Has an unusually pronounced labrusca aroma that can be very pleasant. Alwood has exceptional disease resistance for a labrusca variety. A grower in Tennessee says that Alwood resists all the main fungal diseases (downy and powdery mildew, black rot, anthracnose) better than all the other American grapes he grows. Rather short internodes gives the plant a bushy look. Ripens about 17 days before Concord. A, B, T/J, EM.

America. [JAEGER #70 (VITIS LINCECUMII X V. RUPESTRIS) X OPEN POLLINATED] One of T. V. Munson's varieties. Hardy into Minnesota, being able to withstand −30°F (−34°C) and colder (though it is too acid there), with excellent disease resistance that allows it to grow and do well clear into the South. Tolerates Pierce's disease. Pleasant spicy/blackcurrant flavor, but the berries are small for a table grape. Lots of color in the flesh and juice. Hedrick said it had potential for port or dry wines in warmer regions.[*] Flowers appear perfect, but need a pollinator for best set. Prune to canes. A, BL, T/W/J, M.

Aurore. (SEIBEL 5279) A very early, white wine grape. People who like a soft, juicy grape like it for eating. In the East, it has a foxy flavor, but in the West it is quite neutral. Some wineries that won't admit to growing anything but classic vinifera wine grapes use Aurore as a blending base. Productive almost to a fault. I prune it to two bud spurs. FH, WH, W/J/T, VE.

Baco Noir. (V. RIPERIA X FOLLE BLANCHE) One of the older French Hybrids. Before

---

*U.P . Hedrick, author of *The Grapes of New York*, a massive book of descriptions written about the collection of grape varieties being grown at Cornell University's Geneva, New York, breeding station in the late 1800s and early 1900s.

I first made wine from Baco Noir, I had been dealing with types that took at least one month from the start of fermentation to wine that was clear enough to bottle. My first batch of Baco Noir went from start to clear wine in just over seven days, so fast I thought it had gotten "stuck" and wasn't fermenting, until I tested and found all the sugar gone. Extremely vigorous and productive; moderately hardy, to about −15°F to −20°F (−26°C to −29°C). The fresh juice of well-ripened Baco Noir has a flavor like blackberry. FH, B ,W/J, E.

Bath. [FREDONIA X (CHASSELAS ROSE X MILLS)] From the Cornell breeding station at Geneva, New York. Highly productive, tends to overbear. Sweet, with less foxiness in the flavor than other American types. Berries are almost a blueberry blue, and not much bigger than blueberries. Lower in vigor than most. Prune to spurs. A, B, T/ J, E.

Beaumont. An open-pollinated seedling of Headlight (itself a seedling of Delaware) from the late B. T. Johnson of Ohio. Bred for wine, the berries and clusters of this lavender grape are very small in my area. Johnson said it made a good white wine, but had to be pruned to five-bud canes to be fruitful. Good tolerance or resistance to major insects and diseases. Johnson also produced Beaufort, Joyous, Kee-Wah-Din, Scioto, Chief Wawatam, and others. A, R, W/J, EM.

Bell. (ELVIRA X DELAWARE) Munson. A white grape. Vigorous, but only moderately fruitful here. Flavor is mild for an American grape. Munson said it was resistant to black rot. A, W, T/J, EM.

Beta. (*V. RIPARIA* X CONCORD) This blue grape is the standard of hardiness in much of the Upper Midwest and the East. Bred by Louis Suelter in the 1800s, it is hardy to −50°F and has better disease resistance than its competitor in hardiness, Valiant. Lots of vigor, so it can fill an arbor easily. Very distinctive fresh juice and has high color for jelly. Some wineries use it for winemaking, but the Concord-type flavor and rather high acid keep it from being anything special in that area. Berries are a little small and seedy for a table grape, but if you can't grow other grapes, it's worthwhile. Commercial growers in cold areas often have a few vines around to gauge the effects of winter: If Beta is hurt, almost everything else will be severely damaged. Ripens about one month before Concord. Prune to canes. A, B, J/T/W, E.

Black Spanish (SYN. LENOIR, JACQUEZ). I've never grown this old grape, but it is popular in Texas and could be important as Pierce's disease spreads in California, because it is highly tolerant of that disease. Black Spanish was widely planted in Maderia, Texas, in the 1880s under its synonym, Jacquez. Munson originally classified it as *V. bourquiniana*, named because the oldest vine he knew about was growing on the Borquin plantation in South Carolina before Sherman burned the plantation. Some botanists classify it as a French-American type hybrid because it contains characters of *V. vinifera*, *aestivalis*, and *cineraria*. Today, it is often classified as a southern *V. aestivalis*. It has neutral flavor and doesn't lose its acid in heat, so that it makes decent red wine even in hot areas. One other valuable trait is that several growers report that Japanese beetles leave it alone. For hot climates in Texas, California and the South. A, BL, W/J, L(?).

Note: A very similar variety to Black

Spanish is Favorite, apparently a clone or seedling of Lenoir developed by John Neiderauer, who operated a winery in Brenham from 1895 to 1946. (Pleasant Hill Winery, near the old site of the Neiderauer Winery, is currently growing Favorite grapes.)

The Lenoir is a tough vine and will survive many stresses. It is resistant to phylloxera, has a lot of tolerance to Pierce's disease, and will maintain high acid levels in spite of a lot of heat. Today, it is used primarily for tawny ports in Texas; producing table wines with Lenoir is tricky. Too much oxidation results in flavors reminiscent of Kiwi shoe polish. In the 1800s, there were vast vineyards of Favorite around Paso del Norte, but these were not maintained because Americans were turning to European vinifera wines.

Bluebell. (Beta x unknown labrusca type) Minnesota. You could call this variety a cold-hardy Concord, except that the berries are slightly smaller and the flavor is like Concord at its best, with more sweetness. Ripens about four weeks before Concord, and is hardy to around −35°F (−37°C). Will show chlorosis on some soils, but this is correctable with good nutrition. Prune to canes or spurs. A, B, T/J, E.

Bokay. (Captain x Terret Monstre) From Mountain Grove, Missouri. Berries are quite large, smooth, oval white. An extremely productive grape that only ripens well for me in warm years. I almost pulled it until it got enough heat to ripen well one year. The vigor, quality (when ripe), and yield make this worth testing in warmer areas. Equal to a good vinifera table grape. Prune to spurs. A, Y, T, LM.

Brilliant. (Lindley x Delaware) Munson. If I had only tasted this brick-red grape

from my own vines, I'd veto it for being shy-bearing and too vigorous. But in other climates it has been quite decent, and has an unusual quality to the flavor that makes it interesting. Berries are fairly large, clusters are smaller than Concord. Only hardy to about −15°F (−26°C), though. Prune to canes. A, R, T, EM.

Buffalo. A blue, open-pollinated seedling of the old Rogers Hybrid, Herbert. Pluses include: An upright, open growth habit; pleasant-flavored fruit with sweet taste; early ripening; and (for me) a good secondary crop in the event a late frost takes the primary. However, the skin is quite astringent, which makes it less than a perfect table grape, and the pulp texture is somewhat stringy. Very good for juice, though. Ripens about four weeks before Concord. Produces well when trained either to spurs or canes. A, BL, J/T, E.

Campbell Early. This black grape, with its big berries and big clusters, is one of the first grapes I ever grew. While the flavor is Concord-like, it is sweeter and has less of the musky aftertaste. It ripens about two weeks before Concord, but it colors before it is ripe. While most of the clusters are large, handsome, and well filled, there is always a percentage of small, straggly clusters. A historical variety considered one of the best of its time and still very good. Campbell Early, along with Delaware, are favorites of the Japanese, who have used both extensively in breeding. As hardy as Concord, but it likes a more fertile soil. Train to spurs. A, BL, J/T, EM.

Canandaigua. An old New York variety. Neutral, vinifera-like flavor, but some foxy flavor may develop in other climates. Skin is tough, able to resist spoilage in storage.

Also resists rain, so it can mature in cool, wet, fall weather as long as there is no frost. Its main virtue is that it lasts in cold storage a long time. I have kept it at 32°F (0°C) and the fruit was still good in April, six months after harvest. Full hardiness and disease resistance unknown. Prune to canes. A, B, T, LM.

Captivator. (HERBERT X MELADEL) An old variety from Munson, with reddish-violet grapes. This one varies with climate. For me it is sweet, but undistinguished. Several growers in the East rave about the unusual fruity flavor. Good vigor, but only moderate productivity. Ripens early, so it's useful in cool climates. A, RB, T, E.

Cascade. An old British book on grape growing states that this blue grape was named Cascade because it was so productive the fruit just cascaded off the vine. That isn't the true reason for the name, but it isn't far from the truth. Extremely productive for me, to the point of producing fruit even on watersprouts and suckers. The wine is undistinguished and rather light red, but it makes a fine blending base. Prune to two bud spurs, and you still may need to thin the crop at that. FH, B, W/J, E.

Catawba. A very old American grape, red, ripening too late for many areas, it is still grown commercially for wine and juice in a few areas because of its sweet, distinctive flavor. For me, it ripens too late (two weeks after Concord), when rain makes the tender skin crack badly. After Concord and Niagara, Catawba is the most widely known American grape. Not well suited for many areas, and there are so many excellent grapes that are easier to grow. Only hardy to about −10°F (−23°C); susceptible to diseases. A, R, T/J/W, VL.

Cayuga. (SEYVAL X SCHUYLER) Introduced in 1972 from the Cornell breeding station at Geneva, New York. Very productive, with as many as four clusters to a shoot; large berries on Concord-sized clusters. Bred as a wine grape, though the handsome clusters invite fresh-eating. In my cool climate, the skin is astringent, but a grower in Missouri says the grapes are pure and sweet there, and it's his favorite table grape. Crack-resistant berries. Open, upright growth habit. Prune to spurs. Ripens with or shortly before Concord. A, WH, W/J, M.

Century 1. [SEYVE-VILLARD 20-347 X DUNSTAN 3 (CHASSELAS VIOLET X GOLDEN MUSCAT)] The large, ovoid, black or reddish-black berries of this grape are excellent, fruity, clingskin, like a very good vinifera table grape. But the vine behaves like it is overly sensitive to nitrogen, so that in any normally fertile soil it is excessively vigorous and hardly sets any fruit. In less-fertile soils, it will set large crops. Probably hardy to about −15°F (−26°C). Prune to canes. A, B, T, M.

Concord. Grown from seed of a wild grape planted by E. W. Bull in 1843, bearing for the first time in 1849 in Concord, Massachusetts. Concord was special because it ripened earlier than other varieties of its time and it would grow in a wider range of soils and climates than any other grape. Horace Greeley called it "the grape for the millions." Even Bull admitted that it wasn't the best table grape. Its best use is for cooked grape juice. It should have been replaced as a table grape long ago, but it's so well known, people still ask for it. Does best on deep, fertile soils. Ripens unevenly in hot climates, such as the mid-South. Prune to canes (though mine will set well when spur-pruned, if it is well fed) Ripe about the October 10 for me, in an average year. A, B, T/J, M.

Dattier St. Vallier. (S.V.20.365) A handsome, large, white, "ladyfinger"-shaped grape with firm flesh and neutral, vinifera flavor. A beautiful grape when well grown. Good vigor, but can overproduce if not thinned or pruned to two bud spurs. Reported as resistant to downy mildew. Only hardy to about –10°F (–23°C). FH, WH, T, M.

Delaware. A very early red variety, long the standard of excellence in grapes. In the mid-nineteeth century, it was known as one of the first grapes to ripen (two weeks earlier than Concord). Small clusters and small berries, but sweet and with very little labrusca flavor, it was prized for wines. Very resistant to black rot, it is susceptible to mildews. Some reports suggest it resists Pierce's disease. Still not a bad grape for fresh juice. Train to canes for best yield, though spurs will still give a decent crop. A, R, T/J/W, EM.

Delicatessen. (R. W. MUNSON X DELICIOUS) from Munson, 1902. A bit too acid in my cool climate, but this blue grape still has a very enjoyable, fruity flavor. Berries are a bit small here, but I'm told they are about Concord-size in warmer climates. George Gale in Kansas says Delicatessen is an excellent wine grape there, making a very good fruity red. Prune to canes. A, B, J/T/W, M.

Diamond. (SYN. MOORE'S DIAMOND, WHITE DIAMOND) (CONCORD X IONA) This old white grape has Concord's adaptability to soils and climates and ripens two weeks earlier. For a grape of its time, the flavor is mild, sweet, and not strongly labrusca. Good

vigor, but not excessive like Niagara, to which it is sometimes compared. Diamond is by far the better grape. Has a nice, upright growth habit, but the fruit is rot-prone and will crack in wet weather. Still used for wine in New York and a few other places. Diamond is the ancestor of many modern grapes: It was crossed with Winchell to give Ontario, and Ontario was used extensively in breeding in the Cornell breeding programs at Geneva, New York. About as hardy as Concord, to –20°F (–29°C). Train to cordons and spurs. A, Y, T/J/W, EM.

Dobson. A chance seedling red grape. From a man named Dobson who was a neighbor of Elwyn Meader in New Hampshire. Dobson scattered grape seeds around his property and selected from whatever came up. This red grape looks to be a seedling of Delaware, but for me, it has an odd, musky, metallic flavor. Very likely it has a different quality in other climates. Small, wingless clusters of medium-size berries. Proof that not everyone's tastes are the same. Prune to canes. Ripens about three to four weeks before Concord. A, R, T/J, E.

Dutchess. Once considered excellent, mainly because it had neutral, vinifera flavor when other grapes mainly tasted of labrusca. More "shot" berries (millerandage) than any other variety tested. Not hardy below –10°F (–23°C), almost as susceptible to disease as pure *V. vinifera.* A, WH, W/J/T, EM.

Edelweiss. (MINNESOTA #78 X ONTARIO) From private breeder Elmer Swenson in northern Wisconsin. A white grape with excellent disease resistance. Does not require spraying in a wide region, as far south as northern Kentucky. Ripens early enough to be useful in many climates. Has been grown outdoors in southern Norway. Mild labrusca flavor that gets stronger as the fruit is left on the vine. Hardy to approximately –30°F (–34°C). Has been used for wine in Minnesota, but is primarily a table variety. A, G–WH, T/J, E.

Elizabeth. A variety with this name is passed around the Pacific Northwest by amateurs. When I grew it, it appears to be just "Van Buren" that someone gave a different name.

Erie. [(GOFF X WORDEN) X WORDEN] The late D. C. Paschke of North East, Pennsylvania, told how this grape was named. A grape festival was being held in which samples of grapes named for cities around the Finger Lakes region were being displayed, with a string connecting each sample of fruit to the corresponding city on a large wall map. There was no variety for Erie, Pennsylvania, so someone went to the Cornell University breeding vineyard at nearby Fredonia, New York, selected a variety, and named it 'Erie' for the occasion. Only later was it found that Erie was a female-flowered variety, which meant it had little commercial value. A very early ripening, blue labrusca type somewhat resembling Van Buren, but ripens a few days before it. Clusters are ragged unless well pollinated. It is hardy to –25°F to –30°F (–32°C to –34°C) in New Hampshire. Main value is probably for breeding. A, B, T, E.

Esprit. (PVP) (EDELWEISS X VILLARD BLANC) Swenson variety. The large clusters of round, white berries are technically for wine, but they make a fine table grape as well. Very good disease resistance. Has upright canes like Villard Blanc. The wine often has a strong, almost foxy taste when young, but that ages out after a few months,

and it becomes similar to Chardonnay. Hardy to about –25°F (–32°C). Ripens about two to three weeks before Concord. A, WH, W/T, EM.

Festivee. (ALDEN X VERDELET) Vineland, Ontario, Canada. Sometimes a vine that does well in testing will do something completely unexpected in other areas. This is one. This big, meaty, red-black grape looked like a wonderful table grape when it was released, but when vines reached a few years old, the clusters became loose and straggly, and production dropped. This is not due to disease or anything measurable, it is just an inherited flaw of the variety. Such things are rare, but do happen. *Not* recommended. I include Festivee here because it is new enough that it is still being sold and potential buyers should know of its flaw. A, RB, T, EM.

Frontenac. (VITIS RIPARIA X LANDOT 4511) University of Minnesota, 1995. An interesting and new hardy red wine variety. Hardy to –35°F (–37°C) this vine has excellent wine potential due to its intense color and high sugar (24° Brix is common), as well as lack of any herbaceous flavor. In Minnesota, the grapes must be allowed to hang as long as possible to help reduce the rather high acid. The variety doesn't need that treatment in warmer climates. Test plantings in Missouri produced wine that is close to classic vinifera in quality. A, B, W, EM(?).

Goff. (UNKNOWN PARENTAGE) New York, 1898. In its day, this red grape was considered remarkably good. It is still decent, though hardly outstanding compared to many newer varieties. What makes Goff worth noting is that it keeps amazingly well in ordinary refrigeration, six months or more. The flavor is mild, not labrusca, and the flesh is firm, almost rubbery. It ripens after Concord, but resists cracking from rain, so it succeeds almost every year. A, R, T, LM.

Golden Muscat. (MUSCAT HAMBURG X DIAMOND) An old New York variety that ripens late, one to two weeks after Concord. It will ripen earlier in hot years, and individual berries may ripen one to two weeks ahead of the rest of the cluster. When well ripened, the flavor of the very large berries is excellent, sweet, and rich, though it is *not* a true muscat flavor. Even when not fully ripe, it has a tangy, citrus-like flavor that is very good. Clusters often weigh over 1 pound. The fruit is very sensitive to cracking if there is rain at ripening time and will rot readily once cracked. Vine is only moderately hardy and not particularly disease-resistant. Train to spurs. At its best in a hot, dry climate such as California. A, G, T, L.

Greek Perfume. At a meeting one time, an old fellow approached a friend and me with cuttings of this grape. He said that a Greek researcher in an experiment station had to flee during unrest in Greece, and he took some of his favorite grape with him. The old man said the grape had a perfumed flavor, so the grape was summarily dubbed 'Greek Perfume'. For me, it has been an unremarkable, blue-labrusca type grape, though the berries are larger than Concord. The vine is vigorous and shows there is vinifera in the ancestry. It's possible this grape has a different flavor in other climates. I include it here in hopes that someone can someday identify it. A, B, T/J, M.

Horizon. (SEYVAL X SCHUYLER) From the Cornell breeding station at Geneva, New York. For white wine. A sister seedling of Cayuga, but very different. Berries are green, very juicy, and prone to cracking and bunch rot if rained on at ripening time. Fresh juice has a wonderful, apple-like flavor. The vine is extremely vigorous and is oversensitive to excess fertility. Productive when pruned to spurs, but almost needs to be pruned to canes to have enough crop to reduce vigor. A, WH, W/J, EM.

Isabella. This is a very old American variety, blue, of average quality, and ripening late, with Catawba. Were it not for one trait, I wouldn't include it. However, Isabella has shown an unusual ability to adapt to different climates. It has been found blooming in Hawaii and bearing green and ripe fruit more or less year-round, without having to go dormant. A, B, T/J, L.

Ivan. A chance seedling found in Oregon, named for the man on whose property it was found. Very productive of black, rather small, neutral grapes that ripen extremely early, seven weeks before Concord for me. Looks like a seedling of Cascade. Prune to spurs. Hardy to at least –25°F (–37°C). A, B, J, W, VE.

John Viola. A chance seedling found in New Hampshire by Meader, named for the owner of the farm where he found it. Small clusters of small black berries, this looks like a natural hybrid of *V. riparia* with *V. labrusca*. Vine habit is open and productive. The flavor of the fruit is unremarkable, typical labrusca-type flavor. Hardy to at least –30°F (–34°C), possibly hardier. Spur pruning seems to work, though cane pruning might give a larger total crop. A, B, T/J, EM.

Kay Gray. (PVP) [(MINNESOTA # 78 X GOLDEN MUSCAT) X OPEN POLLINATION] From Swenson. The white berries are not especially large and the clusters are small. Flavor varies from distinctly foxy to mild and fruity. Vine is only moderately vigorous at best, though production is good. Used for wine in Minnesota, but takes heroic measures to make a drinkable wine from it. Very disease-resistant and extremely cold-hardy, to –40°F (–40°C) and a bit more. A, WH, W, T/J/W, E.

KeeWahDin. (OSBU x BACO NOIR) Developed by Johnson, the name means "North Wind." A wine grape hardy to about –35°F (–37°C), with small clusters of very small, blue berries. As many as four clusters per shoot. Good general disease resistance, extremely vigorous on most soils, though it needs regular moisture. Wine is intensely colored, neutral, but often has high acid. A, B, W, E.

Kishwaukee. A chance seedling found by Bill Vose in Illinois, this large-berried, black grape has survived temperatures of –30°F (–34°C) in its place of origin. Oddly, it is very similar to Steuben here, but at Vose's vineyard, it is hardier and has a different flavor than Steuben, according to his reports. Prune to spurs. A, B, T/J, EM.

LaCrosse. (PVP) [(MINNESOTA #78 x SEIBEL 1000) x SEYVAL] A sister seedling to St. Pepin, it is similar to its male parent, Seyval, though hardier. Extremely productive, the crop must be regulated or it will not be hardy. In Minnesota, it is often grafted on rootstocks to increase hardiness and vigor so that it won't overload itself. Wine is similar to Seyval, though with a stronger flavor at first. A, WH, W/J, EM.

Leon Millot. A sister seedling of Marechal Foch, they are similar in appearance and wine quality. Leon Millot ripens about one week earlier than Foch, with smaller berries and clusters, more vigor, and less cold hardiness. Same good fresh juice, too. FH, BL, W/J, E.

Louise Swenson. (E.S. 2-3-17 x KAY GRAY) Swenson. Released in 1999–2000. E.S. 2-3-17 = [(Minnesota #78 x Seibel 1000) x (Minnesota #78 x Seneca)] (description from the Minnesota Grape Growers). In trials, wine is light-bodied and has a delicate "floral-and-honey" aroma. Blending with a variety such as Prairie Star makes it a more complete wine. Louise rarely exceeds 20° Brix, even if left to hang past mid-season. Acidity is moderate and needs no reduction. Clusters are small to medium, conical, and compact. Louise Swenson is also a very good seeded table grape. Little or no winter injury in –40°F (–40°C) winters at several sites. Moderate vigor. Disease resistance generally very good; some susceptibility to anthracnose. May need irrigation on very sandy soils. A, WH, W/T, EM(?).

Lynden Blue. Another variety passed around in the Pacific Northwest by amateurs. There may be more than one grape with this name, but the ones I've seen look like Fredonia.

Marechal Foch. This blue wine grape, along with its sister seedling Leon Millot, is rapidly gaining popularity in the Northwest for organic wines. The intense, very dark red-violet wines have a distinct, complex quality in the cool climates, and the vines need little more than pruning and picking. The intense color is a function of the cool nights: in eastern areas, where nights are warmer, the color is often lacking. This is also an excellent grape for uncooked grape juice—the fresh juice tastes much like sweet cherry juice. I prune mine to both canes and spurs and don't see much difference, but in cooler areas, cane pruning works better. Hardy to about −25°F (−32°C). FH, B, W, J, EM.

McCampbell. A sport of Fredonia with much larger clusters. Quality only fair and not productive. Berries tend to shell off the cluster when ripe. Not much of a grape for me, but it does have vigor and is said to have good disease resistance in the Northeast. A, B, T, EM

Minnesota. (#78) A female-flowered seedling of Beta from the University of Minnesota, produced in the 1930s. Good hardiness, close to Beta, and with less acid and larger clusters than Beta. Mild labrusca flavor, fairly sweet. Its best use, however, has been as a parent in breeding cold-hardy grapes. It passes good hardiness and disease resistance to the offspring, and was the basis for many of the varieties bred by Swenson. A, B, T, J, E.

Munson. (SYN. JAEGER # 70) (*VITIS LINCE-CUMII* X *V. RUPESTRIS*) This female-flowered variety, though named for T.V. Munson, was created by Herman Jaeger. When well pollinated, it sets large crops of decent grapes that make a fair red wine. I include it because it is the American ancestor of a large percentage of the French Hybrids, and it still has potential for breeding due to its excellent disease resistance and hardiness. A, B, J, W, M.

New York Muscat. (MUSCAT HAMBURG X ONTARIO) New York. This grape is always in the top three in tastings. The oval, reddish-blue grapes have the best muscat flavor of any hybrid I have tried. Only pure vinifera muscats are better in flavor, but they aren't hardy. New York Muscat is hardy to about −15°F (−26°C), Only of medium vigor and productivity, but the flavor makes you forget that. Also used for sweet muscat wines in the eastern United States. Prune to spurs. A, RB, T, W, E.

Niagara. (CONCORD X CASSADY) Introduced in 1882 by the Niagara Grape Company of Lockport, Niagara County, New York. Even after more than a century, Niagara is still the main white grape that American home growers choose to grow. Niagara is excessively vigorous, susceptible to disease, and hardy only to about −15°F (−26°C). The berries are not particularly sweet, though fairly large. Niagara's extreme vigor makes it useful on arbors (but give it *room*) and the fruit gives off a pleasant aroma when ripe. However, if you want quality fruit, there are so many better varieties. A, G, T/J, M.

Ontario. (WINCHELL X DIAMOND) New York. Given the percentage of labrusca in the parentage of this grape, it is surprisingly mild-flavored. The white berries have outstanding quality for a grape of its parentage and the period in which it was bred. More important, Ontario proved to be an excellent parent, having contributed its genes to a very large percentage of varieties from the breeding program at Geneva, New York. Ontario ripens early, four to five weeks before Concord, and is hardy to at least −20°F (−29°C). It is productive, but likes a somewhat light, fertile soil; on other soils, it may lack vigor. A, WH, T/J, VE.

Prairie Star. (E.S. 2-7-13 X E.S. 2-8-1) Swenson. A new, very hardy, white wine grape. Released in 1999. (Information from the Minnesota Grape Growers Association). Both parents have the same ancestors: Minnesota # 78, Kendaia, and Villard Blanc. Good sugar, with 20° to 22° Brix.

Medium-sized berries are borne in long, slightly loose clusters. Clusters are heavier on heavy soils or from grafted vines. On lighter soils, cluster size is smaller. The wine is neutral, with a delicate floral nose some years, but most years is best for blending. Very hardy, to –40°F (–40°C) in some locations, though damaged at that temperature on other sites. Resistant to mildew diseases, but moderately susceptible to black rot and anthracnose. Also has a tendency for shoot breakage in strong winds early in the season. Deal with this by using a low cordon or low fan-training system, with catch wires to attach the shoots. A, WH, W, EM.

Price. This complex blue hybrid from Virginia Polytechnic Institute deserves to be better known. The quality is among the best of American grapes. The clusters aren't big, but the Concord-size berries have juicy, tender, very sweet flesh, and tender, non-astringent skin. The vine is productive, with good vigor. I'm told it has withstood –25°F (–32°C), and has very good disease resistance. Best of all, it ripens very early, usually with the first grapes in my collection, and is so well adapted to cool climates that it is one of the few grapes that will ripen around Puget Sound in Washington State. This is my oldest son's favorite grape, and it's one that deserves trial for cool, short seasons everywhere. A, B, T/J, VE.

St. Croix. (PVP) [(MINNESOTA #78 X SEIBEL 1000) X (MINNESOTA #78 X SENECA)] Hardy to nearly –40°F (–40°C), though it needs mulch or snow cover on the ground at those temperatures, as extreme cold can harm the roots. In my area, it makes a very good, fruity, light red wine. Doesn't set fruit well in some locales if temperatures are cold and dewy during bloom. Good vigor. Heavy bearing in Minnesota. Prune to canes. A, B, W/J, E.

St. Pepin. (PVP) [(MINNESOTA #78 X SEIBEL 1000) X SEYVAL] A white wine grape with a fruity quality somewhere between Reisling and Muscat. Also good to eat, but, though clusters are large, berries are small. Unusual in that it has female flowers and needs to be planted near a perfect-flowered grape to set well. LaCrosse and Swenson Red are two possible pollinators. May be slow to reach full production. Prune to canes. A, WH, W, E.

St. Vincent. A red wine grape that apparently was a chance cross of Pinot Noir with either Chambourcin or Vidal. It is just starting to attract a following. The following letter from Fred Dressel of Missouri explains its probable origin:

My father "discovered" St. Vincent in the early 1970s growing as a rogue in a Vidal Blanc vineyard at his winery, Mt. Pleasant, in Augusta, Missouri. He sent it to researchers at Cornell and to Phillip Wagner (where the Vidal originally came from). Neither had ever seen anything like it.

It has no diglucosides like all other red French Hybrids (save Plantet, also called Seibel 5455), only monoglucosides like vinifera. The leaves turn bright red in the fall (like Pinot Noir) and these are certified virus-free vines (so the red isn't due to virus). It makes good dry red wine and has made an excellent rose sparkling wine. It is a vigorous grower and a prolific bearer (6 to 10 tons per acre.) A worthwhile grape in areas that cannot grow vinifera.

When the original St. Vincent vine died, we had Southwest Missouri State Viticulture people on hand at the time.

(The original) St. Vincent looked to have a long tap root [a characteristic of seedlings, but not plants started from cuttings], so maybe this was a chance seedling. We had Pinot Noir on one side of the Vidal and Chambourcin nearby. Best guess is that, if this is a chance seedling, these may be the parents. St. Vincent is really light in color, not much of a tienturier." [Tienturier is a French term, meaning "having colored juice."]

A, B, W, M?

Schuyler. (ZINFANDEL X ONTARIO) from Geneva, New York. Extremely productive, bearing large clusters of very sweet, soft, juicy berries. In the East, it has a very slight labrusca flavor, but in the West, it is totally neutral. Somewhat susceptible to powdery mildew for me, but training it to an open growth habit is usually enough to keep it clean. It must be pruned very short, to two bud spurs, and may still need thinning to prevent overcropping. Hardy to about –15°F (–26°C), but needs a fairly long fall to harden off well. In 1999, we had an early frost that was just enough to take the leaves off, and only Schuyler was affected by it, failing to harden most of its wood that year. Also makes a neutral red wine. A, B, T/J/W, EM

Seneca. (LIGNAN BLANC X ONTARIO) New York. With small, white, oval berries usually having just one seed each, this very early-ripening grape (coming on at least six weeks before Concord) is excellently sweet, with a nice spicy flavor. It also is more susceptible to powdery mildew than any other American grape I have tried. Irregular bearing, extremely vigorous. Must be pruned to canes. A, W, T, VE.

Sonoma (syn. Sonona). (LADY X V. RIPARIA) From Nels Hansen in South Da-

kota. White, with a pink tinge, sometimes turning light red. Very light production reported by most growers. Its main value is hardiness, being hardy to –35°F (–37°C) or colder. A, WH–P, T/J, E.

Steuben. (WAYNE X SHERIDAN) New York. Big, handsome clusters of blue grapes that make excellent juice and are good eaten fresh. This one was kept in testing for a very long time. By the time it was released, interest had shifted to seedless grapes. Good vigor, productivity, general disease resistance, and nice fall leaf color. Good arbor grape. Prune to spurs. A, B, T/J, M

Sunbelt. (PVP) (CONCORD X OPEN POLLINATION) University of Arkansas. 1993. In the South, Concord ripens unevenly in the hot summers: A single cluster will contain green and ripe berries at the same time. This variety was developed because of the increasing commercial interest in juice production in Arkansas. Similar to Concord in most ways, the clusters are smaller and the berries slightly larger. Otherwise, it will ripen uniformly where Concord will not. The variety is also said to be highly resistant to downy mildew and powdery mildew. A, B, J, M.

Swenson Red. (MINNESOTA #78 X SEIBEL 11803) The first grape released from Swenson's grape work, and my personal favorite. The unique, fruity flavor of this firm, meaty grape is like no other. Only grapes with muscat flavor usually tie it in tastings. Hardy to at least –25°F (–32°C), sometimes to –30°F (–34°C) if it hardens off well. While it is generally red, it can be bluish in climates with cool nights. Where nights are very warm, it may not color at all, staying green even though ripe. Swenson says it is susceptible to downy mildew in bad years in his area of northern Wisconsin. I'm told it also makes a good white or light rose wine. The sugar can often get over 21° Brix, which is enough to make good wine. The vine is often rather low-vigor in its early years, but with care will usually increase in vigor and productivity as it gets older. On some of the clusters, flowers in the center section may fail to set, making the mature cluster dumbbell-shaped. Heavy dew or fog may interfere with set, and I find that training it at least 4 to 5 feet tall helps get the clusters up where air circulation is better, improving set. A, R, T, W, E.

Swenson White. (EDELWEISS X E.S. 442 [MINNESOTA #78 X S. 11803]) From Swenson. "Released" in 1999. I once sent cuttings of a collection of grapes to a friend in Colorado for a testing program. When he got a job at a nursery in Boulder, he took some of the cuttings with him. A garden writer visited the nursery, and in tasting the fruits on the place, fell in love with a grape there. She saw it tagged as "Swenson White" and wrote it up for *Horticulture* magazine that way. She didn't know that the tag was just meant as shorthand for "A white grape from Swenson." The item was included in the magazine, and, once the name was in print in a national magazine, that made it an official release.

The grape was worth releasing, but there was a question about its hardiness. Apparently it hardens off differently in different climates. Generally, it is hardy to about –30°F (–34°C). It is an excellent grape, with a very good balance of sugar and acid and a very unusual fruity flavor that has no labrusca overtone at all. I first tried it at Swenson's vineyard, and it had a very good crop and 20-foot canes besides. One odd trait is that,

once in a while, a berry will have six seeds all together in a ball, almost the size of a cherry pit. Ripens about three to four weeks before Concord. Prune to canes. A, W, T, W, EM(?).

Totmur. (BACO 2-16) This very early white wine grape might have value in cool, short-season climates if it had more vigor and productivity. Its name roughly translates to "first early," and it fits. It has high acid in many climates. To be commercially viable, it needs to be grafted to a rootstock that would invigorate it and increase its productivity. FH, WH, W, VE.

Trollhaugen. (2-4-13 X 2-5-5) Swenson, 1998. Here are Swenson's own words about this grape: "Medium size clusters are quite compact, berries medium large, blue with a mild Concord-like flavor, ripens extremely early, yet hangs in good conditions until hard frost. Develops high sugar."

It should be hardy to at least –30°F (–34°C). Prune to spurs. A, B, J/T, VE.

Valiant. (FREDONIA X *V. RIPARIA*) South Dakota Valiant is equal to or better than Beta in hardiness in a dry climate, but in a moist one, Valiant is more susceptible to disease, which keeps it from hardening off as well. (One parent of Valiant was a selection of *V. riparia* hardy to more than –70°F (–57°C), but it came from a dry climate where it had no need for disease resistance.) Valiant has withstood –50°F (–46°C) unharmed in Manitoba, Canada, and it is extremely productive of blue berries that have excellent sugar and acid for highly colored juice and jelly. Letting it overcrop when young may retard its maturity. Prune to spurs of three buds each. A, B, J, T, E.

Van Buren. (FREDONIA X WORDEN) Geneva, New York. Sometimes sold under the incorrect name President Van Buren. Likes light, fertile soils; on other soils it may have thin canes and lower vigor. The flavor of this very early black grape is like Concord, but it has low sugar and acid, too low for good juice. For me, Price is superior in all ways, especially for a grape of this season. Prune to spurs. A, B, T, VE.

Ventura. (CHELOIS X ELVIRA) Vineland, Ontario. A white wine grape that was intended to preserve the good qualities of Elvira without that variety's faults, and it seems to have succeeded. Hardy to about –25°F (–32°C) or colder. Though a little high acid in some climates, it makes a good dry white wine. Very productive, somewhat moderate in vigor. Prune to spurs. A, WH, W/J, EM.

Verdelet (syn. Siebel 9110). Firm, meaty white berries that are neutral and vinifera-like are the main attraction of this grape. Also said to make a good light white wine. Though not particularly disease resistant, it seems to grow well in a range of conditions. FH, WH, T/W, EM.

Vineland #71121. When I was a student at the University of California at Davis, a grape was brought into the testing lab that was brilliant, fluorescent orange. Even the juice had a fluorescent glow to it. However, it was a failure as a wine grape, with such an odd chemistry that it wouldn't ferment, so it was discarded. I thought it was worth keeping, but as a student I didn't have a say in it. I figured that was the only time I would ever see an orange grape. Then along came V. 71121, which may have a common ancestor with the orange seedling, and which is also orange. It's not as brightly colored as the seedling, and it tends to turn brown in

full sun. Neutral, vinifera-type berries. Average vigor, good production. Prune to spurs. A, O, T, EM.

Wapanuka. (ROMMEL X BRILLIANT) Munson. I first tasted this in Geneva, New York and was amazed at the flavor. It had a sweet, rich, fruitiness that was unlike any white labrusca type I had tried. I'm not sure why this grape didn't "take" when it was released in 1893, but it is reported as having good general disease resistance. As hardy as Concord, and two weeks earlier. I haven't had enough grapes from my vine to make final judgment, but it is worth growing. A, W, T/J, EM.

Worden. (SEEDLING OF CONCORD) Two things make this large-berried black seedling of Concord worth growing—it ripens two weeks before Concord and it is hardier than Concord, to –25°F (–32°C) or colder. Less flavor and sweetness than Concord. Prune to canes. A, B, T/J, EM.

Yates. (MILLS X ONTARIO) Geneva, New York. I'd grow this grape just for fruit bowls. The big red berries and handsome clusters are extremely attractive. While the flavor isn't that special, the grape keeps remarkably well, six months or more in refrigeration. Vigorous, good production, good rain resistance (which it needs because it ripens late, about two weeks after Concord). Succeeds most years, though. Prune to spurs. A, R, T, VL.

SEEDLESS AMERICAN GRAPES

While some seeded grapes have been found as chance seedlings, rather than having been intentionally bred, virtually all seedless grapes have been produced by controlled breeding. Further, the type of seed-lessness in most grapes all originates with Sultanina, which is a form of Thompson Seedless. With the American demand for seedless grapes, you can be sure that nearly all the table grapes that will be released in the future will be seedless.

Bronx Seedless. [(GOFF X IONA) X SULTANINA] Geneva, New York. This was the second seedless grape released from the Cornell Station at Geneva, New York. The clusters are quite large, though there is a lot of variation in berry size, and the red color is attractive. Probably not hardy below −10°F (−23°C). The flavor, for me, is quite similar to Reliance. The foliage of this variety is an odd chrome-yellow color that makes it look like it's perpetually starved for nitrogen, but the color is genetic, not a sign of a problem. The fruit will crack in wet fall weather. The variety has been quite popular in California, where the dry climate prevents cracking. A, R, T, EM.

Canadice. (BATH X HIMROD) A seedless red variety from Geneva, New York. Less vigorous than other varieties, but extremely productive, so much so that it must be pruned to two bud spurs on cordons. Even then, it may need cluster-thinning to prevent overcropping. Supposed to be hardy to −25°F (−32°C), but it *must* be kept from overcropping to ripen the wood well. I've seen canes die back at 10°F (−12°C) because of a too-heavy crop. Ripens even in very cool areas—one of few varieties that will ripen around Puget Sound. Growers in Michigan reported Canadice as being more resistant to black rot than other seedless grapes grown there. A, R, T/J, E.

Challenger. Red seedless from Missouri. Red, ovoid berries are attractive, but lack

sugar and acid: They tend to be flat-tasting, and they develop an odd "fish egg" texture when overripe. The vine is only hardy to −10°F (−23°C) at best, and not very disease resistant. A, R, T, EM.

Einset. (FREDONIA X CANNER) Geneva, New York. When properly grown, this red seedless is an excellent table grape with firm, crisp berries, having a unique fruity flavor. Ripens quite early, a few days after Himrod. For me, it has been very particular about soil: Even a little too much fertility makes the vine overly vigorous and nonproductive and causes the clusters to shatter. Twenty feet away, on a strip of slightly heavy soil, two other vines are undervigorous, and their fruit is small and soft. Also, in some years, some of the fruit has an off taste. Like too many grapes, it has wonderful fruit on a fussy vine. Don't count on hardiness much below −10°F (−23°C). Prune to canes. A, R, T/RS, E.

Glenora. (ONTARIO X RUSSIAN SEEDLESS) Blue seedless. The vine vigor is excessive and not as productive as such a large vine could be. Flavor is very mild and pleasant, but the clusters vary. Some may be perfect, with uniform large berries; others are straggly, with various berry sizes on the same cluster. Berries crack if rained on at ripening time, but seem able to "heal" somewhat instead of rotting. One oddity for me is that, almost without fail, the bottom three berries on a cluster are always underripe when the rest of the cluster is ripe. When frozen, berries of Glenora look and taste a lot like blueberries. Hardiness is slightly less than Himrod, perhaps to −15°F (−26°C). Prune to canes. A, B, T, EM.

Himrod. (ONTARIO X SULTANINA) A white seedless from Geneva, New York. Large, loose clusters of flavorful, somewhat soft berries. Vine is excessively vigorous and not very productive: 20 pounds per vine is a good crop, and 15 pounds is more common. Very early, about five weeks before Concord, so it ripens in cool areas. Vine is excessively vigorous. Berry stems are weak and the clusters tend to shatter if fruit isn't picked soon after ripening. Has some susceptibility to powdery mildew, but usually doesn't need control if grown well. Hardiness to about −15°F (−26°C). A, WH, T, RS, VE.

Interlaken. A sister seedling of Himrod (same parents) with seedless green to golden berries. Less vigorous than Himrod, but ripens about a week earlier and is much more productive, up to 30 pounds per vine. Good for cool, short seasons. Hardy to about −15°F (−26°C). Berries are firm, have high sugar (22° Brix) on well-filled to compact clusters and are the best variety I have tried for raisins. They also make excellent frozen fruit. A, WH–Y, T/RS, VE.

Jupiter. (PVP) (COMPLEX PARENTAGE) University of Arkansas. Newly released in 1998. A new reddish-blue to blue seedless muscat variety with firm flesh and resistance to cracking. My own vines have not borne as of this writing, but Arkansas tests indicate that Jupiter bears reliably, even needing thinning in some cases. Vigor is good, hardiness may be about to −20°F (−29°C). Ripens between Venus and Reliance. A, RB, T, E.

Lakemont. Another sibling of Himrod from Geneva, New York, this white seedless is the best producer of the group, able to produce 35 pounds per vine for me. Clusters are very large, well-filled to compact, and quite handsome. In the West, they are neutral in flavor, but in the East they have a mild labrusca flavor. The best keeper in cold storage of all the seedless varieties, Lakemont actually gets better in storage. Ripens about two weeks after Himrod and about as hardy. I cane-prune mine. A, G, T, EM.

Marquis. (ATHENS X EMERALD SEEDLESS) Geneva, New York. 1996. Large, white, spherical, soft, juicy berries on shouldered clusters. Like Einset, it looks like Marquis may lack adaptability. It is prone to cracking of the berry skin. Flavor is unusual, fruity. Hardy to about −10°F to −15°F (−23°C to −26°C). Prune to canes. A, WH, T/W, EM.

Mars. (PVP) (ISLAND BELLE X ARK. 1339) 1986. University of Arkansas. This blue seedless has the largest berries of all American-type seedless grapes. Good vigor; productivity is low when the vines are young, but improves as they mature. At first, clusters are loose and straggly, but they fill better on mature vines. Flavor is labrusca, like its female parent. The fruit is a little pulpy, and it is actually at its best a day after picking, when acids go down a bit. Vine is said to be as healthy as Concord, but some Arkansas growers disagree with this assessment. Can be hardy to −25°F (−32°C) or a bit colder if it has a long fall to aid hardening off. One of the last to bud out in the spring, which helps it avoid late frost. Spur-pruning works for me. Ripens about three to four weeks before Concord. A, B, T, E.

Orlando Seedless. [(NORRIS X SCHUYLER) X (FLORIDA A4-23 X PERLETTE)] Orlando looked very promising as the first seedless grape resistant to Pierce's disease. But the variety needs spraying for fungal diseases, including isariopsis leaf blight, and there are reports it is showing decline from PD after several years. For me, the fruit has been a disappointment, with very small berries and an unattractive blotchy appearance. The clusters can be very large and long, with good care. My vines went into decline when nothing around them was affected and they have never recovered. I have yet to find a reason why. A, P–WH, T, EM.

Neptune. (PVP) (COMPLEX PARENTAGE) University of Arkansas 1998 (from description). White, oval, firm fruit with extremely high resistance to cracking; pleasant, unusual, fruity flavor. Moderate vigor and only moderate yield. Ripens about one and a half to two weeks before Concord. A, WH, T, EM.

Petite Jewel. (MINNESOTA #78 X CANADICE) Swenson, 1999. I don't have this in bearing yet. Folks in Minnesota say the berries are small, but have a wonderful fruity flavor. Extremely early-ripening. Supposed to be the hardiest seedless grape yet developed, but there isn't enough data to know how well it will perform. Assume hardiness to start at –25°F (–32°C), at least. A, R, T, VE.

Reliance. (PVP, but patent expired in 2001) (Ontario X Suffolk Red) University of Arkansas. Reliable might be a better name for this red seedless. It consistently has large crops and good vigor for me. In Arkansas and the East, it has a unique, fruity flavor: I never get that flavor from my grapes, but it's still good. I always know if there are raccoons around—they go for Reliance before anything else in the collection. Good commercial potential variety for farm stands. Hardy to about –25°F (–32°C), and early enough for most areas. Actually edible before it is fully colored. Prune to spurs. A, R, T, EM.

Remaily Seedless. Bred by private breeder George Remaily, released through the Cornell Station at Geneva, New York. Neutral-flavored, firm, very large (for a seedless) white berries. Sets badly if weather is cool and wet at bloom time, producing lots of shot berries. Only moderately productive, with one cluster to the shoot, though clusters are often very large. Flavor can be somewhat flat unless weather at ripening time stays warm long enough to produce high sugar. Tends to develop brown sun-scald areas on the berries unless well shaded. Keeps well in cold storage. A, WH, T, M.

Royal Blue. A parthenocarpic seedless, origin uncertain, having very small berries on small clusters. Vine is low-vigor, though moderately productive. At this time it seems very similar, if not identical, to Seedless Concord. Ripe about two weeks before Concord. A, B, T, M.

Saturn. (PVP) (COMPLEX PARENTAGE) Clusters and berries of this dark red grape can be very large, especially for a seedless, but Saturn shows a tendency to produce all parthenocarpic (small) seedless berries if the weather is cool at bloom time. Neutral-flavored. Since it comes from a hot climate (Arkansas), it may need a hot climate to develop best. Not particularly disease-resistant, it may be grown without spray only in areas with a dry summer climate. Evidence suggests –15°F (–26°C) is the lower limit of hardiness. Prune to canes. A, R, T, M.

Sovereign Coronation. (PATRICIA X HIMROD) Summerland, British Columbia, Canada. This black grape seems to be at its best in very cool climates. Even for me, in a somewhat cool climate, the oval berries have an odd, off taste. Further, people in cooler climates report better production than I have seen on it here. There has been confusion about the female parent. Many sources list it as Lady Patricia, but Lady Patricia is a white grape and couldn't produce a black offspring. There is a Canadian variety named Patricia that is black, and it is more likely to be the real female parent. Prune to canes. A, B, T, E.

Suffolk. Red, firm, meaty berries, with only the lightest of labrusca flavor. A large percentage of the clusters may be irregular, with poor set and variable berry size.

Even though the number of clusters may be fairly large, the crop weight is often small because the clusters are loose. Vigorous vine, only moderately hardy. Large, upright canes. Easy to train to cordons. One grower in Colorado says he loves it for raisins. A, R, T, EM.

Thornton. The old New York State Fruit Testing Association used to send out numbered selections for testing, and, if the varieties didn't work out, they would ask the testers to destroy them. Sometimes a variety grew well enough for some people that they didn't want to destroy the vines. A few people opted to keep and name these selections and "release" them unofficially. Thornton could be one of those old selections, but tracing it would be difficult. Seedless yellow berries are a lot like Interlaken, except that the vine is less productive, and the fruit ripens at least one week before Interlaken, making it extremely early. Oddly, one grower found it to be an excellent grape for growing in an unheated greenhouse in cool climates. Grown thus, it gave a crop at least three weeks before any other variety. Other reports suggest its performance var-

ies a lot in different climates and soils. A, WH, T/RS, VE.

Vanessa. (SENECA X NEW YORK 45910) Vineland, Ontario. Seedless with firm, fruity berries. Red color with no muddiness. A good variety for those who want a Flame Seedless type that will grow in colder climates. Big, open vines, very vigorous when young, needing to be cane-trained to get enough crop. As it matures, the vines settle down and can be cordon (spur) trained, and production increases. One odd trait of this variety is that, if the weather is dry all season long, the fruit can have astringent skin. However, if one good rain occurs after the fruit ripens, the astringency disappears. This is likely connected to its place of origin: Vineland selections are bred to resist rain at ripening time. Ripens early enough to do well in cool climates, about four to five weeks before Concord. Supposed to be hardy to −20°F to −25°F (−29°C to −32°C). A, R, T, E.

Venus. (ALDEN X NEW YORK 46000) Arkansas. Black seedless with an unusual flavor that is both muscat-like and mildly labrusca. Not always perfectly seedless—in some years and some climates, it can have seeds that are full-sized but soft, and a few of those may be hard. In cool climates, it may have astringent skin, but the flavor is good enough to overlook that. Can be spur-pruned, but more productive with cane training. Ripens about four weeks before Concord. Hardy to about −15°F (−26°C). A, B, T/J, EM.

William's Seedless. A red, female flowered variety that will set clusters of parthenocarpically seedless fruit when not pollinated. When pollinated, the berries are very large and have seeds. Flavor is a harsh labrusca that literally makes my mouth itch. I am pretty sure this is the old Rogers Hybrid variety Massassoit.

SEEDED VINIFERA GRAPES

As a group, vinifera grapes are not reliably hardy below 0°F to −5°F (−18°C to −20°C), and are susceptible to the major diseases of grapes.

Early Muscat. (MUSCAT HAMBURG X QUEEN OF THE VINEYARD) U.C. Davis. Bred as a table grape, this large-clustered white muscat with oval berries is excellent to eat. In the cool climate of the Northwest, it also has good sugar-acid balance for wine. Some Oregon vineyards used to make a varietal from it that was excellent, but the name didn't sell well, so it is used only for blending now. Prune to spurs. V, WH, T, EM.

Gold. [(MUSCAT HAMBURG X SULTANINA) X (MUSCAT HAMBURG X QUEEN OF THE VINEYARD)] One of the most striking grapes I've seen, with very large, oval berries that have a gold sheen. Medium vigor, very productive. Needs shelter from rain to have the best flavor and reduce cracking. Prune to spurs. V, WH–Y, T/LV, M.

Katta Kourgane. An old Middle Eastern variety with very large berries and large clusters. However, it has female flowers and needs pollination by another vinifera variety to set fruit. Flavor is neutral, but the texture is firm. I first acquired it to use in breeding, but it's a nice grape by itself when well pollinated. Prune to spurs. V, WH, T, LM.

Muscat Blanc. The classic muscat wine grape, also called Moscato Di Canelli and other names. Not a grape for an amateur,

as it cracks very readily when ripe and rots easily. The flavor is excellent, but between the cracking, rot, and yellow jackets, it's almost impossible to get a useable crop. V, G–WH, W, EM.

Muscat Hamburg. (BLACK HAMBURG X MUSCAT OF ALEXANDRIA) This black muscat is so good that I grow it even though I rarely get a fully ripe crop (raccoons have a lot to do with that). The oval berries are variable in size, but the flavor is consistently excellent. Resists cracking fairly well. Spur pruning works well for me, but other references suggest cane pruning. V, B,T/W, LM.

Muscat Ottonel. This white muscat is only suitable for the coolest areas. Even for me, the climate is too warm and the acid drops before the sugar is at favorable levels, resulting in a very flat-tasting grape and poor wine. Early Muscat has better balance for wine. V, WH, W, T, E.

Orange Muscat. A wine grape, said to be a sport of Muscat Blanc, but I am inclined to think it is a seedling or separate variety. It cracks noticeably less than Muscat Blanc. This variety has the strongest muscat flavor I've found: the "orange" in the name refers to the flavor, which is so strong it is citrus-like. Prune to spurs. V, WH, W/T, M.

Perle de Csaba. The two best features of this grape are that it is very early and it has muscat flavor. It lacks vigor and has thin canes. Prune to spurs. V, WH, T, VE.

Queen of the Vineyard (syn. Skolokertek Kiralynoje). A white variety from Hungary, very early, with firm flesh and an interesting, light muscat flavor with overtones of rose petals. Clusters not especially large by themselves, but some very large, handsome ones can be developed by careful thinning at bloom time. Should be spur-pruned. V, WH, T, E.

SEEDLESS VINIFERA VARIETIES

These are the types of grapes commonly sold in grocery stores. Between the lack of resistance to American grape diseases in vinifera grapes and the fact that most, if not all, are descendants of varieties from the Middle East, the only place it is relatively easy to grow these varieties outdoors is where the growing season is dry and relatively warm, if not hot.

Beauty Seedless. (QUEEN OF THE VINEYARD X BLACK KISHMISH) U.C. Davis. The first black seedless created by breeding. Small, ovoid berries with a light spicy flavor. With thinning, 5-pound clusters are possible, but not advisable. The variety is prone to botrytis bunch rot, and large clusters can be infected internally without outward signs. Infected clusters will collapse in your hands when picked. Survived an early freeze of 5°F (–15°C), with less damage than most other vinifera. Very vigorous, prune to spurs. V, B, T/RS/L, E.

Black Corinth (syn. Zante Currant, and a lot of other aliases). A very old Greek variety. Promoted by a produce dealer as the "Champagne grape" simply because the very small berries looked fancy in a photo next to a glass of champagne. Physiologically, the flowers are essentially male, but have very small ovaries that will sometimes develop into tiny seedless grapes. With girdling or hormone treatment, more berries will set and they will be larger. Without treatment, the cluster is straggly, mostly stem with a sprinkling of pinhead-sized berries. I strongly advise against it as a home grape as you *must* either treat it with hormone or girdle the vine to stimulate berry size; also, the variety is the most susceptible to powdery mildew of my collection. As a vinifera, it has no resistance to other diseases, either. Ironically, there is an old red grape variety called Champagne that is a very coarse, poor-quality labrusca grape.

How did Black Corinth get started? It was probably developed as a pollinator variety. The legend is that a donkey tied to a Black Corinth vine circled the vine repeatedly until the rope girdled the vine, causing the plant to produce more and larger berries on the clusters. Prune to cane. V, B, RS/T, M.

Black Monukka. An old variety that isn't necessarily black—it may be mottled reddish black, or even black and green. Larger berries than Thompson Seedless, but lower sugar than that variety. Seed traces are often large, sometimes even partly hardened. Too prone to cracking and bunch rot in rainy weather in the Northwest. Prune to canes. V, RB, T/RS, M.

Centennial. (PVP) (GOLD X Q25-6) U.C. DAVIS. An excellent grape—firm, crisp, with mild muscat flavor and some of the largest berries of any seedless grape—this variety should have been a winner. However, the berries are uneven sizes, and the stems don't stay green in shipping, two things that destroyed it for commercial sales. An excellent raisin variety, with very large raisins that could be a specialty item, but commercial users want small raisins for baking and processing. Skin is tender, cracking in wet weather. It is an example of how an apparent winner can become an unknown. Prune to canes. V, WH, T/RS, EM.

Dawn. (PVP) (GOLD X PERLETTE) U.C. Davis. Like Centennial, very large berries for a seedless grape. Tougher, more crack-resistant skin, with more uniform berry size than Centennial. Color looks a little like Gold. A very attractive, early grape. Flavor is neutral. Prune to canes. V, WH, T/RS, EM.

Delight. (QUEEN OF THE VINEYARD X THOMPSON SEEDLESS) U.C. Davis. A sister seedling of Perlette, I think it's the better of the two. Fruit is sweeter, ripens a bit earlier, with a hint of muscat, and it doesn't crack quite as much as Perlette. The vine has short internodes that make it more bushy, slower to establish, but easier to handle. Prune to spurs. V, Y, T/RS, E.

DoVine. (COMPLEX PARENTAGE) United States Department of Agriculture (USDA) Fresno. The first variety produced by embryo rescue, it has no visible seed remnant, only an insignificant dot in the flesh where seeds would be. Bred for a new system of producing raisins, the name is short for Dried on Vine, and refers to that system. The canes are cut when the fruit is ripe, leaving the clusters to dry while hanging on the wires instead of being laid on trays on the ground. Then a machine comes through the vineyard and shakes the raisins off. The result is much cleaner, higher-quality raisins than with the old method. DoVine is quite early to ripen and should be a good home table variety because of its high sugar. Prune to spurs. V, WH, T/RS, E.

Fantasy Seedless. (COMPLEX PARENTAGE) USDA Fresno. This grape has large, oval, black berries that are unusual for a seedless

in that you should *not* treat them with gibberellic acid (GA) to enlarge them. Besides the fact that they are large enough without treatment, the vine responds badly to GA and may not be fruitful the following year. Prune to canes. V, B, T/RS, M.

Flame Seedless. (COMPLEX PARENTAGE) USDA Fresno. If you think you know Flame Seedless from the grocery store, you don't know it. The berries are smaller on untreated vines, though still respectable, tend to be darker in color in cooler climates, and the vine is *vigorous* to a fault. I grow mine without watering, and I still get canes 20 feet long. More resistant to cracking than other vinifera grapes, at least partly due to the open clusters, which dry quickly after rain. Prune to spurs, and space vines at least 10 feet apart. V, R, T/RS, E.

Fresno Seedless. (COMPLEX PARENTAGE) USDA Fresno. A white sister-seedling to Flame Seedless, this is mainly a home garden variety. Berries are firm and crisp and ripen about as early as Perle de Csaba, the standard of earliness in vinifera grapes. Does not hang well, as the stems quickly dry and turn brown, so that the clusters break and shatter. Productivity medium at best, vine of average vigor. Prune to canes. V, WH, T, R, VE.

Ruby Seedless. (EMPEROR X PIROVANO 75) U.C. Davis. The red oval berries of this variety have tougher skin than some, which helps keep them from cracking in fall rain. Still, the variety is late enough that it does best with some "help" in the Northwest, such as growing it under the eaves of a south-facing wall. Very vigorous and productive. Keeps well. Prune to spurs. Also known as King's Ruby. V, R, T/LV, L.

Thompson Seedless (syn. Sultanine Blanche, Sultanina, Sultana, Kechmish Jaune, Kis-mis alb, Kismis belil ovalnti, etc.). Why describe such a common variety? Because the form most people see in the grocery stores is anything but typical of the variety. First, Thompson Seedless grapes sold in stores have been treated with gibberellic acid until they are far larger and of a different shape and texture than the untreated ones. The clusters have had parts removed, as the natural Thompson cluster can be 2 feet long and weigh 5 pounds. Natural Thompson, when well ripened, has an excellent balance of sugar and acid that is distinctly different from the GA-treated fruit. Nor is Thompson just for table fruit or raisins: It is also widely used for wine as a neutral, balanced blending base for mixing with other varieties, or in flavored wines. Finally, Thompson Seedless is a very old variety, and as such has many sports and variants: types with larger fruit than usual, some with a pink blush on the berries, some with nearly all red berries, and more. Thompson is also the source of all stenospermocarpic seedless grapes, even the American seedless grape varieties. Breeding has transferred seedlessness to many varieties, but they probably all trace back to Thompson.

One of the reasons for Thompson Seedless's long popularity with growers is that it is a triple-use variety. If the market isn't favorable for table fruit, the grapes can be made into raisins. If raisin sales are soft, it can go to the winery.

If you can grow Thompson Seedless, be sure to prune it to canes, as it is not fruitful when trained to spurs. V, WH, T/RS/W, LM.

MUSCADINE GRAPES

I first tasted muscadine grapes when I was a student at U.C. Davis. That part of California has enough heat to ripen muscadines well, and the university had an interesting collection. The fruit has a wonderful aroma, and I quickly learned to enjoy their flavor. Also, since my thesis involved hybrids of muscadines with bunch grapes, I got to know them fairly well.

While muscadines are generally the most disease-resistant grapes grown in the United States, there is a lot of individual variation. For instance, black rot will attack some cultivars, but not others. Some show no symptoms when they are infected with Pierce's disease, while others show a crisping of the edges of the leaves (though they seem to grow normally otherwise).

While the same general principles apply to growing bunch grapes and muscadine grapes, there are enough differences that I don't have room to include them all. Instead, I'll refer you to two useful Web sites. The first is www.smallfruits.org/MuscadineGro/toc.htm which offers an in-depth guide to muscadine care. For pictures of diseases of muscadines, go to www.ces.ncsu.edu/depts/pp/notes/Fruit/fdin012/fdin012.htm.

Muscadine Varieties

Scuppernong bronze and Thomas black are the cultivars most widely known and asked for by the public. The following are much improved recommended cultivars.

TABLE 10-1

Relative Hardiness and Disease Resistance of Wine, Juice, and Table Grape Varieties

Variety	WH	BR	DM	PM	BOT	PHOM	EU	CG	ALS	Sulfur
Alden	4	?	+	++	++	?	?	?	?	No
Alwood	4	+	+	+	+	?	?	?	?	?
Aurore	4	+++	++	+++	+++	?	?	?	+++	No
Baco Noir	4	+++	+	++	+	+	++	+++	++	No
Beta	6+	+	+	+	+	?	?	?	?	?
Bluebell	6+	?	?	?	?	?	?	?	?	?
Buffalo	4	?	++	+++	++	?	?	?	?	No
Cabernet Franc	3	+++	+++	+++	+	?	+++	+++	?	No
Cabernet Sauvignon	2	+++	+++	+++	+	+++	+++	+++	?	No
Captivator Catawba	5	+++	+++	++	+	+++	+	+	+	No
Cayuga White	4	+	++	+	+	+	+	?	++	No
Chambourcin	3	+++	++	+	++	?	?	++	?	Yes
Chancellor	5	+	+++	+++	+	+++	+	++	+++	Yes and Cu
Chardonel	4	?	++	+++	++	?	?	++	++	No
Chardonnay	2	++	+++	+++	+++	+++	++	+++	++	No
Chelois	4	+	+	+++	+	?	?	?	+++	No
Colobel	3	?	+	+++	+	?	?	?	?	?
Concord	5	+++	+	++	+	+++	+++	+	++	Yes
Cynthiana (Norton)	5	?	?	++	?	?	?	?	?	?

Key to abbreviations:

WH = Winter hardiness
  1 = too tender for all but a few select sites, to about -5°F
  2 = tender, to about -10°F
  3 = slightly hardy, may be grown on better sites, to about -15°F
  4 = moderately hardy, to about -20°F
  5 = hardy, to about -25°F
  6 = very hardy, worthy of trial on cold sites, to -35°F or colder

BR = Black rot
DM = Downy mildew

PM = Powdery mildew
Bot = Botrytis
Phom = Phomopsis
Eu = Eutypa
CG = Crown gall
ALS = Angular leaf scorch
Sulfur = sensitivity to sulfur spray injury
Cu = sensitivity to copper spray injury

Disease categories are rated as follows
  + = slightly susceptible or sensitive
  ++ = moderately susceptible or sensitive
  +++ = highly susceptible or sensitive
  ? = relative susceptibility or sensitivity not established

This table was compiled from several sources and should not be taken as absolute—disease and hardiness ratings can vary by climate and locale.

TABLE 10-1 *continued*

Variety	WH	BR	DM	PM	BOT	PHOM	EU	CG	ALS	Sulfur
De Chaunac	5	+	++	+++	+	++	+++	++	+++	Yes
Delaware	5	++	+++	++	++	+++	+	+	++	No
Dutchess	3	+++	+++	+++	?	?	?	?	+	?
Edelweiss	6	?	+	++	++	?	?	?	?	?
Elvira	6	+	++	++	+++	?	?	?	++	No
Esprit	5	?	++	+++	++	?	?	?	?	?
Fredonia	5	+	+++	++	+	?	?	?	+	No
Frontenac	6	++	++	+	+	?	?	?	?	?
Gewurztraminer	2	+++	+++	+++	++	?	?	?	+	No
Golden Muscat	4	?	++	++	+++	?	?	?	?	No
Horizon	5	?	+	+++	++	?	?	+	+++	No
Ives	5	+	+++	+	+	?	?	?	+	Yes
Kay Gray	6+	+	+	+	+	?	?	?	?	?
LaCrosse	5	+++	+	++	+++	?	?	?	?	?
Léon Millot	5	?	+	++	+++	?	?	+	?	?
Limberger	2	+++	+++	+++	+	?	+++	+++	?	No
Maréchal Foch	5	++	+	++	+	?	+++	?	+	Yes
Melody	4	+++	++	+	+	?	?	?	++	No
Merlot	1	++	+++	+++	+++	+++	+++	+++	Ê	No
Missouri Reisling	5	?	?	?	?	?	?	?	++	?
Moore's Diamond	4	+++	+	+++	++	?	?	?	?	No
New York Muscat	4	?	+	+++	++	?	?	?	?	Yes
Niagara	4	+++	+++	++	+	+++	+	++	+	No
Pinot Blanc	2	+++	+++	+++	++	?	+++	+++	?	No
Pinot Gris	2	+++	+++	+++	++	?	+++	+++	?	No
Pinot Noir	1	+++	+++	+++	Varies	?	+++	+++	++	No
Ravat 34	4	?	+	++	+	?	?	?	?	No
Rosette	6	?	?	?	?	?	?	?	++	?
Rougeon	4	++	+++	+++	++	?	?	?	+++	Yes
St. Croix	6	?	++	++	++	?	?	?	?	?
St. Pepin	5	?	+	+++	++	?	?	?	?	?
St. Vincent	4	++	++	++	++	?	?	?	?	?

TABLE 10-1 *continued*

Variety	WH	BR	DM	PM	BOT	PHOM	EU	CG	ALS	Sulfur
Seneca	3	+	+	+++	++	?	?	?	?	Yes
Seyval	4	+++	++	+++	+++	+	+	+++	++	No
Sheridan	5	?	+	++	+	?	?	?	?	?
Shiraz	2	+++	+++	+++	+++	?	?	?	?	?
Steuben	5	++	+	+	+	?	?	+	++	No
Sunbelt	5	?	?	?	?	?	?	?	?	?
Swenson Red	5	?	+++	++	++	?	?	?	?	?
Traminette	4	++	++	++	++	?	?	?	?	?
Valiant	6+	+	+++	+	++	?	?	?	?	?
Van Buren	5	?	+++	++	++	?	?	?	?	Yes
Ventura	6	++	++	+++	+	?	?	+	+++	No
Vidal Blanc	3	+	++	+++	+	+	+	+++	+	No
Vignoles	5	+	++	+++	+++	++	++	+++	++	No
Villard Blanc	3	+	++	+++	+	?	?	?	?	?
Vincent	4	?	+	++	+	?	?	?	?	?
White Riesling	2	+++	+++	+++	+++	0	++	+++	+	No
Worden Seedless	6	+	+	+	+	?	?	?	?	?
Canadice	4	+++	+	+	++	?	?	?	++	No
Concord Seedless	5	?	+	++	++	?	?	?	?	Yes
Einset	4	+++	++	+++	+	?	?	?	?	?
Glenora	3	++	++	+++	+	?	?	?	?	?
Himrod	4	+++	+	++	+	?	?	?	+	No
Interlaken	3	+++	+	+++	++	?	?	?	?	No
Lakemont	3	++	+	++	++	?	?	?	?	No
Marquis	4	++	++	++	+	?	?	?	?	?
Mars	4	+	+	+	+	?	?	?	?	?
Reliance	5	+++	++	++	+++	?	?	?	?	?
Remaily	3	?	?	?	?	?	?	?	+	?
Saturn	2	++	++	+++	++	?	?	?	?	?
Suffolk Red	3	?	+	++	++	?	?	?	?	Yes
Vanessa	4	+++	++	++	+	?	?	?	?	?
Venus	4	+	++	+	+++	?	?	?	?	?

Carlos. bronze, midseason, medium size, perfect-flowered, very dry stem scar, good fresh or for wine.

Doreen. bronze, very late, medium size, perfect-flowered, dry stem scar, good fresh or for wine.

Magnolia. bronze, early, medium to large size, perfect-flowered, wet stem scar, excellent fresh flavor, good for making wine and juice.

Nesbitt. black, early, large size, perfect-flowered, dry stem scar, good fresh, poor wine color.

Noble. black, early, small size, perfect-flowered, wet scar; good fresh flavor, good for making wine and juice.

Regale. black, mid-season, medium size, perfect-flowered, wet scar, good fresh, good for making wine and juice.

Triumph. bronze, early, large size, perfect-flowered, dry scar, good fresh, fair for making wine.

All of these cultivars are perfect-flowered (have both male and female flower parts) so a single vine will be fruitful. Other available cultivars such as Fry, Higgins, Scuppernong, and Jumbo have flowers with only female flower parts. They must be planted near a perfect-flowered cultivar to ensure pollination.

Muscadine grapes can often be grown successfully without insecticides or fungicides. Japanese beetles are often the most damaging insect pests. Cultivars with some disease resistance such as Carlos, Nesbitt, Noble, Triumph, or Regal will show less severe loss than others without fungicide applications.

When a berry separates from the vine, the stem end of the berry may show a small wound—this is called a wet scar. The wound leaves the fruit more susceptible to deterioration. Dry scar varieties separate cleanly. Magnolia and Scuppernong are wet-scar varieties. Ison's Doreen, Supreme, and Carlos are dry scar types. Wet-scar varieties are usually used mostly for juice or wine, while dry-scar types are more durable and can be sold as fresh fruit.

Some cultivars seem to be "regional" in that they do better in one area than in others. Varieties suited to South Carolina, for instance, sometimes are less vigorous and don't do as well in northern Florida.

Several growers have reported good results from growing seedling muscadines. Muscadines produce a much higher percentage of seedlings with good-quality fruit than other grapes, and, by growing a few seedlings, you increase the chances of getting one that is particularly well adapted to your area. Ideally, get your seed from a vine that has perfect flowers, so you will have a better chance of getting a self-fertile seedling. (See chapter 8 for instructions on how to grow grapes from seed.)

BUNCH GRAPES
for the DEEP SOUTH

Muscadines are not the only grapes for the Deep South and Florida, though they are the predominant types. There are bunch grapes that have been bred using several *Vitis aestivalis*– type grapes in Florida and Mississippi that have good resistance to Pierce's disease (PD). Many of these varieties can resist the intense pressure from fungal diseases in that climate. These are

MUSCAT AND MUSCADINE—both are grapes, but besides that, all they have in common are the first five letters of their names: musca. If you had ever eaten the two types, you wouldn't mistake one for the other.

Muscat most likely started out as the name of the variety known as Muscat of Alexandria. The name Muscat refers to the place it was thought to have originated—the Sultanate of Muscat in northern Africa. The popular flavor has been bred into many other varieties, and Muscat refers to the wonderful, flowery, aromatic flavor of the many varieties of muscat grapes. In my own collection, I have Early Muscat, Muscat Hamburg, Orange Muscat, Muscat Blanc, Morio Muscat, New York Muscat, and several others that have the muscat flavor, but not the name. And there are many more.

Muscadine grapes, now classified as the genus and species *Muscadinia rotundifolia*, are native to the southeast United States, a hot, humid climate that fosters so much disease that any grape not native to the area has little chance of surviving for long. In traditional nomenclature, "muscadine" refers to the form of the species with black fruit, while the large, bronze- or white-berried type was known as Scuppernong. Both are actually the same species, just different varieties. And while there is no one variety named "muscadine," Scuppernong *is* the name of an old variety, first thought to have been selected or found by the natives of the area long before the arrival of Europeans.

To further confuse the issue, a native grape of Texas is the Mustang grape *(Vitis mustangensis, also called V. candicans)*, which is nothing like either of the other two.

also varieties worth testing in other wet, subtropical climates.

Blanc Du Bois. Florida. A white wine grape for the south with a muscat-like flavor. Self-fertile. Susceptible to black rot, ripe rot, and anthracnose in the Florida climate. Resistant to Pierce's disease. California growers should consider planting this grape in areas of the state where PD has become a serious problem. In the much drier climate there, this grape could be grown with no disease control and still produce very acceptable wines.

Blue Lake. (VITIS SMALLIANA X CACO) Florida. Blue; for table, juice, and jelly. Resistant to PD. In some seasons it needs pollination from another variety, such as Lake Emerald, for good fruit set.

Conquistador. [(VITIS SMALLIANA X CONCORD) X (NORRIS X CONCORD)] Florida. A Concord-like grape for Florida conditions; for eating, juice, and jelly. Tolerant of PD. Late bud break.

Daytona. (FL. 133-90 X EXOTIC) Florida. A red table grape that resembles Tokay. Large, red, firm berries. Vine tolerates PD.

Lake Emerald. (VITIS SIMPSONII 'PIXIOLA' X GOLDEN MUSCAT) Florida. Mixed reports on this one. A grower in Florida reports Lake Emerald as one of his heaviest-bearing "old reliable" grapes, while others say it is light-bearing. It's likely that some of the stock of this juicy, green, aromatic grape are infected with virus, so that getting clean stock may make a considerable difference. Has proven tolerant of PD over years of testing, and often needs little or no spray for fungal diseases.

MissBlanc. [GALIBERT 261-12 X (SEEDLING OF EXTRA X MARGUERITE) Mississippi.

Very heavy-bearing, up to 60 pounds per vine, of white grapes. Survived nine years of PD in testing. Ripe in mid-August in Mississippi.

MissBlue. (VITIS CHAMPINI X MOORE EARLY) Mississippi. Rather like a Concord type. Sugar levels not high enough for wine; mainly for table or juice. Heavy yields, 9 to 12 tons per acre. Survived nine years exposure to PD. Ripens in late July to mid-August in Mississippi.

These are only a few possibilities. I know private breeders in South Carolina who have bred hybrids of bunch grapes crossed with muscadines that are some of the toughest, most disease-resistant grapes around. Sadly, there is no commercial source for them, so all I can do is mention that they exist.

Grapes have also been developed in Puerto Rico and elsewhere for rainy, humid, tropical conditions—varieties with names like Esperanza and Valplatinta.

There is no way to cover all possible grapes for all possible growing conditions, but there are varieties for all climates if a grower is serious about seeking them out. The best advice I can give is to keep searching.

SEEDED *or* SEEDLESS

In most grocery stores nowadays the produce section sells only seedless grapes. But go to the gourmet section and you may find grapeseed oil, while the health section offers grapeseed extract at pretty high prices.

Winemakers know that grape seeds contribute several substances to wine that improve its ability to age, so they often leave the juice or must in contact with the skins and seeds for as long as possible during fermentation. This maximizes the amount of tannins, phenols, and other substances that add body and character to the wine. And many of these same substances have now been found to be beneficial to human health (hence the grapeseed extract). However, at least two grape breeders tried to develop seedless red wine grapes that could be used to produce red wine that would be drinkable while very young. Without seeds, the wine would get only enough tannins and color to have the right appearance and body, without needing long aging to mellow out after extended fermentation on the seeds. Neither breeder was able to bring their projects to fruition before the end of their careers.

There is a type of special gourmet cheese that is aged in grape seeds. It was a tradition in the Savoy region of France to keep a few old slabs of cheese called "tommes," and to leave them, once winter had arrived, to macerate in grape marc, the remains of skins and seeds left from the pressing of the grapes. The result of this manipulation, known as Tomme au Marc, was great. Under the crust, which was coarse, black, and studded with grape seeds, was hidden a flesh with a unique flavor, a mixture of softness, finesse, and character. This was also known as Fondu au Raisin or La Grappe.

Given the proven medicinal value of grape seed, as well as the flavors and other characters seeds can impart to food, wine, and cheeses, it seems odd that so many people find grape seeds objectionable. Denture wearers might have trouble with seeds getting under their plates, but for everyone else, grape seeds are small enough to be swallowed unnoticed. There are exceptions, of course. There are giant varieties of grapes bred in Japan in which seed size has increased along with berry size, so the plum-sized fruits have seeds like small cherry pits. But the Japanese like such large fruits for appearance and often use them ceremonially rather than just to pop in the mouth.

Not everyone feels this way. There have been people who came to me looking for grapes who insisted that they only wanted seeded grapes. Some even objected to seedless grapes on Biblical grounds, saying they were an abomination because they couldn't reproduce themselves. Not quite true, but that's another story, told elsewhere in the book.

There are a *lot* of *good* seeded grapes out there. Only seeded grapes can have both size and really high quality. That is, it is possible to treat seedless grapes with a hormone to increase the berry size, but often that makes the berries tough, watery, and lacking sweetness. Even in my collection, although I have some very good seedless grapes, the very best grapes are seeded types.

A few years ago, grocery stores sold many types of seeded grapes. Some of the first of the season, in early summer, were the red, big-berried Cardinal. Of course there were seedless in the mix, usually Thompson Seedless, but most of the varieties had seeds. As the season progressed, there was a cornucopia of varieties: big red, meaty, sweet Flame Tokay; perfumed Italia; solid Malaga of both the Red and Green varieties; and the black, globular Ribier, considered one of the best for generations in Europe because of its excellent firmness and balance of sugar and acid. Winter meant Emperor: solid, red, almost cherry-flavored, and able to keep in cold storage until spring. Then there was Almeria, a very solid, almost olive-green grape that kept forever and almost always showed up in Christmas fruit bowls. Not the best, but still festive when midwinter was at full depth.

Now grocery stores sell seedless grapes almost exclusively, and very few varieties. Once the summer season is over in California, suppliers turn to selling the same varieties, produced in South America, so they play on and on all year long, like a broken record.

Even raisins were once made from a seeded grape, the old Muscat of Alexandria. A few specialty growers still produce them. They are big, meaty, richly aromatic raisins that taste more like candy than dried fruit. And while the seeds can be mechanically removed, I've eaten them with seeds, which added a nutty crunch that made the raisins even more like a confection. In fairness, Muscat of Alexandria, seeds or not, ripens so late that it's difficult to make sun-dried raisins from the fruit in all but a very few places (another important reason it isn't grown much now). Thompson Seedless took over as much because it was earlier as because it was seedless: growers had more chance to sun-dry the fruit and bring it into storage before the fall rains started.

I do eat seedless grapes and I do like them; they definitely have their place. But I also appreciate the excellent quality of many seeded grapes and the healthy virtues of grape seeds.

CHOOSING VARIETIES

Too many people plant grapes on a whim. They see vines offered in a garden center, or more likely in a big chain store, and they plant the vines. They think of homemade jelly or some other fond memory from their childhood without really knowing what they will do with the grapes.

Buying even one grapevine should be a conscious decision, not something done on impulse. Before you plant even one vine, sit down and ask yourself some questions, as follows.

Home Growers

1. *How are you going to use it?*

Fresh fruit to eat. If you just want fresh fruit in season and nothing else, one vine of most varieties will do very well for four people. For comparison, most grapes in the grocery store are wholesaled in 22-pound lugs (flat boxes). One box that size is about all that four people can eat before they spoil, unless you have cold storage for them, and a mature vine of most varieties of bunch grapes will produce at *least* that much fruit.

Juice. That same 22-pound lug will yield 1½ to 2 gallons of raw juice. Be sure you *want* juice before you get juice grapes, though. If you've never made grape juice, buy a lug of grapes from a farmer and make juice from them *before* you plant vines. Then you'll know if you want to do that year after year when your own vines produce.

Home Wine. In good conditions, a mature wine-grapevine should produce 1 gallon of wine, but production of wine grape varieties varies enough that you should plan on ten vines to produce a 5-gallon carboy of wine.

2. *How much work do you want to put into the vine?*

If your climate is a cold one, are you willing to protect a tender vine in the winter, or would you prefer something that doesn't need special treatment?

3. *Is this variety disease resistant?*

Even though proper care can help a vine tremendously, it won't necessarily guarantee that it will be free of disease. Choosing resistant types to start with can make care a lot easier and disease control more certain.

Commercial Growers

Ask yourself questions 2 and 3 from the previous section. Then consider:

1. *What is your market?*

Wine grapes. If you're going to make and sell your own wine, the choice of varieties is your own. But if you plan to sell to a winery, it's best go to them *before* you plant and ask what they will buy from you.

If you live near a population center you may be able to sell to home winemakers, in which case you have more leeway in which varieties you plant. Once you are known, you can often set up contracts with customers and sell your crop in advance.

2. *Do you want to grow table or juice grapes?*

You have lots of options here, including

selling to farm stands, farmers' markets, and local grocery stores. An organic grower I know sells his grapes to hotels and restaurants in a nearby city. For grocery stores and restaurants, the highest demand is for seedless grapes. For farmers' markets and farm stands, customers are often looking for juice grapes, but also will also accept "old-fashioned" seeded grapes in that setting as they are more "rustic." In such markets, you can do a little more educating and personal promoting, so that it is often possible to teach your customers about the flavor and high quality of seeded table grapes.

Juice grapes usually sell by the lug, or at least in large baskets, though the people looking to make juice are fewer than in the past. If you have facilities to make it, fresh raw juice often sells very well.

A range of varieties can extend your market. In my vineyard, I grow varieties with at least a six-week spread in ripening times from the earliest to the latest. Some of the varieties store well enough to stretch the season out past Christmas in most cases. For storage, cold facilities are needed that will keep the grapes as close to 32°F (0°C) as possible.

Ultimately, the best idea to start with is to plant a range of types and see which grapes do best for your needs. From there, you can take cuttings off your favorites to start larger plantings.

COLLECTING GRAPE VARIETIES

People come to me looking for hard-to-find varieties of grapes, but it's surprising how few ever ask, "How did *you* get all these 'hard-to-find' grapes?"

Locating varieties is a mix of networking, knowing how to look, and just plain luck. In many cases, I didn't set out to find grapes, just people. I wanted to meet the rare folk who were interested in breeding grapes, and those were most often the ones who had made "finds" in gathering the material they used in their work.

Deciding What to Collect

Before you just start collecting grapes, there are steps to take that will help you obtain varieties that are truly what you want and need, not just another name to enable you to say, "I have (fill in the blank) grapes."

First, learn to ask the right questions about a grape before you go looking for it.

- Is that grape hardy or disease-resistant enough for your area? Not much future in growing grapes that will die without producing anything.
- Does it ripen early enough to have a chance to mature for you? Unripe grapes are almost useless, and they *don't* ripen off the vine.
- Does the variety truly have characteristics you want? Collecting a variety simply to have it is a good way to fill space without getting grapes you can use.

Sources for Collectors

Many named varieties are easier to find now than they were when I started, thanks to places like the National Clonal Germ-plasm Repository (NCGR). This series of government research stations around the country has been collecting many varieties and species of fruiting plants and their relatives since the late 1980s, and a lot of varieties can be obtained from them. The collections of grapes in the United States are held in two stations. The branch at Geneva, New York, has most of the old American grapes, plus French Hybrids and American species, as well as other reasonably hardy grapes. Vinifera and other less cold-hardy grapes can be found in the collection at the University of California at Davis. Neither of these collections is 100 percent complete for a couple of reasons. First, this institution doesn't even have access to *every* grape—there are an estimated twenty thousand varieties in the world. Secondly, because of limitations of space and people, the NCGR has had to discard, or not acquire, grapes they feel to be duplicates of material they already have, or at least to have the same sorts of genes. The main purpose of the collections is to save potential breeding material.

Besides the NCGR, there are other publicly available collections in North America that can provide many varieties. The Munson Memorial Vineyard at Grayson Community College in Denison, Texas, has nearly one hundred of the over three hundred varieties bred by T. V. Munson in the late nineteenth century and early twentieth century. The Plant Health Centre in Sydney, British Columbia, has an extensive collection of varieties, including many bred in Canada and Europe that would otherwise be extremely hard to obtain in the United States. While it takes some paperwork (which varies with the state you are in) and a fee to obtain plants from these collections, it is much less costly than trying to import varieties yourself from overseas. Current regulations are such that grapes from overseas must be quarantined and indexed for virus, regardless of their origin.

This can take five years or more and costs several thousand dollars per variety.

Many varieties from overseas have already been imported into the United States, or at least to Canada, if you know where to look. Some of these varieties are in the collections already mentioned. Some may be in the collections of universities with grape breeding programs, though you may need to show that you are a serious breeder or grower before you can obtain material from such collections.

Meeting Other Collectors

There are two groups that are a must for a serious grape collector or breeder. The first is the North American Fruit Explorers (NAFEX), a group of amateurs and professionals all joined through their love of the unusual in fruit. NAFEX has members all over the world and offers a wealth of possibilities for serious fruit collectors. For the very modest cost of one year's membership, you receive four issues of their journal, *Pomona*, and a membership roster, as well as library privileges for members around the world. NAFEX has an online discussion list, as well. I have met some of my most important contacts through NAFEX.

The second group for a really serious grape person to join is the North American Grape Breeders. With about fifty members in North America, this group is composed of private, government, and university breeders. It meets every two years. There is no one contact person for the group, but any university with a grape breeding program can tell you how to get on the membership list to be notified of the meetings. I attended my first meeting in

1985, when the group met in Geneva, New York, and met several grape breeders I had known only by name until then.

Sometimes, grapes will literally fall into your lap. Once people know you have a strong interest in grapes, you will hear from home growers with vines that they inherited from grandparents, vines that they found somewhere and started, and vines that just happen to be on the property. Many of these won't amount to much, but you can make a rare find now and then.

If you are looking for species from overseas, the simplest way to obtain them is as seed. There is no restriction on importing grape seed at present. You may not even have to go overseas: There are already nurseries and seed companies in the United States that carry some of the exotic species. The drawback to starting from seed is the length of time it may take the seedlings to come into bearing—sometimes as long as ten years.

After named varieties and species, the serious collector should also look into things such as numbered breeding selections from private breeders. Experienced private breeders often have selections that they have found to be exceptional parents and have saved them for breeding. Often these selections are fine grapes in their own right, but may have one or two flaws, such as having female flowers. In some cases, by growing these selections you may be helping preserve and pass on the work of decades that would otherwise be lost when the breeder died.

You might think using the Internet would make it easier to find odd varieties, but I have tried Internet searches and often found myself in contact with the same people I've known for years. A lot of plant material is in the hands of old-timers who don't use computers (some hardly use the phone).

The best part of hunting for old varieties of grapes (or any plant, for that matter) is the people you meet in the process. I've enjoyed many good phone conversations and exchanged long letters with some fascinating people I met in the process. I've gone to visit some and made friends that I cherished for as long as I was privileged to know them. People like D. C. Paschke in Pennsylvania, who started working with Cornell grape breeder Fred Gladwin before World War I, and was still interested in grapes when he died at age 101½. Or Professor Elwyn Meader in New Hampshire, one of the foremost plant breeders of our time and also one of the kindest, most gentle men I've ever met. Or Byron Johnson, in Ohio, who got interested in wine when he was holed up in a French chateau in World War II and went on to breed wine grape varieties with very high disease resistance. There are many others, whose names crop up in this book in other places. Often when you find one of these special people, he or she will start you on the trail by introducing you to others, who know still more people, on down the line. Take time to meet them and get to know them—the friendships are worth more than the plants you get from them.

11 GRAPE SPECIES

I N THIS CHAPTER, instead of repeating the usual, dry, botanical descriptions of species (which are readily available elsewhere) I've opted to share odd, interesting, and unusual bits of information that I've accumulated through experience and interaction with other "grape people," and that you won't find in standard reference books.

I include: overlooked values of wild species, weaknesses other books don't tell you about, unusual traits worth knowing about, odd bits of interesting lore, and even some (well-grounded) speculation. Much of this information also ties in with grape breeding and rootstocks. I hope this will help you as a grower to expand your view of grapes and see new possibilities in vines glossed over by others.

VITIS VINIFERA

First, for background, let's discuss the oldest cultivated grape species, which established the standard for all others, *Vitis vinifera*.

V. vinifera probably arose in western Asia and the Middle East. Wild, dioecious vines of the species still exist in the wild in Afghanistan. My professor in graduate school, Dr. H. P. Olmo, told of being chased by bandits in Afghanistan while he was collecting wild plant material. (That was about three decades before the Taliban.) I saw some of those vines in the collection at the University of California at Davis (U.C. Davis). One of their odd traits was a tendency to bloom more than once a season. They bloomed in spring, like most grapes do, but also later in the season on some of the new growth. In North America, only muscadine grapes (*Muscadinia rotundifolia*) do this regularly. In uncertain climates, repeat blooming helps ensure that at least some fruit is produced even in poor years. Though not common, repeat blooming does show up in a few modern grapes. A numbered selection in my collection from the Cornell University Agricultural Experiment Station in Geneva, New York, blooms twice every year, producing a small "secondary" crop about three weeks after the main crop. This grape has at least three species in its parentage besides vinifera, so the "second-crop" trait survived dilution through several generations.

V. vinifera was probably first selected for wine and dried grapes, since those were the main types of preserved grapes in pre-industrial times. In those days, "wine" didn't always mean the alcoholic sort we think of (which was more likely the "strong drink" mentioned in the Bible), but a sort of boiled juice, cooked to concentrate the sugar until it had a syrup-like consistency that resisted spoilage.

Later, though still at least as early as Biblical times, various types of grapes were selected specially for table fruit, as ways were found to extend the life of fresh grapes. One early method was to hang clusters "by their tails," meaning by the cluster stem, in caves, where the constant cool temperature and moist atmosphere would keep the fruit in edible condition for months.

It's possible that for a long time there were very few selected table grapes, at least in many parts of the Middle East. Olmo visited a number of oases in Arabia as part of a program to help improve grapes there and found the same two varieties, one red and one white, in all locations. Obviously, new material was very slow to move into new areas in those parts of the world.

There is a little irony in this, because some of the best vinifera table grape varieties have origins in areas of North Africa and the Middle East where the Islamic religion predominates. Because of the Islamic prohibition against alcohol, grapes are not used for wine, so they have been highly selected for quality table-fruit and raisin grapes.

While the wild form of *V. vinifera* has good qualities, the species has been greatly improved and enhanced by countless growers and breeders over thousands of years in cultivation. The qualities of the fruit include: high sugar content, which keeps raisins from spoiling and yields enough alcohol in fermentation to preserve wine; neutral or "vinous" flavor, plus some distinct flavors desired both for wine and fresh eating; stable pigments, tannins, and other substances that contribute to wine quality; firm, meaty flesh and tender skin in fresh grapes; and seedlessness.

Regarding this last quality, *V. vinifera* is the only original source of this trait used in most grape breeding, so that almost all seedless bunch grapes are, of necessity, descended from *V. vinifera*—and mostly from the single variety Thompson Seedless. *V. vinifera* also lends appeal to table grapes by contributing traits such as large berry size and unusual berry shapes, as well as cluster sizes that are larger than those found in other species.

How large can grapes be? In trials of seedling table grapes bred by Olmo at the U.C. Davis, I saw selections with berries 2 inches and more in diameter. The clusters of such large-size berries tended to be small, since clusters of only a half dozen berries would weigh as much as clusters having a much larger number of smaller berries. The result was that a very few large clusters of such monster grapes could weigh as much as an entire crop of normal-sized berries, making them impractical for commercial use.

Clusters can be large, too. In England, greenhouse-grown specimens of the grape

Grape Shape

IF SOMEONE ASKS WHAT SHAPE A GRAPE IS, "round" is not the only answer. In the bygone days of seeded commercial grapes, the form that was fancied was the "ladyfinger" grape. "Ladyfingers" were elongated grapes prized for their appearance in displays and fruit bowls—they weren't bad eating, either. Ladyfingers weren't even the extreme of that particular grape shape, either. Dr. James Moore of the University of Arkansas tried breeding just for this elongated, slightly pointed shape, to see how far he could exaggerate it. The result was berries so long and pointed they were nicknamed "needle berries" (shown below).

Beans and grapes have a shape in common, too. A sport of the old variety Emperor, "Jelly Bean" failed to develop on one side of the berry, leaving it with a curved, kidney bean shape. The technical name for this grape shape is falcoid.

Then there are oval, flattened, oblate, pear-shaped, and even some almost cylindrical grapes.

Nor are grape berries always smooth-skinned. In a group of seedlings bred by Dr. H. P. Olmo, I saw berries that had little flat spots on them, much the way a wax berry will have. These were part of a group that had been bred for crispness, and they were so solid they crunched and cracked when you bit into them, almost like an apple. None was deemed worthy of release, though.

Some grapes even have dimples. The variety old Ribier (also called Alphonse LaValle) can be identified by a sort of tri-part dent in the bottom of the berry, a trait it shares with Cardinal, one of its descendants.

A ball or an egg, a needle or a bean—how many grape shapes there are to be seen.

Trebbiano, given careful attention, including cluster thinning, are reported to have produced clusters weighing 22 pounds. I have seen a variety called Ranspay that produces multi-branched clusters of weighing 10 pounds without any special care. The fruits are small and blue, not particularly good as table fruit, but valuable in breeding new varieties. Crossed with small-clustered American species, Ranspay produces hybrids with much larger clusters than are possible with other vinifera varieties.

As a vine, *V. vinifera* grows easily from cuttings and is generally vigorous, productive, and manageable. The species tolerates alkaline soils better than most and grows in desert regions where temperatures regularly reach 100°F (38°C) and hotter. *V. vinifera* needs less winter chill than other temperate fruits to break dormancy. On the down side, it has little or no tolerance to American grape diseases and pests and is usually hardy only to about −5°F (−21°C), though some varieties from northern Europe are reported hardy to −20°F (−29°C). Some botanists debate if such types are pure vinifera or not. As humans traveled, they commonly took their fruits with them to plant in new locales, and it is likely that vinifera vines interbred with local grape species until the local species were essentially absorbed. From such natural hybrids, people undoubtedly selected types with good fruit that were better adapted to local conditions than the varieties they had brought with them. In the United States, *V. vinifera* grows best where winters are mild and summers have low humidity and little rain. Vinifera vines fail in most areas outside the American West and Southwest unless sprayed heavily, protected in winter, and grafted to rootstocks that tolerate adverse soil conditions and/or root pests and diseases.

VITIS AMURENSIS

V. amurensis is another Old World grape species that has drawn interest because of its hardiness, with forms reported in China and Russia able to withstand temperatures of −40°F (−40°C) and below. As researchers have worked with it in the United States, however, it has shown certain drawbacks.

First, while *V. amurensis* can withstand great cold, it is typical of many species with near-Arctic hardiness in that it is hardy mainly in non-fluctuating winter climates. In its native area, once temperatures go below freezing in the fall, they stay very cold until spring, when they go up and stay above freezing for the whole growing season. Plants adapted to such climates are kept dormant by the cold, ready to burst into growth at the first sign of warm weather. In much of temperate North America, however, winter temperatures fluctuate, with frequent spells above freez-

ing during the winter, later returning to subfreezing. In such conditions, *V. amurensis* tends to de-harden during a warm spell, becoming cold tender, to be killed when the temperature drops again. Further, some researchers who have tried the species report that at least some forms have unpleasant flavors, though other selections have been neutral in flavor, more like *V. vinifera.* Finally, since *V. amurensis*, like *V. vinifera*, evolved in the absence of American grape pests, it has little or no resistance when grown in North America, or other areas where American grape diseases and insects have reached.

There is, however, a good deal of variation in the species. I have seen a presentation by a Chinese researcher who showed slides of Chinese types of *V. amurensis* with white fruit (most selections are blue), and types with clusters one foot or more long (the usual types have 3-inch clusters). The researcher indicated these types were hardy to more than −40°F (−40°C). Further, the Japanese have produced commercial wine from amurensis selections, as evidenced by a bottle sent to me from a Japanese research station. The wine was a red, and was rather acid and lacking in body, but it had no off flavors.

So there is potential in *V. amurensis*, though in North America it would have to be bred with other species to create something useful. For example, if the hardiness of *V. amurensis* could be combined with genes to keep the vine dormant during midwinter warm spells, it could bring vinifera-like flavor into very hardy grapes. A number of amurensis selections also have excellent fall color, with some having red foliage even during the growing season, offering the potential for breeding excellent ornamental vines. Some amurensis selections ripen very early, which suggests that the grapes could be adapted to cool, short seasons. In fact, wine-grape varieties recently observed in the Baltic area by Tom Plocher are some of the earliest grapes yet found, able to ripen in cooler weather than has been seen previously.

While grape species in Asia generally have little more resistance to American diseases than *V. vinifera*, they should still be explored by those seeking new and different traits for grapes. For example, a friend who is a private grape breeder accompanied a group on a plant-hunting expedition to China: He told of tasting grapes with flavors unlike any he had encountered elsewhere.

Unusual vine traits could be used to create highly ornamental grapes. *V. davidii* is a Chinese species with unusual, thick, thorn-like hairs that give the vine a most striking appearance. Its fruit is edible and it could be used to breed grapes that would be both ornamental and edible.

AMERICAN GRAPE SPECIES

At present, the grape species that probably have the greatest potential for breeding work are the American species. These grapes have pest and disease resistance, the ability to grow in many adverse climates and soils, extremely early ripening, and the ability to produce in short, cool seasons where *V. vinifera* would fail.

In looking at the different American grape species, I've noticed that almost all the valuable traits of *V. vinifera* exist in them, just not combined in one species. Even so, it's theoretically possible that grapes having the most desirable vinifera traits could be bred by planned crosses of American grape species, though it might take more than one lifetime to achieve perfection.

One thing that would help in such a project is all the variation within the native species. An unpleasant trait of a species may not exist in all members of that species. Likewise, a useful trait may be stronger in some individuals than others. This is where it's easy to see the value of being able to examine as many members of a species as possible.

For instance, T. V. Munson reported that many of his varieties with *V. lincecumii* in their parentage had good tolerance of alkaline soil in Denison, Texas. However, in another area of Texas, private breeder J. Cottingham has found many of Munson's selections lacking in alkaline tolerance. At the same time, Cottingham found local forms of *V. lincecumii* and other species used by Munson that had much greater tolerance to the "black-waxy" soils of Texas, which are very alkaline.

This shows that if you are looking for grapes that are adapted to difficult conditions, you need to examine as wide a range of material as possible: You may find important qualities in a few individuals that are lacking in the species as a whole.

This doesn't refer just to grapes to be used for breeding for fruit, either. I've heard from more than one private grape grower who traveled the surrounding countryside and collected cuttings of local wild grapes to use as rootstocks. These growers believed that using local vines as rootstock would help the varieties grafted to them adapt to local conditions. I haven't seen any long-term results from such experiments, but so far the growers report no obvious problems and are encouraged by the general performance of the vines.

Private breeder Elmer Swenson found several local selections of *V. riparia* in Wisconsin that have produced favorable increases in cold hardiness in varieties grafted to them. In Texas, Cottingham found several local selections of *V. berlandieri* with alkaline tolerance even greater than that of the commercial rootstocks reported as being alkaline-tolerant. Further, he said that some of the vines had pure, vinous flavor with no off taste, as well as levels of sugar high enough to make wine. I have a selection of *V. aestivalis* from Arkansas that is very pleasant as a table grape. Though seeded and somewhat smaller than commercial grapes, it is firm and meaty and has a very good fruity-spicy flavor.

There may be wild grapes with good qualities growing just feet from your home, if you take the time to look.

VITIS RIPARIA

Probably the most widespread grape species in North America is *Vitis riparia*, the riverbank grape, found from the East Coast to the Rocky Mountains, south into Arizona, and north into Manitoba. Due to its very wide range, there are many forms of it adapted to many different conditions, giving it great potential for breeding.

Botanists are aware that *V. riparia* (sometimes called *V. vulpina* in old texts) has different subtypes, but it seems unlikely that all the differences have been cataloged.

Riparia in the Western United States

In Colorado, an artist who traveled the state looking for scenes to paint also had an interest in grapes. He found what was apparently an alpine form of *V. riparia* growing on Colorado mountainsides and in canyons, practically out of the rock, fed by water from melting snow. It was bushy in habit, almost like *V. rupestris*, and able to tolerate more alkalinity than expected. He sent me some, which I passed along to a breeder in eastern Washington who was trying to breed cold-hardy rootstocks with the ability to tolerate alkaline soil. The exact alkaline tolerance is not known, but the fellow in Washington reported that other grapes planted near some of these same riparia vines become seriously chlorotic due to the soil's alkalinity, whereas the riparia vines were normal.

In Montana and North Dakota, there are (or were) super-hardy types of *V. riparia* with several unusual traits. Able to survive temperatures of −70°F (−56°C), these types adapted to cold by going dormant in response to daylength instead of temperature. These riparias have little warning when the temperature is going to drop, as temperatures can go from 80°F (27°C) down to freezing in a very few days almost any time after late August. To be prepared for this, the vines go dormant automatically as soon as the days begin to shorten. I have seen vines of this form growing in Wisconsin, with dead, dry leaves in late August when other grapes were fully green and still active. I have such a vine in my own collection and it does the same thing even in the mild climate where I live.

Many of these super-hardy grapes were found in the 1960s and 1970s, largely by Dr. Ron Peterson, the South Dakota State University professor who bred Valiant (which is a cross of Fredonia by one of these super-hardy grapes). Sadly, much of the hardy riparia material grew along riverbanks that were the boundaries of wheat fields. The fields were sprayed with herbicides by air, and the planes would turn at the boundaries—the rivers—and those areas were doubly hit by herbicides. I heard a speech by Peterson in 1985 in which he showed maps of areas north of Bismarck, North Dakota where some of the hardiest of these riparias formerly existed, but are now almost certainly extinct due to the spraying.*

Cold hardiness was the greatest virtue of these riparia types. Otherwise, they were adapted to a climate that was dry in summer, and in such a climate there is very little disease. Move them east to more humid climes and they are hit by fungal diseases. Valiant, which has one of these super-hardy riparias as a parent, doesn't have nearly the disease resistance of Beta, which had a more disease-resistant riparia parent from Minnesota or Wisconsin.

Disease-Resistant Riparia

The Canadians have assembled a collection of superior, extra-disease-resistant riparia types at the Morden, Manitoba, station. Most of the best of those were brought to the University of Minnesota for evaluation and breeding. Also, superior riparia material was collected by graduate student Pat Pierquet of the University of Minnesota in

*Personal conversation with Dr. Ron Peterson, at a meeting of grape breeders in Geneva, New York, in 1985.

the 1970s. He spent considerable time in the wild, often in a canoe (riparia vines prefer stream banks), hunting for superior types with extra disease resistance and better-quality fruit (lower acid, higher sugar). One of the Pierquet selections was crossed with Landot 4511 to produce the recently released wine grape, Frontenac.

At the same time, the fruit quality of V. riparia varies within the species considerably. The fruit is generally small and seedy, with very high acid and a herbaceous, "weedy" taste. However, individual selections can be found that have bigger, sweeter berries with lower acid and much less of the weedy taste. Had American colonists found some of these types early on, it could have changed the face of American grape growing. The colonists wanted grapes for wine and, because vinifera types wouldn't grow for them, they wound up using V. labrusca, which has low sugar and acid and strong flavor, making it poorly suited to winemaking.

While fruit of the average riparia vine has high acid, and higher sugar than most American species, as much as 20 to 25° Brix versus about 14° Brix for V. labrusca.

Indeed, Herbert Fritzke in Minnesota has selected and bred pure V. riparia for lower acid and pure flavor, as well as high yield and good disease resistance. In so doing, he produced selections of the pure species with sugar of 24° to 26° Brix and acid of 1.7 and lower. The wine from these selections won local awards. Remember, Fritzke selected only the pure V. riparia: he didn't cross it with other species or varieties. His selections have been collected at the University of Minnesota for further testing and to use in breeding. After all, if relatively ordinary riparia vines produced grapes like Beta when crossed with other grapes, what might come of using these much improved riparia selections as parents?

Riparia in Breeding

In one case, nature seems to be trying to tell us what would happen. In Iowa, a private breeder found several apparently natural hybrids of *V. riparia* with *V. labrusca* (probably Concord) and some extra-large-fruited forms of the species along Lake Okoboji. From his description, it seemed that nature had created some spontaneous Beta-type grapes. He told me that there were sheltered areas along the lake where residents had grown Concord, which could have pollinated some of the local riparia vines. Since Beta is a cross of *V. riparia* with Concord, such natural hybrids should indeed be similar to that famous variety.

From conversations I have had with breeders who have used *V. riparia* in creating cold-hardy grapes, I believe that, in addition to the differences in the behavior of *V. riparia* in various regions, there may be some genetic differences as well. These would take the form of inversions and translocations in chromosomes. That is, a piece of a chromosome can sometimes "trade places" with a piece from another chromosome, or just with another area of the same chromosome. Within a single population or group, all the members would probably have the same change. But when such riparias are crossed with other grapes, the chromosomes wouldn't match up correctly between the two. When that hybrid reproduces, many of its offspring would have unbalanced chromosomes.

To put it in simpler terms, a cross between two closely related grapes will produce offspring that are usually similar in behavior and vigor. But when there is such a large difference between the two, the "grandchildren" tend to contain a much higher percentage of runts, dwarfs, deformed vines, and weak vines.

That sort of behavior has been seen fairly often in the seedlings of Beta. Beta itself is the F1, the "child" of *V. riparia* and Concord. It has a full set of chromosomes from each parent. But when seedlings of Beta are grown, the *V. riparia* chromosomes don't match with their "normal" counterparts and they don't separate normally in the formation of eggs and pollen. The result is seedlings that haven't inherited all the genes that they were supposed to, or that have too many copies of some genes. Many of the offspring are so defective that the seeds don't grow at all, or the seedlings don't live beyond germination, and a large percentage of the survivors are deformed. A breeder can overcome this problem by only using the best, most normal-looking seedlings as parents, and then selecting for normal vines.

For breeding purposes *V. riparia* has shown advantages and disadvantages. Unlike *V. labrusca*, characteristic riparia flavor is easily diluted in crosses with other species, making it easier to get cold-hardy grapes with neutral, vinifera-like flavor. In some viparia/labrusca hybrids, the flavors of the two species tend to cancel each other out, producing hybrids much milder in flavor than might be expected.

Because of its intense pigment of the skin and its high sugar and acid levels, *V. riparia* has been a parent to some hybrids that are particularly good juice grapes, producing bright, well-colored juice with lots of sugar. Beta and Valiant are examples. Both have a diluted Concord-like flavor, but with better sugar and more acid, which makes the juice sweeter and more interesting.

V. riparia has the advantage of rapid, complete seed germination. In my experience, once germination begins, over 95 percent of the seeds germinate within one week of each other. By comparison, labrusca seeds may continue to germinate for one month or longer, and as few as 30 percent of them may produce seedlings, though many of the remaining seeds will germinate after a second stratification (see page 168).

One disadvantage of using *V. riparia* in breeding is that the small cluster size of the species is strongly dominant. In the wild, small berries and clusters are an advantage. The small size of the berries makes them easy for birds to pick, and the small cluster size means one or two birds can pick all the fruit on a cluster and ensure that the seeds are all spread to new locations. When a trait is so useful to the survival of a species, it is often hard to breed it out. One way to overcome this dominant trait is to cross *V. riparia* with grapes that have extremely large clusters.

VITIS LONGII

In the late 1980s, *Vitis longii* was renamed *V. acerifolia* (maple-leaf grape), but the species is better known under its old name, which I prefer. The old name was bestowed in honor of the man who discovered the species, Col. Long.

V. longii is related to *V. riparia* and has many of that species' advantages, plus a few of its own. I find it surprising that this species has been overlooked by most grape breeders. For example, the fruit, though small, lacks the "weedy" taste of its cousin *V. riparia*, and when crossed with *V. vinifera*, the hybrids have no off tastes at all. *V. longii* also has lower acid than *V. riparia*, making it a better parent for producing hybrids that are more balanced in sugar and acid. It is a tienturier (literally means "colored juice") so its hybrids with other grapes have a lot of color, making them useful in blending for red wine.

Dr. A. J. Bell in Ohio made many crosses of *V. longii* with other grapes and found that the hybrids had many good features, including disease resistance, cold hardiness, and early ripening.

An oddity of the species is that, while it has no resistance to Pierce's disease, it rarely suffers from the malady, because the sharpshooter leafhopper, which spreads the disease, doesn't like to feed on *V. longii*. This is probably due to the pubescence (downy fuzz) on the leaves. Crosses of *V. longii* with other species inherit the fuzzy leaves and keep most of the resistance to the leafhopper.

V. longii has a rather bushy growth habit, halfway between the very bushy *V. rupestris* and the vining *V. riparia*. The habit comes through in hybrids, making them very upright, and easier to train.

V. longii is second only to *V. riparia* in cold hardiness, but with some variations in growth. It will continue growing later in the fall than other grapes, but is able to stop growth and harden off very quickly when temperatures drop—often in as little as a week. It seems to pass its hardiness down to its offspring very well, according to Bell.

Also like *V. riparia*, the seeds of longii germinate very fast and essentially all of them germinate at one time.

One possible difficulty of *V. longii* is that it is more variable than other species. Some botanists think it is a recently created species, with *Vitis rupestris*, *V. candicans,* and *V. monticola* in it. Perhaps this is true, because different selections of *V. longii* vary in disease resistance and fruit quality. In his breeding work, Bell found that the female-flowered selection N74 from the U.C. Davis collection was one of the best parents for producing hybrids with *V. vinifera* that combined the health and hardiness of the *V. longii* parent and the fruit quality of *V. vinifera*. There is also a variant, called *V. longii microsperma,* with unusually small seeds, found growing along the Red River in Texas. Munson was one of the few to have found this variant, and it may not exist much in the wild now due to land development.

In any event, *V. longii* is definitely a species that has been overlooked by grape breeders.

VITIS RUPESTRIS

This native of washes and streamsides usually tends to grow with many short shoots, in a bush-like form rather than as a climbing vine. Many selections of *Vitis rupestris* are quite healthy and very cold hardy, depending on where they are collected. Rupestris vines from the drier areas of Texas, for instance, show less disease resistance than forms from Kansas, where summers are more humid.

V. rupestris is in the ancestry of many French Hybrids: Its influence is sometimes visible in those hybrids that have short, upright canes. A complaint among the French was that the rupestris genes in French Hybrid grapes imparted black-currant flavor that was objectionable in wine. Perhaps that same black-currant flavor could be interesting and valuable in developing new table grapes.

VITIS LABRUSCA

The variety Concord is usually given as an example of a *Vitis labrusca* grape, though it is felt by many botanists to contain some vinifera blood. However, its basic character is enough like pure *V. labrusca* to give the average person a fair idea of the species. One question often asked about *V. labrusca* is how it comes by the common name "fox grape." Some say it is because the fruit smells like foxes. Then there are historical references that people drunk on wine from the grapes were said to be "foxed." An assumption that may come closer to the truth is that the fruit is favored by foxes. One writer reported that the fruit is an ideal bait for trapping foxes. Consider the following characteristics of *V. labrusca* and judge for yourself.

The purpose of fruit in the wild is to induce animals to eat it, spreading the seeds so that new plants will sprout some distance from the parent. But while most grapes are adapted to being spread by birds, *V. labrusca* is suited more for being spread by medium-sized animals in woodlands.

First, *V. labrusca* has larger berries than

most other grapes—too large to be easily eaten by birds. Birds tend to peck holes in labrusca grapes, rather than to eat the whole fruit, so they don't often carry away the seeds. Next, a widespread labrusca trait, found even in some cultivated varieties, is a tendency for the berries to "shell," or fall off the cluster when ripe. Since the species is a woodland dweller, the fruit would be lost in the leaf litter on the forest floor, or under shrubs, where birds would have a hard time locating it. However, the pronounced aroma of the fruit makes it easy for foxes and other animals to find the fruit, and it is large enough for them to pick up readily. And finally, the seeds are large and hard, well suited to survive the journey through a fox's digestive tract, but too large to pass through a bird's gizzard without being damaged. It's interesting to note that white- and red-fruited forms show up more often in *V. labrusca* than other grape species, and both colors would make the fallen fruit easier for animals to see on the ground. Maybe this is the real reason to call *V. labrusca* the "fox grape."

It's interesting to note that muscadine grapes, *Muscadinia rotundifolia*, share these traits and exhibit them to an even greater degree than labrusca grapes. These characteristics—large, aromatic fruit and berries that fall when ripe—are apparently recognized instinctively by animals. My son has several Eastern box turtles that come from the area where muscadines are native. Even though the turtles had never seen labrusca grapes in their native area, they responded readily to them and will eat them in preference to almost anything else when they are offered a choice.

VITIS CORDIFOLIA

In the central United States, from mid-Ohio south, you'll find this grape with heart-shaped leaves (hence the name, which means "heart-shaped leaves"). *Vitis cordifolia* is another example of overlooked potential. It has very good to excellent resistance to fungal diseases, and very good resistance to phylloxera, but has been neglected because the fruit of the pure species has an unpleasant, acrid flavor. However, it could be the forerunner of grapes with many new, very pleasant flavors.

In many grapes, even *V. vinifera*, flavors are imparted by combinations of several chemical compounds, each of which is controlled by different genes. When grapes are crossed with other species, the genes for the different compounds are separated, so that offspring may inherit only some of the compounds. This can lead to surprises, because some of the flavor or odor substances can be quite different by themselves, or in new combinations with substances from other species. In the case of *V. cordifolia,* Johnson used it in his crosses and found that in the second and third generations he could detect new flavors, apparently due to the recombination of flavor compounds. He reported flavors of black currant, almond, and apricot in some of the selections. Dr. Herbert Barrett made crosses using *V. cordifolia* when he was grape breeder at the University of Illinois. This series of Illinois selections was put into the National Clonal Germplasm Repository branch at Geneva, New York, but as far as

I know, no varieties were ever produced and released from the material. Hopefully, breeders will use *V. cordifolia* further, and possibly produce some very healthy table grapes with unusual flavors.

VITIS AESTIVALIS, VITIS LINCECUMII, VITIS BICOLOR

Depending on the botanist you ask, you may be told that *Vitis aestivalis, Vitis lincecumii,* and *Vitis bicolor* are three separate species, or three forms of *V. aestivalis.* They are quite similar in several important ways, but there are some distinct differences. This group has some of the best potential for grape breeding in North America. In these species, the berries have firm flesh; high sugar; light, fruity flavor; moderate acid; and good tannins. All are among the most disease-resistant of the bunch grapes (as opposed to the muscadine grapes). *V. bicolor* has the added advantage of being second only to *V. riparia* for cold hardiness. *V. lincecumii* is extremely resistant to drought and can grow on soils that are too dry for most other species. It also has the largest berries of the three.

The fruit quality of the group is high enough that selections found in the wild have been used directly. For instance, Norton, a wine grape selected from *V. aestivalis,* has been a standard of quality in North America for well over a century. I have had red wine made from Norton that equaled many of the classic vinifera wines in quality. It has sufficient tannin for the wine to have body as well as excellent, fruity flavor and attractive color. Further, Norton can be grown without spray in areas where vinifera vines would need very heavy spray, and it is tolerant of Pierce's disease as well.

I have been growing an aestivalis selection from Arkansas that produces berries that I enjoy eating just as they are, though they are a bit smaller than many commercial types.

Considerable resistance to Pierce's disease can also be found in southern forms of the species, something that may be needed more as the glassy-winged sharpshooter leafhopper spreads in California, and, in turn, spreads Pierce's disease.

Munson thought so highly of the group that he bred many grapes from *V. lincecumii.* It is distinguished by its larger berries and by lobing of the leaves, while *V. aestivalis* has entire leaves with no sinuses.

Unfortunately, one counterproductive trait of the group is that dormant cuttings resist rooting, a trait that is passed down to the hybrids in many cases. This is one reason that of the hundreds of varieties of grapes that Munson is known to have bred, fewer than one hundred have survived to present times. At present, varieties that don't root well from dormant cuttings can be rooted easily as green cuttings in mist benches, or even grown in tissue culture. But nurserymen in the nineteenth century and early twentieth century would have had to layer these varieties to produce nursery stock, and layering is a much more labor-intensive process than growing cuttings, and with a lower yield of plants.

However, not all hybrids with these species are hard to root. Munson's hybrid America is a hybrid of *V. lincecumii* and *V. rupestris,* and it will root readily from dormant cuttings, having inherited the trait of easy rooting from *V. rupestris*.

I earnestly hope that anyone interested in grapes who lives where these species are native will take time to explore the material in their area. There could be another Norton out there, or other material that could become the parents of new, hardy, extra-healthy grapes.

VITIS CALIFORNICA

Dismissed in the past as without value, *Vitis californica* is no hardier or more resistant to disease than *V. vinifera*. It would seem to offer nothing to the grape breeder. Research indicates the strain of Pierce's disease in California is genetically different from that in the Southeast, suggesting that it has existed there for several centuries, at least. If so, *Vitis californica* has been exposed to the disease long enough for resistant vines to have arisen. When I was a student at U.C. Davis, I saw some natural californica-vinifera hybrids in a collection, and the fruit was very much like vinifera, with no unpleasant or off flavors. If resistance to PD came through in the hybrids, such material might offer at least a partial solution to the PD problem in California.

VITIS MUSTANGENSIS

Vitis mustangensis (formerly *V. candicans*), the mustang grape of Texas, is definitely a vine worth studying. Vigorous to a degree hardly seen in other grapes, it can grow in alkaline soils where "cotton root rot" would kill other grapes, and it is highly resistant to Pierce's disease. At the same time, though the fruit of the pure species has a strong "peppery" flavor, the berries are large, and hybrids of it with other species quickly lose the flavor. C. O. Foerster, Jr., a grape breeder in Brownsville, Texas, produced several fine grapes that were at least one quarter *V. mustangensis*, but which had no off flavor at all. Some of the varieties included Mother Gloid, Wiesser, and more. Ironically, C. O. ("Call me Crude Oil") Foerster was a grandson of the staunch prohibitionist Carry Nation, yet he included wine grapes in his work.

Foerster often grafted tiny seedlings on massive old vines of *V. mustangensis* as a means of bringing them into bearing in as short a time as possible. The pictures he showed of the grafted vines weren't half as impressive as the old mustang vines, which had trunks that looked to be 3 feet thick.

Recent work has indicated that the mustang grape, when used as a rootstock, is able to confer some resistance to PD on varieties grafted to it.

Other Texas Grapes

There are many chances for a fruit explorer or breeder to find wild species of value. J. Cottingham of Medina, Texas, told me of finding wild grapes that appeared to be natural hybrids of *V. monticola* with *V. berlandieri*. He said that the fruit of these vines was pure and sweet like vinifera, and was able to grow in soil more alkaline than the standard rootstocks bred from *V. berlandieri*. Perhaps these could be the basis for new wine grapes adapted to the difficult alkaline soils that are common in the Southwest.

MUSCADINIA ROTUNDIFOLIA

While most grapes are classified in the genus *Vitis*, muscadines have been placed in their own genus, *Muscadinia,* because muscadines have forty chromosomes whereas *Vitis* grapes have thirty-eight. Muscadines can tolerate a lot of heat and ripen two months or more after most bunch grapes. Because of that, I haven't found any muscadines that will succeed in the Pacific Northwest.

Muscadines have a labrusca-like flavor, but without the musky aftertaste. The skin has no astringency, though it is acid. To me, muscadine juice is like a very smooth labrusca juice with a dash of apple. Most muscadines are *very* tough skinned, grow in small clusters of as few as three to five berries, and drop from the cluster when ripe. Many of the newer muscadines have been bred to form a dry scar when the berries separate from the cluster, so the berries don't leak when they come off the stem. Even with dry stem scars, however, the berries don't keep very long and must be used or processed within about one week.

Muscadinia rotundifolia requires a lot of heat to mature and grows best in the hot, humid Southeast, though it also does well in the hot interior valleys of California. The vines are very vigorous, requiring as much as three times the space between vines as bunch grapes. The berries are mainly purple-black or "bronze." Traditionally, the white or bronze types were treated as a separate sort and called "scuppernongs," after an Indian tribe in the area of South Carolina where they are native, while the black and purple-black types were called muscadines. Now the term muscadine refers to the species as a whole, and Scuppernong refers to just one variety. The fruit of all varieties is highly aromatic, so much so that sailors on ships were supposed to have been able to smell it even when anchored out in the ocean.

Space muscadines with 15 to 20 feet between vines when planted in rows. Prune the vines to spurs on cordons, either on wire trellises or on arbors. For home growers, an arbor is usually the preferred way to grow them, so they can be harvested by shaking the vine over a tarp or sheet spread underneath the vine.

Muscadines produce their fruiting shoots on new growth, instead of out of the previous year's buds. They also bloom over a much longer time, with some clusters still setting in mid-summer. This continuous cycle extends the ripening season, though most varieties have a season of three weeks at most.

The aromatic elements of the grapes are stable: Eat a quantity and you can smell them in your urine or bowel movements. The fruit's skin is so tough that it just kind of bursts when you bite it, and most people who eat them swallow the pulp and spit out the "hulls."

Select breeding of muscadines only began in the early twentieth century. Considerable progress has been made in developing new varieties, given the comparatively short time the species has been domesticated. Originally there were only male or female vines, but there are now perfect-flowered types, which eliminates the need to grow unproductive male vines for pollination. More recently, types have been developed that are seedless as well, though this is parthenocarpic type seedlessness.

12 *GRAPES in COLD CLIMATES and the TROPICS*

T<small>HE MORE WE LEARN</small> about grapes, the more we appreciate their tremendous adaptability. In this chapter, I will describe methods that make it possible to extend the range of grape growing farther than most people would believe possible.*

GRAPES *in* COLD CLIMATES

In recent years, grape growing has been moving farther and farther north, into climates thought in times past to be too cold for grape vines. Grapes are now grown commercially in places where winter cold may reach or exceed −40°F (−40°C), with commercial vineyards as far as 56° north latitude. With special care, grapes can be grown even farther north than that. Partly this is due to improved methods, partly to

*Thanks to Tom Plocher for much of the information in this section. His book on cold climate viticulture, *Northern WineWork,* co-authored by Bob Parke, is available from the Minnesota Grape Growers Association.

hardier varieties, and partly because we simply understand the vines better, what they need and what must happen to them in cold climates.

Many pests and diseases are absent or less of a problem in northern areas. The grape leafroller, for example, cannot overwinter in areas where the soil freezes deeply, and may only show up in northern area when winds bring adults from the south; the leafrollers will not survive long enough to become a problem. In the cooler climate of northern areas, fungal diseases may be less virulent and produce fewer generations.

In some ways, northern climates have some of the best growing conditions for development of high-quality wine grapes. The milder days and cooler nights of northern climates, especially during ripening, allow for development of more intense flavors and aromas than in areas with warmer growing seasons. The winter itself may even be related to wine quality. Helmut Becker of the Geisenheim Research Institute in Germany felt that grapes needed cold in winter as part of the regimen that would bring out the best flavor in wines.

Table grapes grown in cold climates will often have different, sometimes more intense, flavors than ones raised in hotter climates, as well as different textures. I have tasted the same varieties of table grapes grown in different climates and, while they were all acceptable, the climate made an easily recognizable difference in the character of fruit from each location.

Varieties for Cold Climates

The easiest way to deal with cold winters, especially for beginners, is to plant varieties that are hardy enough for the climate, ones that don't need special care to survive the winter. A fair number of cold-hardy grapes have been developed, and with the expanding commercial wine and grape industries in Minnesota and Wisconsin, new hardy grapes are being tested and bred both by the University of Minnesota and by private individuals, such as Elmer Swenson and members of the Minnesota Grape Growers Association. Additionally, there are varieties from public and private breeding programs in Canada, as well as varieties from the Baltic area of eastern Europe, that show promise. Cold-climate growers will have more and more grapes to choose from as time goes on. For information on specific varieties for cold climates, see chapter 10.

When you begin trying to grow grapes that are less hardy, and you know you will need to protect them over the winter, one of the most important things to remember is that your chosen varieties must be able to ripen well in the available growing season. Too often, growers learn how to protect grapes in cold climates, but then try to grow varieties that ripen too late for the length of the season. Winter protection cannot make up for lack of heat during the growing season, too. Planting varieties that won't ripen well every year means that sooner or later you will go broke, if you are growing them commercially, either from lack of crop or from having the vines freeze out because they failed to mature and harden off in time before frost.

Grapes begin to prepare for winter way back in early August. Until then, the vine has been producing food to grow new shoots. But once fruit starts to ripen, there is a change.

First, the vine starts moving more food to the fruit. Once the crop has been harvested, carbohydrates start moving to the roots and into woody parts of the vine. The shoots stop growing and start showing more and more brown as they become woody and start "hardening off."

Research at Cornell University has shown that the longer a vine has from harvest until a killing frost occurs, the more likely it is to be fully hardened off. When crop was removed at the earliest possible time from a given variety, that vine hardened off more and showed better winter survival than did the same variety when crop was left on the vine as long as possible. This effect doesn't mean that a cold-tender variety can be made hardy by picking the crop early, but it does indicate why many cold-hardy varieties also ripen early.

Hardening off is affected by both day-length and decreasing temperatures. In August, vines "recognize" decreasing daylength and begin getting ready for cold days ahead. Some exceptionally cold hardy forms of *Vitis riparia* are so sensitive to daylength that they are completely hardened off by early September, even if there has been no frost at that time. Other grapes are stimulated to harden off by decreasing temperatures in the fall, with decreasing daylength being a secondary stimulus.

By early October, the woody parts of cold-hardy varieties are already adapted to withstand temperatures below zero. Less-hardy varieties may continue the hardening-off process as long as no freezes occur that are cold enough to kill the leaves (below 30°F [–1°C] or so). No matter how much time grapevines have for hardening off, there is a limit to how cold hardy a given variety can ultimately become, which depends on its heritage. In this discussion, I am talking about varieties able to handle –30°F (–34°C) or colder.

When temperatures dip below 20°F (–7°C), the vines pass into another stage of adjusting to cold, known as supercooling. In supercooling, most of the water in the vine's tissues freezes, except for a small fraction that becomes bound in the tissues in such a way that it doesn't freeze. This phase continues into early winter and varies according to temperature.

The supercooling effect is a natural mechanism that protects the vine from cold. This effect varies with species—some are better at it than others. Eventually, though, at a certain low temperature, even the supercooled water will freeze and the vine will be injured. Also, this phase of cold acclimatization occurs very slowly over a period of many days, and sudden subzero cold spells in early winter may catch the

vine unprepared if the hardening-off process hasn't proceeded far enough. The ability of a vine to supercool appears to correlate directly with hardiness.

By comparison, dehardening caused by mid-winter spells above 32°F (0°C) occurs rather quickly. Early and mid-winter warm spells can reverse acclimatization, so that vines can be hurt by sudden temperature drops. Fortunately, vines have a natural, built-in dormancy that protects them to some extent. This dormancy is controlled by the vine's biochemistry and until the substances controlling it have broken down, the vine will not break dormancy completely. After these inhibiting substances are gone, the vine is kept dormant mostly by cold temperatures. This biochemical regulation is a mechanism that protects the vine from breaking bud in mid-winter when temperatures are most apt to fluctuate. In most areas, as the winter moves into January and February, the cold is more constant and the vines are held dormant more by cold.

To demonstrate this, try to root grape cuttings in November and early December. Even cold-tender vinifera will root only sparsely at this time and will not break bud. By January, though, inhibition has broken down enough so that the cuttings will root and shoots will grow.

Vitis amurensis, as mentioned elsewhere, is native to a climate where temperatures are less prone to mid-winter fluctuations. As a result, this species is more prone to deharden quickly in warm spells. All of twenty-two *V. amurensis* selections tested in late-winter controlled-freezing tests at the University of Minnesota Horticultural Research Center suffered much more injury than *V. riparia*, even though the *V. amurensis* material was as hardy as *V. riparia* in early winter.

Staying dormant isn't the only quality needed to survive cold, though. *V. vinifera* vines stay dormant all winter and bud out late in the spring, but they are much less hardy than all but the most southern American species.

Increasing Hardiness

Practices that promote vine health can also increase vine hardiness. Vines that receive maximum sunlight, for example, can withstand the most cold. Studies at Michigan State University found that, in mid-winter, well-exposed canes could withstand temperatures 10°F to 20°F (5.5°C to 11°C) colder than could shaded canes on the same vine.

Regulating crop load can increase hardiness also. Overcropped vines have weak, poorly nourished canes that don't survive well, while undercropped vines may produce rampant growth that stays vegetative too long and doesn't harden soon enough before frost. An ideal vine has well-hardened canes of moderate size for the variety.

Controlling disease plays a role in hardiness, because diseased foliage can't produce food well, and thus diseased vines don't develop enough carbohydrates to harden wood thoroughly.

Beyond attending to vine health, you can help vines better withstand cold by training them to multiple trunks.

Multiple trunks. In New York, in the winter of 1966, the late Nelson Shaulis observed that of vines of Delaware with single trunks, 95 percent were killed to the ground; but in vines with two trunks, only 40 percent lost both trunks. That means that at least 60 percent of the vines with two trunks were still able to produce a crop that season. Further work in this area suggests that of vines that have three trunks, fewer than 15 percent will lose all three trunks in a severe winter. Further, with multiple trunks, each trunk remains flexible longer, making it easier to lay one or more of the trunks down on the ground to be covered for the winter.

A grower in Canada uses a multiple-trunk training system as insurance against cold damage. In this system, each vine is trained to two trunks. In some cases, the vine starts as one trunk with four canes (a standard Kniffen system), and a second trunk is added after the first has grown for a few years and has developed enough vigor.

Once a vine has two trunks, the grower trains two canes from one trunk to the right, and trains two canes from the other trunk to the left. When a trunk becomes distorted or damaged from cold, a sucker is trained up as a third trunk. Once this new trunk is three to four years old, the defective trunk is removed, returning the vine to two trunks again.

If one trunk is lost, the surviving trunk is trained like a four-cane Kniffen vine until a new sucker is ready to become a replacement second trunk.

Using cover crops. Sod or other cover crops can moderate soil temperature. Sod slows both the freezing of soil in early winter and the thawing of soil in the spring. The slow thawing in spring might help delay budding in varieties that are otherwise prone to budding too early, such as amurensis hybrids, like Michurinetz.

Winter Protection

The simplest form of winter protection is having vines that are known to be hardier than any winter lows recorded in your area. However, that limits your selection and potential markets, especially if you are in an area that is Zone 4 or colder. This will change in the future as new higher-quality cold-hardy varieties are released from programs such as the one at the University of Minnesota and from private breeders such as Swenson.

Winter protection of vines usually means taking the vines off the trellis and laying them on the ground, either to be covered with mulch or to be pinned down to allow snow to cover and insulate them. This is an area where multiple trunks have an added use, because dividing the vine's energies between three trunks means that each will stay smaller in diameter and keep its flexibility longer, thus allowing each trunk to be laid down easily.

Burying vines. In northern China, there is a system used for table grapes in which a short trunk has a single cordon that is tied to a low wire 7 inches above the ground. In the fall, the cordon is dropped into a trench dug under the wire. Most of the cordon is easily buried; the trunk and the bit of cordon attached to it need to be covered with a mound of soil. The trunk does not need to bend, the cordon bends gradually and can be replaced as needed to keep it flexible.

In spring the mound is leveled and the cordon is hauled up and tied back to the wire.

Where cold winters are infrequent, a variation used in New York is to leave a single spur at the base of the trunk, usually made by cutting back what would otherwise be an unwanted sucker. By the fall, a cane should have grown from the basal spur. The cane can be easily laid on the ground and buried, sometimes by using a plow to push the soil over the cane. In the spring, the cane is dug up, and the soil is placed back in the row. If the winter was mild and the vine is unhurt, the cane is cut back to a spur, and the process is repeated. If the vine was hurt badly or killed by cold, the cane is brought up as a new trunk, and it should bear a small crop that year.

When covering vines with mulch, the type of material you use can make a difference. With hay, mice can be a serious problem, nesting in the hay and eating the vine's buds. Sawdust should be baked or composted well so there are no resins in it that could harm the vine. One grower reported that cornstalks made a good mulch, able to protect the vine and hold snow, but too coarse to serve as mouse cover. Covering the vine with soil may cause rot in the vine if the soil is a wet, heavy type. This is where good, healthy soil containing mycorrhizal fungi and other soil life can help by combatting and displacing pathogens, so buried vines are healthy when they are unearthed in spring. The time to uncover vines varies with climate, but they should be unearthed by the time the buds on the unburied "indicator" vines (see page 132) have started to swell. After unearthing the vines, the mulch can be worked into the soil around the vines to provide organic matter.

How Cold Did It Get?

The only way to know how cold it gets in your vineyard is to take records right there. Temperature reports from television and radio meteorologists can be as much as 5 to 10 degrees different from those in your area. Even the heat given off by your house can have great effects on temperature readings.

One reasonably low-tech solution is to place a reliable min-max thermometer enclosed in a white-painted, three-sided wooden shelter in your vineyard. The thermometer should face north, and be about 4 feet above the ground. The Taylor Mini-Max Thermometer is constructed with a small metal indicator that rides on top of the mercury column. When the mercury drops on cold nights, the metal indicator is pushed up in the U-shaped column. When the weather warms and the mercury recedes in the column, the metal indicator remains "stuck" in place at the minimum temperature. In fact, it will stick there all winter long at the coldest temperature if you don't reset it with a magnet.

More high-tech solutions are available, such as electronic temperature sensors that can be downloaded to your computer to provide a complete temperature record at all times for the whole season. More sophisticated monitoring systems are being created, and will likely be on the market by the time you read this book.

Another aid to measuring the effects of cold is to plant a few vines of known hardy grapes, such as Valiant, Beta, or local selections of *V. riparia*, if it is native where you live. If these grapes suffer cold damage, the winter had to have been a real killer! Marechal Foch is a good vine to test the middle hardiness range. You can hope that your winters will never be harsh enough to hurt this variety, which is hardy to about −25°F (−32°C).

Recognizing Winter Injury

Learning to know what to look for in terms of winter injury means that you can plan your growing season accordingly. That's because winter-injured vines need different care than unharmed ones.

In late winter to early spring, when all serious cold has passed, but temperatures are still at or slightly below freezing, collect cane samples from the lower and middle sections of the canes of the still-dormant vines. Select them all from the same area on each vine, to be consistent. Put the pieces in a plastic bag in a refrigerator for about one week so they can gradually get used to warmer temperatures. Just before you are going to examine the buds, leave the canes out at room temperature for about one day.

To examine the material for cold damage, use a razor blade to slice away the bark and expose the cambium. If the cambium is bright green, it is alive. If brown or grayish, it is dead or seriously harmed. To examine the buds, start at the tip and slice horizontally (parallel to the cane) to make cross-sections. Use a magnifying glass to examine the bud. The first slice should show the primary bud or shoot primordia. Live buds will be bright green, dead ones will be brown or black. The second slice should reveal the secondary bud, lying like a crescent moon to one side of the large primary. Further slicing will show the tertiary bud, appearing as a smaller crescent between the primary and secondary bud. Be sure you can tell the difference between the three bud primordia.

You may find: all three buds green and alive; the primary dead, but the secondary and tertiary alive; only the tertiary alive; or, in the worst case, all three dead. This is important because if even one of the three is alive, the vine can produce a partial crop, though each successive bud usually pushes later and with less initial vigor.

When the temperature begins to warm up, healthy vines should also be able to produce globs of sticky sap at the ends of cut canes, showing that the sap is able to flow in the vine. No sap flow means the vine's trunk may have been killed or injured, and that the vine will die back soon even if you find live buds. Buds on such severely damaged vines may push, only to wilt and die later. Here is where your known standards of hardiness, the varieties Beta and Valiant, can help, by showing what normal sap flow should look like. Compare them to cold-tender varieties to help decide how bad winter damage may have been.

What To Do with Winter-Injured Vines

When you know that vines have been injured, be prepared to put extra time and effort into repairing them. It's worth it in terms of helping them face the next winter and making them maintain or return to productivity.

Maximize leaf area. Healing and repair of cold damage can use up all the vine's resources, which means that the vine needs as many leaves as possible to produce food. So, if your examination showed that more than 50 percent of the primary buds on a vine were injured, simply don't prune it in the spring. It will need all the buds to produce enough leaves for food synthesis. If less than 50 percent of the buds are dead, prune it lightly, leaving more buds in proportion to the damage.

Leave suckers on badly damaged vines. Suckers can help make food, and you may need one or more as a replacement trunk if the old trunk is badly injured. Choose the ones you want as new trunks and tie them up, pinching the tips of others to slow their growth without preventing them from making food.

Pinch "bull" canes. Vines with fewer than usual live buds will push lots of vigor into the remaining ones, making massive "bull" canes. Keep such canes pinched back at the tips, repeatedly if needed, to force the development of lateral shoots that will redistribute the excess vigor and help the vine harden off better in the fall, as well as making the shoots more useful as future fruiting wood.

Control vigor. A winter-injured vine with only a few live buds may produce very vigorous shoots, since the root system will still be intact. The danger is that such vigorous shoots may produce soft wood that won't harden off properly in the fall. Even if you think trunks or canes are injured, don't be in a hurry to cut them off. Wait until well after bud break, so as not to encourage so much overly vigorous growth. Also, withhold any nitrogen fertilizer from vines with dead trunks or with over half their buds dead. Watch the new growth for three weeks or so and, if it is vigorous, don't fertilize that year. Only add fertilizer if the vine is making slow, weak growth.

This regimen may not necessarily apply to vines that have been inoculated with mycorrhizal fungi, because the fungi, in combination with application of organic matter (especially compost), can regulate the uptake of nutrients to the vines and help improve their health. Full work on the use of fungi in cold climates has not been done at this time, but results from milder climates indicate that vines harden better and should have better winter survival when fungi are present.

Make sure crop load Is balanced. On vines where more than half the primary buds have been damaged, more secondary buds can be left to bear, as their crop is smaller in most varieties. Crown suckers also may produce some fruit. The trick is to allow enough crop to balance the very vigorous vegetative growth of some of the shoots without overloading the vine. Don't worry if it seems hard—it takes experience and familiarity with one's vines to be able to perfect this balance.

Choose new shoots. By mid- to late June, you'll be able to tell which shoots will serve as replacements for missing vine parts. Train and tie up those shoots well so they will be exposed to sun for proper hardening off. If you didn't have multiple trunks on your vines, this is a good time to start—choose two or three suckers you can train up as future trunks.

For more information on growing grapes in cold climates, check the Web site of the Minnesota Grape Growers Association at www.mngrapes.com.

TROPICAL GRAPES

The ability of grapes to adapt to different climates makes them the most versatile of fruits. While grapes are commonly thought of as a fruit for temperate climates, they can be adapted to tropical climates as well. There are two main limiting factors that must be dealt with: disease and lack of cold weather.

Disease Problems

In Florida, the heat and high humidity of summer mean that diseases of grapes run rampant: black rot, downy mildew, anthracnose, powdery mildew, Pierce's disease, isariopsis blight, various fruit rots, and more. Grapes that might grow and succeed a few hundred miles north are rapidly overcome by disease unless seriously protected. Yet there are very similar climates in other parts of the world where even *V. vinifera*, which is susceptible to all the American diseases of grapes, can be grown with no serious disease problems. Why? Because American grape diseases don't exist in many tropical areas.

So the first step in growing grapes in the tropics is knowing what types of disease you may or may not have to deal with. However, even in the tropics, there are apt to be mitigating conditions. Grapes growing in a climate with constant high humidity and very little air movement will have more disease problems than grapes growing in an area that is humid, but has good breezes and air movement.

Further, there isn't always an easy way to know where serious diseases may exist: surveys of American grape diseases are not complete (that I am aware of) and it may be necessary to plant a few vines as a test and see if they develop symptoms before progressing. In the New World (that is, North and South America and the Caribbean), there is a good chance that at least some disease organisms are present, especially if cultivated grapes were ever grown there, or if native species of grapes are in the area. Of course, there are always isolated locations, such as areas at high altitude or on remote islands, where disease has never reached. Hawaii apparently has never been infected with grape diseases from the mainland United States, as grapes grow in Hawaii with few problems. In short, you may have a disease-free location, but it's a good idea to plant a small test planting first if you aren't certain. Better to find potential problems before investing in a large acreage of vineyard.

Even if disease organisms are present, you may be able to grow disease-resistant varieties without having to resort to heavy spraying (see chapters 5 and 10 for specific variety suggestions). And if you are in it for the really long haul, you could try crossing cultivated grapes with native grapes to breed new varieties suited to the local climate. Nature sometimes even cooperates in this venture. In Florida, there are forms of the native *V. smalliana* that have very large clusters, and some that have white fruit, both of which are unusual for a wild species. Some botanists believe these are the result of natural crosses between the native grapes and European grapes brought by Spanish explorers. The European grapes certainly didn't live long in that climate, but even if they only bloomed once, their pollen could have reached the flowers of native vines and created natural hybrids that survived and passed their traits to later generations.

Lack of Cold

The second obstacle to raising grapes in the tropics is the lack of any cold weather. Most grapes must go through a dormant period to "rest" and need temperatures between 32°F and 45°F (0°C and 7°C) to help them break dormancy and be able to resume growth in the spring. Even before that, the vines need frost to kill the old leaves, so the leaves will fall from the vine.

If such conditions don't exist, though, it is possible to replace them with a little trickery. When I was a graduate student, I studied with Dr. H. P. Olmo, who traveled to India to help develop a system to allow grapes to be grown in tropical conditions. He based it on traditional methods already in use in the area. His procedure proved successful. Here is his method.

About one month after harvest (longer if the variety ripens early, so the dormancy period doesn't start too early), remove the leaves from the vine. With small numbers of vines, this can be done by hand-stripping. With commercial vineyards, methods may include using a chemical such as urea to burn and kill the leaves so they will fall off.

At the same time, stop watering the vine at least one week before the leaf removal. Allow the naked, unpruned vine to "rest" for anywhere from two to four months, depending on the variety and other factors. You have some latitude in this and can use it to advantage. For instance, the dormancy period can be shortened to allow the vines to resume growth early enough that the crop will ripen before similar grapes from other climates. In some cases, it is possible to shorten the rest period sufficiently that the vine can be tricked into producing two crops in a year.

Obviously, this system works best in tropical areas where there are distinct wet and dry seasons, and the dry season corresponds to the time the vines are to be dormant.

When you are ready for the vine to start growing again, prune the vine and resume watering. A dose of mild fertilizer, preferably one with a low percentage of available nitrogen, helps give the vine a jump start. The vine breaks bud, starts to grow, and blooms.

This method isn't perfect, as vines treated this way have a tendency to break buds only at the outer ends of the vine. After a few years, the center of the vine is "bald," with few or no shoots, and the bearing wood moves farther and farther from the center of the vine. Some growers have addressed this problem by training up a shoot from the base of the vine to become a second trunk. Once the new trunk is established, the old one is cut off, solving the problem for a few years.

This system was devised for use with *V. vinifera* grapes, and should work with other species, though I have no information on it being used with other grapes.

This method was developed mainly for use with table grapes, but the traditional methods from which it was adapted work with wine grapes. I have corresponded with a commercial grower in India who produces wines from the classic grapes such as Chardonnay, and he has sent reports of Indian wines that have been winning acclaim.

Vines Adapt Themselves

Another possibility in adapting grapes to the tropics could be in letting a grape "go native." The late Dr. Norman Good, a friend of mine who was a plant physiologist and private grape breeder, visited Hawaii and found vines of the old American grape Isabella that had adapted to a tropical climate. It bore flower buds, immature fruit, and ripe fruit all on the same vine, apparently bearing year-round. Since Isabella originated in New England, it was quite a change for this vine to adapt to a tropical climate. Good said the vines bore less fruit than they would have in a temperate climate, because the vines were dividing energy among flowers, green fruit, and ripe fruit. For a home grower, the tradeoff between smaller individual pickings and having fruit year-round seems worthwhile. However, there is no way to be sure in advance which grapes might react this way, so it would be necessary to try different varieties.

Contradictory though it seems, in one way, varieties from extremely cold climates might adapt very easily to tropical and subtropical climates. This is because they need very little cold to satisfy their dormancy requirements, as the cold itself is what keeps them dormant. For example, *V. amurensis* needs very few hours of chilling to fill its requirement to break dormancy. This is because, in its native lands in the extreme climates of Siberia and northern Asia, there may be less than one month between the end of the growing season and the time when temperatures dip below freezing and stay there for the winter. So the vines may have only three or four weeks when temperatures are in the correct range to satisfy chill requirements. After that, only the deep cold keeps the vines dormant. The cold is constant throughout the winter. Usually, once temperatures rise above freezing in the spring, the weather warms above the ideal range for fulfilling chill hours. The vines have to be ready to start growth immediately in the spring—there's no waiting around to finish satisfying a chilling requirement. In this one requirement then, this northern species is well adapted to subtropical conditions since it requires very little chilling to break dormancy. Unfortunately, it lacks resistance to the diseases of the tropical and subtropical areas, as the cold, dry climate of its native area is inhospitable to most disease, allowing the species to have evolved without developing any disease resistance.

13 BREEDING GRAPES

After you've been growing grapes for a while, you may realize that you don't have *the* variety that really suits your needs, so you set out to develop one that truly suits *you*. Or, you may enjoy grape growing so much that you want to leave a legacy in grapes in the form of your own new grape variety. Exotic as it may sound, creating new varieties of grapes, or any plants, is surprisingly easy. All you need to start breeding grapes is some fundamental gardening skills.

If you decide to dabble in grape breeding, what traits might you "personalize"? Flavor, for starters. Few grapes taste the same in all the climates in which they grow. I've tasted Concord grown along the shores of Lake Erie, and those grapes have an aromatic, fruity flavor that they never quite develop in other areas. That's why Welch's grows most of the Concord grapes they use in their juice in that area. Reliance, a red seedless grape bred in Arkansas, has a distinct flavor when grown in that climate.

Where I live, a Reliance grape is pleasant enough, but never has its "signature" flavor. If I wanted to achieve those same flavors where I live, I would attempt it in one of two ways. One way, such as with a seeded grape like Concord, would be to grow seedlings of the variety and look for one that had the special flavor. In the case of a seedless variety, it might be possible to cross the original parents and grow seedlings, hoping that one might produce fruit with the desired flavor. The odds of producing a variety exactly like the one you are trying to duplicate are small, however.

Breeding for flavor applies to wine grapes as well as table grapes. For instance, a wine grape grower I knew in New Jersey couldn't grow Cabernet, so he bred his own variety that yielded Cabernet-style wines in his climate. I never tried his wine, so I couldn't say how well he succeeded, but *he* was satisfied with the results.

You can also breed grapes with the goal of ability to survive in difficult climates. In northern Wisconsin, Elmer Swenson developed dozens of grapes adapted to that cold climate because he was unsatisfied with the few existing varieties that were hardy there. In South Carolina, Robert Zehnder has bred grapes with extremely high resistance to disease for that fungus-ridden climate. These breeders are private individuals who decided they could do better than just accepting what existed before they started.

One of the adventures of breeding new varieties is that, if you succeed, you may create something that not only suits you, but may be a boon to many others as well. In breeding cold-hardy grapes, Swenson produced selections that also perform well where the growing season is short and cool, even if the winters aren't unusually cold. If you plant even one seedling, there's always the chance it could be *the* one that will be the new "grape for the millions."

Does breeding require special equipment or training? Nope. Any good gardener can easily learn to do it with items found around the house and garden. And learning to breed grapes will teach you other skills that will make you a better grape grower, such as:

- Learning how to choose varieties that are as well suited to your climate and needs as possible. To breed new grapes, you have to start with the best of the existing ones and learn all their strengths and weaknesses, in order to decide which ones to choose as parents.
- Tracing the ancestry of a variety. Following the family tree back a few generations helps you understand the source of a variety's strong and weak points. For example, many of the French Hybrid grapes have *Vitis rupestris* in their back-

ground, which is species with a growth habit of short, upright canes. This growth habit shows up in many of its descendants, even after several generations of dilution by other types of grapes. You might even decide to go back a step and use one of the ancestors in your breeding work, as a stronger source of a trait. In American grapes, for instance, you will frequently find Concord in the background somewhere. It was often used as a parent because of its ability to grow in many different conditions.

- Knowing who bred and selected a grape may give you insights into the breeder's goals and why the grape has a certain set of traits. For example, most breeders of French Hybrids were primarily interested in wine grapes, and they used *V. riparia* and *V. rupestris* because (in addition to being resistant to disease and phylloxera) both have high sugar and intense color, desirable qualities for red wine grapes. However, *V. riparia* prefers somewhat acid soil, while *V. rupestris* will tolerate a degree of alkalinity. Thus, in searching for a wine grape with tolerance to alkaline or acid soil, finding these species in the ancestry can be a guide.

Of course, the degree to which a species will affect a variety will depend on factors such as how far back the species appears in the ancestry, how many times the species appears in the pedigree, and what the conditions were where the variety was selected.

In short, grape breeding is neither hard nor expensive, and it needn't take a lot of space. It can be fun, and it is definitely personally rewarding. Plus, learning about grape breeding will give you the answer to the age-old question: "How do they get seedless grapes?"

A BRIEF HISTORY *of* PRIVATE GRAPE BREEDING

In the days when only a few fruits could be shipped easily, fruit varieties were bred or selected for almost every growing area, so that each region supplied itself with locally grown fruit. Now most fruit is shipped from just a few growing areas, vulnerable to being cut off by a change in climate or a shift in politics. If even a few people in areas that are now considered marginal for fruit took up grape (or other fruit) breeding, there is a very good chance they could create varieties to supply fruit to their area if other sources failed.

Before you dismiss private grape breeding as a mere hobby, consider that private breeders have contributed as much, if not more, to grape culture in America and other countries as have many university and government programs.

Here's proof of my point. If you ask someone to name a grape (in the United States), it is likely to be Concord. Did you know that Concord was developed by a private grape breeder? Ephraim W. Bull planted seeds in 1843 collected from a wild *V. labrusca* vine. When the seedlings bore fruit in 1849, he selected one of the vines as the best, and it became the variety known as Concord. He didn't try to make a controlled cross and probably didn't know what the male parent might have been. The main thing he did was to compare the seedlings and choose one that looked the best. From that uncomplicated beginning came the grape that is the basis for most commercial juice and jelly and that is still the single most widely grown variety in the United States.

T. V. Munson

The same year Concord was planted, the "granddad" of grape breeders, T. V. Munson (1843–1913) was born. His work in grape botany and breeding set such high standards that his 1906 book *Foundations of American Grape Culture* is still a revered reference. A version of the book is still in print, and can be ordered from the Denison Public Library, in Denison, Texas (see Resources).

Munson bred over three hundred varieties of grapes using disease-resistant American species not used by most other breeders, particularly *V. lincecumii*, the "Post Oak" grape. Equally as important, he allowed disease to cull weak seedlings so only the strongest, most resistant survived. Sadly, many of his varieties have been lost over the years, at least partly due to his use of *V. lincecumii* in the parentage. The species is hard to propagate from dormant cuttings, and many of the varieties bred from this species inherited that disadvantage. Nurserymen were reluctant to grow the varieties because it was hard to propagate commercial quantities of plants.

Over seventy-five of the surviving Munson varieties have been collected in the Munson Memorial Vineyard in Denison, Texas, the town where he did most of his work. A few of Munson's best varieties are still available from nurseries. His grapes are so tolerant of pests and diseases, including

Pierce's disease, that some can be grown in as much as 75 percent of the United States.

Munson knew that the major diseases of grapes are native to North America, and that only American grapes have good resistance to these diseases. While other breeders used pure *V. vinifera* in their crosses, which contributes little disease resistance to hybrids, Munson used mainly the most resistant American species. His variety America has only the American species *V. rupestris* and *V. lincecumii* in its parentage. America will grow without spray well into the South. It is hardy as far north as Minnesota, though conditions are too cool there for the grape to ripen to full sweetness. Munson also developed Champanel, a cross between Concord and *V. champini*. It is one of few varieties that grow in the "black waxy" soils of Texas where cotton root rot is severe. Old vines of Champanel have grown and borne good crops without spray for decades.

No other breeder developed as many widely adapted grapes as did Munson. While other breeders mainly used *V. labrusca* and *V. vinifera*, Munson used other American species such as *V. lincecumii, V. rupestris*, and more. Those species have flavors different from *V. labrusca,* yielding varieties that were sweeter and often more refreshing. Combine that with the higher disease resistance of Munson's varieties compared to varieties derived from *V. labrusca*, and it more than makes up for the fact that none of the varieties is seedless. Munson did know of seedless grapes, but the methods for breeding new seedless grapes weren't discovered until around the time of Munson's death.

Munson also developed grape rootstocks, which helped save French vineyards when the American insect pest phylloxera devastated the roots of vinifera vineyards. The French followed Munson's methods and crossed classic vinifera varieties with disease-resistant American species, developing Hybrid Direct Producers, better known in America as French Hybrids. These were intended to produce good wine without the need to graft vinifera vines on resistant rootstock. A variety used very frequently in the ancestry of the hybrids was Jaeger #70, a *lincecumii* x *rupestris* hybrid produced by Herman Jaeger, a contemporary of Munson. Munson also used Jaeger #70 in some of his breeding work. Though the primary goal of the French breeders was to develop grapes that could produce good wine without needing to be grafted, many of the hybrids also inherited cold hardiness and disease resistance and can be grown in many climates where pure *V. vinifera* would suffer without spray or protection from the cold.

Most of the French Hybrids bear breeders' code numbers that include the name or initials of the breeder. Surprisingly few have been given names; most are still known by their number designations. Some of the more well-known breeders include Baco, Couderc, Seibel, Seyve (or Bertille Seyve, his full name), Seyve-Villard (Seyve married the daughter of another breeder, Villard, and Seyve-Villard is the son of that marriage), and others. Thus, a grape with the nomenclature S.V. 5-276 is the French Hybrid Seyve-Villard 5-276, also known as Seyval. Seyval is an excellent white wine grape that has been used extensively in breeding programs. The majority of the French Hybrids are wine grapes, but some are also fine table grapes, though few of those resist all diseases. Ironically, the French are now banned from using French Hybrids commercially, as it was feared that vintners would flood the market with cheap wine from the hybrids, which were easier to grow than the classic vinifera varieties, displacing those classic wines. At the same time, many of the French Hybrids have become widely planted in parts of North America, especially where there is interest in varieties that can be grown organically, without need for spray to combat disease.

Elmer Swenson

Munson's method of letting Nature weed out the weaklings is how private breeder Elmer Swenson in northern Wisconsin does it too. Swenson has produced some amazing grapes, some hardy to −40°F (−40°C) and colder. This is not surprising, since Swenson cut his grape-breeding teeth on Munson's book in the 1930s and continued over sixty years, still working at grape breeding into his eighties. His formal education was minimal, but this gentle, modest man's experience and his great enthusiasm for breeding grapes suited to cold climates are respected by university and government breeders, who travel far to see his work.

Swenson's grapes are so good that they have become the basis for breeding programs in various parts of the world, and a wine industry based on his varieties has sprung up in Minnesota and surrounding states. Since his primary goal was winter hardiness, Swenson did spray his grapes, but only enough to protect ones with at least a fair level of resistance. He weeded out any varieties with poor disease resistance. As a result, much of his material needs little or no spray in Wisconsin and Minnesota, and some varieties show good disease resistance even farther south in areas where disease is more intense. His Edelweiss variety grows without spray in a wide range of climates, as far south as Kentucky, and ripens early enough to succeed in very short summers. With hardiness to −30°F (−34°C), it has even been grown successfully in Norway. He has selections that look even better than Edelweiss, and though some are available through a few nurseries, he doesn't expect to name any more than the seven he already has (Swenson Red, Edelweiss, Kay Gray, St. Croix, LaCrosse, St. Pepin, and Esprit). He prefers to leave that task to those who come after him, if the varieties prove out. In fact, breeder/nurseryman David MacGregor has named several of Swenson's selections, and one was named elsewhere. The varieties include Trollhaugen, Petite Jewel, Prairie Star, Louise Swenson, and the one named elsewhere, Swenson White.

One of Swenson's contemporaries, the late Byron T. Johnson, in southern Ohio, bred wine and juice grapes (Scioto, Beaumont, Beaufort, Chief Wauwautan, Kee-WahDin, Joyous, etc.) for that area, also using the Munson methods. These varieties have enough disease resistance that they can be grown without spray in much of the central Midwest. Several of Johnson's varieties, though released, haven't been taken up by commercial nurseries yet, so aren't available.

Sadly, private breeders have produced a number of excellent varieties that are extremely "care-free," but the varieties are apt to be lost or never be well-known because they have been ignored by universities and government programs. Most commercial nurseries look to such programs as either the direct sources of varieties they sell, or follow their recommendations, and with few private varieties making it into such programs, they tend to be overlooked. Some of these varieties can be found through groups such as the Seed Savers Exchange or the North American Fruit Explorers, but others are much harder to locate.

As part of my graduate thesis, I studied the material of one of these private breeders, Dr. Robert Dunstan, who was the first breeder to produce hybrids between bunch grapes and muscadine grapes. Muscadines have the greatest resistance or tolerance to disease of all American grapes, but they do not cross readily with other grapes, so it was quite an accomplishment to produce varieties that have the very high disease resistance of muscadines and the fruit quality of bunch grapes. Even so, none of the varieties are available commercially, though some are finally being examined in California because of their resistance to Pierce's disease.

Each of these breeders had two simple qualities in common: They wanted grapes that would grow and do well where they lived, and they were persistent in their efforts.

BREEDING *Your Own* GRAPES

The first step in breeding grapes is collecting varieties that will grow in your area. In extreme cases, that might mean collecting wild grapes. When Louis Suelter began grape breeding in Minnesota in the late nineteenth century, the only truly hardy grapes he had to work with were pure *V. riparia*. He found a rare, white-fruited form of that species and crossed it with Concord, which had much better fruit than the wild grape, but was neither hardy enough nor able to ripen early enough for Minnesota. From this he selected Beta, one of the first varieties hardy enough and sufficiently early ripening to be useful for Minnesota. One of Beta's offspring, Minnesota #78, a seemingly modest grape, became one of the most important parents in Swenson's breeding work.

At present, there are enough cultivated varieties developed for almost all areas that it is rarely necessary to go back to a pure species for breeding work. Yet, even with this groundwork already laid, there is still much room for improvement. For instance, in the Deep South, where fungus and Pierce's disease are rampant, there are few bunch grapes approaching the quality of vinifera that are able to grow without considerable spraying. There is still plenty of need in all areas for varieties of better quality, greater disease resistance, and ability to adapt to a range of soils. And once these things have been achieved in a variety with vinifera quality, other traits will need to be added, such as seedlessness, firm berries, special flavors, and more. Even in the most ideal climates, such as the commercial vinifera-growing regions of California, there is still room for new varieties. For specifics on possible varieties, see chapter 10.

One big advantage that modern grape breeders have is that they don't have to grow all the varieties they want to use. Breeders of the past, such as Suelter, were limited to making crosses between whatever vines they could grow themselves. Suelter probably had to give winter protection to the Concord he used in his breeding. Or perhaps he grew it in a pot in a greenhouse. While the latter method is still used by university and government breeders, it isn't necessary for a private breeder to do such things. It is possible to obtain pollen of desirable varieties from many sources, such as other private breeders, or university or government grape collections or breeding programs. I've received pollen from the National Clonal Germplasm Repository grape collections at Geneva, New York, and Davis, California, as well as United States Department of Agriculture breeding programs in Fresno, California, and various university breeding programs.

Northern breeders have an advantage because they can look to southern growers for pollen, because grapes bloom earlier in the South than in the North. Pollen can be stored dry in a freezer for up to one year if the pollen parent blooms after the variety being used as a female parent. (More on this later). Neither are breeders limited to using varieties suited only to their area. If the female parent has the right genetic makeup, it can often be crossed with a variety that has some valuable traits, but is otherwise unsuited to the area where the breeding is being done. Grape breeders in both the North and the South have used as parents vinifera varieties that, by themselves, wouldn't survive unprotected or unsprayed in either locale.

Examples of such female parents are Minnesota #78, a female-flowered seedling of Beta, developed at the University of Minnesota in the 1940s, and Florida W 1521, a female aestivalis type from the University of Florida. Minnesota #78 has contributed earliness, cold hardiness, and disease resistance in crosses with varieties that have very little of those traits, but do have high fruit quality. Florida W 1521 has been crossed with vinifera to produce high-quality grapes that survive unsprayed in the intense disease pressure of Florida and South Carolina.

Things to Look for in Choosing Parents

When choosing parent plants, be sure the male and female parent do not have weaknesses in common. If one parent is susceptible to a disease, the other should be resistant. Whenever possible, choose parents that both have a desired trait, to reinforce the chances that the trait will occur in the offspring. The ideal situation would be to have two varieties that share all the ideal traits but one. Statistically, that would ensure that a high percentage of the offspring would carry all the desired features.

Sometimes there are different degrees of a trait, and parents with these may produce offspring with variations in the trait. For instance, when very cold-hardy grapes are crossed with grapes having only medium hardiness, about half the offspring will be very hardy, and half will be only medium hardy. But if very hardy grapes are crossed with cold-tender grapes, there will often still be a percentage of the seedlings with a high degree of hardiness. Surprisingly, crossing cold-tender selections may sometimes produce a very small percentage of seedlings with greater hardiness than either parent.

This situation shows that there are hidden genes for many traits. However, the percentage of seedlings that get enough hidden genes is often pretty small, so it doesn't pay to count on them in most crosses.

In almost all cases, a given variety has more recessive genes than you would guess. You won't know that these recessive genes are present in a parent plant unless the character they control shows up in a seedling. Concord, for example, is a blue grape, but both red- and white-fruited seedlings will show up in its offspring, indicating that it has hidden recessive genes for those colors.

One way to deal with this is by using a technique known as backcrossing. For example, say you wanted a Reisling-type grape with strong resistance to black rot. Using backcrossing, you would cross Reisling with a grape having strong resistance to black rot. Among the seedlings, there would be some that would have resistance to black rot and at least some of the character of Reisling. You would then cross those selections back to Reisling, which was one of their parents. Among the seedlings of this cross there should be some with black rot resistance and character even more like Reisling. In other words, this process aims at selecting a seedling that has a desired trait and then crossing it with one of its parents in hopes of eventually producing a variety that has all the desired characteristics of one parent, but only one or a few traits from the other parent. German breeders have used this method with a lot of success.

One drawback to backcrossing is that more runts and weaklings are produced than in a cross of two unrelated varieties. Usually, though, after a few generations of careful selection, most of the genes that cause these weaklings will have been weeded out.

It is also possible to cross two sibling seedlings resulting from the same cross, to increase the chances that all the right traits will be combined in *their* offspring.

Ultimately, experience will be your most important teacher in breeding grapes. Producing even one generation of seedlings will help you learn more about potential parents and the inheritance of traits than you could learn from reading books.

Pollen Sources for Breeding

Even if you are growing all the varieties that you intend to use in breeding, you'll have to contend with the problem that they don't always bloom at the right time. If a variety intended as a pollen source blooms before a female, it is a simple matter to collect and store pollen until the female parent is ready. However, if the desired female blooms before your pollen source, there are things you can do to help the male and female get together. (I've already mentioned obtaining pollen from someone who grows the male parent in an area where it blooms earlier than in yours.) You can collect and store pollen, so it is available when the female variety is receptive the following year. Or, you can delay blooming of the intended maternal variety by growing it in a pot and holding it in a cooler or similar place to keep it dormant. You would bring it out to bloom when the male is available. The drawback of this method is that it limits the number of clusters that will be available for breeding: A potted vine usually doesn't bear as large a crop as a vine grown in the ground.

Another way to delay bloom is to strip all the shoots off the female vine. This will force the secondary buds to grow, and the

The first step for all methods of collecting pollen for breeding is to bag the clusters. This is also the way to protect a cluster that will be used as a female parent.

base of shoot

cotton (optional)

end of shoot

unopened flower cluster

slit or tear

seam of bag should always be facing down

1- or 2-pound size bag

twist tie

slit fitted around shoot

♀ parent either a pistillate cluster or an emasculated ☿ cluster.

cluster for used pollen

When pollinating the female parent, the bag containing the cluster used as a pollen source replaces the bag that was put on the female cluster.

CUTAWAY VIEW

flower clusters on these secondary shoots will bloom later, hopefully when the pollen source is ready. When you strip shoots be sure to get the entire shoot out of its "socket." If even a short piece of shoot is left, it will regrow instead of allowing the secondary bud to start growing. The secondary flowers generally bloom one to two weeks later than the primary ones.

Collecting pollen. There is more than one way to collect and handle pollen for making crosses. The first step for all methods is to bag the clusters.

Choose the variety(ies) you want to use as the pollen source. To bag them, use a 1-pound-size brown paper bag (there will be a "1" on the bottom of the bag), or just standard-size school lunch bags. Before proceeding, write the name of the variety on the bag with a permanent marker pen.

With the bag still folded flat, make a cut in the top of the bag. There is usually a small semicircular notch in one edge of the top of the bag—make a 2- to 3-inch cut straight down toward the bottom of the bag, through both sides of the bag. Now, open up the bag. The bag will now fit over the cluster, with the slits fitting around the shoot. Be sure the seam on the bag, where the paper is glued, faces downward. This keeps moisture from settling on the seam and loosening it.

Choose a cluster for pollen that has few or no open flowers on it: flowers that have already opened will have shed a lot of pollen, so bagging a cluster already in bloom means you will gather much less pollen.

There is always a leaf on the opposite side of the shoot from the flower cluster. When you put the bag over the cluster, the slits will fit around the green shoot, and the top of the bag can be gathered around the stem of the leaf opposite the cluster. Tie the bag shut around the leaf stem with a twist tie.

The number of clusters to be bagged for pollen will depend on the method of crossing you plan to use, which will be covered later in this chapter.

There are usually at least two clusters on a shoot, so you can usually bag one cluster and use the other as a barometer: when the unbagged cluster is in bloom, the bagged cluster next to it will likely be in bloom. Otherwise, open the bag carefully and peek in to see if it is in bloom. It should be 75 to 90 percent in bloom before you collect the pollen. If you bag clusters when other clusters on the vine are in bloom, you will probably need to wait about one to three days for the pollen-bearing clusters to be ready, longer in cool weather.

When the flowers on the clusters are open, you can use the pollen in one of two ways.

First, to collect pure pollen, reach into the bags and cut the clusters off, into the bag. Take the bags indoors. You will need a sheet of clean glass about 2-by-3 feet. Use a clean cloth to wipe the glass with rubbing alcohol. Wait for the alcohol to dry, then dump the contents of the bags onto the glass. Tap the bags over the glass to dislodge any shed pollen in the bag. Take each cluster in turn and hit it against the glass several times to knock off anthers and pollen onto the glass. Depending on the size of the cluster, do up to three clusters at a time. Now, carefully tip the glass and tap it or gently shake it to dislodge all the flower caps and debris. A film of pure pollen will be left on the glass. Using a single-edged razor blade, carefully scrape and push the pollen into a small ziplock storage bag. (You can buy small bags at shops that sell rockhound and jewelry supplies.)

The pure pollen can be used immediately or stored. If you plan to store it, leave the bag open and put it in a closed jar with a desiccant to promote drying. You can use the little desiccant packets from vitamin bottles if you first warm them in a very low oven (100°F to 110°F) for a few minutes to a half hour to drive off moisture. You can also buy desiccant from craft shops, where it is sold for use in drying flowers, or from some mail-order seed catalogs. Or, use a small cloth bag filled with powdered milk from a *fresh* box. Put the pollen in a half-pint canning jar (still in the bag, left slightly open) along with the desiccant, seal the jar, and store it in the freezer. Pollen can be held up to one year this way and still have sufficient viability to make crosses.

Pollination

In making crosses, you can either use a perfect-flowered variety as the female, or a female-flowered type. Female-flowered types are rare among modern commercial varieties, but some old grape varieties are female. More important, breeders often find female-flowered types among the offspring of their crosses, and it's common for them to save such types. If you correspond with other breeders, odds are good you will be able to obtain a few of the favorite female selections they have accumulated.

If you want to make crosses involving wild species, all of the bearing vines will be female, since all wild American grapes have male and female flowers on separate vines.

The big advantage to using female-flowered vines is that you can make crosses without tedious emasculation, and seed set generally be higher because the flowers are undamaged: emasculation damages a percentage of the flowers so that they won't set. The disadvantage of using a female-flowered variety is that a smaller percentage of offspring from crosses with seedless grapes will be seedless, and with seeded grapes, you may wind up with half the seedlings being female, and thus not useful for anything except breeding.

The value of a female selection may not be fully apparent until it is used in a cross. For example, Dr. H. P. Olmo produced a white-fruited seedling (code number F2-35) that was a better wine grape than its sibling, the red wine variety Ruby Cabernet, but the seedling couldn't be released because it had female flowers. However, Olmo used the seedling as a parent for his first successful cross of *V. vinifera* with *Muscadinia rotundifolia*. Before that, all seedlings produced from crosses of those two species had been sterile.

When using a female-flowered grape as a parent, bag the cluster before it has started to bloom in the same manner as described for bagging male clusters. If you want to be sure no unwanted pollen gets into the bag, wrap a bit of cotton around the shoot and the leaf stem so that the bag fits around the cotton when it is tied in place. The cotton will act like a filter to keep any stray pollen out.

Once or twice a day, check the flower cluster that you intend to pollinate. When the flowers have opened and the tips of the pistils are shiny, they are ready for pollen: The shininess is a secretion that stimulates germination of the pollen so it will grow a pollen tube down to the ovary and fertilize the eggs.

If the "male" has bloomed at the same time as the female, there is an easy way to pollinate the female flower cluster. First, carefully clip the male cluster, leaving it in its bag. Carefully remove the bag from the female cluster and replace it with the bag containing the male cluster, making sure the seam on the bag is still facing down. Shake the bag to stir up the pollen and allow it to settle on the female flowers. Shake the bag daily for the next two days to ensure full pollination.

If the female blooms later than the male, use a fine camel hair paint brush to dab pollen on the stigmatic surfaces from the pollen you collected earlier. Wash the brush with alcohol and allow it to dry well for several minutes before using a different variety of pollen. You can use your clean finger to dab on pollen, but fruit set tends to be lower.

An alternate way to pollinate clusters with collected pollen is to transfer the pollen to a larger plastic bag, such as a pint, and then carefully slip the plastic bag over the female cluster and shake it enough to dust pollen on the female flowers. I have achieved higher percentages of set with this method than any other, at least on some varieties.

Within one week or less after pollination, the berries will have set, and it will no longer matter if the bag is completely intact. However, if you live where summer rains, birds, animals, or disease might harm the fruit, it's a good idea to cover the bag and cluster with a nylon or other fabric bag that will keep out marauders. There is nothing more frustrating than to find that the cluster from your pollination work has been stolen by a raccoon or birds. Be sure to include an indelible tag on the fabric bag so you will know what the male parent is. A plastic or metal tag that can be wired onto the bag is a good idea.

Emasculating perfect flowers. When you use a perfect-flowered grape as a female parent, you must remove the anthers before they shed pollen and pollinate the flower. The process isn't complicated, but it does take practice.

First, emasculating grape flowers should be done in early morning or late evening, when the air is still, to prevent pollen from being blown onto the flowers on which you are working. You will need a stool to sit on, a screen to help block breezes, a fine-pointed pair of forceps (tweezers), and patience. It may also help to have a magnifying glass mounted on a headband so you can magnify

Removing the cap and anthers of a grape flower to emasculate the flower.

your work while leaving your hands free.

Keep in mind that grape flower petals don't open from the top down like most flowers. Instead, they release at the base and come off the flower like a cap. Once the cap is off, the anthers open and the pollen is shed. To emasculate, choose a cluster that has buds that are full size, but not yet open. To be sure, look for a cluster that has just a few flowers starting to open, and pull those off with the forceps before starting to emasculate. To emasculate, use the forceps to grab the cap of petals from the side, near the tip. If you squeeze and pull the cap just right, it will come off and the anthers will come with it, leaving a naked ovary and pistil intact. This takes practice, and not all grape varieties have identical flower characteristics. Some have pistils that protrude farther up than others; these are harder to emasculate without damaging the pistil.

Eventually you will master the technique. Even then, it can take up to one hour to fully emasculate a large cluster.

Once emasculated, the cluster should be bagged and left alone for that day. If the flowers were mature enough, the stigmas should be shiny and receptive to pollen the next morning. If so, proceed as previously described. If not, try again the next morning.

SEX *of* GRAPE FLOWERS

Just about all grape varieties sold today are perfect-flowered and are self-fertile hermaphrodites: The flowers contain both functional ovaries and anthers, produce viable pollen, and can set fruit without a second variety around. In wild species, however, almost all vines are dioecious—the sexes are separated on separate vines.

In Nature, having the sexes separate ensures that all seed produced on a female vine is the result of a cross with a different, male vine, so that there is always more genetic recombination. With perfect flowers, the seedlings of such a vine are largely the result of reshuffling of the same genes, with no new variation added. That is no problem for us, since we usually reproduce our chosen grapes by growing cuttings, rather than seeds, but it would be less desirable in the wild because vines would have less chance to create new gene combinations for new environments.

Sex in grapes is not absolute, either male, female, or perfect. There are varieties that appear to be perfect-flowered but which behave as females. That is, the pollen they produce is sterile and unable to fertilize a flower. Sometimes such varieties have anthers that are only slightly recurved—bent back from the pistil a little—and some appear to be completely normal hermaphrodites. The way to determine such types is to bag clusters before they bloom. This keeps any outside pollen from them. If they don't set any fruit, or if the fruit is small and seedless, the variety is considered female, no matter what the flowers look like.

Males are not absolute, either. Dr. H. P. Olmo devised an experiment in which flowers of known male vines were dipped in the hormone kinetin at an early stage, and when these flowers bloomed, they were functionally perfect and set normal, seeded fruit. Further, I once met a breeder who had found wild males of *Vitis cordifolia*

that set a few small seedless fruit. He used pollen from those on normal females and was able to select male seedlings that set a large number of the small, seedless fruit. He used pollen of those partly fruitful males to pollinate some of their sister females and got males in the offspring that had even more small seedless fruit, and a few seeded fruits. This demonstrated that it was possible to develop perfect-flowered selections out of wild, dioecious species. Further, perfect-flowered types have been selected in muscadine grapes, which are dioecious in the wild. All these examples show that perfect flowers, in grapes at least, arise from males rather than females. It seems that it is easier for the ovaries and pistil of the male to develop and become functional than it is for the nonfunctional anthers of a female to become functional again.

Even the cultivated grape *V. vinifera* is dioecious in its wild form, and there are still many old varieties of it that are female-flowered. One that could be one of the early steps to perfect-flowered types in that species is Black Corinth. It has large, upright, well-developed anthers, but the ovaries are very small and the pistil is very short. In its natural state, the clusters are straggly and produce only scattered pinhead-sized berries. If the vine is girdled, or sprayed with gibberellic acid at bloom time, the ovaries develop and most set fruit, although the small, black seedless berries, rarely, if ever, contain any seed.

In most cultivated grapes, the sex of the flowers is controlled largely by one gene with several alleles. That is, cross a male and a female and the offspring will be half female and half male. Cross a perfect-flowered grape with a female-flowered grape, and if the perfect-flowered grape has only the alleles for perfect flowers, the cross will result in all perfect-flowered seedlings. But cross one of those seedlings (which has one allele for female and one for perfect flowers) with a female, and the offspring will be half perfect-flowered, and half female-flowered. Or cross two of them together and three-quarters of their seedlings will have perfect flowers and one quarter will have female flowers.

Good female-flowered grapes can be a useful tool in breeding in several ways:

- They don't require tedious emasculation.
- Crosses with them usually give a higher percentage of viable seeds per cross. That is, when perfect-flowered types are crossed by emasculating one of the varieties to use as the female parent, a fair number of the seeds will often be empty, having no viable embryo. But there are often almost no empty, nonviable seeds in a cross using a female-flowered parent.
- Female flowers can be used to make wholesale crosses. Plant a female-flowered grape in the midst of good quality perfect-flowered types and just collect the fruit that sets. All seed has to be from crosses of the female to one of the other grapes, since the female can't pollinate itself.

One drawback to females is that, if you use a seedless grape as the pollen parent and it carries one gene for female, you will only get the possibility of seedless selections in the seedlings that have perfect flowers, reducing the total possible number of seedless offspring by half compared to using a seedless parent that has only the genes for perfect flowers. You can't be sure of the latter case most of the time, however, unless you have made other crosses with the seedless parent and gotten female flowers in the offspring.

Extracting Seed

Once the fruit is ripe, you can harvest seeds. If you have a very few fruits, the seed can be extracted by cutting the berries with a razor blade or sharp knife and removing the seed. If you can be sure of yourself, you can also carefully eat the berry and spit the seeds out. As soon as you have the seeds, put them in a cup of water and stir gently to see which seeds float and which ones sink. The floaters are almost always inviable; you can discard them. Just be sure the seed is floating on its own, rather than because an air bubble is stuck to it.

If you have a lot of seed to extract and aren't worried about losing a few, you can extract seeds en masse by putting the fruit in a blender with at least an equal amount of water and blending it at very low speed —just enough to break up the pulp. The pulp, skins, and "floaters" can then be poured off. Repeat washing the seed until you have floated off most, if not all, the skins and pulp. Rinse the seeds in a tea strainer and spread them on a paper towel to dry.

If you plan to keep the seed for awhile or send it elsewhere, let it dry for several days so it is dry and loose. But if you intend to grow it yourself and want to get a higher percentage of seedlings, put it right into moist peat for stratification.

I have put fresh seed into moist peat without first drying the seed and without putting it immediately into refrigeration, and on two occasions, one or two seedlings germinated right away. I didn't find the seedlings in time, and they rotted off in the dark. I have found that the percentage of seeds that germinate is higher when seed is put directly into stratification, rather than if it is dried, soaked, and put into stratification later in the fall. Seed stored dry seems to go into a deep dormancy: It is difficult to stimulate it to germinate after regular stratification. (Some of these "stubborn" seeds will grow when stratified twice.)

Preparing Seeds for Planting

If the seeds have been dried and stored, soak them in water for three days, changing the water each day, before stratifying them.

Stratify the seeds in moist peat moss in the refrigerator for a minimum of one-and-a-half to three months. The ideal temperature is 35°F to 40°F (1°C to 3°C). Only enough peat to cover the seeds is needed: 1 to 2 tablespoons per 100 seeds. The peat should be moist enough that water can be squeezed out, but it should not feel soggy or have water dripping from it. I prefer peat because it has anti-fungal properties that help keep mold from forming on the seeds.

Grape seeds can be held in stratification for one year or more without harm; they will not sprout in refrigeration.

Planting Seeds

Plant seeds in flats 1½ inches apart in all directions, or plant in small 2-inch pots, one seed per pot. Growing temperatures should be 70°F (20°C) or warmer during daytime and 60°F (17°C) at night. One way to ensure uniform heat for the seeds is by using a heat source under the flat. Rubberized heat mats help speed germination and make it more uniform. The same mats also work for rooting grape cuttings.

Seed germination is also affected by day length: I've always had grape seeds germinate faster and in greater percentages when day length is over fifteen hours. Before the days are that long, germination is often slower and more irregular. You can help things along earlier in the year providing supplemental light to increase the day length. Full-spectrum lights are best, and they only need to be on for a few hours at the end of the day. Just figure how much extra daylight the seeds need to give them a full fifteen and a half hours per day and hook the light fixture to a timer set so as to provide the needed light.

In ideal conditions, seeds may begin to germinate in two to three weeks, but they can take up to two months, or more. Once seeds start to grow, all of a given lot may come up in as little as one week, or over one month. Germination percentages vary from less than 40 percent to close to 100 percent. If less than 70 to 80 percent of the seeds germinate, it can be worthwhile to re-stratify the remaining seeds and try again. Some of these "second-year" seedlings have exceptional vigor and health when they do finally germinate, as though the best was being saved for last (see chapter 8 for more information on seed germination).

Note: If you re-stratify the seeds by overwintering the flats or pots with seeds in them, be sure to cover them with metal screening or otherwise protect them from rodents, because mice love grape seeds.

Bulk planting of seeds. Making controlled crosses isn't the only way to produce good seedlings. Often, seed from open-pollinated vines, especially female-flowered ones, can produce good offspring. In the case of open-pollinated seed, however, it's easier to plant mass-extracted seed in bulk. One way to do this is to plant the seed directly into the ground in the fall and let the seed stratify in the soil naturally. Then, when the seedlings grow, select only those that are strongest and healthiest to continue.

When planting this way, sow seeds ½ to 1 inch apart and cover the seedling row with metal screening. Use a strip of fine-mesh hardware cloth about 8 inches wide and as long as you can handle, bent into a "U" and placed over the row to make a protective tunnel that will keep mice and slugs out. Pin the hardware cloth tightly to the soil with wire hoops and close the ends with boards. Leave it in place until the seedlings have at least two true leaves, or more if possible. The larger the seedlings are when the screen is removed, the less likely they are to fall prey to animals.

Handling Seedlings

Seedlings in flats can be transplanted to pots when the second true leaves show. From this point, there are two ways to handle the seedlings. Seedlings may be grown through the summer in the greenhouse in 2½-inch or larger pots and planted in test rows when they go dormant. This type of fall planting allows the roots to grow for a while into the winter and establish the plant well for faster growth the following spring.

However, if winters are cold enough that frost heaving of the plants may be a prob-lem, or that some of the seedlings could be killed by the cold because they are too small and tender, it may be more practical to set the seedlings in a nursery row to be selected by cold and disease before trans-planting them to permanent locations in a test row. If you have started the seedlings early, or they have grown well enough that they are at least 6 inches by early summer, they may be set out either into nursery rows or directly into the test rows. Seedlings planted in nursery rows can be set at close spacing—6 inches apart in the rows—let-ting disease and climate weed out the weak and unfit plants. The seedlings are then transplanted into the test rows as dormant vines—which are less susceptible to stress than young, actively growing seedlings—in winter or early spring.

Planting seedlings directly into the test rows from the greenhouse can save one to two years time, since vines grown in the nursery and transplanted must usually take a year to reestablish themselves before they can be trained. However, such seedlings require careful watering, weeding, and fer-tilizing, and some of them will prove weak or disease-susceptible before ever coming into bearing, which will leave empty places in the test rows. However, with good care, it is possible to bring some seedlings into bearing in as little as two years from seed. (The average time is closer to five years and can go as long as seven or more.) Ultimately, the method you choose depends on how much care you can give the seedlings. Direct planting in the test row gives faster results, but requires more labor. Growing plants in a nursery row takes longer, but preselects out some of the seedlings, and the remainder will be easier to handle.

If you grow seedlings planted directly in the ground, you should be able to remove a fair number due to disease. Many of the survivors can be left in place to continue growing to fruition, with the rest being transplanted to other rows. The vines left in place from the time the seed germinated will often bear faster than transplanted vines.

Test Rows

Since most of the seedlings in test rows will be grown only long enough to come into fruit and bear one or two crops before being eliminated, they can be planted at close spacings. In most cases, 2 to 4 feet between seedlings is sufficient. Rows should be at least 6 feet apart. Unlike regular vineyard rows, test rows need only a single wire for supporting the vines, and the stakes for the vines do not need to be treated to prevent rot, since they will only be in the rows a few years at most. Also, the poles or stakes for the vines need only be about 1 inch diameter.

Train a single trunk and leave two to four short (1-foot) fruiting canes at pruning time, depending on the vigor of the vine. Most seedlings will bear within three to five years after they are trained up, though some can take as long as seven years. Where space is limited, it may be better to remove such slow-to-bear vines. Also, eliminating slow types from the breeding helps select for precocity in later generations.

Selecting Seedlings

When vines start to bear, the first crop is not always typical of what crops will be when the vine is more mature. Traits such as flavor, skin toughness, pulp texture, color, and seedlessness will not change much, and vines with serious flaws in those areas can be removed immediately. However, cluster and berry size can increase and crop yields generally increase as a vine matures, so if the fruit characteristics are otherwise good, it may be worthwhile to let the vine bear a crop for another year or two before making your final evaluation.

As you gain experience, you will learn to judge from a first-year crop whether the vine is apt to improve enough to be useful. In commercial table-grape breeding, less than one-tenth of 1 percent of seedlings may pass all selection criteria and be considered good enough to become new varieties. Selection is even more rigorous in wine grapes, because fruit may produce high-quality wine one year and poor wine the next. So selection of wine grapes has to take longer to be sure all the desired qualities are consistent.

On the other hand, if you are breeding grapes just for your own use, you may be willing to accept traits that would be considered flaws in a commercial variety. You might find a grape that suits you by growing as few as fifty seedlings. You can also simplify your process by crossing varieties that are already known to be good parents, capable of producing a high percentage of useful offspring. This is *not* the same as using high-quality varieties as parents. A grape may be supremely delicious or make excellent wine, but at the same time may be totally incapable of producing seedlings with any merit. Conversely, some varieties that seem like ordinary, unassuming grapes are able to pass just the right traits to their offspring to create excellent new selections. Swenson's female-flowered selection, E.S. # 5-14, seems like a somewhat nondescript white grape with odd, jelly-like flesh. However, 5-14 has produced several excellent table *and* wine grapes among its seedlings. So don't dismiss a grape because it seems unimpressive—try it in breeding first.

Disease resistance. One of the first goals of breeding should be to select varieties that are capable of being grown without spray in the area where they are selected. Selecting for complete absence of disease isn't necessary. The vines only have to tolerate disease without any serious effects, not necessarily be totally immune to it. With powdery mildew, for example, damage may not be serious if the fungus only appears late in the season, particularly after the fruit is harvested.

If any disease appears as more than an occasional small patch on a leaf or cane and causes visible damage, mark the vines for removal. Seedlings showing symptoms of any disease serious enough to require spray for control should be eliminated.

Select for vine health *first* and then look for fruit quality among those vines. You may not harvest a lot of good-quality fruit at first, but in later generations the overall quality will go up, and you will have vines that are much more resistant and better able to tolerate problems than vines selected for fruit quality first, and vine health second.

Ripening time. It's important to select varieties that will ripen well every year without having to supply additional heat. However, if a vine shows many good traits and only fails to ripen some years, think about try-

ing it in sheltered areas, or send cuttings to people in warmer parts of the country: It might be a good grape for other climates.

Hardiness. In areas where winter cold is severe, select only vines that can be grown without winter protection: It defeats the purpose of breeding hardy grapes if the vines require protection.

Fruit quality. Selecting for fruit quality will reflect the tastes of the person doing the selection. For table grapes, color should be bright and uniform, not dull or muddy-looking. Skin should not be excessively tough, sour, or astringent. Different people like different flavors, but some grapes have such distinct flavors that you will know right away that you have a winner.

Other fruit traits depend on personal criteria, since some people prefer soft or juicy flesh, while others may like firm, crisp flesh. Wine and juice types should be evaluated by testing sugar and acid, and by making actual samples of the product. How you make wine or juice can make an important difference. Wine samples should be made with basic techniques. When I helped make test wines as a graduate student, we used the general-purpose Montrachet strain of yeast and simple glass bottles with airlocks, to make sure the varieties could perform well without special handling. Some of the selections might have made excellent wine with extra care, but why release something that vintners have to baby?

Sex of the flowers. Female-flowered vines will show up in the seedlings of many grapes—don't be too quick to discard these vines, especially if the vine has many good traits. Such female vines can be very useful for breeding as they are much easier to use in controlled crosses. Saving such selections to use as breeding stock can be more useful in the long run than finding a new variety right away.

Vigor and productivity. Seedlings half the size or less of the majority of the population generally have too little vigor to be useful and should be eliminated. Such vines may have good fruit, but their low vigor is hard to manage in a normal vineyard. There is one exception to this rule: Some bonsai enthusiasts are interested in such dwarf or undersized vines.

Note that some selections have very short internodes, but are nonetheless vigorous and healthy enough to keep. The seedless grape Delight has internodes that are about half the length of the internodes on the canes of its sister variety Perlette, but Delight is very productive and the vine is large enough to be reasonably easy to grow. Look at the overall size of the vine and how well it performs.

Productivity of a vine isn't always obvious in seedling vines, since only a few clusters can set on the small vines. However, experience and comparing the vines in a population can usually help you decide which vines will be heavy producers and which won't. For instance, heavy-bearing vines will usually produce as many as four clusters per shoot, while lighter bearing types may have only one per shoot and may not form a cluster on every shoot. Remember that productivity should not be judged by just one crop, but don't keep a seedling in the hope that productivity will improve unless the fruit is of very good quality.

In general, the best way to select a vine is to ask yourself: "Would I want to grow this as a variety if someone else had developed it?" Don't keep something if it is no better than an existing variety: Be ruthless, or you will be overrun with junk.

Breeding Seedless Grapes

Before trying to breed seedless grapes, it helps to understand how seedlessness in grapes works. There are two types of seedlessness: parthenocarpic and stenospermocarpic.

Parthenocarpic seedlessness. *Parthenocarpic* is when the grape ovary develops without fertilization of the ovules. That is, the grape is stimulated to develop without the seeds developing at all. This usually produces a very small, totally seedless berry. In many seeded varieties, such berries are often produced along with normal, seeded berries and are called "shot" berries. (In Europe, this condition is called coulure.) Such "shot" berries can even be produced in clusters of seedless grapes, where the rest of the grapes are seedless by stenospermocarpy. In this case, the only way to tell the difference is that the parthenocarpic berries are smaller and have no seed traces in them. Female-flowered varieties often produce large quantities of such shot berries when incompletely pollinated.

Some years ago I acquired a grape called William's Seedless, a red labrusca-type grape. The first year it bore, it had female flowers, and set clusters of fairly good, red seedless grapes. At that time, the vineyard was young and no other vines near it had started to bear.

The next year, however, several other grapes near William's Seedless came into bearing and pollinated it thoroughly. From then on, it produced only large, coarse, strong-flavored berries with very large seeds. I now believe this vine is the old Roger's Hybrid variety Massasoit.

Rarely, some normally seeded varieties produce sports that have all parthenocarpi- cally seedless clusters. Seedless Concord is believed by some to be such a variety, but I believe it is a separate variety.

The variety Black Corinth (also known as Zante Currant, and by several other names), which probably originated in Greece, is a parthenocarpic seedless grape.

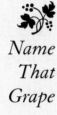

Name That Grape

BREEDERS KNOW THEY WILL PRODUCE many selections that look good at first glance, but after further testing won't prove worthy of releasing as new varieties. Rather than waste names on these seedlings, breeders have devised several types of code numbers to identify selections until they have been tested enough to be named or discarded. Here are some basic ones.

University of California at Davis numbers usually look something like B2-12. This would mean that the selection was found in the planting block labeled "B," in the second row, twelfth vine from the start of the row. A new block is planted every year, so the letter of the block would refer to a specific year. A record book would identify what the actual parents of the seedling were, and what type of grape it was supposed to be—wine or table grape.

At Cornell University, in Geneva, New York, numbers generally are prefaced with "NY." In the early days, seedling selections were simply numbered as found, so the numbers got rather large for a while—five digits or more—and a record book was needed to identify the year and the cross. An example would be NY 30454. Later, a system was adopted that includes the year, the number of the cross, and the number of the selection. So NY 65.483.2 means that the cross was made in 1965, it was cross number 483 (they make a *lot* of crosses) and it was selection number 2 from that cross. The breeders at Vineland, Ontario, use a similar code, but without any punctuation—hence numbers like V. (for Vineland) 71121.

Names may reflect the place where the grape was bred, as well. Vineland always gives their varieties names that start with "V," such as VeeBlanc and Ventura. Most of the older New York selections were named after places around the Finger Lakes, mostly in New York: Buffalo, Himrod, Interlaken, Steuben, Lakemont, and Schuyler. In the last two decades of the twentieth century, they switched to naming varieties after people (Einset) or just chose a pleasant sounding name (Horizon, Traminette, etc.).

Names can be taken from places, people, or combinations of the names of the parents (America X Delaware = Mericadel). Names can be descriptive (Ruby Seedless), poetic (Per- lette means "little pearl"), or refer to relatives of the breeder (Fern Munson, R. W. Munson). Sometimes, even previously used names are acceptable if the older variety is extinct or no longer common. Ruby was an old variety produced at Geneva, New York, but it has all but disappeared, so Dr. H. P. Olmo was free to name one of his selections Ruby Seedless.

However you name or number your grapes, be sure to record it, so that breeders and growers can understand and follow your system.

When the breeding of seedless grapes was first explored, during the first decade of the twentieth century, Black Corinth was crossed with several other grapes. It was found that the parthenocarpic type of seedlessness wasn't consistent, and crosses produced fewer than 1 percent seedless offspring. Parthenocarpic seedlessness is also a less desirable type, as the berries are usually quite small.

Stenospermocarpic seedlessness. In *stenospermocarpic* seedlessness, the ovules are fertilized and the berry and its seeds begin to develop, but at some stage, the embryos in the seeds abort and the seeds stop developing. If the embryos stop developing early enough, the seeds remains very small and soft. If development stops later, the seeds may be normal size, but have a soft or only partially hardened seed coat. The American hybrid seedless variety Venus is an example of the latter type. In normal conditions, it has seeds that are the size of normal seeds, but they are soft, hollow, and easy to eat. Sometimes, however, the seeds develop completely and become normal, hard, viable seeds. (A member of the Minnesota Grape Growers Association found five normal seeds out of several hundred Venus berries, and two of those germinated and produced vines.)

Stenospermocarpic seedlessness is more commercially useful because the berries can reach a much larger size than parthenocarpic berries, and because stenospermocarpic varieties respond well to girdling of the vine and hormone (i.e., gibberellic acid) treatments, so large seedless fruit can be produced. Since the pollen of stenospermocarpic varieties is normal, new seedless varieties are produced by using the seedless parent as the male, applying it to normally seeded varieties. Since the gene for seedlessness is dominant, you would expect 50 percent of the seedlings to be seedless. However, the gene does not act the same in every variety, so that some vines with it will have only very small seed traces, while others may have nearly normal seeds. The result is that even in the best cases, usually less than 25 percent of the seedlings have useful seedlessness (seeds small and soft enough to be unnoticeable when the berry is eaten), and more often the level is 10 percent or less.

Results of years of grape breeding indicate that there are additional genes besides the main one affecting the expression of stenospermocarpic seedlessness. If you cross a seedless grape with a seeded grape that has a seedless grape in its ancestry, you will get a higher percentage of seedless offspring than if the female parent had no seedless ancestors. For instance, when a wild species is the female parent, there may be less than 1 percent seedless offspring from the cross, since wild American species contain no genes associated with seedlessness.

The history of breeding for seedlessness. Controlled breeding for seedlessness in grapes—which has only been done since shortly before World War I—has brought surprises, as more genes affecting seedlessness have been accumulated in single varieties. For instance, early seedless grapes had very small berries, while newer ones such as Centennial have berries reaching a little over 1 inch long, as large as Thompson Seedless grapes after they have been treated with gibberellic acid. Further, older theories said that grape berries would only enlarge if the seeds were almost fully developed. That is, it was thought that berry size was due to hormones produced by the developing embryo. Thus, the sooner the embryo aborted, the smaller the seed trace would be, but the smaller the berry would be, too. Obviously, other factors are at work, because some of the newer seedless grapes are large and still have little or no seed trace.

All-American Grapes

WHILE MOST GRAPE BREEDERS use varieties that have at least some percentage of *Vitis vinifera* in them, it is possible to breed good grapes that have only American species in their parentage. In fact, American grapes have all the qualities that vinifera grapes do, just not all in the same species. For example, *V. labrusca* has large, attractive berries. *V. riparia* is juicy, has high sugar levels, and is cold-hardy. *V. lincecumii* and *V. aestivalis* have firm-fleshed berries and exceptional resistance to disease, including Pierce's disease in many cases. About all that *V. vinifera* has that hasn't been found in American bunch grapes is seedlessness and certain flavors for wine grapes. Otherwise, combining even three of the above American species gives at least the possibility of sorting out large, sweet, firm-fleshed, mild-flavored selections. Done right, by letting disease weed out the "weaklings," such selections could also have very high levels of disease resistance and even cold hardiness.

Embryo rescue is a recent technique that has improved breeding for seedlessness in grapes. In this method, a seedless grape is used as the female parent and is fertilized with pollen from another seedless grape. However, before the developing embryo can abort and be lost, it is removed and cultured on sterile media such as agar, similar to tissue culture, allowing it to grow into a vine. This way, the resulting vine has more genes for seedlessness than would be possible with ordinary breeding methods.

Selections produced in this way have shown results such as seedless berries that are not only larger than the berries of either parent, but often larger than any seedless grapes seen before. Seed traces in such selections are so small they virtually cannot be seen. These new vines even offer new possibilities for breeding seedless grapes by conventional methods. When used as male parents, they will produce a higher percentage of seedless offspring than when ordinary seedless types serve as the male parent. It's theoretically possible that as many as 50 percent of the seedlings might be seedless. At the time of this writing, however, this is only speculation, as no crosses of seeded grapes with embryo-rescue seedless grapes have been brought to fruition.

The first variety produced by embryo rescue to be released for commercial use in the United States, is DoVine, produced in Fresno by the USDA breeding program there. DoVine (short for Dried on Vine) is a new type of raisin grape, though it could be a good early table grape as well. Raisins are produced from DoVine by cutting the fruit-bearing canes, but without taking them or the clusters down. This allows the clusters to dry while hanging in air, instead of being laid on trays on the ground, as with the old method. Then a mechanical harvester goes through and shakes the raisins off. The new variety ripens as much as six weeks ahead of Thompson Seedless, so it can be dried while the weather is hotter and drier, and less prone to unexpected rains than when Thompson matures. With this new system, the raisins are cleaner, have few or no insects in them, and have a much higher percentage of the best-quality raisins. There is considerably less labor involved. One person can cut the canes on a substantial acreage, and no workers are needed to lay the grapes or handle the raisins—it is all done by machine, faster and cleaner.

Once you start down the road of grape breeding, you will find a kind of excitement unlike that from any other aspect of growing grapes. It's exciting when you see the flowers that you pollinated by hand develop into grapes, and when you harvest seed from those fruits. But the true excitement begins when you see the first little grape seedling start to emerge from the soil, the seed leaves unfurling like pennants. Then you realize that, with luck, this tiny seedling could be starting a lifetime that could last for centuries and spread over a large part of the world. Long after you are dust, this vine and its descendants bring wonderful fruit to generations far beyond your span of years. Even if the grape is a modest one that you keep mostly for your own use, it could still continue through your friends and neighbors in your own community, and through their children and grandchildren.

So if anyone asks why you are doing grape breeding, just tell them: "It's for posterity."

T. V. Munson produced a very good example of the value of using only American grape species with his variety America. A second-generation seedling from a cross of *V. lincecumii* with *V. rupestris*, America can be grown without spray well down into the South, even resisting Pierce's disease. It is quite drought resistant, and is hardy enough to grow in northern Wisconsin, though it fails to ripen well there: the acid levels stay too high even though the fruit colors. I've tasted America, and the flavor is an unusual fruity one, much smoother and milder than most varieties derived from *V. labrusca*. It's a firm/juicy grape, unlike the slippery-pulped labrusca grapes, though the juice is highly colored, so your lips are soon stained. The berries are smaller and seedier than today's palates would find ideal, but most of its other qualities are good. This example shows that it doesn't have to take centuries to develop useful varieties from native American species.

This is the sort of project that will most likely have to be undertaken by a private breeder, as it is a rather long-term experiment, and most university programs need to produce results within a short time to maintain their funding. Dr. James Moore, retired grape breeder at the University of Arkansas, once told me that he would have preferred to use more species and varieties like America in his breeding, but he had to produce quality grapes in as short a time as possible, even if they needed spray, or risk losing funding. So he used parents that had a high percentage of *V. vinifera* to get seedless, high-quality fruit, though the vines

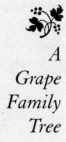

A Grape Family Tree

WHEN TRYING TO DECIPHER the ancestors of a grape (or any plant), you'll see a lot of the following: A x B. This notation just means "variety A *crossed with* variety B." It's easy to follow if you always remember that it's "ladies first." The female parent is always listed first, reading left to right, in the outline of the cross. So in the cross of Ontario x Suffolk Red, you would know that Ontario was the seed parent and Suffolk Red was the pollen parent.

There are different ways to list the parentage of a plant family, either as a branching tree, or as a series of crosses in parentheses. Here's an example of the branching tree:

Pedigree of Reliance

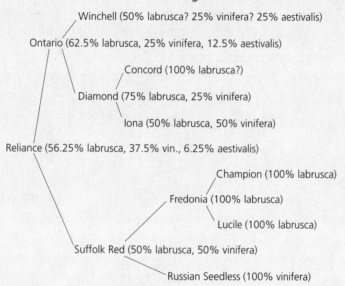

In this chart, start at the left with the variety you are trying to trace. The first branch is where it forks to Ontario and Suffolk Red. The upper parent, Ontario, is the female (seed) parent and the lower parent, Suffolk Red, is the male (pollen) parent. At each branch, the seed parent is always the upper parent. In this case, the farthest back we can trace the family is three generations. Iona could be traced back two more, but it wasn't necessary when I made the chart, the purpose being to show which species went into Reliance.

To restate it in another form:

Reliance = Ontario x Suffolk Red.
Ontario = Winchell x Diamond
Winchell = exact parentage unknown; possible parentage = 50% *labrusca*, 25% *vinifera*, 25% *aestivalis*
Diamond = Concord x Iona
Concord = 100% *labrusca*
Iona = self-pollinated seedling of Diana

Diana = self-pollinated seedling of Catawba
Catawba = appears to be *labrusca* x *vinifera*
Suffolk Red = Fredonia x Russian Seedless (probably Black Monukka)
Fredonia = Champion x Lucile (both are pure *labrusca*)
Russian Seedless = pure *vinifera*

had to be sprayed regularly. Had he used the very healthy types, with their slightly lesser quality fruit, he would have needed more to produce a commercial-quality grape and would have lost the funding to continue his work.

So, dear reader, when you start your own grape-breeding program, one that doesn't have to rely on someone else's funding to keep going, think of producing a truly All-American grape. Growers may be thanking you for ages to come.

Glossary of Viticultural Terms

absorption: The uptake of nutrients or other substances by roots or through stomata or cuticle of the foliage.

acid soil: Soil having a pH of less than 7.0.

adsorption: The concentration of molecules or ions on the surface of colloidal particles or on solid material.

adjuvants: Materials that are mixed with spray materials and act as wetting or spreading agents, stickers, or penetrants, to aid in the action of the active ingredient.

adventitious roots: Roots formed from areas where there were no pre-existing roots, i.e., roots that develop from callus tissue or from nodes.

adventitious bud: A bud developing from an area where there were no pre-existing buds. These occur on fruit trees and other types of plants, but not on grapes.

after-ripening: A period of chilling required by seeds before germination will take place.

alkali soil: Soil with levels of sodium high enough to interfere with plant growth.

alkaline soil: Soil with a pH greater than 7.0.

American hybrid: A hybrid cultivar (either intra- or interspecific) created in North America by crossing American grape species or cultivars with *Vitis vinifera* in an effort to develop cultivars that have the hardiness and disease resistance of the American parent and fruit quality more like that of *V. vinifera*. See also **native American variety.**

ampelography: The science of identifying grape varieties by detailed description of the appearance of the vine, especially its leaves, clusters, and berries.

anther: The pollen-bearing part of a stamen.

anthesis: The time of full bloom in a flower, just after the calyptra has fallen.

anthocyanins: Pigment compounds that impart red, blue, or purple colors to the fruit and leaves of the grapes.

aoutement: The period just after ripening of the fruit, beginning when the vine's rate of growth slows until the shoots stop growing and begin to show woodiness developing. As it proceeds, the shoots and leaves may even start to turn color.

apex (pl. apices): The tip of a shoot or of a lobe of a leaf.

apical dominance: The inhibition of lateral bud growth by the apical meristem.

apical meristem: The tip of a growing shoot of a plant.

asexual propagation: Propagation by use of plant parts other than seeds, such as cuttings, buds, and shoots.

astringency: A puckery taste sensation, caused mainly by tannin in fruit or wine made from the fruit.

available water: The part of the soil moisture, usually the capillary fraction, that the plant can readily absorb.

axil: The upper angle between a petiole and the stem to which it is attached. A true leaf will always have a bud in the axil.

balanced pruning: Pruning a vine based on its growth in terms of the amount of one-year-old wood that it produced the previous growing season. A method of determining the fruiting capacity of a vine for the upcoming season by weighing the wood removed at pruning time.

bark: The tough external covering of a woody stem or root outside the cambium. Bark is largely composed of dead tissue that is slowly shed by the plant.

basal bud: A small bud lying at the base of a cane or spur, as part of a whorl of buds laid down when a shoot arises from older wood.

biological control: Controlling disease or pests through the use of predators, parasites, or disease-producing organisms.

bilateral cordon: A vine-training system in which the trunk is divided into two branches extending horizontally on a supporting wire. Often referred to as cordon training.

blade: The expanded portion of a leaf.

bleeding: The exudation of sap from cut canes; usually occurs when pruning is done at the end of the dormant season.

bloom: The delicate, waxy or powdery substance on the surface of grape berries.

Brix: Grams of sugar per 100 grams of liquid at 68°F. The percentage of sugar in a solution. The Brix and Balling scales, though discovered separately, are essentially the same, and are used to indicate soluble solids content.

bud: An undeveloped shoot, usually protected by scales and usually located in the axil of a leaf at a node.

bud scales: Protective scale-like leaves of a bud that cover the bud during winter. Bud scales are hairy and impregnated with suberin.

bud sport: A branch, flower, or fruit that arises from a bud and differs genetically from the rest of the plant. Caused by a spontaneous mutation of a gene or genes in one cell that gave rise to the bud. .

calcareous soil: Soil containing calcium carbonate or magnesium carbonate that effervesces when treated with dilute hydrochloric acid. Usually has an alkaline reaction.

callus: Undifferential tissue that grows over a wound or graft and protects it from drying or injury. Callus also forms at the base and nodes of cuttings being prepared for rooting.

calyx: The external part of a flower consisting of sepals.

calyptra: The petals of a grape flower, which stay together and are shed as a "cap" when the flower blooms.

cambium: A very thin layer of undifferentiated meristematic tissue between the bark and the wood. All tissues in the vine originate from the cambium.

cane: A shoot after it becomes mature, brown,

and woody. A shoot is usually called a cane only after leaf fall. Canes are the previous year's fruiting or renewal shoots.

cane training: A form of training the vine whereby the fruiting wood is pruned to canes, which have five or more fruiting buds on them.

canopy: The above-ground parts of the vine, mainly the canes, shoots, and leaves.

canopy management: Manipulating the canopy to allow the vine to produce the best quality grapes in the largest practical quantity.

cap stem (pedicel): The stem of an individual flower or berry.

carbohydrates: Starches and sugars produced by plants as a means of storing energy. Carbohydrates are produced mainly in the leaves and are stored in the roots, wood, and fruit of the vine.

catch wire: A wire that serves as an attachment point for developing grape shoots. It can be fixed or movable, and there may be one or several, depending on the training system.

certified planting stock: Propagation material that has been tested and found to be free of known virus diseases.

chlorosis: Yellowing or blanching of green portions of a plant, especially the leaves, which can result from nutritional deficiencies, disease, or various stress factors.

clone: A group of vines of a uniform type propagated vegetatively from a single original mother vine, which was selected for some particular attribute(s).

cluster stem: See **rachis.**

compatibility (graft compatibility): Ability of stock and scion varieties to unite in grafting and make a strong, enduring graft union.

contact herbicide: A chemical that kills the portion of the weed or plant with which it comes in contact. See also **Systemic herbicide** and **Pre-emergent herbicide.**

cordon: An extension(s) of the grapevine trunk, usually horizontally oriented and trained along the trellis wires. Cordons are considered permanent (or perennial) wood and carry fruiting spurs that are renewed annually.

coulure: Flowers that were not pollinated and should have dropped, which remain on the cluster and develop into small seedless (shot) berries.

cross: The process of pollinating one variety with pollen of a second in hopes of producing a seedling that favorably combines the traits of both parents. Also, a variety or cultivar that is the result of crossing. Crosses are usually artificial, but can happen naturally.

crown: The juncture of the vine's trunk(s) with the roots.

cultivar: Literally, cultivated variety. A distinct form selected by humans, of a plant grown under human care/domestication for a specific reason. This is different from a "variety," which can also be a specific type within a species, but not necessarily selected by humans, nor always grown in cultivation.

curtain: A portion of the canopy composed of the current season's shoot growth. It may be oriented upward or downward, depending on the variety and type of training system.

debourrement: The period between bud break and the appearance of the first inflorescence.

dioecious: Having the male (staminate) and female (pistillate) flowers on separate plants.

dormancy: That stage when the plant is leafless and not actively growing. For grapevines, it is usually characterized by average air temperatures below 50°F, though it can be induced artificially in special circumstances.

emasculation: Removal of the male parts of a flower before they can shed their pollen to prevent self-pollination of the flower.

embryo rescue: The process of removing the embryo from a seed of a stenospermocarpic grape before it aborts. The embryo is then grown on culture media into a small vine, which is planted into soil and grown to mature size.

enology: The science and study of winemaking.

eye: A compound bud of a grape.

fasciation: Flattening of the stem as a result of multiple buds growing in the same place. May indicate that the vine has been infected by a virus, but can also be caused by a shock to the vine, such as intense heat or herbicide damage.

field grafting: Grafting a new variety onto an established vine or rootstock.

filament: A stalk supporting a stamen.

foliar feeding: Fertilization of a plant by spraying nutrient solutions on it, for direct absorption by the foliage.

foxy: The distinctive taste of the grapes and wine of some native American cultivars, especially *Vitis labrusca* and some of its hybrids.

French/American hybrids: Controlled crosses between certain native American species and *Vitis vinifera* created in Europe, as a result of the phylloxera devastation of the late nineteenth century, in an effort to create high-quality, pest-resistant, cold-hardy, direct-producing (able to survive on its own roots) grapes. Also known as Hybrid Direct Producers.

fruit: A mature ovary (berry) or a cluster of mature ovaries.

fruit set: The stage of cluster development after the drop of flowers that did not become fertilized during bloom. The small, developing berries are also called "set."

fruiting wood: One-year-old wood, which will produce the current season's crop.

fruiting zone: The area within the vine where most of the fruit clusters can be found. Under most training systems, it will be found within a horizontal band extending down the vine row.

fungicide: A chemical or physical agent that kills fungus or inhibits its growth.

gall: An abnormal growth of plant tissue. Generally caused by insects such as phylloxera or bacteria such as crown gall.

gibberellins or gibberellic acid (GA): A plant-growth regulator that promotes cell elongation and growth of shoots. This is the substance used to increase the size of seedless grapes.

green-manure crop: A crop grown and plowed under to add organic matter to the soil.

grafting: Attaching specially prepared pieces of one plant (scions) on to another plant in such a way that they unite and grow as one plant. A grafted vine consists of a scion (the fruiting portion of the vine) and a rootstock (the root system and possibly some or most of the trunk, depending on how the grafting was done).

growing season: For grapevines, the growing season is defined as the number of days between spring and fall (last and first frost) with a mean average temperature of 50°F (10°C) or more.

grow tube (vine shelter): A hollow tube (usually made of plastic) sometimes placed over vines in an effort to enhance the growth environment of the vine.

guard cells: Specialized cells in the epidermix of leaves that control opening and closing of stomates (openings into the leaf through which gasses enter the plant).

guttation: Harmless loss of liquid from intact plants. Usually visible as very small, clear "beads" on young, fast-growing grape shoots.

hardpan: A hardened or compacted soil layer below the soil surface that can restrict movement of water through the soil.

head: That portion of the trunk from which spurs, canes, or cordons can originate.

heading: To prune a new, developing shoot being trained as a trunk when it reaches the desired height. Done to stimulate the breaking of buds and the growth of shoots that will become canes or cordon arms.

hermaphrodite: A flower in which both male and female parts are functional.

hybrid: A cross of two species. A plant created by the intentional genetic combination of two varieties, in an effort to combine the best traits of each parent .

hydathode: A structure that releases liquid during guttation.

hypha: A fungal thread or filament, a structure of the fungus.

indexing: Determining the presence of virus in a plant, either by serological means, or by grafting parts of the plant onto a susceptible indicator variety whose reaction will show whether the virus is present.

indoleacetic acid (IAA): A plant hormone and growth regulator. Forms of this hormone are used to stimulate the formation of roots.

inflorescence: A flower cluster consisting of many individual blossoms, each attached by an individual stem (capstem or pedicel) to a larger stalk.

internode: The portion of a cane or shoot between two nodes.

lateral: A branch of the main axis of a flower cluster; shoots arising from a main shoot.

latent bud: A dormant bud, usually hidden or buried in the wood, which is over one year old and which may remain dormant indefinitely unless the vine suffers a major injury that makes it necessary to produce new shoots.

leaf: The primary structure of photosynthesis and food production. Also used in viticulture to refer to the age of a vine; as in: a vine in its "third leaf" is three years old.

leaf bud: A bud that develops into a stem with leaves, but no flower clusters.

leaf scar: A scar left on the stem after a leaf falls.

lenticel: A porelike, slightly raised spot on pedicels and grape berries.

lesion: A wound or delimited disease area.

light saturation: The light intensity at which an increase in light does not result in an increase in the rate of photosynthesis.

maturity: The stage of fruit development when the fruit has reached the maximum quality for its intended purpose.

meristematic: Pertaining to an area of undifferentiated cells that can actively divide and differentiate.

microflora: Microscopic plants in the soil, air, and water that interact with the vine (and all plants) in either beneficial or harmful ways. They include bacteria, fungi, and viruses. Black rot is an example of a harmful microflora, while mycorrhizal fungi are types of beneficial microflora.

microfauna: Microscopic animal life in the soil, air, and water that interact with the vine. They include nematodes, protozoa, mites, and many others. An example of microfauna harmful to the vine is root knot nematodes, while parasitic nematodes help vines by attacking insect larvae that would feed on the vine.

millerandage: Abnormal and uneven fruit set in which bunches contain berries of very different sizes, particularly many small parthenocarpic seedless berries, because of poor fertilization; often caused by unfavorable weather or improper thinning of unfertilized clusters. Also known as shot berries.

monoecious: Having male and female flowers on the same plant.

mulch: Organic materials, such as straw, used on the soil surface to promote moisture retention, control temperature, control weeds, and supply nutrients and organic matter to the soil.

muscadine: A native American species of grape indigenous to the south Atlantic region of the United States. With the scientific classification *Muscadinia rotundifolia.*

Muscat: A unique flowery aroma/flavor originating in the variety Muscat of Alexandria, but transfered to other varieties by breeding.

must: In making wine, the crushed and stemmed grapes that are ready to be inoculated with yeast to start fermentation.

Mustang: A native American grape indigenous to central and southern Texas; *Vitus mustangensis.*

mutation: Genetic change in a mother plant or stock that may influence the character of the sexual or asexual offspring (seeds, buds, cuttings). These changes can be large and readily visible, or may take careful measurement to detect.

mycelium: A group or mass of fungus filaments.

mycorrhizal fungi: A group of fungi that form a mutually beneficial relationship with a plant's roots. As such they act as an extension of the root system, increasing the roots' ability to absorb nutrients and water, as well as helping protect the plant from disease.

native American variety: A cultivar whose primary parents are species native to North America.

nematode: Microscopic soil animal that may be a parasite on plants or other soil-dwelling organisms, or that may break down soil organic matter.

noble rot: The benevolent form of botrytis (q.v.). Usually caused by an early-morning fog or dew, allowing for primary infection, which is followed by a windy, warm day.

node: A thickened portion of a shoot or cane where the leaf and its compound bud are attached.

nonsaline-alkali soil: A soil that contains sufficient exchangeable sodium to interfere with the growth of some plants, but which does not contain appreciable quantities of soluble salts.

nouaison: When the ovaries of the blossoms on each inflorescence have properly self-fertilized successfully and they become small, hard, green berries. The inflorescences thus are transformed into grape clusters. Also known as berry or fruit set.

parenchyma: Tissue composed of living, thin-walled cells with intercellular spaces that often fit together rather loosely. It makes up the soft parts of plants, such as the pith and the berries.

parthenocarpy: Development of fruit without seed production, as in the Black Corinth grape.

pedicel: A stalk of one flower or fruit in a cluster.

peduncle: A cluster stem. Usually refers to a stem from the point of attachment to a shoot to the first lateral branch on a cluster.

permanent wilting percent: The moisture content of a soil at which a plant wilts and fails to recover when in a relative humidity atmosphere of 100 percent.

perennial wood: The permanent wood of a grapevine; the wood of the trunk and cordons of the vine, which is two years old or older.

perfect flower: A flower having both functional stamens and pistil.

petiole: A leaf stalk that attaches a leaf blade to a shoot.

pH: Refers to the degree of acidity or alkalinity as a scale of numbers from 1 (extremely acid) to 14 (extremely alkaline). A pH of 7.0 is neutral, while pH 6.5 to 7.2 is the ideal soil pH for most plants.

phloem: Region of tissue in a plant composed of sieve tubes and parenchyma; translocates food materials produced by the leaves.

photosynthesis: The process by which water and carbon dioxide are converted to carbohydrates in the vine by use of radiant energy from the sun.

pistillate flower: A flower in which only the female parts are functional; male parts may be present, but non-functioning.

pith: The tissue in the central part of shoots or stems, usually made up of soft parenchyma cells.

pre-emergent herbicide: A chemical or substance that kills seedlings as they germinate, before they emerge to become visible plants.

primordial shoots: The buds that develop on the current year's fruiting wood. They will give rise to the fruiting shoots for next vintage.

pruning: The removal of portions of a plant for the purpose of maintaining its size and productivity.

pubescent: Covered with fine hairs or soft, downy fuzz. Many labrusca grapes are pubescent.

rachis: The main stem of a flower or fruit cluster. It is subdivided into branches and thence into berry stems.

renewal zone: Refers to the area of the shoots that will produce the following season's fruiting spurs or canes.

rosette: Leaves with a bunched appearance caused by development of short internodes. Some causes of rosetting include virus, herbicide damage, insufficient chilling to break dormancy well, and nutrient deficiency.

rootstock: A grapevine to which other varieties of grapes are grafted to produce a commercially acceptable vine. Rootstocks may be chosen for resistance to pests or disease, adaptability to unfavorable soil, or ability to influence the scion's bearing habits or hardiness.

scion: A cutting (or bud wood) taken from one vine and grafted onto a root system of another vine.

selective herbicide: A chemical or other substance, or possibly a biological agent, that can attack or kill some plants but has little or no effect on the crop plant.

self-pollination: Fruit and seed set resulting from pollen of the same flower or another flower on the same plant landing on the stigma and fertilizing the ovules.

shatter: A condition in which an abnormal number of flowers are shed from the cluster either before, during, or after bloom, leaving the cluster with very few berries, resulting in a straggly or very loose cluster.

shelling: A condition in which ripe berries drop from the cluster, either due to weak berry stems or weak attachment of the berry to the stem.

shoots: Current season's stem growth that bears leaves, fruit, and buds.

shot berry: A very small berry that fails to develop to normal size; usually seedless.

shouldered cluster: A fruit cluster in which the basal laterals are larger than the other laterals, giving the cluster a triangular outline.

sod culture: Type of management in which a permanent perennial groundcover is maintained at all times and is usually mowed periodically during the growing season.

soil structure: The aggregate arrangement of individual soil particles.

spur: A cane pruned to four or fewer nodes, either on a cordon or on a head-trained vine.

stamen: The pollen-producing organ of a flower, consisting of an anther and a filament.

staminate flower: A flower that has stamens but no pistil.

stenospermocarpy: A condition in which fertilization occurs and seeds are produced, but the embryos soon abort, stopping the development of the seed but allowing a seedless fruit to develop. Mature berries contain only rudimentary, soft seed traces.

stigma: The upper surface of the pistil, where the pollen grain must land in order to germinate and produce a tube down the style to the ovary to allow the sperm cells to reach the ovules.

stomate (pl. stomata): A pore in the epidermis of the leaf or young stem surrounded by two guard cells. It is an opening where gas exchange takes place in the leaf.

stratification: A process of subjecting seeds to temperatures between 32°F and 45°F in moist conditions to break conditions that keep the seeds dormant. Most grape seeds need a period of one month to three months in such conditions before they will germinate.

style: The section of the pistil between the stigma and the ovaries.

suberin: A waxy, waterproof substance present in the cell walls of cork tissue in plants. Suberin accumulation occurs as the new green shoots of a vine begin to turn brown and become woody.

sucker: A shoot arising from a bud below ground level.

suckering: Removal of unwanted shoots from the vine head and trunk while the shoots are still young.

sunscald: Injury to tissues due to excess heat; sunburn on fruit.

surfactant: A chemical that modifies the surface tension of spray droplets so they will spread out more evenly on plant surfaces in a thin film for more efficient distribution of spray materials.

systemic herbicide: A chemical that is taken up by a plant and causes the death of the entire plant at once, roots and all.

tannin: A phenolic compound in grapes that can impart an astringent taste. Commonly found in skins and seeds.

tendril: A slender structure arising from some nodes of a shoot that can coil around objects to help support the shoot and allow a vine to climb. Tendrils may be simple, bifurcated (forked), or trifurcated (with three tendrils coming off one stem).

tensiometer: An instrument used to measure water tension (available water) in the soil.

tetraploid: Having twice the usual number of chromosomes.

tomentum: Densely matted, tiny epidermal hairs; pubescence. Common on some American grape species.

training: Arranging the fruiting buds of a vine for greatest efficiency of management and production of fruit according to the climate, soil, and growing conditions. Training systems usually refer to the relation of the fruiting wood to the permanent parts of the vine (trunk and cordon arms).

translocation: The movement of water, nutrients, or food materials within a plant.

transpiration: Water loss by evaporation from the leaf surface and through the stomata.

trunk: The main upright structure of a vine from which cordons, shoots, and canes can arise.

veraison: The physiological stage in the development of a grape berry when it begins to ripen, as indicated by a softening of the fruit and a change in color (red for dark varieties and translucent for white varieties.)

vigor: A vine's tendency/ability to both grow and bear fruit. Vines with high vigor sometimes (but not always) produce excess growth at the expense of productivity.

vine density: The number of vines planted per unit of area.

vine shelter: See **grow tube.**

vintage: Can mean either the particular year in which a crop was harvested, or the actual process of the annual crop's growth and harvesting.

viticulture: The science or study of grapevine production and natural drying of raisins.

Vitis: The botanical genus of grapes.

vertical shoot positioning (VSP): This is a training technique of forcing the growing shoots of a vine into a vertical position, perpendicular to the ground. With low-wire trained systems, the shoots are trained "up," while with high-wire trained systems they are trained down.

waterlogged: A condition of soil with poor drainage that lacks sufficient oxygen for proper root functioning.

watersprouts: Rapidly growing shoots arising from latent buds on branches or trunks. Generally unfruitful.

weed: Any plant growing where a grower doesn't want it. Most weeds are "pioneer plants" whose function is to anchor soil and prepare the way for other species to follow.

wettable powder: A formulation of a solid that forms a suspension when mixed with water and can be sprayed on as though it were a liquid.

wing: A well-developed basal cluster lateral that projects from the main stem and is separated from the main body of the grape cluster, rather like a small cluster attached to the main cluster stem, but separate from the rest of the cluster.

xylem: The woody portion of conducting tissue whose function is the conduction of water and minerals up from the roots. In grapes, xylem makes up a large portion of the wood.

yield: The amount of wine or grapes produced per unit area, usually measured either as tons per acre, tons per hectare, or in much of Europe, hectoliters per hectare (for wine).

Resources

Information in this resource section is as current as possible, but products and companies do change. There are online sources with more current listings. They are the author's Web site, www.bunchgrapes .com, and the Organic Materials Review Institute, www.omri.org.

If you notice an entry needing updating, please contact the publisher at editors@chelseagreen.com and we will make the change in the next printing. Thank you.

FURTHER READING

General Interest

Basiouny, Fouad M., and David G. Himelrick, eds. *Muscadine Grapes.* Alexandria, Va.: American Society for Horticultural Science Press, 2001. Very complete assemblage of the history and work done on muscadines. Excellent variety chapter. Good culture information, though pest and disease control methods are mainly with pesticides.

The Brooks and Olmo Register of New Fruit and Nut Varieties, 3rd ed. Alexandria, Va.: American Society for Horticultural Science Press, 1997. Source of descriptions and parentage of a very large number of varieties.

Cox, Jeff. *From Vines to Wines.* Pownal, Vt.: Storey Books, 1999. Good basic information on pruning and winemaking. Shows heavy California influence.

Galet, Pierre. *A Practical Ampelography: Grapevine Identification,* translated and adapted by Lucie T. Morton. Ithaca, N.Y.: Comstock Publishing Associates, 1979.

Hedrick, U. P. *The Grapes of New York.* Report of the New York Agricultural Experiment Station for the Year 1907, II. Outstanding historical reference for American species and older American varieties, with color plates of many varieties.

Munson, Thomas Volney. *Foundations of American Grape Culture.* New York: Orange Judd Company, 1909. Hardbound reprint version available from the Denison Public Library, 300 West Gandy St., Denison, TX 75020; phone: 903-465-1797; can also be read online at http://cdl.library.cornell.edu/ cgi-bin/chla/chla-cgi?notisid=AFR6278. Excellent reference for species, many old varieties, and much basic information. Munson literally laid the foundation for many modern methods.

Plocher, Tom, and Robert Parke. *Northern Winework.* North Hugo, Minn.: Eau Claire Printing, 2002. Order directly at: Northern Winework, 9040 152nd Street, North Hugo, MN 55038. http://northernwinework.com/ cms/. Excellent work on growing grapes in cold climates. Includes some very useful material on wine characteristics of many cold hardy varieties and how best to vinify them.

Weaver, Robert J. *Grape Growing*. New York: John Wiley and Sons, Inc., 1976. More eastern grape-growing information than *General Viticulture* (see below), but less complete in other areas.

Winkler, A. J., et. al. *General Viticulture*. Berkeley, Calif.: University of California Press, 1974. The original standard of grape growing information, but dated, and slanted to California conditions.

Online Help

grapesrus@yahoogroups.com
growgrapes@yahoogroups.com

Rootstocks

Galet, P. *Grape Varieties and Rootstock Varieties*, translated by Jaqueline Smith. Chaintre, France: Oenoplurimedia, 1998.

Hardie, W. J., and R. M. Cirami. "Grapevine Rootstocks." In *Viticulture*, volume 1, ed. B. G. Coombe, and P. R. Dry. Adelaide: Winetitles, 1988, pp. 154–76.

May, P. *Using Grapevine Rootstocks: The Australian Perspective*. Adelaide: Winetitles, 1994.

Pongracz, D. P. *Rootstocks for Grape-Vines*. Cape Town: David Philip Publishing, 1983.

Wolpert, J. A., M. A. Walker, and E. Weber, eds. *Proceedings Rootstock Seminar: A Worldwide Perspective*, Reno, Nevada, 24 June, 1992. Davis, Calif.: American Society for Enology and Viticulture, 1992. The proceedings include updates on rootstock research and recommendations from France, Australia, South Africa, California, and New York.

Grapevine Disease Information

Database of Integrated Pest Management Resources
http://ipmnet.org/cicp/fruit/grape.html

SUPPLIES *for* GROWERS

Trellising, Planting, Training, and Pruning the Vines

Many of these suppliers have everything needed for the vineyard, though companies with special items are noted.

A and P Ag Structures
11266 Ave 264
Visalia, CA 93277
phone: 877-780-6985
fax: 559-685-8266
e-mail: aandpag@msn.com
Web site: www.aandpag.com

Grow tubes (vine protectors), vine ties, trellising, pruning shears, hand-held sprayers, etc. Source of braces for Geneva Double Curtain trellis system, a heavy-duty "universal" crossarm.

A.M. Leonard, Inc.
241 Fox Drive, P.O. Box 816
Piqua, OH 45356-0816
phone: 1-800-543-8955
fax: 1-800-433-0633

Bio-Organics
P.O. Box 5326
Palm Springs, CA 92263
phone: 888-332-7676
e-mail: infor@bio-organics.com
Web site: www.bio-organics.com

Mycorrhizae inoculants.

BLUE-X Grapevine Shelters
McKnew Enterprises
P.O. Box 2128
Elk Grove, CA
phone: 888-47-BLUEX
Web site: www.growtube.com

Grow tubes (vine protectors).

California Vermiculture, LLC
P.O. Box 95
Cardiff by the Sea, CA 92007
phone: 760-942-6086
fax: 760-942-5356
e-mail: geohahn1@juno.com
Web site: www.wormgold.com

Bulk and bagged WORMGOLD (WG) worm castings, WG Tea, WG Premium Mix, and bulk and bagged KELZYME (fossilized kelp).

Central Elastic Corp.
phone: 604-390-6212,
fax: 604-390-8052
e-mail: Central@po.jaring.my
Web site: www.cec.com.my

Anchor Band UV-resistant rubber ties.

Clip-it Systems
4930C Eisenhower Avenue
Alexandria, VA 22304
phone: 888-925-4748
fax: 703-751-7179
e-mail: infor@ clipitsystems.com
Web site: www.clipitsystems.com

The Clip-it System secures vines quickly and easily to wires or stakes, holds catch wires together, and secures drip irrigation tube to the wire. Free samples available.

DRiWATER, Inc.
600 East Todd Road
Santa Rosa, CA 95407
phone: 800-255-8458 or 707-588-1444
fax: 707-588-1445
e-mail: driwater@driwater.com
Web site: www.driwater.com

"Packaged" water to help start plants where no irrigation is available.

Farm and Home Supply Center
50 N Canal Boulevard-Basin City
Mesa, WA 99343
phone: 509-269-4403

fax: (509) 269-4404
Web site: www.farm-home.com

Fence tools and other supplies.

Farm Wholesale Products
3740 Broolake Rd. NE.
Salem, OR 97303
phone: 1-800-825-1925
fax: 503-393-3119
Web site: www.farmwholesale.com

Greenhouse supplies. grow tubes, coconut peat substitute (for rooting), and more.

Forestry Suppliers, Inc.
205 West Rankin Street, P.O. Box 8397
Jackson, MS 39284-8397
phone: 601-355-5126

Many unusual items, including weather measuring devices, tools, etc. Excellent catalog.

Hydrolysate Company of America
LLC P.O. Box 271
Isola, MS 38754805 474-8562
Web site: http://multibloom.com/

Fish fertilizer made from farmed catfish.

Jim's Supply Company, Inc.
P.O. Box 668
Bakersfield, CA 93302
phone: 800-423-8016
Web site: www.jimssupply.com

Grow tubes (vine protectors).

Maxicrop USA, Inc.
900 Lively Boulevard
Elk Grove Village, IL 60007
phone: 1-800-KELP-964
fax: 847-364-7374
e-mail: maxicrop@maxicrop.com
Web site: www.maxicrop.com

Sells seaweed extract, an excellent fertilizer that improves plant's resistance to diseases.

Midwest Vineyard Supply, Inc.
2300 S. Twin Bridge Road
Decatur, IL 62521
e-mail: sales@midwestvineyardsupply.com
Web site: www.midwestvineyardsupply.com

Sells a number of useful items and distributes Snap-N-Grow tubes east of the Rockies.

Neptune's Harvest
P.O. Box 1183
Gloucester, MA 01931-1183
Web site: http://www.neptunesharvest.com/

Fish fertilizer, kelp fertilizer, garlic based pest repellants.

Orchard Valley Supply
1521 Mountain View Drive
Quakertown, PA 18951
phone: 888-755-0098 or 215-529-8445
e-mail: maggie@orchardvalleysupply.com
Web site: www.orchardvalleysupply.com

Oregon Vineyard Supply
2700 St. Joseph Road
McMinnville, OR 97128
phone: 800-653-2216
fax: 503-474-0476
e-mail: solutions@ovs.com
Web site: www.ovs.com

Tape gun for tying up vines, most other vineyard products and tools.

Oregon Wire Products, Inc.
P.O. Box 20279
Portland, OR 97294-0279
e-mail: sales@oregonwireproducts.com
Web site: www.nwnetcom/oregonwire or www.oregonwireproducts.com

Wire and metal posts.

Premium Home and Garden
417 South 13th Street
Omaha, NE 68102

phone: 877-541-4076 or 402-344-3536
Web site: www.premiumknives.com

Pruning tools.

S and H Farm Supply
Frank Hobson
2732 Country Club Road
Yadkinville, NC 27055
phone: 336-679-6244
fax: 336-679-3158
Web site: www.sandhfarmandvineyard supply.com

SPEC
39 Indian Drive
Ivyland, PA 18974
phone: 800-237-4594
fax: 215-357-3122
e-mail: wire@spechardware.com
Web site: www.spechardware.com

Factory-direct dealer of hi-tensile smooth and crimped vineyard/fence/orchard wire. All wire and staple inquires welcome.

T&J Enterprises
Thomas Giannou
2328 W. Providence Avenue
Spokane, WA 99205
phone: 509-327-7670
fax: 775-206-1613
Web site: www.tandjenterprises.com

Mycorrhizae inoculants to help vines grow better.

Treessentials Company (MN)
2371 Waters Drive
Mendota Heights, MN 55120-1163
phone: 800-248-8239
Web sites: www.treessentials.com and www.growtubes.com

Grow tubes (vine protectors), bird netting.

Insect and Disease Controls

AgBio, Inc
9915 Raleigh Street
Westminster, CO 80031
phone: 877-268-2020
phone: 303-469-9221
fax: 303-469-9598
e-mail: info@agbio-inc.com
Web site: www.agbio-inc.com

Produces MycoStop. European Grape Berry Moth traps.

AgBioChem, Inc.
3 Fleetwood Court
Orinda, CA 94563
phone: 925-254-0789
Web site: www.agbiochem.com/www
    .agbiochem.com/

Galltrol (crown gall control).

AgraQuest, Inc.
1105 Kennedy Place
Davis, CA 95615
phone: 530-750-0150
fax: 530-750-0153
Web site: http://www.agraquest.com/

Serenade powdery mildew control.

Associates Insectary
P.O. Box 969
Santa Paula, CA 93061-0969
phone: 805-933-1301
Web site: www.associatesinsectary.com

Cryptolaemus, N. californicus, G. helveolus, Aphytis melinus, *and decollate snails.*

BigPower vacuum cleaner
CleanSweeps Vac Shop
712 E. Main Street
Bozeman, Montana 59715
phone: 888-581-9929
e-mail: bigpower@cleansweepsvacshop.com
Web site: www.cleansweepsvacshop.com

Bio-Integral Resource Center (BIRC)
P.O. Box 7414
Berkeley, CA 94707
phone: 510-524-2567
fax: 510-524-1758
e-mail: birc@igc.org
Web site: http://www.birc.org/

BIRC produces a Directory of Least-Toxic Pest Control Products, *updated every November. Products are listed by the pest for which they are used and are divided into the categories of Identification and Monitoring, Physical Controls, Horticultural Controls, Biological Controls, and Least-Toxic Chemical Controls. In the Chemical Controls section, one can easily find all botanical pesticides we know of used for the particular pest. Manufacturers are referenced after the pesticide brand name and their addresses and phone numbers are listed in the back of the publication.*

BioSafe Systems
22 Meadow Street
East Hartford, CT 06108
phone: 860-290-8890
fax: 860-290-8802
Web site: www.biosafesystems.com

Oxidate, Nontoxic fungicides.

BioWorks, Inc.
100 Rawson Road Suite 205
Victor, NY 14564
phone: 800-877-9443
fax: 585-924-4362
Web site: http://www.bioworksinc.com/

Biological and nontoxic disease and insect control.

California Vermiculture, LLC
P.O. Box 95
Cardiff by the Sea, CA 92007
phone: 760-942-6086
fax: 760-942-5356
e-mail: geohahn1@juno.com

Bulk and bagged WORMGOLD (WG) worm castings, WG Tea, WG Premium Mix, and bulk and bagged KELZYME (fossilized kelp). Worm casting tea is used to suppress disease, including armillaria root rot.

Foothill Agricultural Research (FAR)
550 Foothill Parkway
Corona, CA 92882-6305
phone: 888-760-0120
e-mail: xfarinc@aol.com
Web site: http://www.far-inc.com/

Anagyrus pseudococci, Leptomastidea abnormis, Aphytis melinus, and decollate snails.

Gemplers, Inc.
100 Countryside Drive, P.O. Box 270
Belleville, WI 53508
phone: 800-332-6744
e-mail: customerservice@gemplers.com
Web site: www.gemplers.com

Botanical insecticides and horticultural supplies of all kinds.

IPM Technologies, Inc.
4143 N. Vancouver Avenue, #105
Portland OR 97217 USA
phone: 888-476-8727
fax: 503-288-1887
e-mail: semiochem@aol.com
Web site: www.ipmtech.com

A range of traps and lures available for monitoring pests.

Leinbachs, Inc.
4995 Reynolda Road, P.O. Box 11786
Winston-Salem, NC 27116-1786
phone: 800-334-6119
fax: 910-924-6847
Web site: http://www.leinbachs.com/inc.html

Sprayers.

Natural Insect Control
R.R.#2
Stevensville, ON
Canada L0S-1S0
phone: 905-382-2904
fax: 905-382-4418
e-mail: nic@niagara.com
Web site: www.natural-insect-control.com

Beneficial insects, bird feeders and accessories, beneficial nematodes, bird and bat houses, traps and lures.

Naturalis-L
Troy Biosciences
2620 N. 37th Drive
Phoenix, AZ 85009
phone: 602 233-9047
fax: 602 254-7989
Web site: www.troybiosciences.com

Insect-killing fungus.

Rincon-Vitova
Everett Dietrick
P.O. Box 2506
Ventura CA 93002
Web site: http://www.rinconvitova.com/
    d-vac.htm

Commercial insect vacuum.

Rincon-Vitova Insectaries
P.O. Box 1555
Ventura, CA 93002
phone: 800-248-2847
e-mail bugnet@rinconvitova.com
Web site: www.rinconvitova.com

Lacewing (Chrysoperla spp.), Trichogramma, Rhyzobius (=Lindorus), and fly parasites. Rhyzobius is a scale predator. Fly parasites control flies that build up on pommace and other compost materials. Rincon-Vitova can supply materials to control a wide range of pests.

SoilGard (part of W.R. Grace, Co.)

Natural fungus that fights soil pests. Sold widely in garden stores throughout the US.

Stylet-Oil
JMS Flower Farms, Inc.
1105 25th Avenue
Vero Beach, FL 32960
phone: 561-567-9241
fax: 561-567-9394
e-mail: styletoil@aol.com
Web site: www.stylet-oil.com

Nontoxic oil used as insecticide, miticide, and fungicide.

Surround
AgNova Technologies Pty Ltd
PO Box 590
Eltham VIC 3095
Australia
phone: +61 (0)3 9840 2333
fax: +61 (0)3 9840 2555
Web site: www.agnova.com.au/
    surround-crop-protectant.htm

Surround is sold in the US. Clay-based product that protects plants from insects, fungus, and more.

Trécé Incorporated
1143 Madison Lane
Salinas, CA 93907
phone: 831-758-0204
Web site: www.trece.com

Pheromone lures for a very wide range of insects.

Animal Pest Controls

Bird-X, Inc.
300 N. Elizabeth Street
Chicago IL 60607
phone: 800-662-5021
fax: 312-226-2480
Web site: www.bird-x.com

Bird-control products.

D and C Distributing
300 #81 Road
Ellensburg, WA 98926
phone: 509-968-3307
fax: 509-968-3660
e-mail: dancplastics@elltel.net
Web site: http://www.dandcdistributors.com/

Twine, sisal, bird netting, weed barrier, and other plastic products.

Deer Fence by Benner
P.O. Box 875
Bala Cynwyd, PA 19004
phone: 800-753-4660
fax: 215-477-9429
e-mail: benners@erols.com
Web site: www.bennersgardens.com/

Deerbusters
phone: 888-422-DEER
Web site: www.deerbusters.com

Deer and animal repellents, fencing, and scaring devices.

Maplehurst Deer, Inc.
P.O. Box 697
Dellville, TX 77418
phone: 409-865-9601
fax: 409-865-9922
Web site: www.maplehurstfence.com/

Fencing.

Reed-Joseph International Company
P.O. Box 894
Greenville, MS 38702
phone: 601-335-5822
fax: 601-335-8850
Web site: www.reedjoseph.com/

PROPAGATION SUPPLIES

Anderson Die and Manufacturing Company
2425 SE. Moores
Portland, OR 97222-6362
phone: 503-654-5629
Web site: http://andersonpots.com/

Pots for starting vines. Many sizes, good prices.

Dip 'N Grow, Inc.
P.O. Box 1888
Clackamas OR 97015-1888
phone: 866-DIPNGROW (866-347-6476)
fax: 503-445-0101
e-mail: sales@dipngrow.com
Web site: www.dipngrow.com/
dipngrow.html

Rooting hormone.

Grow for It
300 N. Elizabeth Street
Chicago IL 60607
phone: 800-662-5021
fax: 312-226-2480
Web site: www.cozy-products.com/
germinateseeds-grow-seeds-warming-tray
.html

Heat mat, well suited to grape cuttings because the amount of heat can be varied by how close the flat/pot is to the mat.

Hummert International
phone: 800-325-3055
Web site: www.hummert.com/

Heat mats, Omega grafting machine, other grafting supplies.

Monarch Manufacturing, Inc.
13154 County Road 140
Salida, CO 81201
phone: 800-284-0390
fax: 719-539-3900
Web site: www.monarchmfg.com

Offers a system of collapsible flats and tall paper pots that make it easy to root grape cuttings on a heat mat.

Phytotronics
phone: 314-770-0717
e-mails: sales@phytotronics.com
Web site: www.phytotronics.com

Second-level supplier for small purchases.

Southeastern Outdoor Supplies, Inc.
Route 3, Box 503
Bassett, VA 24055
phone: 800-368-5924

Propagation supplies

U.S. Sources for Grapevines and Grape Cuttings

Brigdoon Vineyards
25166 Ferguson Road
Junction City, Oregon 97448
phone: 541-998-8708
Web site: http://www.brigadoonvineyards
    .com/

Grape rootstocks.

Classical Fruits
8831 AL Hwy. 157
Moulton, AL 35650
phone: 205-974-8813

Muscadines.

Cummins Nursery
18 Glass Factory Bay
Geneva, NY 14456
Web site: www.cumminsnursery.com

Double A Vineyards
10275 Christy Road
Fredonia, NY 14063
phone: 716-672-8493
Web site: www.rakgrape.com

Foster Concord Nurseries
10175 Mileblock Road
North Collins, NY 14111
phone: 800-223-2211
Web site: www.concordnurseries.com/

*American and French-American Hybrid wine
grapes in all quantities.*

Grafted Grapevine Nurseries
Herman Amberg
2399 Wheat Road
Clifton Springs, NY 14432
phone: 315-462-3288 or 716-526-6742
Web site: http://www.graftedgrapevines.com/

*Vinifera, French-American hybrids; custom
grafting services.*

Ison's Nursery and Vineyards
P.O. Box 190
Brooks, GA 30205
phone: 770-599-6970
e-mail: Info@isons.com
Web site: www.isons.com

Muscadines. Ask for color catalog.

Johnson Nursery
Rt. 5, Box 29-J
Ellijay, GA 30540
phone: 888-276-3187
Web site: http://www.johnsonnursery.com/

Muscadines.

Lake Sylvia Vineland Nursery
David MacGregor
13835 51st Avenue
South Haven, MN 55382

*Specializes in cold-hardy grapes, particularly the
grapes of Elmer Swenson and the University of
Minnesota; offers some of his own selections,
including some excellent new wine grapes.*

**Barb and John Marshall's Great River
Vineyard**
35680 Highway 61 Boulevard
Lake City, MN 55041
phone: 877-345-3531
Web site: www.greatrivervineyard.com

Cold-hardy grapes.

Plaisance Viticulture
16955 Water Gap Road
Williams, OR 97544
phone: 541-846-7175
joeginet@plaisanceviticulture.com
www.plaisanceviticulture.com

Oregon Certified grafting and propagation.

Lon J. Rombough, B.S., M.S., ATM.
P. O. Box 365
Aurora, OR 97002-0365
e-mail: lonrom@bunchgrapes.com
Web site: www.bunchgrapes.com

*Send S.A.S.E. for printed list of 130 + varieties
of grape cuttings or visit Web site.*

St. Francois Vineyard
Ed Daugherty
1669 Pine Ridge Trail
Park Hills, MO 63601
phone: 573-431-4294
e-mail: winevine@I1net
Web site: www.stfrancoisvineyard.com

*Supplies vines of American and French Hybrid
vines.*

Tinga Nursery
2918 Castle Hayne Road
Castle Hayne, NC 28429
phone: 910-762-1975

*Muscadines. Varieties include Carlos, Doreen, Mag-
nolia, Nesbitt, Noble, Tara, Tarheel, and Triumph.*

Walter S. Voltz Vinifera Vineyard and Nursery
109 Gibson Street
Bath, NY 14810
phone: 607-776-2270

Weeks Berry Nursery
6494 Windsor Island Road
Keizer, OR 97303
phone: 503-393-8112
Web site: www.weeksberry.com

Table grapes and other berries, wholesale only.

Herman J. Wiemer Vineyard, Inc.
Rt.14, Box 38
Dundee, NY 14837
phone: 607-243-7971
Web site: www.weimer.com

Winterhaven Vineyard & Nursery
18103-628th Ave.
Janesville, MN 56048
phone: 507-234-5469
cell phone: 507-317-7914
Web site: http://www.winterhaven
    grapevines.com/

Cold hardy grapes

Womack's Nursery
Rt. 1, Box 80
De Leon, TX 76444-9660
phone: 817-893-6497

Muscadines. Munson grape varieties.

Canadian Grape Sources

Alain Breault
313 Begin Street
Brigham, QU
J2K 4Y5 Canada
phone: 450-263-7127
e-mail: Coquine@enDirect.qc.ca

Swenson selections in Canada; Vandal-Cliché grapes.

Hardy Grapes
Bert Dunn
RR4
Tottenham, ON
L0G 1W0 Canada
phone/fax: 905-880-4423
Web site: http://www.littlefatwino.com/
    bertslist.html

European Grape Sources

Latvian Growers Club
Dr. Andris Dishlers
Madonas iela 27 dz. 104
Riga LV-1035 Latvia
phone: 371 2 588 340
e-mail: dishlers@biomed.lu.lv

Baltic grape varieties.

Ole Bonsdorff Nursery
Ejbyvej 98
DK-4632 BjaverskovDenmark
phone: 45 5682 1094

Reform, Rondo, Castel, Don Muscat, and other early-ripening varieties.

Sunnybank Vine Nursery
Cwm Barn
Rowlestone,
Herefordshire,
HR2 0EE UK
email: sarah@sunnybankvines.co.uk
phone: 01981 240256
Web site: http://www.sunnybankvines.co.uk

Swedish University of Agricultural Sciences
Balsgard Experiment Station
Kimmo Rumpunen
Department of Horticultural Plant Breeding
S-291 94 Kristianstad
Sweden
phone: 46 44 755 33
fax: 46 44 755 30

Baltic grape varieties from heat-treated material.

Index

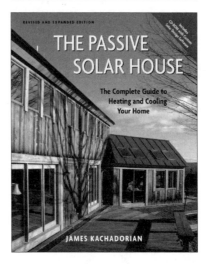